INTESTATES AND OTHERS

FROM THE

ORPHANS COURT BOOKS

OF

MONMOUTH CO., N.J.

1785 -1906

Compiled by

Judith B. Cronk

CLEARFIELD

Printed for
Clearfield Company, Inc. by
Genealogical Publishing Co., Inc.
Baltimore, Maryland
2002

International Standard Book Number: 0-8063-5179-9

Made in the United States of America

For Jeff and Dan,
my pride and joy.

INTRODUCTION

The Orphans Court Books of Monmouth County, New Jersey, held by the county Surrogate's Office, are a valuable resource for genealogists seeking ancestors who were residents of the county. The records span the years 1785 to 1906 and are arranged in Books A to I, K to S, and 1 to 8. There was no Book J, and the books skip from April 1816 to December 1817 and from 1868 to 1882. The books, handwritten until 1868, are often difficult to read. Hidden on the faded pages, wedged between entries of repetitive legalese, one will find parents for orphans, spouses for daughters and remarried widows, property descriptions, and heirs of intestates. The information contained in the books is so extensive, it would require multiple volumes to produce a comprehensive abstract of every entry. This book focuses on intestates, heirs and other family members found in estate allotments, guardianships, and an assortment of miscellaneous records.

Each entry begins with the main surname in the record, followed by the page number in the Orphans Court Book where it was found. The date following the page number refers to the month and year of the court term, not the actual date of the record. To conserve space, the abstracts are as brief as possible. Besides the standard abbreviations for states, the reader will find the following: yr. for year, tshp. for township, dec'd. for deceased, Esq. for Esquire, and dau. for daughter. As the cases worked their way through the court, either from postponement or due process, records with duplicate information appeared. Duplicated records were not abstracted. In some cases, when a subsequent record contained further information on the family, a cross-reference supplies the information, without abstracting the entire source record.

The early records made heavy use of the phrase "children and heirs." Care should be taken in interpreting the phrase; all those listed may not be children of the deceased. The records used the term "late" to refer to a woman's maiden name, as well as a remarried widow's previous married name. The old handwriting produced the usual problems, especially when it came to distinguishing between the capital letters I and J, and S and L. Words and letters that were difficult to interpret have been underlined to alert the reader to the problem.

Petitions for divisions of real estate and distributions of estates identify the heirs of intestates who will receive a share of the estate. Generally, the early years contain simple lists of children and heirs. By the mid-1800s the lists expand, with heirs identified by share portions or relationships. Lunacy hearings were included among the miscellaneous records; the subjects of the hearings were future intestates, and the records identified their heirs. A lunacy hearing resulted in the individual being declared a lunatic. Concerned that some might find the terminology offensive, the compiler used sanity hearing and mentally incompetent to replace the harsher terms. The books contained so many guardianship records that those decreed by a parent's will and those lacking family information were omitted. Over 2200 records were abstracted. Although it may be necessary to acquire other records to untangle some of the less explicit estate divisions, the researcher should find the Orphans Court Books a rewarding resource.

TABLE OF CONTENTS

BOOK A
1785 – 1793

TOMSON –pg. 3; July 1785. Benjamin VanCleaf and Mary, his wife who was a legatee in the last will and testament of Lewis Tomson, dec'd., were complainants against Thomas Tomson, executor of the estate of Lewis Tomson, dec'd.

CRAIG –pg. 3; July 1785. John Craig and Jane Craig, executors of the estate of James Robinson, dec'd., were complainants against Anna West, executor of the estate of Henry Robinson, dec'd.

CLAYTON –pg. 6; Jan. 1786. Robert Clayton and David Clayton were complainants against John Clayton, administrator of the estate of John Clayton, dec'd.

COVERT –pg. 10; April 1786. William Covert, son of Francis Covert, dec'd., was a complainant against Sarah Covert, administrator of the estate of Francis Covert, dec'd.

JOHNSTON –pg. 11; April 1786. William Lemman and other legatees of Benjamin Johnston, dec'd., were complainants against Sarah Johnston, John Johnston, and Daniel Johnston, executors of the estate of Benjamin Johnston, dec'd.

FORMAN –pg. 14; July 1786. Abraham Probasco and his wife, Elenor, were complainants against Samuel Forman, executor of the estate of Jonathan Forman, dec'd.

HOLMES –pg. 14; July 1786. William Holmes was a complainant against Catherine Wright, administrator of the estate of John Holmes, dec'd., and against her husband, Thomas Wright.

BOGGS –pg. 15; July 1786. Ann Allen, the mother, and others near of kin requested that guardianship of Ann's children Elizabeth Boggs and William Boggs, minors under 14yrs., be granted to Richard Kinnan, also near of kin to the children.

MORGAN –pg. 16; July 1786. Mary Wheatly and Hannah Wheatly were complainants against Obediah Holmes and Richard Crawford, nominated executors on a writing purported to be the last will and testament of Abel Morgan, dec'd. The court declared the paper to be a valid last will and testament. Samuel Morgan appealed judgement.

HOLMES –pg. 25; Jan. 1787. William Holmes, son of John Holmes, dec'd., late of Stafford, petitioned for division of his father's real estate; ownership had passed to John Holmes' children (not named).

GARRISON –pg. 28; Jan. 1787. Timothy Murphy and Mary, his wife, were complainants against Mary Bailey, executor of the estate of Abraham Garrison, dec'd., and against her husband, Elias Bailey.

WHITE –pg. 40; July 1787. William Brinley and wife were complainants against John Tucker, executor of the last will and testament of Vincent White, dec'd. William Brinley's wife was a legatee of the deceased Vincent White.

RANDOLPH –pg. 44; Oct. 1787. Stephen Randolph, a minor and a son of Deliverance Randolph, dec'd., requested sale of his mother's estate as a means of paying for his maintenance and education.

BILLS –pg. 50; Oct. 1787. Sarah Parker requested Thomas Parker be appointed guardian of her son Sylvanus Bills, 11yrs. old.

KNOTT –pg. 57; Jan. 1788. Peter Knott and David Knott, sons and heirs of David Knott, dec'd., petitioned for a division of their father's real estate.

HOLMES –pg. 61; April 1788. Leah Holmes, widow of Daniel Holmes, dec'd., requested guardianship of William Holmes, her 10yr. old son.

ENGLISH –pg. 65; April 1788. James English, guardian of the minor David English, petitioned for the sale of land his ward inherited by will and testament from his grandfather James English, dec'd.

HOLMES –pg. 65 - 74; April 1788. The commissioners divided the real estate of Daniel Holmes, dec'd., amongst the legatees of his will where applicable and when not applicable, according to law. Daniel Holmes, dec'd., owned a farm and plantation in Freehold Tshp. and a salt meadow lot at Canascunck in Middletown Tshp. This land was divided equally between James Holmes, Philip Holmes, and William Holmes, his three surviving sons. The deceased also owned two other lots in Freehold Tshp. that he left to his son Jonathan Holmes, now deceased. This land was divided between the siblings of Jonathan Holmes, dec'd., identified as his heirs.
Siblings of Jonathan Holmes, dec'd., son of Daniel Holmes, dec'd.: James Holmes, Philip Holmes, William Holmes, Catherine Stoutenburgh, Sarah Holmes, Jane Holmes, and Mary Holmes.

HOULET (HEULET) –pg. 79; July 1788. The real estate of George Houlet, dec'd., was divided between his dau. Margaret Heulet and her younger sister, Arney Heulet, the two surviving children of George Heulet, dec'd. Note: surname was spelled Houlet and Heulet in this record.

FLEMMING –pg. 81; July 1788. A petition by Jacob Flemming stated his children, Joseph Flemming, Stephen Flemming, Jacob Flemming, Sarah Flemming, and John West Flemming, had an estate bequeathed to them by their grandfather James West, dec'd., whose executors wanted the land taken out of their hands by a legally authorized person. He asked appointment as guardian of his children.

COX –pg. 83 - 86; Aug. 1788. Benjamin Loxley and Robert Jones, in behalf of their wives who were daus. of John Cox, dec'd., were complainants against James Cox and William Cox, executors in "an instrument of writing purported to be the last will and testament of John Cox, dec'd." The deceased had two wills prepared; the first by a Mr. Blackwell, and the last, now being contested, by Robert Lawrence. Several witnesses were called and asked about the mental soundness of the testator at the time he wrote his will. Those claiming he was sound of mind outnumbered those who doubted his mental state. Among the witnesses, Mary Ashton testified that she lived in the house with John Cox, dec'd., and Edward Taylor testified the deceased had once mentioned a desire to leave a substantial legacy to an unnamed dau. who lived in England. John Cox, dec'd., was declared competent, and the document contested as being his last will was admitted into probate.

KNOTT –pg. 87; Oct. 1788. Anna Knott, widow of David Knott, dec'd., late of Shrewsbury, petitioned the court for a yearly allowance from her late husband's estate for the maintenance and education of her three youngest children: Catherine Knott, 12yrs. old; Lydia Knott, 9yrs. old; and Jane Knott, 13mon. old.

HOLMES –pg. 89; Oct. 1788. Catherine Wright, administrator of the estate of John Holmes, dec'd., petitioned for a division of the real estate owned by the deceased. William Holmes was named as an heir of John Holmes, dec'd.

BENNIT –pg. 96; Jan. 1789. Richard Merrill was a complainant against John Bennit who was administrator of the estate of John Bennit, dec'd., late of Middletown, who was the executor of the estate of John Bennit, dec'd., late of Long Island.

HANKINSON –pg. 100; April 1789. In 'settlement of accounts': Kenneth Anderson, Esq., was administrator of the estate of William Hankinson, son of Kenneth, dec'd.

VANNORTE –pg. 107; July 1789. Thomas White and Catherine, his wife, were complainants against the executors of the estate of Thomas Vannorte, dec'd.

KNOTT –pg. 119 - 141; Jan. 1790. The record provided a lengthy description of how the extensive real estate of David Knott, dec'd., was divided amongst his heirs.
Widow: Anna Knott.

Children of David Knott, dec'd.: Elizabeth (Knott) Merriman; Mary (Knott) Holmes, wife of John Holmes; Sarah (Knott) Boyd; Peter Knott; John Knott; David Knott; Jane Knott; Lydia Knott; Catherine Knott; Abigail (Knott) Maxson; Ann Knott; and Joseph Knott.

HULET –pg. 143; April 1790. Thomas Hulet of Shrewsbury, grandfather of 9yr. old Daniel Hulet and 4yr. old Michael Hulet, requested guardianship of his grandchildren.

ALLEN –pg. 146; July 1790. Samuel Allen and David Allen, sons of Samuel Allen, dec'd., along with Abraham Osborn and Robert James in right of their wives, Elizabeth and Catherine, who were daus. of said deceased, petitioned the court for a division of the real estate owned by Samuel Allen, dec'd., late of Shrewsbury. Samuel Allen, dec'd. left a will, dated June 19, 1782, attested to by only two witnesses; as a result, he was considered to have died intestate.

GRIGGS –pg. 148; July 1790. The honorable David Brearley, Esq., was a complainant against Joseph Griggs, administrator of the estate of Daniel Griggs, dec'd.

WEST –pg. 149; July 1790. John Errickson, guardian of Rebecca West, was a complainant against Stephen Flemming, administrator of the estate of Lydia West, dec'd.

ALLEN –pg. 152; July 1790. Martha Allen, widow of Samuel Allen, dec'd., requested guardianship of her son Joseph Allen, a minor under 14yrs.

LEONARD –pg. 152; July 1790. Moses Sheppard, guardian of Sarah Leonard, a dau. of Joseph Leonard, dec'd., late of Middletown, petitioned the court for a division of the real estate owned by Joseph Leonard, dec'd., who died leaving several children, all under 21yrs. of age. Joseph Leonard's widow had remarried to Benjamin Cooper who now possessed,and was wasting, the real estate of the said deceased. Note: A complaint in Book A, pg. 153, July 1790, identified Benjamin Cooper's wife as Sarah Cooper who was administrator of the estate of Joseph Leonard, dec'd.

ALLEN –pg. 161 – 166; Oct. 1790. The division of the real estate owned by Samuel Allen, dec'd., identified his children and heirs.
Children and heirs: David Allen; Joseph Allen; William Allen; Hannah Knott, wife of John Knott; Catherine James, wife of Robert James; Elizabeth Osborn, wife of Abraham Osborn; Samuel Allen; and Marcy/Mapey? Cook, wife of James Cook.

KIRKPATRICK –pg. 170; Jan. 1791. John Woodhull and Kenneth Anderson petitioned for guardianship of 8yr. old Nancy Huggins Kirkpatrick, dau. of William Kirkpatrick, dec'd. Both her parents were deceased.

TALLMAN –pg. 176; Jan. 1791. John Wardell and Sarah, his wife, Joseph Tallman, Rachel Tallman, Thomas Seabrook and Martha, his wife, James Tallman, and Mary Tallman, administrators and heirs of the estate of Stephen Tallman, dec'd., late of Shrewsbury, petitioned for a division of the real estate owned by the said deceased.

JEFFREY –pg. 178; April 1791. David Jeffrey requested guardianship of Thomas Jeffrey and William Jeffrey, minors under 14yrs.

SMITH –pg. 180; April 1791. Samuel Emmans and his wife, Surviah, a legatee of Abijah Smith, dec'd., were complainants against Benjamin Wooley, executor of the estate of Abijah Smith, dec'd.

IVINS –pg. 184; April 1791. Mary Ivins, widow of Solomon Ivins, dec'd., requested guardianship of her sons Samuel Ivins, about 11yrs., Thomas Ivins, about 10yrs., Ezekiel Ivins, about 6yrs., and Joseph Ivins, about 5yrs.

ALLEN –pg. 185; July 1791. William Hartshorne, guardian of Nancy Allen and Hannah Allen, daus. of Ebenezer Allen, dec'd., late of Shrewsbury, asked to sell 27 acres of their land in Shrewsbury.

WILLET –pg. 190; July 1791. Thomas Seabrook, Esq., requested the court appoint John Willet Jr guardian of John Willet, a minor about 5yrs. of age, son of Joseph Willet, dec'd. The child was the nephew of John Willet Jr.

MOUNT –pg. 194; Oct. 1791. A settlement of accounts was filed by Jane Anderson, formerly Jane Mount, administrator of the estate of James Mount, dec'd.

STOUT –pg. 198; Oct. 1791. James Stout, son of John Stout, dec'd., late of Dover, petitioned for a division of his father's real estate. His father died intestate leaving considerable real estate and several children.

THROCKMORTON –pg. 199; Oct. 1791. A portion of the real estate owned by John Throckmorton, dec'd., was divided between his three heirs, identified as Joseph Throckmorton, Hannah Lawrence, and Anna Scoby, wife of Timothy Scoby.

BRINLEY –pg. 208; Jan. 1792. Apollo Brinley, heir of Sylvester Brinley, dec'd., was a complainant against Margaret Brinley, administrator of the estate of the said deceased.

CHAMBERLAIN –pg. 210; April 1792. Richard Chamberlain and other legatees of the last will and testament of William Chamberlain, dec'd., were complainants against Catherine Anderson, formerly Catherine Chamberlain, executor of the estate of William Chamberlain, dec'd., and against Elias Anderson, her husband.

VANMATER –pg. 212; April 1792. Jacob Schenck, in behalf of his wife and other legatees of Chryne VanMater, dec'd., was a complainant against Joseph Throckmorton and Aaron Vanderbilt who were executors of the estate of Guisbert VanMater, dec'd., who was the executor of the estates of John VanMater, dec'd., and said Chryne VanMater, dec'd.

TALLMAN –pg. 216 – 225; April 1792. The real estate of Stephen Tallman, dec'd., late of Shrewsbury, was divided amongst his heirs.
Heirs identified: Joseph Tallman; Sarah Wardell, wife of John Wardell; Mary Tallman; Martha Seabrook, wife of Thomas Seabrook; James Tallman; and the heirs of Samuel Tallman, dec'd., whose widow was one of the petitioners. The widow and heirs of Samuel Tallman, dec'd., were alive, and the claim was made in their behalf. The mention of the "widow Rachel Tallman," whose name appeared amongst the petitioners, implied she was the widow of Samuel Tallman, dec'd., but, on this point, the wording was ambiguous.

LEONARD –pg. 226; April 1792. A division of the real estate owned by Joseph Leonard, dec'd., late of Middletown Tshp., identified his children.
Children: oldest dau., Sarah Leonard; second dau., Ann Leonard; Nathaniel Leonard; and Samuel Leonard.

STOUT –pg. 239; July 1792. Enoch Potter and his wife, Rachel, were complainants against Ruth Stout, administrator of the estate of John Stout, dec'd.

EDWARDS –pg. 253 – 258; Jan. 1793. A division of the real estate owned by Philip Edwards, dec'd., as requested by his son John Edwards, identified his heirs.
Children and heirs: Abiah Edwards, oldest son; John Edwards, son; Daniel Edwards; Joseph Edwards; Stephen Edwards; James Edwards; Sarah Edwards; Abigail Edwards; and Deborah Edwards.

HENDRICKSON –pg. 269; July 1793. The heirs of Abraham Hendrickson, dec'd., petitioned for a division of his real estate. The petition was signed by Jacob Hendrickson, Matthias Hendrickson, Altia Hendrickson, all children and heirs of Abraham Hendrickson, dec'd., late of Freehold.

SMITH –pg. 280; Oct. 1793. A division of the real estate owned by James Smith, dec'd., late of Shrewsbury, was made between his children and heirs.
Children and heirs: George Smith, Matthew Smith, Ann Smith, Deborah Smith, Jane Smith, and Margaret Poole, wife of George Poole.

BOOK B
1794 – 1801

VANKIRK –pg. 1; Jan. 1794. A petition signed by John VanKirk, Garrit Schanck, and Daniel Peacock stated John VanKirk was the son and heir of James VanKirk, dec'd., late of Freehold, and Garrit Schanck and Daniel Peacock were husbands of two daus. of James VanKirk, dec'd. They requested a division of the real estate owned by the deceased.

COOK –pg. 2 – 8; Jan. 1794. A division of the real estate owned by Jasher Cook, dec'd., identified his children and heirs who received a share. Although his name appeared as Jasher Cook in the record, in the index it was written Jasper Cook.
Children and heirs: Jasher Cook; William Cook; Samuel Cook; Joseph Cook; Lydia Cook; Margaret, wife of John White; Hannah, wife of James Howland; and the heirs of James Cook, dec'd.

HENDRICKSON –pg. 9 - 11; Jan. 1794. A report on the division of the real estate owned by Abraham Hendrickson, dec'd., revealed some of the petitioners had sold their shares. Jacob Hendrickson sold his share to Elias Conover. Altie Hendrickson sold her share to Elias Conover and Mathias Hendrickson. As a result of the sales, the two buyers owned all the real estate.

VANKIRK –pg. 11; Jan. 1794. Jane VanKirk requested Stephen VanBrackle be appointed guardian of her two sons, 11yr. old James VanKirk and 9yr. old Peter VanKirk, children of James VanKirk, dec'd.

WHITE –pg. 13; April 1794. James Tallman and his wife, Charity, petitioned for a division of the real estate owned by Jacob White, dec'd., father of the petitioner Charity (White) Tallman. By his last will and testament, written in 1782, the deceased left his wife, Charity White, the use of his lands and house during her widowhood, after which, they passed to his daus. Elizabeth Tallman, Hannah Tallman, Charity Tallman, and Zilpha Tallman. Since their father's death, the daus., or husbands for them, had purchased the widow's rights.

COX –pg. 15; April 1794. Richard Mason and his wife, Letitia, late Letitia Cox, dau. of Nathaniel Cox, dec'd., requested a division of her father's real estate amongst his children and heirs.

WAINWRIGHT –pg. 16; April 1794. Joseph Wainwright requested guardianship of his dau. Jerusha Wainwright, a 4yr. old.

BOYCE –pg. 16; April 1794. Adam Pease and his wife, Elizabeth, late Elizabeth Boyce, were complainants against John Combs executor of the estate of Adam Boyce, dec'd., and against Richard Prest executor of the estate of Richard Prest, dec'd., who was one of the executors of the estate of said Adam Boyce, dec'd.

VANKIRK –pg. 17 – 23; April 1794. The real estate of James VanKirk, dec'd., was divided for his heirs.
Children and heirs receiving a share: Peter VanKirk; James VanKirk; Phebe VanKirk; Nelly (Ellenor) VanKirk; John VanKirk; Anne VanKirk, alias Anne Peacock; and Jean VanKirk, alias Jean Schenck. Nelly VanKirk was also referred to as Ellenor VanKirk in the same document.

MAXON –pg. 23; July 1794. The real estate of Joseph Maxon, dec'd., who died intestate owning land in Middletown Tshp., was divided between his two daus.
Daughters, both under 21yrs. of age: Anna Maxon, oldest dau., now Anna Smith, wife of Daniel Smith; and Rebecca Maxon.

WHITE –pg. 26 – 29; July 1794. The lands of Jacob White, dec'd., were divided amongst his

6 Intestates and Others

children.
Children: Elizabeth Knott, Charity Tallman, Zilpha White, and Hannah Wikoff.

COX –pg. 34 – 39; Oct. 1794. The real estate of Nathaniel Cox, dec'd., late of Upper Freehold, was divided into nine equal shares, one for each child of the deceased. Children of said deceased were not identified by name. Despite the reference to nine shares, the land was divided into ten shares. Note: See Book B, pg. 60, Jan. 1796.

COX –pg. 40; Oct. 1794. Nathaniel Cox, son and heir of Nathaniel Cox, dec'd., was a complainant against Richard Mason and his wife, Letitea. He wanted the land division report set aside.

TAYLOR –pg. 44; Jan. 1795. John Alwood and his wife, Priscilla, late Priscilla Taylor, were complainants against Garret Vanderveer, executor of the estate of John Vanderveer, dec'd., who was the administrator of the estate of Joseph Taylor, dec'd.

WIKOFF –pg. 55; Oct. 1795. Ezekiel Forman, in right of his wife and in behalf of his children, was a complainant against the executors of the estate of William Wikoff, dec'd.

BOWNE –pg. 56; Oct. 1795. John Combs Jr., Elizabeth Combs, and Sarah Bowne requested the appointment of Stephen VanBrackle as guardian of 8yr. old Polly Bowne, 6yr. old William Bowne, and 4yr. old John Bowne, all children of Jonathan Bowne, dec'd., who died intestate.

SOPER –pg. 57; Oct. 1795. Gabriel Woodmansee requested appointment as the administrator of the estate of Joseph Soper Jr., dec'd., at the request of his widow, Phebe Soper, who refused to accept responsibility for the administration.

TAYLOR –pg. 58; Jan. 1796. Edward Taylor, one of the executors of the estate of Edward Taylor, dec'd., who was administrator of the estate of Lawrence Taylor, dec'd., filed a settlement of accounts. Joshua Taylor, Edward Taylor, and Ezekiel Taylor, noted as heirs of Lawrence Taylor, dec'd., hired a lawyer to place exceptions on the settlement.

COX –pg. 60; Jan. 1796. The court accepted the division on the real estate owned by Nathaniel Cox, dec'd., late of Upper Freehold, but the fee for the division remained outstanding. The fee of 30 pounds, 17 shillings and 9 pence was divided between the beneficiaries of the land division. Those named as owing money: Meribah Cox; Richard Mason and his wife, Latitia; Ann Cox; Nathaniel Cox; James Cox; Parthenia Cox; and Sarah Cox. Note: See Book B, pgs. 34 – 39, and 40, Oct. 1794.

BORDEN –pg. 63; Jan. 1796. A settlement of accounts was filed by John Cook and his wife, Lydia, executrix of the estate of Joel Borden, dec'd., who was an executor of the estate of Samuel Borden, dec'd.

COX –pg. 73; Oct. 1796. David Johnston and Mary, his wife, late Mary Cox, administrator of the estate of Nathaniel Cox, dec'd., filed a settlement of accounts.

LAIRD –pg. 76; Jan. 1797. Thomas Astin and his wife, Sarah, late Sarah Laird who was the executrix of the estate of Archibald Laird, dec'd., were complainants against Thomas Cook, guardian of Sarah Laird.

CHEW –pg. 80; Jan. 1797. Rachel Chew requested guardianship of her dau. Mary Chew, a minor under 14yrs. of age.

COVENHOVEN –pg. 83; Feb. 1797. Samuel I. Forman and his wife, Mary, Nelly Covenhoven, Jane Covenhoven, Hendrick Hendrickson and his wife, Franshinke, requested a division of the real estate owned by Cornelius R. Covenhoven, dec'd., late of Middletown. The deceased left a will dated Jan. 16, 1796 in which he devised a plantation he received from his father, Rulef Covenhoven, dec'd., to his children and grandchildren, to be divided equally.
His children named in the will: Rulef, Sally, Lointie, Polly, Caty, Peggy, Nelly, and Jane.
His grandchildren named in the will: Stephen Covenhoven and Rulef Covenhoven, sons of Tunis Covenhoven, dec'd., a son of the deceased Cornelius R. Covenhoven.

WIKOFF –pg. 85; April 1797. Ezekiel Forman and his wife, Catherine, late Catherine Wikoff, were complainants against Anne Wikoff, administrator of the estate of Nancy Wikoff, dec'd.

COVENHOVEN –pg. 91 - 94; April 1797. A division of the real estate owned by Cornelius R. Covenhoven, dec'd., was made.

Children receiving one lot each: Jane Covenhoven, Elinor Covenhoven, Mary Forman, Rulef Covenhoven, Fransinche Hendrickson, Margaret Hubbard, Catherine Vanderveer, and Sarah Ashton.
Grandchildren who were children of Tunis Covenhoven, dec'd., receiving one lot total: Stephen Covenhoven and Rulef Covenhoven.

CHEW –pg. 97 – 100; July 1797. A division of the real estate owned by Richard Chew, dec'd., identified his widow, and his children and heirs.
Widow: Rachel Chew.
Children and heirs of Richard Chew, dec'd.: William Chew; Mary Chew; Phebe Chew; John Chew; and Hannah Chew, alias Hannah Emmons.

JAMES –pg. 103; Oct. 1797. Elizabeth James requested guardianship of Rebecca James, a minor under 14yrs., dau. of Richard James, dec'd.

JAMES –pg. 103; Oct. 1797. Joseph James requested guardianship of Lewis James, a minor under 14yrs., son of Lewis James, dec'd.

GREEN –pg. 105 – 111; Oct. 1797. The division of the real estate owned by John Green, dec'd., identified his children and heirs.
Children and heirs of John Green, dec'd.: Elizabeth Cooper, Zilphey Green, John Green, Henry Green, Lidia Green, Nancy Green, and Rebecca Green.

HOLMES –pg. 118; April 1798. Daniel Hendrickson requested guardianship of Sarah Holmes, Catharine Holmes, Remsen Holmes, Obediah Holmes, Maria Holmes, and William Holmes, all minors under 14yrs., children of Obediah Holmes, dec'd.

SMOCK –pg. 118; April 1798. Daniel Schanck and his wife, Catherine, late Catherine Smock, were complainants against the executors of the estate of Jacob VanDorn, dec'd.

BRAY –pg. 119; July 1798. Nicholas Morrell and his wife, Rebecca, late Rebecca Bray, were complainants against the executors of the estate of Samuel Bray, dec'd.

WHITE –pg. 127; April 1799. Amos White, of full age, and William Parker, guardian of Humphrey White and Joel White who were both under 21yrs., requested a division of the real estate owned by Amos White, dec'd., late of Shrewsbury Tshp., who died intestate. Petitioner Amos White and the wards of William Parker were sons of Amos White, dec'd. They and Scott Herbert, son of Deborah Herbert, dec'd., who was a dau. of the said deceased, were his only children and grandchildren.

SCHENCK –pg. 130; April 1799. Sarah Schenck requested guardianship of Sarah Covenhoven Schenck, a minor under 14yrs., dau. of Garret Schenck, dec'd.

BOWNE –pg. 136; July 1799. The real estate of Jonathan Bowne, dec'd., late of Freehold Tshp., was divided amongst his heirs. He died leaving five children: Sarah Bowne, now Sarah Antonides, wife of Vincent Antonides; Elizabeth Bowne, now Elizabeth Combs, wife of John Combs Jr.; Mary Bowne; John Bowne; and William Bowne. Note: See Book D, pg. 74 - 78, July 1808.

TALLMAN –pg. 141 – 146; Oct. 1799. The real estate of Samuel Tallman, dec'd., was divided amongst his children and grandchildren.
Children: James Tallman Jr.; Stephen Tallman; Samuel Tallman; Nancy Tucker, wife of John Tucker; Phila Goble, wife of Runah R. Goble; and Rachel Tallman.
Grandchildren: Samuel Williams and Mary Williams.

WOOLLEY –pg. 150; Jan. 1800. Montilian Woolley and Joseph Woolley, devisees of Daniel Woolley, dec'd., late of Shrewsbury Tshp., petitioned for a division of the real estate owned by the said deceased. The deceased was the father of petitioner Montilian Woolley and the grandfather of petitioner Joseph Woolley.

STOUT –pg. 151; Jan. 1800. Amos Phar, Esq., Garret D. Covenhoven, and his wife, Ruth, late Ruth Stout, executors of the estate of James Stout, dec'd., reported a settlement of accounts.

JOHNSTON –pg. 159; July 1800. James Reynolds and his wife, Abigail, late Abigail Johnston, were complainants against William Eugene Imlay, administrator of the estate of John Johnston, dec'd.

VANDERVEER –pg. 163; Oct. 1800. George Smith and his wife, Jane, along with other legatees were complainants against Garrit Vanderveer, executor of the estate of John Vanderveer, dec'd.

BORDEN –pg. 163; Oct. 1800. Richard Divinney and his wife, Elizabeth, late Elizabeth Borden, one of the devisees of Joel Borden, dec'd., requested a division of the real estate owned by the deceased. By his will Joel Borden, dec'd., left a 23 acre lot in Rumson, Shrewsbury Tshp. to his three youngest daus., viz., Elizabeth Borden, Mary Borden, and Hannah Borden. Elizabeth Borden, now Elizabeth Divinney, had reached 18yrs. of age. Mary Borden and Hannah Borden were still under 18yrs.

BORDEN –pg. 169; Jan. 1801. Elizabeth Borden, Samuel Borden, and Joel Borden were complainants against John Cook and his wife, Lydia, late Lydia Borden, who was executrix of the estate of Joel Borden, dec'd.

WOOLLEY –pg. 171 – 176; Jan. 1801. The real estate of Daniel Woolley, dec'd., late of Shrewsbury, was divided amongst his heirs: Montilian Woolley, his son; Daniel Woolley, his son; Joseph Woolley; and the heirs of Jedidiah Woolley, a deceased son of Daniel Woolley, dec'd.

BOOK C
1801 – 1807

JAMES –pg. 2; Feb. 1801. Robert James, son of Robert James, dec'd., through his guardian William Laird, petitioned for a division of real estate amongst the heirs of the deceased. Robert James, dec'd., late of Freehold Tshp., died intestate leaving two sons and three daus., some under 21yrs. of age. The court had sold several tracts of land to pay the debts of the deceased, but a part of the homestead farm was still owned by the heirs as tenants in common, and it was this tract the petitioner requested divided.

BROWN –pg. 4; April 1801. John White requested guardianship of Jeremiah Brown and Sarah Brown, minors under 14yrs., children of Samuel Brown, dec'd.

JAMES –pg. 8; April 1801. Robert James had requested a division of the real estate owned by Robert James, dec'd. William Wilson and his wife, Catherine, late widow of Robert James, dec'd., objected to the request for themselves and the children of the said deceased, other than his son Robert.

JAMES –pg. 10 – 14; July 1801. The court upheld the division of the real estate owned by Robert James, dec'd., and it was divided amongst his children, viz., Robert James, Samuel James, Anner James, Ame James, and Elisa James.

COOPER –pg. 20; Jan. 1802. Uriah Cooper, son and heir of William Cooper, dec'd., requested a division of his father's real estate amongst the said deceased's children. William Cooper, dec'd., late of Shrewsbury Tshp., died intestate leaving children.
Children of William Cooper, dec'd.: Uriah Cooper; Samuel Cooper; William Cooper; Benjamin Cooper; Brittain Cooper, under 21yrs.; Elizabeth Cooper, under 21yrs.; Sarah Cooper, under 21yrs.; and Abigail Cooper.

KIRBY –pg. 25; April 1802. Abel Kirby and Robert Kirby were complainants against Israel Kirby and Job Kirby, administrators of the estate of Robert Kirby, dec'd.

VANDERVEER –pg. 28; April 1802. John Lloyd asked that he, David Vanderveer, and Eleanor Vanderveer be appointed guardians of Sarah Vanderveer, David Vanderveer, Catherine Vanderveer, Rulif Vanderveer, and Tunis Vanderveer, all minors under 14yrs., children of Rulif Vanderveer, dec'd.

SCHENCK –pg. 35; April 1802. Sarah Schenck requested Chrineyonce Schenck be appointed guardian of Jacob Schenck, Lydia Schenck, Anna Schenck, and Tiley Schenck, minors under 14yrs., children of Rolef H. Schenck, dec'd.

WILLIAMS –pg. 38; July 1802. Robert Morris and his wife, Abigail, late Abigail Williams, were complainants against Benjamin Jackson, guardian of said Abigail.

ALLEN –pg. 41; July 1802. James Whiting and his wife, Deborah, along with John Wilkins and his wife, Philadelphia, were complainants against John Rolph and his wife, Margaret, late Margaret Allen, administrator of the estate of Judah Allen, dec'd.

WOOLLEY –pg. 43; Sept. 1802. Judiah Woolley and Daniel Woolley, children and heirs of Judiah Woolley, dec'd., petitioned for a division of the real estate owned by the said Judiah Woolley, dec'd., late of Shrewsbury Tshp., who died intestate owning lands bequeathed to him by his father, the late Daniel Woolley, dec'd.

BRINLEY –pg. 46; Oct. 1802. Thomas Brinley, Gabriel Brinley, Silence Brinley, and John Brinley, through their guardian Samuel Brinley, petitioned for a division of the real estate owned by their grandfather Gabriel Woodmansee, dec'd., late of Dover Tshp., who died intestate.

JOHNSTON –pg. 47; Oct. 1802. Benjamin Lawrence and Catherine Johnston requested the appointment of Benjamin Lawrence as guardian of David Johnston, a minor under 14yrs., son of John Johnston, dec'd.

HOLMES –pg. 49; Oct. 1802. Joseph L. Holmes, son of John Holmes, dec'd., requested a division of his father's real estate. John Holmes, dec'd., late of Upper Freehold Tshp., died intestate leaving children.
Children: Joseph Holmes; John Holmes; Eliza Holmes who died leaving a dau.; and Alice Holmes who died intestate leaving no issue.

BRINLEY –pg. 50; Oct. 1802. Samuel Brinley requested appointment as guardian of his children Thomas Brinley, Gabriel Brinley, Silence Brinley, and John Brinley, minors under 14yrs. They were his children by his late wife, Hannah Brinley, dec'd.

FORMAN –pg. 53; Jan. 1803. Samuel Whitehouse, Charlotte Whitehouse, and Thomas Shinn requested the appointment of Thomas Shinn as guardian of Mary Forman, Nancy Forman, and William Forman, minors under 14yrs., children of Thomas Forman, dec'd.

WOOLLEY –pg. 56 – 60; Jan. 1803. The real estate of Judiah Woolley, dec'd., was divided amongst his heirs: Joseph Woolley, Jedidiah Woolley, Daniel Woolley, Hugh Woolley, Abigail White, and Elizabeth West. Note: Jedidiah was also used in the report as the given name for the deceased and for a son referred to as Judiah in earlier records.

FORMAN –pg. 60; Jan. 1803. Samuel Whitehouse and his wife, Charlotte, late Charlotte Forman, administrator of the estate of Thomas Forman, dec'd., filed a settlement of accounts.

HOLMES –pg. 65 – 73; April 1803. The lands of John Holmes, dec'd., and those of his dau. Alice Holmes, dec'd., (she was entitled to 1/4 of her father's estate) were divided between Joseph L. Holmes, John Holmes, and Elizabeth H. Ellis who was the dau. of Rolean Ellis who married Eliza Holmes, dec'd., late dau. of John Holmes, dec'd.

QUAY –pg. 74; April 1803. Lucy Quay requested guardianship of Ann Quay, Caroline Quay, Eleanor Quay, Alexander Washingtion Quay, and Martha Quay, minors under 14yrs., children of Samuel Quay, dec'd.

COWARD –pg. 74; April 1803. Jonathan Coward and Elizabeth Coward requested petitioner Jonathan Coward be appointed guardian of Susannah Coward, a minor under 14yrs., dau. of Daniel Coward, dec'd.

VOORHEES –pg. 79; July 1803. Levi Platt and his wife, Margaret, late Margaret Voorhees who was administrator of the estate of John Voorhees, dec'd., filed a settlement of accounts.

WOODMANSEE –pg. 80 – 89; July 1803. The real estate of Gabriel Woodmansee, dec'd., was divided amongst his heirs: Thomas Woodmansee, Amela Woodmansee, and the heirs of Hannah Brinley, dec'd. The heirs of Hannah Brinley, dec'd., were grandchildren of Gabriel Woodmansee, dec'd., and four of them were minors identified in the heading as Thomas Brinley, Gabriel Brinley, Silence Brinley, and John Brinley.

JOURNEY –pg. 96; Oct. 1803. Stephen Applegate and his wife, Catherine, late Catherine Journey, were complainants against the executors of the estate of James Journey, dec'd.

VANDERVEER –pg. 96; Oct. 1803. The administrators of his estate, viz., John Lloyd, David Vanderveer, Charles Dubois and his wife, Eleanor, late Eleanor Vanderveer, filed a settlement of accounts on the estate of Ruleff Vanderveer, dec'd.

ALLEN –pg. 98; Oct. 1803. Elizabeth Allen requested guardianship of Robert W. Allen, a minor under 14yrs., son of Samuel Allen, dec'd.

GOLDEN –pg. 106; April 1804. Joseph Golden, a minor over 14yrs., requested Mathias Golden be appointed his guardian.

DENISE –pg. 106; April 1804. Tunis Denise, dec'd., died intestate leaving children Samuel Denise and Margaret Denise, minors under 14yrs. without a guardian. The court appointed George Cook their guardian.

BRAY –pg. 109; April 1804. A settlement of accounts for the estate of Samuel Bray, dec'd., was filed by the administrators of his estate, viz., Samuel Ogburn, Stout Holmes, and Mary Holmes, the late Mary Bray.

BROWN –pg. 113; April 1804. Amos Elmer and Elizabeth Elmer petitioned for guardianship of Abigail Brown, Sarah Brown, and William Brown, minors under 14yrs., children of John Brown, dec'd., who died intestate. Amos Elmer and Elizabeth Elmer were noted as "the father in law and mother of said infants."

HIGHT –pg. 114; April 1804. Jacob Hight stated his father, Nicholas Hight, dec'd., late of Middlesex County, died without assigning a guardian for his son John Hight, a minor under 14yrs. who lived in Monmouth County. Jacob Hight asked the court to appoint John Clark guardian of the minor.

HIGHT –pg. 115; April 1804. Daniel Hight, a minor over 14yrs., son of Nicholas Hight, dec'd., requested John Clark be appointed his guardian.

CONOVER –pg. 116; April 1804. Joseph Conover and Anne Conover, minors over 14yrs., children of Isaac Covenhoven, dec'd., requested Lewis Conover be appointed their guardian.

VANMATER –pg. 118; July 1804. Cornelius VanMater, Daniel Polhemus, Garret VanMater, Jacob Holmes, Aaron VanMater, John Bennet, and Benjamin VanMater petitioned the court for a division of the real estate owned by Abigail VanMater, dec'd., late of Shrewsbury Tshp., who died intestate without issue. Said deceased was the only child of Cornelius VanMater, dec'd., and his surviving heir at the time of his death. It was from him she inherited the real estate. Abigail VanMater, dec'd., had two uncles and two aunts, brothers and sisters of her father: Jacob VanMater; Cyrenius B. VanMater; Nelly Covenhoven, wife of Garret Covenhoven; and Sebanchea Bennet, wife of William Bennet. All the aunts and uncles named were then deceased. By this means the real estate had descended to the children of the said deceased aunts and uncles of Abigail VanMater, dec'd.
Children of Cyrenius B. VanMater, dec'd.: Benjamin VanMater Jr.; Aaron VanMater; Jacob VanMater; Cornelius VanMater; Garret VanMater; Peter VanMater, under 21yrs.; John VanMater, under 21yrs.; Elizabeth Bennet, wife of John W. Bennet; Catherine Golden, wife of Mathias A. Golden; Eleanor Wikoff, wife of William Wikoff; and Sarah VanMater, under 21yrs.
Children of Jacob VanMater, dec'd.: Benjamin I. VanMater; Nelly Holmes, wife of Jacob Holmes; Elizabeth Polhemus, wife of Daniel Polhemus; and Hendrick VanMater.
Children of Nelly Covenhoven, dec'd., late wife of Garret Covenhoven: Garret G. Covenhoven; Caubauchea Schenck, wife of John Schenck; and Catherine Ellison, wife of Samuel Ellison.
Child of Sebanchea Bennet, dec'd.: Idah Smith, wife of James Smith.
NOTE: See Book C, pg. 171, Oct. 1807 for additional children of Cyrenius VanMater.

PERINE –pg. 130; July 1804. Ira Condit and Ephram Woolley were appointed guardians of Hannah Perine, Abigail Perine, and Jeremiah W. Perine, all minors under 21yrs., children of Lewis Perine, dec'd.

PERINE –pg. 130; July 1804. Joseph Rue and Jeremiah Woolley asked the court to appoint Ira Condit and Ephram Woolley guardians of Mary Perine, Lewis Perine, Henry Perine, and John Perine, minors under 14yrs., children of Lewis Perine, dec'd.

BARCALOW –pg. 137; Jan. 1805. James Tapscott, Esq., and his wife, Ann, late Ann Barcalow, requested guardianship of Eleanor Barcalow and William Barcalow, minors under 14yrs., children of Derick Barcalow, dec'd. Note: two separate entries on the same page.

BARCALOW –pg. 137; Jan. 1805. Helenor Barcalow, a minor over 14yrs., dau. of Derick Barcalow, dec'd., requested Tunis D. Vanderveer as her guardian.

BARCALOW –pg. 138; Jan. 1805. Zebulon Barcalow, a minor over 14yrs., son of Derick Barcalow, dec'd., requested Tunis D. Vanderveer as his guardian.

BOWNE –pg. 140; Jan. 1805. Mary Bowne, a minor over 14yrs., dau. of Jonathan Bowne, dec'd., requested Tunis G. Vanderveer be appointed her guardian.

MOUNT –pg. 141; Jan. 1805. Timothy B. Mount, Elizabeth Covenhoven, and Lydia Mount, brother and sisters of the children's father, requested petitioner Timothy B. Mount be appointed guardian of Elizabeth Mount and Margaret Mount, minors under 14yrs., daus. of William

Mount, dec'd.

VANMATER –pg. 141; Jan. 1805. Cobauche VanMater, widow of Cyrenus VanMater, dec'd., requested William A. Wikoff be appointed guardian of her son John VanMater, a minor under 14yrs., son of Cyrenus VanMater, dec'd.

SMITH –pg. 142; Jan. 1805. Elizabeth Smith, widow of Henry Smith, dec'd., requested guardianship of her children Elsey Smith, Clark Smith, and Maryan Smith, minors under 14yrs., children of her late husband, Henry Smith, dec'd.

ARROWSMITH –pg. 144; March 1805. Henry Arrowsmith requested guardianship of Joseph Arrowsmith, Thomas Arrowsmith, Mary Arrowsmith, and Peter Arrowsmith, minors under 14yrs., children of Thomas Arrowsmith, dec'd.

ROGERS –pg. 145; March 1805. Elihu Rogers, a minor over 14yrs., son of Elihu Rogers, dec'd., chose Brittain Rogers as his guardian.

ROGERS –pg. 148; April 1805. John Rogers, a minor over 14yrs., son of Elihu Rogers, dec'd., elected Benjamin Jackson as his guardian.

ROGERS –pg. 148; April 1805. Lucretia Rogers, widow of Elihu Rogers, dec'd., requested guardianship of her children Susannah Rogers, Samuel Rogers, and Garret Rogers, minors under 14yrs., children of Elihu Rogers, dec'd.

DUBOIS –pg. 152; April 1805. Benjamin Dubois, a minor over 14yrs., son of Joseph Dubois, dec'd., requested Tunis D. Dubois be appointed his guardian.

DUBOIS –pg. 152; April 1805. Tunis G. Vanderveer and Tunis D. Dubois requested guardianship of John Dubois, a minor under 14yrs., son of Joseph Dubois, dec'd.

ALLEN –pg. 153 – 154; April 1805. Caleb Lloyd, attorney for Elizabeth Allen as the guardian of Robert Allen who was an infant interested in the estate of Samuel Allen, dec'd., presented a case and won a motion declaring all interested in the estate of Samuel Allen, dec'd., show cause or the estate would be distributed. Samuel Allen, dec'd., died intestate. Children of Samuel Allen, dec'd.: Thomas Allen, Samuel Allen, William Allen, Charles Allen, Mary Allen, Elizabeth Allen, and Sarah Allen.

COMBS –pg. 156; May 1805. Catherine Combs, widow of Solomon Combs, dec'd., requested guardianship of their children Maryann Combs and Jonathan Combs, minors under 14yrs.

HOPKINS –pg. 158; July 1805. Rebecca Hopkins requested guardianship of her children Anne Hopkins, Joseph Hopkins, Sarah Hopkins, and Samuel Hopkins, all minors under 14yrs., children of Joseph Hopkins, dec'd.

HOPKINS –pg. 158; July 1805. Mary Hopkins, a minor over 14yrs., dau. of Joseph Hopkins, dec'd., requested her mother, Rebecca Hopkins, be appointed her guardian.

MORRIS –pg. 159; July 1805. Joseph Applegate requested guardianship of Elizabeth Morris, a minor under 14yrs., dau. of Elisha Morris, dec'd.

CURTIS –pg. 159; July 1805. David Curtis Jr. requested guardianship of Robert Curtis and Elizabeth Curtis, minors under 14yrs., children of Thomas Curtis, dec'd.

BURTON –pg. 160; July 1805. Obadiah Hollinbak and his wife, Sarah, late Sarah Burton, were complainants against Joseph Dennis, executor of the estate of Jesse Burton, dec'd.

LAYTON –pg. 160; July 1805. Thomas Layton and his wife, Mary, late Mary Layton, were complainants against James Frost, Esq., executor of the estate of Andrew Layton, dec'd.

MEIRS –pg. 161; July 1805. James Allen, Esq., and his wife, Sarah, late Sarah Thomas, were complainants against Jacob Herbert and his wife, Hannah, late Hannah Meirs, and against Benjamin Jackson, where Hannah and Benjamin were executors of the estate of John Meirs, dec'd.

ROGERS –pg. 164; July 1805. Benjamin Jackson, guardian of John Rogers, son of Elihu Rogers, dec'd., petitioned for a division of the real estate owned by said Elihu Rogers, dec'd., who

died intestate leaving children.
Children: Brittain Rogers, Elihu Rogers, John Rogers, Samuel Rogers, Garret Rogers, and
Susannah Rogers.

VANMATER –pg. 171; Oct. 1805. William A. Wycoff, in behalf of his ward John VanMater,
petitioned for a division of real estate that belonged to Cyrenius VanMater, dec'd., father of
his ward. The petition stated: Abigail VanMater, dec'd., dau. of Cornelius VanMater, dec'd.,
died intestate and without issue, but holding real estate in Shrewsbury Tshp. At the time of
her death she had neither brother, sister, aunt, nor uncle on her father's side living to inherit
her real estate; therefore, the real estate descended to the children of her deceased aunts and
uncles, namely the children of Jacob, Cyrenius, Eleanor and Sibache. After the division, the
share belonging to Cyrenius VanMater, dec'd., remained undivided and owned by his thirteen
children: Benjamin, Aaron, William, Anne, Jacob, Cornelius, Elizabeth, Garret, Eleanor,
Catherine, Peter, Sarah, and John. The said John, Peter, and Sarah were under 21yrs. of age.
Note: See Book C, pg. 118, July 1804.

BEAKES –pg. 181; Oct. 1805. James Allen, Esq., and his wife, Sarah, late Sarah Thomas, were
complainants against Edmund Beakes, surviving executor of the estate of William Beakes,
dec'd.

FORMAN –pg. 182; Jan. 1806. Garret Forman and his wife, Ann, late Ann Ker, petitioned for a
division of the real estate belonging to her father, Ebenezer Ker, dec'd., who died intestate
owning real estate in Upper Freehold Tshp. The deceased left three children: Ann Forman,
the petitioner; Euphame Ker, under 21yrs.; and Phebe Ker, under 21yrs.

KER –pg. 183; Jan. 1806. Phebe Ker, a minor over 14yrs., dau. of Ebenezer Ker, dec'd., requested
the appointment of Dr. John A. Scudder as her guardian.

COX –pg. 183; Jan. 1806. James Cox, a minor over 14yrs., son of Nathaniel Cox, dec'd., requested
Dr. Edward Taylor be appointed his guardian.

CLAYTON –pg. 183; Jan. 1806. Thomas Clayton, a minor over 14yrs., son of Joel Clayton, dec'd.,
requested James Morris as his guardian.

CLAYTON –pg. 184; Jan. 1806. Zebulon Clayton, a minor over 14yrs., son of Joel Clayton, dec'd.,
elected James Morris as his guardian.

CLAYTON –pg. 187; Jan. 1806. James Perine filed his accounts as executor of the estate of David
Clayton, dec'd. The record revealed David Clayton, dec'd., was the administrator of the
estate of his son John Clayton, dec'd.

SEXTON –pg. 195; April 1806. Asher Cox requested appointment as guardian of Asher Sexton, a
minor under 14yrs., son of William Sexton, dec'd.

MOUNT –pg. 195; April 1806. Cornelius S. Mount, a minor over 14yrs., son of William Mount,
dec'd., selected Richard Applegate as his guardian.

SEXTON –pg. 196; April 1806. Daniel Sexton, son of William Sexton, dec'd., requested a division
of real estate amongst him and his brothers, Joseph Sexton and Asher Sexton who was under
14yrs. His father, William Sexton, dec'd., and grandfather Daniel Sexton, dec'd., both died
owning real estate in Upper Freehold Tshp.

HONCE –pg. 197; April 1806. George Thompson and his wife, Mary, late Mary Honce, petitioned
for a division of real estate. John Honce, dec'd., died owning land in Freehold Tshp. He left
no issue, but he had siblings.
Siblings: David Honce; Cornelius Honce; Hendrick Honce, under 21yrs.; Jane Tice, wife of
Peter Tice; Phebe Honce; Elsey Honce, under 21yrs.; and the petitioner, Mary Thompson,
wife of George Thompson.
Note: See Book C, pg. 229, July 1806, where Jane Tice was referred to as Jane Tyson in the
actual division of real estate.

CORLIES –pg. 198; April 1806. William Tilton and his wife, Margaret, the late Margaret Corlies,
petitioned for a division of her father's real estate. Timothy Corlies, dec'd., late of
Shrewsbury, wrote his last will and testament without disposing of certain lands he then
owned.
Children: Hannah Woolley, wife of Samuel Woolley; Deborah Corlies; Elizabeth Allen, wife

of William Allen; Lydia Lloyd, wife of Robert Lloyd; George Corlies, a minor; Edna Corlies, a minor; Phebe Corlies, a minor; Rebecca Corlies, a minor; and Margaret Tilton, wife of William Tilton.
Grandchildren, unnamed, who were children of his son Joseph Corlies, dec'd., who died intestate.

MOUNT –pg. 199; April 1806. Rebecca S. Mount, a minor over 14yrs., dau. of William Mount, dec'd., requested the appointment of Richard Applegate as her guardian.

COX –pg. 199; April 1806. Abel Cox requested guardianship of Gilbert Cox and Maryan Cox, minors under 14yrs., children of Benjamin Cox, dec'd.

CORNELIUS –pg. 200; April 1806. Sarah Cornelius requested guardianship of Allen Cornelius, Rebecca Cornelius, and Hyram Parent Cornelius, all minors under 14yrs.

HERBERT –pg. 216; July 1806. James Herbert Jr., a minor over 14yrs., son of Daniel Herbert, dec'd., chose James Herbert, Esq., as his guardian.

REID –pg. 224; July 1806. Jasper Smith and his wife, Theodocia, late Theodocia Reid, were complainants against the executors of the estate of Samuel Reid, dec'd., who was the executor of the estate of Col. John Reid, dec'd.

CORLIES –pg. 232; July 1806. Abigail Edwards, late Abigail Corlies, was a complainant against Britton Corlies, surviving executor of the estate of Jacob Corlies, dec'd.

WOOLLEY –pg. 233; Oct. 1806. Abraham Woolley and Adam Woolley Jr., children and heirs of William Woolley, dec'd., petitioned for a division of real estate. William Woolley, dec'd., died intestate owning a farm in Dover Tshp., a half interest in a saw mill, and several smaller tracts of land. He left five children, some being under the age of 21yrs.

WOOLLEY –pg. 237; Oct. 1806. William Woolley, a minor over 14yrs., son of William Woolley, dec'd., chose Samuel Allen as his guardian.

CRAIG –pg. 238; Oct. 1806. Capt. David Craig requested appointment as guardian of Eleanor Craig and Ann Craig, minors under 14yrs., children of James I. Craig, dec'd.

HERBERT –pg. 240; Oct. 1806. James Herbert, administrator of the estate of Daniel Herbert (son of Daniel Herbert), dec'd., filed a settlement of the accounts.

HERBERT –pg. 240; Oct. 1806. James Herbert, administrator of the estate of Ann Dorothy Herbert, dec'd., filed a settlement of accounts.

SCHANCK –pg. 258; Jan. 1807. Tunis D. Dubois and Daniel I. Schanck requested guardianship of Catherine Schanck, Maria Schanck, David Schanck, Sarah Schanck, and Jane Schanck, all minors under 14yrs., children of Tunis Schanck, dec'd.

WHITE –pg. 258; Jan. 1807. Jacob White requested guardianship of John Hedger White, a minor under 14yrs., son of John White, dec'd., late of Shrewsbury.

WOOLLEY –pg. 260 – 267; Jan. 1807. The real estate of William Woolley, dec'd., was divided amongst his heirs: Abraham Woolley; Elizabeth Allen, wife of John Allen; Adam Woolley; Ann Allen, wife of James Allen; and William Woolley.

HORSFULL –pg. 268; March 1807. Elizabeth Horsfull, mother of Martha Horsfull and Sarah Horsfull, minors under 14 yrs., children of William Horsfull, dec'd., requested Job Kirby be appointed guardian of her children.

WILLIAMSON –pg. 268; March 1807. Elizabeth Williamson requested guardianship of her children Deborah Williamson and Mary Williamson, minors under 14yrs., children of Cornelius Williamson, dec'd.

WILLIAMSON –pg. 269; March 1807. Tunis Williamson, a minor over 14yrs., son of Cornelius Williamson, dec'd., requested Cornelius P. Vanderhoef, Esq., be appointed his guardian.

BOOK D
1807 – 1813

HOLMES –pg. 4; April 1807. John Stoutenborough along with Philip Holmes, brother of the children's father, requested John Stoutenborough be granted guardianship of Leah Holmes and Catherine Holmes, minors under 14yrs., children of William Holmes, dec'd., late of Freehold.

SOUTHARD –pg. 4; April 1807. Mary Southard, widow of Job Southard, dec'd., requested guardianship of Elizabeth Southard, Rachel Southard, and Mary Southard, minors under 14yrs., children of Job Southard, dec'd., late of Stafford Tshp.

ALLEN –pg. 4; April 1807. Joseph Allen along with Edmund Lafetra the grandfather of Elizabeth Allen, Hannah Allen, and Ebenezer Allen, asked the court to appoint petitioner Joseph Allen as guardian of the children, all minors under 14yrs., children of Daniel Allen, dec'd.

SCHANCK –pg. 5; April 1807. Tunis D. Dubois and Daniel I. Schanck were appointed guardians of Tunis Schanck, a minor under 14yrs., son of Tunis Schanck, dec'd., late of Freehold.

CONKLIN –pg. 5; April 1807. Joseph Conklin, a minor over 14yrs., son of John Conklin, dec'd., chose Silas Crane, Esq., as his guardian.

SKIDMORE –pg. 14; July 1807. A request to sell the real estate owned by Robert Skidmore, dec'd., to pay his debts was filed by Robert Holman and his wife, Sarah, late Sarah Skidmore, administrator of the estate of Robert Skidmore, dec'd.

STILLWELL –pg. 21; Oct. 1807. Lewis Dye, Catherine Dye, Mary Stillwell, and Lydia Stillwell, children and heirs of Gershom Stillwell, dec'd., petitioned for a division of the real estate owned by Gershom Stillwell, dec'd., who died intestate.

BOWNE –pg. 22; Oct. 1807. William Bowne, a minor over 14yrs., son of Jonathan Bowne, dec'd., chose John Hull, Esq., as his guardian.

BOWNE –pg. 23; Oct. 1807. John Bowne, a minor over 14yrs., son of Jonathan Bowne, dec'd., chose John Hull, Esq., as his guardian.

SMITH –pg. 23; Oct. 1807. Benjamin Wardell and Elizabeth Smith, widow of the child's father, requested the appointment of Benjamin Wardell as guardian of Emilina Smith, a minor under 14yrs., dau. of Benajah Smith, dec'd.

DENISE –pg. 27; Oct. 1807. Tobias Polhemus, guardian of Catherine Conover, late Catherine Denise, filed a settlement of accounts.

WILLIAMS –pg. 31; Jan. 1808. Daniel Williams requested appointment as guardian of his sister Ann Williams, a minor under 14yrs., dau. of Israel Williams, dec'd.

ALLEN –pg. 31; Jan. 1808. David Lewis and William Allen requested the appointment of David Lewis as guardian of Thomas Jeffrey and Catherine Jeffrey, minors under 14yrs., children of Thomas Jeffrey Jr., dec'd. William Allen was the children's brother.

VANDERHOEF –pg. 32; Jan. 1808. Peter Vanderhoef, a minor over 14yrs., son of Samuel Vanderhoef, dec'd., elected Cornelius P. Vanderhoef, Esq., as his guardian.

STILLWELL –pg. 36; Jan. 1808. The real estate of Gershom Stillwell, dec'd., was divided into three shares.
Heirs receiving one share each: Lydia Stillwell and Mary Stillwell.

Heirs receiving one share total: Lewis Dye and Catherine Dye.

WILLIAMSON –pg. 47; April 1808. Senah Williamson (mother of the minor) and John Holsart requested John Holsart be appointed the guardian of Mary Williamson, a minor under 14yrs., dau. of William Williamson, dec'd.

ANTRIM –pg. 47; April 1808. Elisha L. Antrim, a minor over 14yrs., son of John Antrim, dec'd., requested Ann Antrim be appointed his guardian.

VANMATER –pg. 48; April 1808. Chrineyonce B. VanMater and Elizabeth VanMater, minors over 14yrs., children of William VanMater, dec'd., elected James Smith as their guardian. Note: two separate entries on the same page.

VANMATER –pg. 48; April 1808. William A. Wikoff and his wife, Eleanor, dau. of Cyrenius B. VanMater, dec'd., were complainants against Cornelius VanMater who was executor of the estate of said Cyrenius B. VanMater, dec'd.

VANMATER –pg. 49; April 1808. Hendrick G. Hendrickson and his wife, Phebe, dau. of Cyrenius Vanmater, dec'd., were complainants against William Vanmater, surviving administrator of the estate of Cyrenius Vanmater, dec'd.

BOWNE –pg. 53; April 1808. Tunis G. Vanderveer, guardian of Mary Towers, late Mary Bowne, filed a settlement of accounts.

BARCALOW –pg. 53; April 1808. Tunis D. Vanderveer, guardian of Helena Lanier, late Helena Barcalow, filed a settlement of accounts.

CRAIG –pg. 60 – 67; June 1808. John I. Craig and John P. Covenhoven asked the court to establish the mental status of Lewis Craig and appoint a guardian for him. Lewis Craig of Freehold Tshp. was the brother of the petitioner John I. Craig, and had been deprived of reason and understanding for over a year. The court established Lewis Craig was about 33yrs. of age and his closest heirs were his siblings. Lewis Craig was declared mentally incompetent. Siblings: William J. Craig; John I. Craig; Ann Lloyd, wife of James Lloyd; and Mary Drummond, wife of Robert Drummond.

WILLIAMSON –pg. 67; July 1808. William Williamson, a minor over 14yrs., son of William Williamson, dec'd., elected John Holsart as his guardian.

CORNELIUS –pg. 68; July 1808. A joint petition by Gabriel Woodmansee and Sarah Ferguson, late Sarah Cornelius and the mother of Allen Cornelius, Rebecca Cornelius, and Hyram P. Cornelius, minors under 14yrs., children of Daniel Cornelius, dec'd., requested Gabriel Woodmansee be appointed guardian of the said minor children.

BOWNE –pg. 74 - 78; July 1808. The record was concerned with the 1795 court order to divide the real estate of Jonathan Bowne, dec'd., and the division that occurred in 1798; an error was found and the land re-divided.
Children of Jonathan Bowne, dec'd.: William Bowne; John Bowne; Sarah Bowne, wife of Vincent Antonades; Mary Bowne, wife of Mr. ____ Towars; and Elizabeth Bowne, wife of John Combs. Note: See Book B, pg. 56, Oct. 1795, and Book B, pg. 136, July 1799.

ARROWSMITH –pg. 80; Aug. 1808. Joseph Arrowsmith, a minor over 14yrs., son of Thomas Arrowsmith, dec'd., elected John P. VanPelt as his guardian.

SICKLES –pg. 81; Oct. 1808. Sarah Sickles and John Sickles, minors over 14yrs., children of Duncan Sickles, dec'd., chose Jacob Holmes as their guardian. Note: two separate entries on the same page.

SICKLES –pg. 82; Oct. 1808. Jacob Holmes requested guardianship of Zachariah Sickles, a minor under 14yrs., son of Duncan Sickles, dec'd.

HOWLAND –pg. 82; Oct. 1808. Christianna Howland, widow of James Howland, dec'd., requested guardianship of Charles Howland, Ann Howland, and Lydia Howland, minors under 14yrs., children of James Howland, dec'd.

WILLIAMS –pg. 93; Jan. 1809. George McCully and his wife, Ann, late Ann Williams and widow of John Williams, dec'd., requested guardianship of Hannah Williams, Samuel Williams,

Jonathan Williams, and Isaac Williams, minors under 14yrs., children of John Williams, dec'd. Note: A request by George McCully to sell the children's property in Book D, pg. 160, April 1810 reported the recent death of his wife, Ann McCully.

VANPELT –pg. 94; Jan. 1809. John P. VanPelt requested guardianship of Walter VanPelt and Mary VanPelt, minors under 14yrs., children of Jacob VanPelt, dec'd.

HOWLAND –pg. 94; Jan. 1809. Cook Howland requested guardianship of his brother Asher Howland, a minor under 14yrs. Both were sons of James Howland, dec'd.

JEFFREY –pg. 115; April 1809. Thomas Jeffrey, a minor over 14yrs., son of Thomas Jeffrey, dec'd., chose James Morris as his guardian.

BENNET –pg. 116; April 1809. William I. Bennet, a minor over 14yrs., son of John Bennet, dec'd., elected James Smith as his guardian.

VANPELT –pg. 116; April 1809. John VanPelt, a minor over 14yrs., son of Jacob VanPelt, dec'd., requested John P. VanPelt as his guardian.

VANPELT –pg. 117; April 1809. James VanPelt, a minor over 14yrs., son of Jacob VanPelt, dec'd., requested John P. VanPelt as his guardian.

VANPELT –pg. 117; April 1809. John P. VanPelt requested guardianship of Hendrick VanPelt, William VanPelt, and Sarah VanPelt, minors under 14yrs., children of Jacob VanPelt, dec'd.

WOODMANSEE –pg. 117; April 1809. Louisa Woodmansee, widow of Reuben Woodmansee, dec'd., requested guardianship of John Woodmansee, Martha Woodmansee, and Deborah Woodmansee, minors under 14yrs., children of Reuben Woodmansee, dec'd.

SMITH –pg. 123; July 1809. Elisha Reynolds and his wife, Elizabeth, late Elizabeth Smith the administrator of the estate of Henry Smith, dec'd., filed to sell real estate belonging to the deceased.

DENISE –pg. 128; July 1809. Margaret Denise, a minor over 14yrs., dau. of Tunis Denise, dec'd., elected William I. Covenhoven as her guardian.

HORNOR –pg. 128; July 1809. Rebecca Hornor, widow of Aaron Horner, dec'd., requested guardianship of her children John Hornor, Sarah Hornor, Aaron Hornor, and William Hornor, minors under 14yrs., children of Aaron Hornor, dec'd.

GIFFORD –pg. 131; Oct. 1809. Joshua Gifford, son of Joshua Gifford, dec'd., petitioned for a division of his father's real estate. Joshua Gifford, dec'd., died intestate about nine years earlier.

ELLIS –pg. 133; Oct. 1809. Eliza Ellis, a minor over 14yrs., dau. of Rowland Ellis of the city of Philadelphia, filed a petition for a guardian. Her father had lived in Philadelphia for several years, renounced his rights as her father, and left her estate in the care of an aged grandmother. She requested Jacob Hendrickson and William Lawrie be appointed her guardians.

HOPKINS –pg. 133; Oct. 1809. Moses Hopkins, a minor over 14yrs., son of Barzillai Hopkins, dec'd., elected Ann Hopkins as his guardian.

HOPKINS –pg. 134; Oct. 1809. Ann Hopkins, widow of Barzillai Hopkins, dec'd., requested guardianship of Barzillai Hopkins and Ann Hopkins, minors under 14yrs., children of Barzillai Hopkins, dec'd.

REYNOLDS –pg. 134; Oct. 1809. Elizabeth Reynolds, widow of Elisha Reynolds, dec'd., requested guardianship of Enoch Reynolds, Maria Reynolds, and Hiram Reynolds, minors under 14yrs., children of the said Elisha Reynolds, dec'd.

LEFFERTSON –pg. 134; Oct. 1809. Benjamin Leffertson and William T. Croxson requested the appointment of William T. Croxson as guardian of Leffert Leffertson, a minor under 14yrs., son of Oukey Leffertson, dec'd. Benjamin Leffertson, the petitioner, was the brother of Leffert.

LEFFERTSON –pg. 135; Oct. 1809. Garret Leffertson, a minor over 14yrs., son of Oukey Leffertson, dec'd., elected William T. Croxson as his guardian.

CORNELIUS –pg. 142; Oct. 1809. Gabriel Woodmansee, guardian of Allen Cornelius, Rebecca Cornelius, and Hyram Parent Cornelius, was a complainant against Joshua Ferguson and his wife, Sarah, late Sarah Cornelius the administratrix of the estate of David Cornelius, dec'd., and against John Cornelius, adminstrator of the same estate. Note: See Book D, pg. 68, July 1808, where an earlier guardianship petition for the children named their father Daniel Cornelius, dec'd.

DENISE –pg. 142; Oct. 1809. Samuel Denise, a minor over 14yrs., son of Tunis Denise, dec'd., chose William I. Covenhoven as his guardian.

ANTRAM –pg. 143; Jan. 1810. Ann Antram Jr. and Abigail Scattergood, late Abigail Antram, wife of Jonathan Scattergood, petitioned for a division of the real estate owned by their father, John Antram, Esq., dec'd., who died intestate leaving children and heirs.

SMITH –pg. 144; Jan. 1810. Elizabeth Smith, a minor over 14yrs., dau. of William Smith, dec'd., elected Mathias Golden as her guardian.

SICKLES –pg. 144; Jan. 1810. Zachariah Sickles, a minor over 14yrs., son of Duncan Sickles, dec'd., elected Thomas Slocum as his guardian.

CRAIG –pg. 145; Jan. 1810. Ann Craig, a minor over 14yrs., dau. of James I. Craig, dec'd., chose Samuel Craig as her guardian.

SOPER –pg. 145; Jan. 1810. A request to sell the real estate of Joseph Soper Jr., dec'd., for payment of his debts, was filed by Joseph Wills and his wife, Phebe, late Phebe Soper the administrator of the estate of Joseph Soper Jr., dec'd.

GIFFORD –pg. 156; Jan. 1810. Stephen Frazer and his wife, Amy, late Amy Gifford the administrator of the estate of Joshua Gifford, dec'd., filed a settlement of accounts.

CHEESEMAN –pg. 158; Jan. 1810. George Reid and his wife, Lucy, late Lucy Cheeseman the administrator of the estate of Joseph Cheeseman, dec'd., filed a settlement of accounts.

ANTRIM –pg. 161; April 1810. The real estate of John Antrim, Esq., dec'd., was divided amongst his heirs.
Widow: Ann Antrim.
Heirs: Charity Wineright, late Charity Antrim; Isaac Antrim; Caleb Antrim; Ann Antrim; Abigail Scattergood, late Abigail Antrim; Thomas Antrim; John Antrim; Elisha Antrim; and Henry Antrim. Ann Antrim was the only heir in this record actually specified as a dau. of the deceased.

COTTRELL –pg. 174; April 1810. Jane Cottrell, widow of Gershom Cottrell, dec'd., requested guardianship of Enoch Cottrell, Getty Cottrell, Isaiah Cottrell, Harvey Cottrell, Tylee Cottrell, Israel Cottrell, and Gershom Cottrell, all minors under 14yrs., children of Gershom Cottrell, dec'd.

BREWER –pg. 174; April 1810. Ann Brewer, widow of David Brewer, dec'd., requested guardianship of John Brewer, Ann Brewer, and Lydia Brewer, minors under 14yrs., children of David Brewer, dec'd.

COX –pg. 175; April 1810. Margaret Cox, widow of William Cox, dec'd., requested guardianship of Lydia Cox, Joshua Cox, William Cox, and Catherine Cox, minors under 14yrs., children of William Cox, dec'd.

GIFFORD –pg. 175; April 1810. Sarah Gifford and Amos Gifford, minors over 14yrs., children of Joshua Gifford, dec'd., requested Annaniah Gifford Jr. be appointed their guardian. Note: two separate entries on the same page.

COX –pg. 176; April 1810. Phebe Cox, Richard Cox, and Thomas Cox, minors over 14yrs., children of William Cox, dec'd., selected Margaret Cox as their guardian. Note: three separate entries on the same page.

CAMPBELL –pg. 177; July 1810. Jane Campbell, widow of Benjamin Campbell, dec'd., requested appointment as guardian of John Campbell, William Campbell, Catherine Campbell, and Benjamin Campbell, minors under 14yrs., children of Benjamin Campbell, dec'd.

CAMPBELL –pg. 177; July 1810. Hannah Campbell, a minor over 14yrs., dau. of Benjamin Campbell, dec'd., elected Duncan Campbell as her guardian.

CAMPBELL –pg. 178; July 1810. Eleanor Campbell, a minor over 14yrs., dau. of Benjamin Campbell, dec'd., elected Duncan Campbell as her guardian.

GIFFORD –pg. 179 – 182; July 1810. The real estate of Joshua Gifford, dec'd., was divided amongst his heirs: Annaniah Gifford; Amos Gifford; Joshua Gifford; Mary Connett, wife of Matthew Connett; and Sary Gifford.

WILGUS –pg. 184; July 1810. A settlement of accounts was filed by Solomon Ridgway and his wife, Margaret, late Margaret Wilgus, administrator of the estate of Asa Wilgus, dec'd.

DAVIDSON –pg. 194; Oct. 1810. Caroline H. Davidson, a minor over 14yrs., dau. of Jedediah Davidson, dec'd., elected Thomas Henderson, Esq., as her guardian.

PHARO –pg. 195; Oct. 1810. Timothy Pharo, a minor over 14yrs., son of Timothy Pharo, dec'd., elected Stephen Willits of Burlington Co. as his guardian.

LAWRENCE –pg. 201; Jan. 1811. As administrator of the estate of Joseph Lawrence, dec'd., Benjamin Lawrence was ordered to distribute the money to the children of the intestate. Children of Joseph Lawrence, dec'd.: Benjamin Lawrence, Meribah Barton, and Mary Imlay, wife of Isaac Imlay.

COX –pg. 202; Jan. 1811. Margaret Cox requested guardianship of Morgan Cox and Horatio J. Cox, minors under 14yrs., children of General James Cox, dec'd.

COX –pg. 203; Jan. 1811. Ezekiel T. Cox and Jonathan Cox, minors over 14yrs., sons of General James Cox, dec'd., chose Margaret Cox as their guardian. Note: two separate entries on same page.

COX –pg. 204; Jan. 1811. David Cox, a minor over 14yrs., son of General James Cox, dec'd., elected Margaret Cox as his guardian.

BRAY –pg. 204; Jan. 1811. Ann Bray and David Bray, minors over 14yrs., children of James Bray, dec'd., elected Rachel Bray as their guardian. Note: two separate entries on the same page.

GREEN –pg. 205; Jan. 1811. Tylee Williams and Ezekiel Forman, grandfather of the minor, requested Tylee Williams be appointed guardian of Henrietta Green, a minor under 14yrs., dau. of Henry Green, dec'd.

HOLMES –pg. 205; Jan. 1811. Eleanor Holmes, widow of Philip Holmes, dec'd., along with Peter Johnston, grandfather of the minors, requested the said Peter Johnston be appointed guardian of Ida Holmes, Eliza Holmes, Eleanor Holmes, Ann Holmes, and Mary Jane Holmes, minors under 14yrs., children of Philip Holmes, dec'd.

TILTON –pg. 206: Jan. 1811. Ann Tilton, widow of Samuel Tilton, dec'd., requested guardianship of Sarah Tilton and Lydia Tilton, minors under 14yrs., children of Samuel Tilton, dec'd.

ANDERSON –pg. 206; March 1811. John Anderson requested guardianship of his sisters Elizabeth Anderson and Sarah Anderson, minors under 14yrs., children of Samuel Anderson, dec'd.

BRAY –pg. 207; April 1811. Rachel Bray, widow of James Bray, dec'd., requested guardianship of Catherine Bray, Samuel Bray, and Laurietta Bray, minors under 14yrs., children of James Bray, dec'd.

HORSFULL –pg. 213; April 1811. Mary Harper requested guardianship of her granddaughter Maryan Horsfull, a minor under 14yrs., dau. of Ezekiel Horsfull, dec'd.

PHARO –pg. 213; April 1811. Anne Pharo, widow of Robert Pharo, dec'd., petitioned for guardianship of Allen Pharo and Charlotte Pharo, minors under 14yrs., children of Robert Pharo, dec'd.

MORRIS –pg. 219; July 1811. John King and his wife, Margaret, late Margaret Morris, and William Morris, administrators of the estate of Lewis Morris, dec'd., filed to sell the deceased's real estate to pay his debts.

CAMPBELL –pg. 223; July 1811. John Campbell, a minor over 14yrs., son of Benjamin Campbell, dec'd., requested William Campbell as his guardian.

LITTLE –pg. 223; July 1811. Thomas Little, a minor over 14yrs., son of Thomas Little, Esq., dec'd., selected Robert Evelman as his guardian.

KLINE –pg. 223; July 1811. James Montgomery requested guardianship of Jane Kline, a minor under 14yrs., dau. of Jesse Kline, dec'd.

SKIDMORE –pg. 232; Jan. 1812. Robert Holman and his wife, Sarah, late Sarah Skidmore, administrator of the estate of Robert Skidmore, dec'd., filed a settlement of accounts.

FORMAN –pg. 234; Jan. 1812. Thomas Shinn, guardian of Ann Simms, late Ann Forman, filed a settlement of accounts.

TAYLOR –pg. 245; April 1812. Martha Taylor, a minor over 14yrs., dau. of John W. Taylor, dec'd., elected Nancy Taylor as her guardian.

CHAMBERS –pg. 246; April 1812. Jane Chambers, a minor over 14yrs., dau. of John Chambers, dec'd., elected Hendrick Smock as her guardian.

CHAMBERS –pg. 246; April 1812. Elizabeth Chambers, a minor over 14yrs., dau. of John Chambers, dec'd., elected John H. Smock as her guardian.

TAYLOR –pg. 247; April 1812. Nancy Taylor, widow of John W. Taylor, dec'd., requested appointment as guardian of Joseph Taylor, John Taylor, and James Taylor, minors under 14yrs., children of John W. Taylor, dec'd.

CHAMBERS –pg. 247; April 1812. John H. Smock requested guardianship of Eleanor Chambers, a minor under 14yrs., dau. of John Chambers, dec'd.

HOLMES –pg. 247; April 1812. Ann Holmes, widow of Joseph L. Holmes, dec'd., requested guardianship of Mary Ann Holmes and Charles Holmes, minors under 14yrs., children of Joseph L. Holmes, dec'd.

WOODMANSEE –pg. 254; July 1812. Isaac Woodmansee and his wife, Abigail, dau. of John Woodmansee, dec'd., requested a division of the real estate owned by John Woodmansee, dec'd., who died leaving heirs, some under 21yrs. Note: See Book E, Pg. 45 - 50, April 1814.

TRUAX –pg. 255; July 1812. Salyer Morrell and his wife, Catherine, were complainants against Catherine Truax, administrator of the estate of John Truax, dec'd.

INMAN –pg. 256; July 1812. Job Inman, a minor over 14yrs., son of Job Inman, dec'd., elected Esther Inman as his guardian.

INMAN –pg. 257; July 1812. Sarah Inman and Esther Inman, minors over 14yrs., children of Job Inman, dec'd., elected Esther Inman as their guardian. Note: two entries on the same page.

THROCKMORTON –pg. 258; July 1812. Edmund Throckmorton, Joseph W. Throckmorton, and Samuel Throckmorton, minors over 14yrs., sons of Joseph F. Throckmorton, dec'd., elected Tylee Williams as their guardian. Note: three separate entries on the same page.

SEXTON –pg. 259; July 1812. Asher Sexton, a minor over 14yrs., son of William Sexton, dec'd., chose Thomas Britton as his guardian.

RIDGWAY –pg. 259; July 1812. Mary Ridgway, widow of Richard Ridgway, dec'd., asked for guardianship of Amos Ridgway, Harriet Ridgway, Mary Ridgway, John Ridgway, and Susan Ridgway, minors under 14yrs., children of Richard Ridgway, dec'd.

INMAN –pg. 260; July 1812. Esther Inman, widow of Job Inman, dec'd., requested appointment as guardian of Ann Inman, Mary Inman, and Hannah Inman, minors under 14yrs., children of Job Inman, dec'd.

HOLMES –pg. 260; July 1812. Garret P. Wikoff was appointed guardian of Deborah L. Holmes, a minor under 14yrs., dau. of John Holmes, dec'd.

THROCKMORTON –pg. 260; July 1812. Tylee Williams and Margaret Throckmorton, widow of Joseph F. Throckmorton, dec'd., requested Tylee Williams be appointed guardian of James Forman Throckmorton, a minor under 14yrs., son of Joseph F. Throckmorton, dec'd.

BREWER –pg. 261; July 1812. Meriam Brewer, widow of John Brewer, dec'd., requested guardianship of William Brewer, Margaret Brewer, and Mary Brewer, minors under 14yrs., children of John Brewer, dec'd.

VANDERVEER –pg. 266; July 1812. David Vanderveer, John Lloyd, Enoch Coward and his wife, Eleanor, late Eleanor Vanderveer, guardians of John L. Vanderveer, Sarah Vanderveer, David R. Vanderveer, Catherine Vanderveer, Rulef Vanderveer, and Tunis Vanderveer, filed a settlement of accounts.

GOLDEN –pg. 269; Oct. 1812. Chatherine Golden, widow of Elias Golden, dec'd., requested appointment as guardian of Ann Golden and John Golden, minors under 14yrs., children of Elias Golden, dec'd.

MCKNIGHT –pg. 269; Oct. 1812. John McKnight, a minor over 14yrs., son of Lewis McKnight, dec'd., chose William McKnight as his guardian.

HIMES –pg. 279; Oct. 1812. Andrew Smith and his wife, Susannah, late Susannah Himes, were complainants against the executors of the estate of George Himes, dec'd.

HORSFULL –pg. 285; Jan. 1813. Martha Horsfull who reached the age of 14yrs. asked Job Kirby continue as her guardian.

HORSFULL –pg. 285; Jan. 1813. William Blackwell and his wife, Martha, were complainants against John Horsfull and Richard Horsfull, executors of the estate of Richard Horsfull, dec'd.

FORMAN –pg. 287; Jan. 1813. Rev. Dr. John Woodhull requested guardianship of his granddaughter Sarah Marsh Forman, a minor under 14yrs., dau. of William G. Forman, Esq., dec'd.

CAMPBELL –pg. 287; Jan. 1813. Eleanor Campbell, a minor over 14yrs., dau. of Benjamin Campbell, dec'd., requested Caleb Lloyd, Esq., as her guardian.

CONOVER –pg. 288; Jan. 1813. Peter Conover, a minor over 14yrs., son of Garret Covenhoven, Esq., dec'd., requested Job Walter as his guardian.

GORDEN –pg. 297; Feb. 1813. William Tenant Gordon, a minor over 14yrs., son of William Gordon, dec'd., elected John Hall as his guardian.

DENISE –pg. 297; Feb. 1813. Elizabeth Denise, widow of Garret Denise, dec'd., requested guardianship of William Denise, Jane Denise, Elizabeth Denise, Margaret Denise, and Eleanor Denise, minors under 14yrs., children of Garret Denise, dec'd.

DENISE –pg. 298; Feb. 1813. Catherine Denise and Ann Denise, minors over 14yrs., children of Garret Denise, dec'd., elected Elizabeth Denise as their guardian. Note: two separate entries on the same page.

WOODHULL –pg. 299; March 1813. John T. Woodhull requested guardianship of Mary Ann Woodhull, a minor under 14yrs., dau. of William Hedge Woodhull, dec'd.

HULSE –pg. 300; March 1813. Thomas Hulse, a minor over 14yrs., son of Silvenus Hulse, dec'd., elected Joel Hulse as his guardian.

HULSE –pg. 301; March 1813. Samuel Hulse, a minor over 14yrs., son of Silvenus Hulse, dec'd., elected Joel Hulse as his guardian.

HULSE –pg. 301; April 1813. Richard Longstreet and Mahalah Hulse, widow of John Hulse, dec'd., requested Richard Longstreet be appointed guardian of Lydia Hulse, a minor under 14yrs., dau. of John Hulse, dec'd.

ALLEN –pg. 302; April 1813. Hannah Allen, widow of David Allen, dec'd., requested guardianship
    of Deliah Allen, Joseph Allen, Elizabeth Allen, John Allen, and Lydia Allen, minors under
    14yrs., children of David Allen, dec'd.

LITTLE –pg. 309; April 1813. Theophilus Little requested guardianship of his granddaughter Betsy
    Little, a minor under 14yrs., dau. of John Little, a non-resident of New Jersey.

DAVISON –pg. 309; April 1813. Elizabeth Davison, widow of William Davison, dec'd., requested
    guardianship of John Davison, Benjamin Davison, William Davison, Marian Davison, James
    Davison, Sarah Davison, and Ezekiel Davison, minors under 14yrs., children of William
    Davison, dec'd.

IMLAY –pg. 309; April 1813. Hannah Imlay and Richard L. Beatty requested guardianship of John
    H. Imlay and Jacob T. Imlay, minors under 14yrs., children of James Imlay, dec'd.

MORLATT –pg. 314; June 1813. James Morlatt, a minor over 14yrs., son of James Morlatt, dec'd.,
    requested Garret D. Conover as his guardian.

MORLATT –pg. 322; July 1813. John G. Taylor requested guardianship of Mary Morlatt, Sarah
    Lloyd Morlatt, Hannah Ruth Morlatt, Ida Ann Morlatt, Garret D. Conover Morlatt, Eleanor
    Cole Morlatt, and Lenah Morlatt, minors under 14yrs., children of James Morlatt, dec'd.

ALLEN –pg. 322; July 1813. David Allen, a minor over 14yrs., son of David Allen, dec'd., elected
    Samuel Allen as his guardian.

BRAND –pg. 323; July 1813. Malson Brand, a minor over 14yrs., son of Thomas Brand, dec'd.,
    elected John Morton as his guardian. Note: The ink was smeared over the minor's given
    name.

BRAND –pg. 323; July 1813. White Brand, a minor over 14yrs., son of Thomas Brand, dec'd.,
    elected John Morton as his guardian.

BRAND –pg. 324; July 1813. Latitia Brand, a minor over 14yrs., dau. of Thomas Brand, dec'd.,
    elected John Morton as her guardian.

BOOK E

1814 – 1816

WOOLLEY –pg. 2; Jan. 1814. Britton Woolley and Montillion Woolley petitioned for a division of the real estate owned by Montillion Woolley, dec'd., late of Shrewsbury Tshp., who died intestate.

MORRISON –pg. 4; Jan. 1814. Daniel Connolly and his wife, Mary, and James Egbert and his wife, Sarah, petitioned for a division of the real estate owned by William Morrison, dec'd. Mary Connolly and Sarah Egbert were daus. of William Morrison, dec'd., who died intestate. See Book E, pg. 43, April 1814.

CAMPBELL –pg. 5 – 11; Jan. 1814. The lands of Duncan Campbell, dec'd., were divided into three portions for his heirs who were identified as Casper Fetter, William Campbell, and the heirs of Benjamin Campbell, dec'd. The heirs of Benjamin Campbell, dec'd., who shared one portion, were identified as his children, viz., Hannah Campbell, Eleanor Campbell, William Campbell, Catherine Campbell, Benjamin Campbell, and John Campbell.

BROWN –pg. 21; March 1814. Mary Brown, widow of Samuel Brown, dec'd., requested guardianship of William Brown, Rebecca Brown, and John Brown, minors under 14yrs., children of Samuel Brown, dec'd.

CONK –pg. 21; March 1814. Stephen Conk, a minor over 14yrs., son of Matthias Conk, dec'd., requested Jeremiah Stillwell as his guardian.

ALLEN –pg. 22; March 1814. Abraham Allen and John Allen, minors over 14yrs., sons of William Allen, dec'd., elected Samuel Allen as their guardian. Note: two entries on the same page.

ALLEN –pg. 23; March 1814. Mary Allen, widow of William Allen, dec'd., requested appointment as guardian of Isaac Allen, Joseph Allen, James Allen, William Allen, and Mary Allen, minors under 14yrs., children of William Allen, dec'd.

ALLEN –pg. 28 – 36; April 1814. The real estate of William Allen, dec'd., was divided amongst his heirs: Samuel Allen, Catherine Miller, John Allen, Abraham Allen, Isaac Allen, Joseph Allen, James Allen, William Allen, and Mary Allen. The record stated seven of those named were under 21yrs., and the relationship of the heirs to the deceased was not given, with the exception of Mary Allen who was specifically mentioned as a dau.

ALLEN –pg. 37 – 42; April 1814. The real estate of David Allen, dec'd., was divided amongst his heirs, viz., Thomas Allen, William Allen, David Allen, Elisha Allen, Lewis Allen, Joseph Allen, John Allen, Delila Allen, Elizabeth Allen, and Lydia Allen. Eight of the named heirs were under 21yrs.

MORRISON –pg. 43; April 1814. The real estate of William Morrison, dec'd., was divided amongst Daniel Connolly, James Morrison, James Egbert, Ann Brewer, and Ezekiel Davison, Esq. Note: See Book E, pg. 4, Jan. 1814.

WOODMANSEE –pg. 45 – 50; April 1814. The real estate of John Woodmansee, dec'd., was divided into five shares for Abigail Woodmansee, Almanah Holmes, Elizabeth Brinley, John Woodmansee, and the heirs of Reuben Woodmansee, dec'd., who were not identified. Elizabeth Brinley, John Woodmansee, and all the heirs of Reuben Woodmansee, dec'd., were under 21yrs. of age. Note: See Book D, pg. 254, July 1812.

SCHENCK –pg. 51; April 1814. John R. Schenck Jr., heir of Rulif H. Schenck, dec'd., requested a division of the real estate owned by Rulif H. Schenck, dec'd., late of Freehold Tshp., who died intestate leaving several heirs.

WILSON –pg. 54; April 1814. A settlement of accounts was filed by Ezekiel Morris and his wife, Mary, late Mary Wilson, and Samuel Pintard, Esq., administrators of the estate of Joseph Wilson, dec'd. Joseph Wilson, dec'd., was noted as the son of Benjamin Wilson.

ELLIS –pg. 59; April 1814. William Lawrie, surviving guardian of Eliza H. Vanderveer, late Eliza H. Ellis, filed a settlement of accounts.

JONES –pg. 60; April 1814. Deborah Jones, a minor over 14yrs., dau. of Christopher Jones, dec'd., elected Robert Shafto as her guardian.

JONES –pg. 60; April 1814. Robert Shafto requested guardianship of William Jones and Mary Jones, minors under 14yrs., children of Christopher Jones, dec'd.

IMLAY –pg. 61; April 1814. Richard Beatty requested guardianship of James Holcomb Imlay, a minor under 14yrs., son of James Imlay, dec'd.

SLOCUM –pg. 61; April 1814. Peter Slocum and John Williams requested guardianship of Ruth West Slocum, a minor under 14yrs.

MALSBURY –pg. 61; April 1814. William Malsbury, a minor over 14yrs., son of Gilbert Malsbury, dec'd., elected Sarah Malsbury as his guardian.

MALSBURY –pg. 62; April 1814. Phebe Malsbury, a minor over 14yrs., dau. of Gilbert Malsbury, dec'd., elected Sarah Malsbury as her guardian.

WHITE –pg. 62; April 1814. Mary White requested guardianship of Ann White, William White, Elizabeth White, John White, Asher White, Rachel White, and David White, minors under 14yrs., children of Asher White, dec'd.

MALSBURY –pg. 63; April 1814. Sarah Malsbury, widow of Gilbert Malsbury, dec'd., requested guardianship of Alice Malsbury, Thomas Malsbury, Abigail Malsbury, and Sarah Malsbury, minors under 14yrs.

BENSON –pg. 66; July 1814. Hannah Benson requested guardianship of James Benson, Jesse Benson, and Elizabeth Benson, minors under 14yrs., children of James Benson, dec'd.

BRAND –pg. 79 – 85; July 1814. The real estate of Thomas Brand, dec'd., was divided amongst his heirs.
Heirs: Thomas Brand, Jonah Brand, Dorling Brand, Maxson Brand, White Brand, Mary Newman, Lydia Newman, Ruth Alger, Blessing Brand, Jael Jeffrey, Sary (also given as Sarah) Brand, and Lettee Brand.

WOOLLEY –pg. 85 – 90; July 1814. The real estate of Montillon Woolley, dec'd., was divided amongst his heirs, viz., Ruth Cooper, Montillon Woolley, Britton Woolley, Daniel Woolley, Deborah Woolley, Abigail Woolley, and Mariah Woolley.

ALLEN –pg. 127; Jan. 1815. Tunis Covert requested guardianship of Joseph Allen, James Allen, William Allen, and Mary Allen, minors under 14yrs., children of William and Mary Allen, now deceased.

CHADWICK –pg. 128; Jan. 1815. Lewis Chandler and his wife, Hulda, late Hulda Chadwick, contested the accounts of Taber Chadwick, administrator of the estate of Francis Chadwick, dec'd.

COVENHOVEN –pg. 134; Jan. 1815. Elizabeth Covenhoven, widow of Cornelius C. Conover, dec'd., requested guardianship of William Conover, Sidney Conover, Harmon Conover, and Sarah Ann Conover, minors under 14yrs., children of Cornelius C. Conover, dec'd.

COVENHOVEN –pg. 134; Jan. 1815. John Covenhoven, a minor over 14yrs., son of Cornelius C. Covenhoven, dec'd., requested his mother, Elizabeth Covenhoven, as his guardian.

WOOLLEY –pg. 135; Jan. 1815. Ann Woolley, widow of Adam Woolley Jr., dec'd., requested guardianship of William Woolley, Hannah Woolley, Ann Woolley, and Elizabeth Woolley, minors under 14yrs., children of Adam Woolley Jr., dec'd.

COVENHOVEN –pg. 135; Jan. 1815. Daniel Covenhoven, son of William Covenhoven, dec'd., late

of Middletown Tshp., petitioned for a division of the real estate owned by his father who died intestate leaving nine children.
Children: Daniel Covenhoven; Asher Covenhoven; Timothy Covenhoven; Charles Covenhoven; Elizabeth Covenhoven, under 21yrs.; William Covenhoven, under 21yrs.; Margaret Covenhoven, under 21yrs.; Ann Covenhoven, now wife of James Schenck; and Ellen Covenhoven, now wife of Elihu Woolley.

JEFFREY –pg. 139; April 1815. Samuel Jeffrey along with Thomas Haywood and his wife, Ann, late Ann Jeffrey, were complainants against the executors of the estate of Thomas Jeffrey, dec'd.

ARROWSMITH –pg. 150; April 1815. Mary Arrowsmith and Peter Arrowsmith, minors over 14yrs., children of Thomas Arrowsmith, dec'd., elected Peter Arrowsmith as their guardian.

BULLUS –pg. 150; April 1815. John Bullus, a minor over 14yrs., son of William Bullus, dec'd., requested Dr. Edward Taylor as his guardian.

SCHANCK –pg. 151 – 155; April 1815. The real estate of Rulif H. Schenck was divided amongst his heirs; this included about 30 acres inherited by his heirs from Ann Holmes, wife of Jonathan Holmes, dec'd. In naming the heirs, the record did not specify the relationship of the heirs to Rulif H. Schenck, dec'd., but certain transactions prior to the division, also recorded in the record, revealed relationships between the heirs and other information. Children: Hendrick Schenck, then deceased; John R. Schenck; Jonathan Schenck; Elenor Schenck, now Elenor Shepherd; Mary Schenck, now Mary Conover; Lydia Schenck; Ann Schenck, now Ann Walters. Other heirs named: Jacob Schenck and Tylee Schenck. Jacob Schenck, Tylee Schenck, Lydia Schenck, and Ann Schenck were wards of Chrineyonce Schenck. Note: See Book C, pg. 35, April 1802.

CRADDOCK –pg. 163; June 1815. Ann S. Craddock, a minor over 14yrs., dau. of William Craddock, dec'd., chose Thomas Lettson as her guardian.

WILLIAMSON –pg. 176 - 150; July 1815. The real estate of Cornelius Williamson, dec'd., was divided between Tunis Williamson, Deborah Williamson, and Mary Williamson.

ALLEN –pg. 181; Oct. 1815. Elisha Allen and Lewis Allen, minors under 21yrs., children of David Allen, dec'd., chose Thomas Allen as their guardian.

WILLIAMSON –pg. 188; Oct. 1815. John Williamson, a minor over 14yrs., son of Hendrick Williamson, requested John Holsart as his guardian.

ROUZE –pg. 188; Oct. 1815. William Sinclair and Mary Rouze, widow of Daniel Rouze, dec'd., asked the court to appoint William Sinclair guardian of Clementine Rouze, William Clark Rouze, and Elizabeth Rouze, minors under 14yrs., children of Daniel Rouze, dec'd.

QUAY –pg. 196; Jan. 1816. Martha Quay, a minor over 14yrs., dau. of Samuel Quay, dec'd., elected Rev. John Cornell as her guardian.

HUTCHIN –pg. 201; Jan. 1816. Rebecca Hutchin and William Hutchin, minors over 14yrs., children of Isaac Hutchin, dec'd., chose Samuel Craft as their guardian.

BROWN –pg. 208; Feb. 1816. On the same page, three separate complaints by David Brown identified daus. of Joseph Brown, dec'd., and their husbands.
Daughters of Joseph Brown, dec'd.: Edith Ridgway, wife of Peter Ridgway; Sybil More, wife of Samuel More; Mary Pridmore, wife of Ephraim Pridmore; Phebe Pridmore, wife of Benjamin Pridmore; Hannah Pierson, wife of Henry Pierson; Elizabeth Perrine, wife of Clark Perrine.

BUCK –pg. 216; March 1816. Halstead Wainwright petitioned the court for guardianship of the children of Elizabeth Buck, dec'd. Elizabeth Buck, dec'd., late of Shrewsbury Tshp., died intestate leaving children under 14yrs. of age, viz., Susannah Buck, Mary Elizabeth Buck, and Hannah Buck. Peter Buck, father of the children, was in a state prison in New York.

BOOK F

1818 – 1823

CAMPBELL –pg. 1; Jan. 1818. Pierson Thompson and his wife, Eleanor, late Eleanor Campbell, were complainants against Daniel Stillwell and his wife, Jane, late Jane Campbell who was the administrator of the estate of Benjamin Campbell, dec'd.

PARKER –pg. 1; Jan. 1818. Joseph Lafetra requested guardianship of Benjamin Parker, Mary Parker, Sarah Parker, George Parker, and Catherine D. L. Parker, minors under 14yrs., children of George Parker.

IMLAY –pg. 2; Jan. 1818. Hetty Imlay requested guardianship of John Reynolds Imlay, Joseph Imlay, and George Augustus Imlay, minors under 14yrs., children of George W. Imlay, dec'd.

CONOVER –pg. 2; Jan. 1818. Hendrick P. Conover, John Rue Conover, and Garret P. Conover, minors over 14yrs., elected John W. Holmes, Aaron Smock, and Patience Conover as their guardians.

CONOVER –pg. 3; Jan. 1818. John W. Holmes, Aaron Smock, and Patience Conover requested guardianship of Ann Conover, Ellen Conover, Margaret Conover, Peter Conover, and Mary Conover, minors under 14yrs., children of Peter H. Conover, dec'd.

HOFFMIRE –pg. 3; Jan. 1818. Martha Hoffmire, Sarah Lilley, and Thomas Hoffmire petitioned for a division of the real estate owned by Isaac Hoffmire, dec'd.

LAYTON –pg. 6; Jan. 1818. John Patterson and his wife, Deborah, late Deborah Sowden, petitioned the court for a division of real estate. Deborah Patterson was a dau. of Nancy Sowden and a devisee of Andrew Layton, dec'd. The petition stated Andrew Layton, dec'd., left a will leaving, under certain circumstances, all his real estate in Middletown Tshp. to the heirs of Nancy Sowden and to Mary Layton, wife of Thomas Layton. The land was divided into two shares; one for Mary Layton, and one for the heirs of Nancy Sowden.

LAKE –pg. 10; Jan. 1818. James Smith, guardian of Elizabeth Lake, was a complainant against William Lake and his wife, Elizabeth, late Elizabeth VanMater.

HOLMES –pg. 12; Feb. 1818. William Davis and Alice Davis requested Peter Bruere of Burlington Co. be appointed Alice's guardian. Alice Davis was a minor over 14yrs. and the dau. of Joseph Holmes Jr., dec'd.

HOLMES –pg. 12; Feb. 1818. Peter Bruere requested guardianship of Sarah Holmes, a minor under 14yrs., dau. of Joseph Holmes Jr., dec'd.

AUMACK –pg. 16; April 1818. Mary Aumack requested guardianship of Eliza Ann Aumack and Deborah Aumack, minors under 14yrs., children of David Aumack, dec'd.

SCHENCK –pg. 16; April 1818. William Herbert requested guardianship of Alice Schenck, a minor under 14yrs., dau. of John Schenck, dec'd.

SCHENCK –pg. 16; April 1818. Garret Schenck, a minor over 14yrs., son of John Schenck, dec'd., elected William Herbert as his guardian.

CONOVER –pg. 17; April 1818. Margaret Conover, a minor over 14yrs., dau. of William Conover, dec'd., chose Jehu Patterson, Esq., as her guardian.

VANBRUNT –pg. 21; April 1818. A settlement of accounts was filed by John Schanck and Auke Wikoff, executors of the estate of Eleanor Forman, formerly Eleanor VanBrunt, dec'd.

GIFFORD –pg. 25; April 1818. Annaniah Gifford, guardian of Sarah Wilbur, late Sarah Gifford, filed a settlement of accounts.

ALLEN –pg. 32 – 34; April 1818. The real estate of Sarah Allen, dec'd., was divided amongst her heirs:
Heirs entitled to one share each: John Allen, Jonathan T. Allen, Samuel C. Allen, and James P. Allen.
Heirs entitled to one share total: Elizabeth C. H. Pennington, Paulina Allen, and Ann M. Allen.

ALLEN –pg. 35; April 1818. Joseph Allen, guardian of Hannah Allen and Ebenezer Allen, children of Daniel Allen, dec'd., petitioned for a division of real estate. The children of Daniel Allen, dec'd., were grandchildren of the sister of John Scott, dec'd., late of Shrewsbury Tshp., who died intestate owning real estate. The real estate was held by his wards and others as tenants in common, and it was this real estate he requested divided.

HOLMES –pg. 37; May 1818. Deborah L. Holmes, a minor over 14yrs., dau. of John Holmes, dec'd., chose Samuel P. Wikoff as her guardian.

THORNE –pg. 38; July 1818. Joseph H. Walling, Hannah Walling, and Garret Thorne petitioned for a division of the real estate belonging to John Thorne, dec'd. Hannah Walling and Garret Thorne were two children of John Thorne, dec'd., late of Middletown Tshp., who died intestate. The children and heirs of John Thorne, dec'd., were John Thorne Jr., Thomas Thorne, Hannah Walling, and Garret Thorne. Within the record, a restatement of the names included Sarah Walling as an heir.

REYNOLDS –pg. 58; Oct. 1818. Mary Holman, late Mary Reynolds, administrator of the estate of Matthew Reynolds, dec'd., filed a settlement of accounts.

IMLAY –pg. 61; Oct. 1818. Richard L. Beatty, Esq., guardian of John H. Imlay and Jacob T. Imlay, filed a record of his accounts. Note: record is a duplicate of another in Book F, pg. 48, July 1818.

HEULITT –pg. 66; Jan. 1819. Robert Heulitt, son of John Huelitt, dec'd., petitioned for a division of his father's real estate. John Heulitt, dec'd., late of Howell Tshp., died intestate owning real estate. The petitioner and John Heulitt, a minor under 21yrs., were his only children and heirs.

HOLMES –pg. 67; Jan. 1819. Jerusha Holmes requested guardianship of Jacob Holmes, John L. Holmes, Abraham Holmes, and Hannah L. Holmes, minors under 14yrs., children of Abraham Holmes, dec'd.

STEWARD –pg. 83; April 1819. Leticia Steward requested guardianship of Lewis Steward, Martha Steward, and John Steward, minors under 14yrs., children of Aaron Steward, dec'd.

HULSART –pg. 83; April 1819. Garret Hulsart, a minor over 14yrs., son of Garret Hulsart, dec'd., chose James VanNote as his guardian.

CONOVER –pg. 84; April 1819. Mary Conover requested guardianship of Jane Conover, Holmes Conover, and Lenah Conover, minors under 14yrs., children of Cornelius R. Conover, dec'd.

CRAIG –pg. 84; April 1819. Sarah Craig, a minor over 14yrs., dau. of Samuel Craig, dec'd., elected Charles Craig as her guardian.

SCHENCK –pg. 84; April 1819. Eliza Ann Schenck requested guardianship of Margaret Schenck and William Schenck, minors under 14yrs., children of Rev. William C. Schenck, dec'd.

SMITH –pg. 86; April 1819. Edward Smith, son of Edward Smith, dec'd., petitioned for a division of his father's real estate. Edward Smith, dec'd., late of Shrewsbury Tshp., died intestate and his real estate had descended to the petitioner, Edward Smith, and to John Smith, Sarah Smith, Ann Eliza Smith, Louisa Smith, and Alfred Smith, other children and heirs of the deceased.

SCOTT –pg. 94; July 1819. John Mount, Esq., on behalf of his wards Ann Scott, John Scott, William Scott, Ebenezer Scott, Clayton Scott, Catherine Scott, and Charles Scott, petitioned for a division of the real estate owned by Samuel Scott, dec'd. Samuel Scott, dec'd., late of Saint John Tshp., Lancaster County, Province of New Brunswick, died intestate owning considerable real estate in Shrewsbury Tshp., Monmouth County, New Jersey. The said minors were the only children and heirs of the said deceased.

MOUNT –pg. 95; July 1819. John Mount, Esq., on behalf of his wards Mary Mount, Susan Mount, and Elisar Mount, petitioned for a division of the real estate owned by Ann Mount, dec'd. His wards were the only children and heirs of Ann Mount, dec'd., late of St. John Tshp., Lancaster County, Province of New Brunswick, who died intestate. As grandchildren of Ebenezer Scott, dec'd., said minors were entitled to a portion of the estate of John Scott, dec'd., late of Shrewsbury Tshp., Monmouth County, New Jersey.

TAPSCOTT –pg. 97; July 1819. Richard Crum requested guardianship of Catherine Tapscott and Elizabeth Tapscott, minors under 14yrs., children of William Tapscott, dec'd.

HULSART –pg. 97; July 1819. Alche Hulsart requested guardianship of Hannah Hulsart, Amos Hulsart, Elias Hulsart, and Alice Hulsart, minors under 14yrs., children of Garret Hulsart, dec'd.

WEST –pg. 97; July 1819. William West, a minor over 14yrs., son of Bartholemew West, dec'd., elected James West as his guardian.

SCOTT –pg. 104 – 111; July 1819. The real estate of John Scott, dec'd., was divided amongst his heirs.
Heirs receiving shares: John Pintard; Almy Millet; Edmund Lafetra; the heirs of Ann Mount, dec'd.; Almy Lafetra; Glencross Pintard; Hannah Tilton; the heirs of Samuel Scott; Ann Pintard; William Pintard; Samuel Pintard; Hannah Pintard; and the heirs of Elizabeth Allen, wife of Daniel Allen, dec'd.

HORSFULL –pg. 112; July 1819. Job Kirby, guardian of Sarah Marshall, late Sarah Horsfull, filed a record of his accounts.

HORSFULL –pg. 113; July 1819. Job Kirby, guardian of Martha Potter, late Martha Horsfull, filed a record of his accounts.

SCOTT –pg. 121; Oct. 1819. The record reported on the application John Mount, Esq., made on behalf of his wards Ann Scott, John Scott, William Scott, Ebenezer Scott, Catherine Scott, Clayton Scott, and Charles Scott for a division of the real estate owned by Samuel Scott, dec'd. The previously mentioned wards all resided in St. John Tshp., Lancaster Co., Province of New Brunswick.

MOUNT –pg. 121 – 122; Oct. 1819. This record reported on the division of the real estate owned by Ann Mount, dec'd. There were 16 acres to be divided into three parts for Mary Mount, Susan Mount, and Elizar Mount, children and heirs of the said deceased. The heirs lived in St. John Tshp., Lancaster Co., Province of New Brunswick.

SCOTT –pg. 122; Oct. 1819. Herbert Scott, a minor over 14yrs., son of William Scott, dec'd., elected Samuel Pintard, Esq., as his guardian.

WARDELL –pg. 129; Jan. 1820. Henry Conine requested guardianship of Harriet Wardell, a minor under 14yrs., dau. of Elizabeth Conine, dec'd.

COOK –pg. 130; Jan. 1820. Mary Cook, a minor over 14yrs., dau. of Peter Cook, dec'd., elected John L. Cottrell as her guardian.

WHITE –pg. 130; Jan. 1820. William White, a minor over 14yrs., son of Thomas White, dec'd., chose Samuel W. Tenbrook as his guardian.

JONES –pg. 143; April 1820. Robert Shafto, guardian of Deborah Jones, now Deborah White, filed a record of his accounts.

WOLCOTT –pg. 147 – 156; April 1820. The real estate of Peter Wolcott, dec'd., was divided after setting off 1/3 for the widow's dower. Children who received a share of the estate: Joseph Wolcott, John Wolcott, Samuel Wolcott, Henry Wolcott, Clementine (Wolcott) VanNote, and Lydia (Wolcott) Branson.

WILLIAMSON –pg. 159; June 1820. David Brewer, grandson of William Williamson, dec'd., petitioned for a division of his grandfather's real estate. William Williamson, dec'd., died

intestate owning land in Freehold Tshp.
Children: Peter Williamson; William Williamson; Ann Williamson; Sarah Williamson; Eleanor Mason, wife of John Mason; and Mary Cook, wife of James Cook.
Grandchildren who were children of his dau. Jane Brewer, dec'd.: David Brewer, Gilbert Brewer, William Brewer, Johnston Brewer, and Elizabeth Brewer.

ESTILL –pg. 161; July 1820. John Dennis and William Dennis, through their guardian John Chamberlain, Esq., petitioned for a division of the real estate owned by their grandfather John Estill, dec'd., who died intestate owning real estate in Shrewsbury Tshp. He left two sons and three grandchildren.
Children: William Estill and Samuel Estill.
Grandchildren: John Dennis, William Dennis, and Lydia Dennis.

CAMPBELL –pg. 162; July 1820. John Campbell, Hannah Campbell, Pearson Thompson and his wife, Eleanor, late Eleanor Campbell, petitioned for a division of the real estate owned by Benjamin Campbell, dec'd., late of Freehold Tshp., who died intestate.
Children and heirs: John Campbell, Hannah Campbell, William Campbell, Benjamin Campbell, Catherine Campbell, and Eleanor (Campbell) Thompson.

QUAY –pg. 166; July 1820. Martha W. Quay, a minor over 14yrs., chose Caroline Quay as her guardian.

WELLS –pg. 179 - 181; Oct. 1820. Rebecca Ely, dau. of James Wells, dec'd., petitioned for a division of her father's real estate. Her father, James Wells, dec'd., late of Stafford Tshp., died intestate in Jan. of 1800 owning real estate in Dover Tshp., Stafford Tshp., and elsewhere.
Children of James Wells, dec'd.: Carvel Wells, James Wells, Joseph Wells, Isaiah Wells, John Wells, Elizabeth Wells who married Levi Anderson, and petitioner Rebecca (Wells) Ely.
Grandchildren who were children of his son Jonathan Wells, dec'd., who predeceased his father: James Wells; Maria Wells; Joseph Wells; Charles Wells, under 21yrs.; Israel Wells, under 21yrs.; and Francis Wells, under 21yrs.
Grandchildren who were children of his dau. Mary Headley, dec'd., late wife of Moses Headley: Samuel Headley; Joel Headley; James Headley; Martha McCoy, wife of William McCoy; and Levinia Warden, wife of Albert Warden.
Since the death of the said James Wells, dec'd., his son John died intestate and without issue. His other son Carvel Wells also died leaving issue, viz., John Wells, Carvel Wells, Bloomfield Wells, and Rebecca Wells. Only Rebecca was over 21yrs. of age. Note: In Book F, pgs. 215 – 218, April 1821, a report on re-dividing the real estate included a Susan Wells as another dau. of Carvel Wells, dec'd., and replaced Bloomfield Wells' name with that of Gabriel Wells.

ESTILL –pg. 185 – 189; Oct. 1820. The real estate of John Estill, dec'd., was divided amongst his heirs.
Children: William Estill and Samuel Estill.
Grandchildren who were the children of Lydia Dennis, dec'd.: John Dennis, William Dennis, and Lydia Dennis.

HOLMES –pg. 193; Jan. 1821. Lyttleton White and his wife, Nancy, late Nancy Holmes, petitioned for a division of her father's real estate. Her father, Jacob Holmes, dec'd., late of Shrewsbury Tshp., died intestate owning real estate in Shrewsbury Tshp. and elsewhere.
Children: Nancy White, the petitioner; Jacob R. Holmes; and Abigail White, wife of Jacob White.
Grandchildren who were children of his dau. Hannah Voorhees, dec'd., late wife of Joseph Voorhees: Peter Voorhees, Jacob Voorhees, Nancy Voorhees, Eleanor Voorhees, and Hannah Voorhees.
Grandchildren who were children of his son Abraham Holmes, dec'd., who predeceased his father: Jacob Holmes, Israel Holmes, Abraham Holmes, and Hannah Holmes.

LEFFERSON –pg. 197; Jan. 1821. Robert Covenhoven requested guardianship of William Lefferson, Benjamin Lefferson, Garret Lefferson, Lydia Lefferson, and Leffert Lefferson, minors under 14yrs., children of Benjamin Lefferson, dec'd.

LEFFERSON –pg. 197; Jan. 1821. Joseph Lefferson and Sarah Lefferson, minors over 14yrs., children of Benjamin Lefferson, dec'd., chose Elijah Combs as their guardian.

NEWELL –pg. 198; Jan. 1821. Elizabeth Newell, a minor over 14yrs., dau. of John Newell, chose

John J. Ely, Esq., as her guardian.

HALL –pg. 199; Jan. 1821. A account for the estate of John Hall, dec'd., was filed by Richard S. Hartshorne, administrator of the estate, and by John A. Vanderbilt and his wife, Alice, late Alice Hall, where Alice was also an administrator of the estate of John Hall, dec'd.

TAYLOR –pg. 210 - 212; Jan. 1821. William Taylor and Joseph Taylor filed several separate complaints in regard to probating a will, combined here into one entry. Pg. 210 - against John Cooper and his wife, Idah, and against James Rowland and his wife, Hetty. Idah Cooper and Hetty Rowland were children of Grover Taylor, dec'd., and legatees of William Taylor, dec'd. Pg. 211 - against Mary Jacobus, against John Stricker and his wife, Ann, and against Charles Taylor. Mary Jacobus, Ann Stricker, and Charles Taylor were legatees in the will of William Taylor, dec'd. Pg. 211 - against Ann Taylor, Phebe Taylor, Eliza Taylor, and James Grover Taylor who were all children of Grover Taylor, dec'd., and legatees in the will of William Taylor, dec'd. Pg. 211 - against Fanny Taylor, a dau. of Grover Taylor, dec'd., and a legatee in the will of William Taylor, dec'd. Pg. 212 - against Patty Taylor, Joseph Taylor, James Taylor, and John Taylor, all children of John Taylor, dec'd., and legatees in the will of William Taylor, dec'd. Pg. 212 - against Hannah Taylor, against John Conine and his wife, Caty, and against Caty Ann VanCleve. Hannah Taylor was the widow and legatee, Caty Conine was the dau. and legatee, and Caty Ann VanCleve was the granddaughter and legatee of William Taylor, dec'd. Pg. 212 - against Daniel Applegate and his wife, Esther, and against Lewis Throp and his wife, Phebe. Esther Applegate and Phebe Throp were daus. and legatees of William Taylor, dec'd.

GOLDEN –pg. 219; April 1821. Ann Golden and John Golden, minors over 14yrs., children of Elias Golden, dec'd., elected Denise Hendrickson as their guardian.

WILLIAMSON –pg. 219; April 1821. Mary Williamson, a minor over 14yrs., dau. of Cornelius Williamson, dec'd., elected Andrew Crawford as her guardian.

HOOPER –pg. 221; April 1821. Caroline Hooper, a minor over 14yrs., dau. of Stephen Hooper, dec'd., requested John J. Ely, Esq., as her guardian.

HEWLIT –pg. 222; April 1821. The real estate of John Hewlitt, dec'd., was divided between Robert Hewlitt and John Hewlitt.

INMAN –pg. 229; July 1821. Job Inman, son of Esther Inman, dec'd., petitioned for a division of his mother's real estate. Esther Inman, dec'd., late of Stafford Tshp., died intestate in 1821. Children and heirs of Esther Inman, dec'd.: Job Inman; Sarah Conkling, late Sarah Inman, wife of Benjamin Conkling; Esther Inman; Nancy Inman; Mary Inman; and Hannah Inman. Note: Record heading stated "Joel" Inman was the petitioner, but, thereafter, he was referred to as "Job" Inman.

COTTRELL –pg. 233; April 1821. Garret P. Hyer and his wife, Jane, late Jane Cottrell, filed an application to sell the real estate of Gershom Cottrell, dec'd., to pay his debts. Jane Hyer, late Jane Cottrell, was the administrator of the estate of Gershom Cottrell, dec'd., late of Freehold Tshp.

BORDEN –pg. 239; July 1821. William Borden and Mary Borden, minors over 14yrs., children of Richard Borden, dec'd., elected Catherine Borden as their guardian.

BORDEN –pg. 241; July 1821. Catherine Borden requested guardianship of Ann Borden and Catherine Borden, minors under 14yrs., children of Richard Borden, dec'd.

HULSE –pg. 244; Oct. 1821. Thomas Hulse, son of Sylvenus Hulse, dec'd., petitioned for a division of his father's real estate. His father died intestate owning land in Howell Tshp. Children: Thomas Hulse; William Hulse; Anthony Hulse; Mary Mitten, wife of Joel Mitten; Joel Hulse; Deborah Longstreet, wife of Aaron Longstreet; and Samuel Hulse. Grandchild who was the child of his son John Hulse, dec'd.: Lydia Hulse.

STILLWELL –pg. 248; Oct. 1821. William Stillwell requested guardianship of Mary Stillwell, Elizabeth Stillwell, and Catherine Stillwell, minors under 14yrs., children of Samuel Stillwell, dec'd.

BEDLE –pg. 253; Jan. 1822. Thomas Bedle, son of Thomas Bedle, dec'd., petitioned for a division of his father's real estate. Thomas Bedle, dec'd., late of Middletown Tshp., died intestate.

The real estate was now held as tenants in common by Thomas Bedle, Joel Bedle, Joseph Bedle, James Bedle, Mary Vanderbilt, Martha Stout, Catherine Hendrickson, Lydia Burrows, Elizabeth Bedle, Nancy Bedle, and Sarah Stout who were children and grandchildren of the said deceased. The grandchildren were children of his two sons, Richard Bedle, dec'd., and Elijah Bedle, dec'd., who died before their father. Note: The record did not distinguish the children from the grandchildren.

SMITH –pg. 270; Jan. 1822. Joseph Voorhees, guardian of Louisa Smith, was a complainant against the administrators of the estate of Edward Smith, dec'd.

MORRELL –pg. 277; April 1822. Mary VanCleve, late Mary Morrell, through her guardian William T. Conover, petitioned for a division of the real estate owned by James Morrell, dec'd., late of Middletown Tshp., who died intestate before Jan. 29, 1817.
Children and heirs of James Morrell, dec'd.: Elizabeth Conover, wife of William T. Conover; Ann Morrell; John Morrell; Jane Morrell; and Mary VanCleve, petitioner and wife of Daniel VanCleve.

HEWLITT –pg. 283; April 1822. John Hewlitt, a minor over 14yrs., son of John, chose Annaniah Gifford Jr. as his guardian.

MIDDLETON –pg. 284; April 1822. William Tilton requested guardianship of Sarah Ann Middleton and George Fox Middleton, minors under 14yrs., grandchildren of Nathan Middleton, dec'd.

ROGERS –pg. 285; April 1822. David Sutfin and his wife, Elizabeth, late Elizabeth Rogers, and Dr. Samuel Forman filed a second account for the estate of John Rogers, dec'd. Said Elizabeth Sutfin and Samuel Forman were executors for the said estate. Note: Sutfin was also spelled Sutphen in other reports on this estate.

JONES –pg. 295; July 1822. George White, as guardian of William Jones and Mary Jones, petitioned for a division of the real estate owned by Christopher Jones, dec'd., late of Howell Tshp., who died intestate before Jan. 29, 1817.
Children of Christopher Jones, dec'd.: Elizabeth Hurley, wife of Robert Hurley; Sarah Jones; Ruth Hunter, wife of John Hunter; Deborah White, wife of George White; William Jones; and Mary Jones.

HOLMES –pg. 315; Oct. 1822. Catherine Holmes, guardian of Catherine Holmes, petitioned for a division of the real estate owned by William Holmes, dec'd., late of Freehold Tshp., who died intestate prior to Jan. 29, 1817. His only children and heirs were her wards, Catherine Holmes, and Leah Hayfield, late Leah Holmes.

HOOPER –pg. 321; Oct. 1822. Sarah Hooper and Cornelian Ann Hooper, minors over 14yrs., children of Stephen Hooper, requested Clement Hooper as their guardian.

HOLMES –pg. 322; Oct. 1822. Catherine Holmes, a minor over 14yrs., dau. of William Holmes, elected John Stoutenborough as her guardian.

HOLMES –pg. 328; Oct. 1822. Thomas Holmes and Caty Richmond, executors of the estate of John R. Holmes, dec'd., filed an account of their records. Caty Richmond, late Caty Holmes, was then the wife of Anthony Richmond.

IVINS –pg. 330; Jan. 1823. George W. Ivins and Aaron Ivins, sons of Aaron Ivins, dec'd., petitioned for a division of their father's real estate. Aaron Ivins died intestate, prior to Jan. 29, 1817, owning real estate in Upper Freehold Tshp.
Children and heirs: George W. Ivins; Aaron Ivins; Ann Comfort, wife of Ellis Comfort; Eliza Ivins; Barclay Ivins; Caleb Ivins; and Lydia Ivins.

HORNER –pg. 331; Jan. 1823. Sarah Hopkins, Aaron Horner, and William Horner, by their guardian, Rebecca Horner, petitioned for a division of the real estate owned by their father, Aaron Horner, dec'd. Fuller Horner, dec'd., grandfather of the petitioners, left a will giving his son Aaron Horner, father of the petitioners, half of the land called "Leavells" and the other half went to another son Isaiah Horner. Aaron Horner died before the real estate was divided.

BEEDLE –pg. 338; Jan. 1823. Cornelius Walling requested guardianship of Daniel Beedle, Timothy Beedle, and Edith Beedle, minors under 14yrs., children of Richard Beedle, dec'd.

BEEDLE –pg. 338; Jan. 1823. Hendrick Beedle, Jeremiah Beedle, and Sarah Beedle, minors over 14yrs., chose Cornelius Walling as their guardian.

BEEDLE –pg. 339; Jan. 1823. Thomas J. Walling requested guardianship of Amy Beedle, Furetta Beedle, Aaron Beedle, and Louisa Beedle, minors under 14yrs., children of Elijah Bedle, dec'd. Note: The surnames of the children and the father were spelled differently in this record, and in Book N, pg. 416, Sept. 1854, Furetta was identified as Phiatta.

BEEDLE –pg. 339; Jan. 1823. Mary Beedle, a minor over 14yrs., elected Thomas J. Walling as her guardian.

CONOVER –pg. 340; Jan. 1823. Charles Conover requested guardianship of his children William Conover, Ellen Conover, and Daniel Conover, minors under 14yrs.

KIRBY –pg. 341; Jan. 1823. John Kirby, a minor over 14yrs., requested Nathaniel B. Kirby as his guardian.

PYLE –pg. 341; Jan. 1823. Abigail Pyle requested guardianship of Simon Pyle, a minor under 14yrs.

THROCKMORTON –pg. 357; Feb. 1823. Richard Throckmorton, David Forman, and Isaac K. Lippencott requested guardianship of Catherine Throckmorton, Mary Ann Throckmorton, and Richard S. Throckmorton, minors under 14yrs.

NEWELL –pg. 362; April 1823. Hugh Newell, son of John Newell, dec'd., and John J. Ely, guardian of Elizabeth Butcher, wife of Joseph Butcher, late Elizabeth Newell and dau. of John Newell, dec'd., petitioned for a division of real estate. Hugh Newell, dec'd., father of said John Newell, dec'd., wrote a will dated Sept. 26, 1816 in which he left real estate to his son John, father of the petitioners. The will stipulated that after John Newell's death, half of John's legacy was to go to John's son Hugh Newell, the petitioner. The other half of the legacy was to go to his daughter-in-law Susannah Newell who was the widow of John Newell, dec'd., and to his granddaughter Elizabeth Newell, dau. of said John and Susannah Newell.

VANDERBILT –pg. 364; April 1823. Gitty Jane Vanderbilt, a minor over 14yrs., dau. of Jeremiah Vanderbilt, chose John P. VanPelt as her guardian.

HOLMES –pg. 364; April 1823. Alice Holmes and Peter Wikoff requested guardianship of Edward T. Holmes, a minor under 14yrs.

WARDELL –pg. 364; April 1823. Harriet McCabe, late Harriet Wardell, wife of Elisha McCabe, a minor over 14yrs., requested her husband, Elisha McCabe, be appointed her guardian.

COWARD –pg. 368; April 1823. Jonathan Coward, guardian of Susannah Karr, late Susannah Coward, filed a settlement of accounts.

SCHENCK –pg. 374; April 1823. Tunis D. Dubois and Daniel I. Schenck, guardians of Catharine Smock, late Catharine Schenck, filed a settlement of accounts.

SCHENCK –pg. 375; April 1823. Tunis D. Dubois and Daniel I. Schenck, guardians of Sarah Robinson, late Sarah Schenck, filed a settlement of accounts.

BOOK G

1823 – 1827

STEWARD –pg. 1; July 1823. Charles Steward, son of Aaron Steward, dec'd., petitioned for a division of his father's real estate. Aaron Steward, dec'd., late of Upper Freehold Tshp., died intestate owning real estate in Upper Freehold Tshp. and elsewhere.
Children and heirs of Aaron Steward, dec'd.: Charles Steward; Margaret Palmer, wife of John Palmer; Hannah Taylor, wife of George W. Taylor; Aaron Steward; Lewis Steward; Martha W. Steward; and John Steward.

SHEPHERD –pg. 7; July 1823. Mary Shepherd requested guardianship of Adaline Shepherd, a minor under 14yrs.

SHEPHERD –pg. 7; July 1823. Thomas Shepherd and Mary Shepherd, minors over 14yrs., elected Mary Shepherd as their guardian.

DRUMMOND –pg. 20; Oct. 1823. Peter Drummond, John C. Drummond, and Mulford Drummond, grandchildren and heirs of Gavine Drummond, dec'd., petitioned for a division of real estate. Gavine Drummond died owning land in Shrewsbury Tshp. and leaving a will that bequeathed land to his son Robert Drummond, the petitioners' father. The will further stipulated, upon the death of Robert, which recently occurred, the land would pass to Robert's children who were the petitioners and Robert Drummond Jr. (under 21yrs.). It was this land the petitioners wanted divided. Note: In Book G, pg. 27, Jan. 1824, another petition gave 'Craig' as the middle name for John C. Drummond and 'Milford' as the given name for Mulford Drummond.

DRUMMOND –pg. 24; Oct. 1823. Robert Drummond, a minor over 14yrs., elected Mary Drummond and Dr. John P. Lewis as his guardians.

CONOVER –pg. 28; Jan. 1824. John C. Conover, son of Cornelius C. Conover, dec'd., petitioned for a division of his father's real estate. Cornelius C. Conover, dec'd., late of Freehold Tshp., died intestate prior to Jan. 29, 1817. John C. Conover, William Conover, Sidney Conover, Harmon Conover, and Sarah Ann Conover were named as the only children and heirs of Cornelius C. Conover.

BROWN –pg. 31; Jan. 1824. William S. Brown, son of Samuel Brown, dec'd., petitioned for a division of his father's real estate. Samuel Brown, dec'd., late of Stafford Tshp., died intestate prior to Jan. 29, 1817.
Children and heirs of Samuel Brown, dec'd.: Rebecca Brown, John L. Brown, and William S. Brown.

WOODWARD –pg. 34; Jan. 1824. John Ridgway and Nicholas Waters, guardians of Lucy Lucas, late Lucy Woodward, filed a settlement of accounts.

EASTWOOD –pg. 39; Jan. 1824. Sarah Eastwood requested guardianship of John Eastwood and Lewis Eastwood, minors under 14yrs., children of Enos Eastwood, dec'd.

EASTWOOD –pg. 40; Jan. 1824. Nathaniel Eastwood and Enos Eastwood, minors over 14yrs., elected Sarah Eastwood as their guardian.

STILLWELL –pg. 40; Jan. 1824. Mary Stillwell, a minor over 14yrs., dau. of Samuel Stillwell, dec'd., elected William Leonard as her guardian.

CLAYTON –pg. 40; Jan. 1824. Sarah Clayton requested guardianship of Matilda Clayton, Lucy Edith Clayton, Moses Clayton, and Elizabeth Clayton, minors under 14yrs., children of John Clayton, dec'd.

ELY –pg. 40; Jan. 1824. Lucy Ely, mother of William Ely, Elizabeth Ely, John Ely, Joseph Ely, Mary Ely, and Lucy Ely, minors under 14yrs., children of Isaac Ely, dec'd., requested Edward Taylor Jr. be appointed guardian of her children.

VANDERVEER –pg. 41; Jan. 1824. Mary Vanderveer, a minor over 14yrs., dau. of Garret G. Vanderveer, dec'd., chose Garret H. Smock as her guardian.

VANDERVEER –pg. 41; Jan. 1824. Garret H. Smock requested guardianship of Sarah Vanderveer and Benjamin Schenck Vanderveer, minors under 14yrs.

PYLE –pg. 63; April 1824. Job Throckmorton and his wife, Rebecca, late Rebecca Pyle, and Samuel L. Pyle requested a division of the real estate owned by Simon Pyle, dec'd., who was the father of Rebecca and Samuel. Simon Pyle, dec'd., late of Shrewsbury Tshp., died intestate owning real estate in Shrewsbury Tshp. and elsewhere.
Children and heirs: Rebecca Throckmorton, Samuel L. Pyle, and Simon Pyle.

BREWER –pg. 69; April 1824. Richard M. Freeman requested guardianship of David Brewer, Morris Freeman Brewer, and Robert Brewer, minors under 14yrs., children of Isaac Brewer, dec'd.

PEACOCK –pg. 70; April 1824. David Hance requested guardianship of Catherine Peacock, a minor under 14yrs., dau. of David Peacock, dec'd.

ENGLISH –pg. 70; April 1824. Elizabeth English and Rebecca English, minors over 14yrs., chose Dr. James English as their guardian. Note: two separate entries on the same page.

PEACOCK –pg. 70; April 1824. Phebe Ann Peacock, a minor over 14yrs., chose David Hance as her guardian.

HALL –pg. 71; July 1824. John A. Vanderbilt and his wife, Alice, guardians of Mary Hall, Cornelia Hall, and John Hall, minor children of John Hall, dec'd., petitioned to sell some of their wards' real estate to offset expenses.

THROCKMORTON –pg. 72; July 1824. Richard Throckmorton, Isaac K. Lippincott, and Dr. David Forman, guardians of Catherine Throckmorton, Mary Ann Throckmorton, and Richard S. Throckmorton who were children of Samuel Throckmorton, dec'd., along with Dr. Samuel Forman and his wife, Sarah, late Sarah Throckmorton, and Richard Throckmorton were exceptants to the accounts of Mathias Van Brackle, surviving executor of the estate of Richard Francis, dec'd.

OAKERSON –pg. 82; July 1824. Gilbert Miller and his wife, Rebecca, late Rebecca Oakerson who was administrator of the estate of Daniel Oakerson, dec'd., filed a settlement of accounts.

PYLE –pg. 88; Oct. 1824. Samuel L. Pyle, one of the children and heirs of Susannah Pyle, formerly Susannah Leonard who was a devisee of Samuel Leonard, dec'd., petitioned for a division of real estate. Samuel Leonard, dec'd., late of Monmouth County, left a will dated March 10, 1790. By this will the deceased left real estate to his five children, viz., Mary, Deborah, Lucy, Susannah and Samuel Leonard. Lucy Leonard died without issue while her father was still alive. After their father's demise, Samuel, Mary and Deborah Leonard sold their shares to Simon Pyle, father of the petitioner. The said Susannah Leonard married the said Simon Pyle and had since died, leaving two children named Rebecca and Samuel Pyle. After the death of Susannah, Simon Pyle married Abigail Thorpe and had one son, Simon Pyle who was under 14yrs. of age at the time. Simon Pyle Sr. was now deceased.

PYLE –pg. 89 – 90; Oct. 1824. Samuel L. Pyle petitioned to have the dower of Abigail Pyle, widow of Simon Pyle, dec'd., set off. The record noted his sister Rebecca Pyle was then Rebecca Throckmorton, wife of Job Throckmorton, dec'd.

WILLIAMSON –pg. 90; Oct. 1824. Peter H. Williamson, son of Hendrick Williamson, dec'd., petitioned for a division of his father's real estate. Hendrick Williamson, dec'd., died intestate. His real estate was held as tenants in common by the following people: Daniel Williamson; Jane Barcalow, wife of Nicholas Barcalow; Catharine Barcalow, dec'd., late wife of Daniel Barcalow; Achly Lawrence, wife of Daniel Lawrence; Arthur Williamson; Peter H. Williamson, the petitioner; and John Williamson.
Catharine Barcalow, dec'd., late wife of Daniel Barcalow, left five children, viz., Ellen Barcalow, Derrick Barcalow, Lydia Barcalow, Hendrick Barcalow, and Catharine Barcalow.

PERRINE –pg. 94; Oct. 1824. William M. Perrine, a minor over 14yrs., son of Matthew Perrine, elected Thomas M. Perrine as his guardian.

SMITH –pg. 94; Oct. 1824. Alfred Smith, a minor over 14yrs., son of Edward Smith, chose Francis Smith as his guardian.

NEWELL –pg. 94; Oct. 1824. Phebe Newell, a minor over 14yrs., dau. of William Newell, elected William J. Ely as her guardian.

PERRINE –pg. 94; Oct. 1824. Esther H. Perrine, a minor over 14yrs., dau. of Matthew, elected Thomas M. Perrine as her guardian.

ROGERS –pg. 99; Jan. 1825. David Rogers, son of John Rogers, dec'd., petitioned for a division of his father's real estate. John Rogers died intestate owning real estate which had descended to his children and grandchildren.
Children of John Rogers, dec'd.: David Rogers; Jesse Rogers; Penelope Anderson, wife of Elias Anderson; Alice Jeffery, wife of Jesse Jeffery; James D. Rogers; George Rogers; Catherine Rogers; Samuel Rogers; and Hannah Lanyard, wife of Abraham Lanyard.
Grandchildren who were children of his son Isaac Rogers, dec'd.: William C. Rogers; Abigail Akins, wife of Benjamin Akins; Solomon B. Rogers; Susan Rogers; Rebecca Rogers; and David Rogers.
Grandchildren who were children of his son John Rogers, dec'd.: Esther Rogers and Abigail Rogers.

RUE –pg. 99; Jan. 1825. John Rue petitioned to have the dower for the widow of William M. Rue, dec'd., set off. John Rue, the petitioner, was the brother of said deceased. William M. Rue, dec'd., late of Middlesex County, died owning real estate in Monmouth County which had descended to his brothers, John Rue and Matthias Rue, subject to the dower of his widow, Catherine Rue.

NEWELL –pg. 100; Jan. 1825. Mary Newell, widow of William Newell, dec'd., petitioned to have her dower set off.

ELLIS –pg. 103; Jan. 1825. Elizabeth T. Ellis requested guardianship of Abraham T. Ellis, Charles R. Ellis, John Borton Ellis, and Amos P. Ellis, minors under 14yrs., children of John Ellis Jr., dec'd. Note: John Borton Ellis' middle name was also given as Barton.

NEWELL –pg. 108; Feb. 1825. Robert Conover requested guardianship of James T. Newell, Lydia Newell, Hugh C. Newell, and Mary Ann Newell, minors under 14yrs., children of William Newell, dec'd.

NEWELL –pg. 108; Feb. 1825. William S. Newell, a minor over 14yrs., son of William Newell, dec'd., elected James A. Reed as his guardian.

THROCKMORTON –pg. 109 – 112; April 1824. The real estate of Holmes Throckmorton, dec'd., was divided amongst his children and his grandchildren. The shares went to Joseph Throckmorton, Elizabeth Brittain, Mary Throckmorton, Jane Scott, Forman Throckmorton, the heirs of John Throckmorton, dec'd., and the children of Sarah Obart, dec'd., dau. of the said Holmes Throckmorton, dec'd.

FROM PAGE 109 TO 123 THE TERM DATES WERE OUT OF ORDER, BUT THE PAGE NUMBERS REMAINED SEQUENTIAL.

CONOVER –pg. 117 - 123; Jan. 1824. The real estate of Cornelius C. Conover was divided amongst his heirs. The records of the division supplied middle initials for the names of some of the heirs previously mentioned in the petition for a division. Heirs receiving a share: John C. Conover, William C. Conover, Sydney Conover, Harmon C. Conover, and Sarah Ann Conover. Note: record dated July 23, 1824.

JOHNSTON –pg. 129; April 1825. Amos Gifford and his wife, Mary, who was the dau. of David Johnston, dec'd., petitioned for a division of her father's real estate. David Johnston, dec'd., late of Howell Tshp., died intestate leaving Mary Gifford and Rebecca Johnston, a minor, as his only children and heirs.

WIKOFF –pg. 129; April 1825. Amanda Wikoff, a minor over 14yrs., dau. of William Wikoff, elected John T. Woodhull as her guardian.

FORMAN –pg. 130; April 1825. Sarah W. Forman, a minor over 14yrs., dau. of William Gordon Forman, dec'd., late of the Mississippi Territory, chose John T. Woodhull as her guardian.

KEARNEY –pg. 130; April 1825. Thomas Kearney, a minor over 14yrs., son of Capt. Edmund, dec'd., (as written) elected Joseph Taylor as his guardian.

PEARCE –pg. 130; April 1825. Jacob Curtis and his wife, Prudence, requested guardianship of Mary Pearce and Abraham Pearce, minors under 14yrs., children of Lewis E. Pearce, dec'd.

PEARCE –pg. 135; April 1825. Jacob Curtis and his wife, Prudence, late Prudence Pearce who was the administrator of the estate of Lewis E. Pearce, dec'd., filed a record of their accounts.

STILLWELL –pg. 147; July 1825. William Leonard requested guardianship of Elizabeth Stillwell and Catherine Stillwell, minors under 14yrs., children of Samuel Stillwell, dec'd.

SHINN –pg. 170; Oct. 1825. Aaron B. Shinn, heir of James Shinn, dec'd., petitioned for a division of real estate. James Shinn, dec'd., late of Upper Freehold Tshp., left a will dated Jan. 25, 1806 devising certain real estate to his son George Shinn who died before the said testator. The real estate was owned as tenants in common by Aaron B. Shinn, Margaret Lawrence, James Shinn, Ezra Shinn, Hannah Shinn, Thomas Shinn, Emily Shinn, Elann Shinn, Rebecca Burtis, Richard Burtis, and others including Hugh Bell. In subsequent records Elann was spelled Elam.

LITTLE –pg. 172; Oct. 1825. Ellen Little requested guardianship of Thomas Little, Jane Amanda Little, Arthur Little, John Little, and Robert E. Little, minors under 14yrs., children of John T. Little, dec'd.

CAMPBELL –pg. 172; Oct. 1825. Benjamin Campbell, a minor over 14yrs., son of Benjamin Campbell, chose Isaac K. Lippincott as his guardian.

ALLGOR –pg. 173; Oct. 1825. Jeremiah Newman Jr. requested appointment as guardian of Eliza Ann Allgor and William Allgor, minors under 14yrs., children of Benjamin W. Allgor, dec'd.

PEACOCK –pg. 184; Jan. 1826. John C. Conover and his wife, Eleanor, dau. of Daniel Peacock, dec'd., petitioned for a division of her father's real estate. Daniel Peacock died intestate owning real estate now held as tenants in common by Eleanor Conover, Margaret Peacock, Phebe Ann Peacock, John Peacock, Catharine Peacock, and Sally Schenck, wife of Jonathan Schenck.

COMPTON –pg. 187; Jan. 1826. Cornelius C. Compton and Job Compton petitioned for a division of the real estate owned by Cornelius Compton, dec'd., late of Middletown Tshp., who died intestate on Jan. 22, 1816 leaving a widow and eight children.
Children of Cornelius Compton, dec'd.: Cornelius C. Compton, Hannah Compton, Jonathan Compton, Mary Holmes, Job Compton, Deborah Compton, Matthias Compton, and Isaac Compton.

BEEDLE –pg. 187; Jan. 1826. Sarah Beedle, a minor over 14yrs., dau. of Richard Beedle, elected Hendrick Beedle as her guardian.

BEEDLE –pg. 188; Jan. 1826. Daniel Beedle, a minor over 14yrs., son of Richard Beedle, chose Hendrick Beedle as his guardian.

REED –pg. 188; Jan. 1826. Noble Reed, a minor over 14yrs., son of Joseph Reed, elected Samuel Craft as his guardian.

BLACKWELL –pg. 188; Jan. 1826. Sarah E. Blackwell, a minor over 14yrs., dau. of William Blackwell, elected Austin D. Blackwell as her guardian.

BLACKWELL –pg. 189; Jan. 1826. Mary C. Blackwell and Margaret D. Blackwell, minors over 14yrs., daus. of William Blackwell, chose Austin D. Blackwell as their guardian. Note: two separate entries on the same page.

REED –pg. 189; Jan. 1826. Samuel Craft requested guardianship of Julia Reed, Johnston Reed, William Reed, and Aaron Reed, minors under 14yrs., children of Joseph Reed, dec'd.

BEEDLE –pg. 189; Jan. 1826. Hendrick Beedle requested guardianship of Timothy Beedle and

Edith Beedle, minors under 14yrs., children of Richard Beedle, dec'd.

COTTRELL –pg. 196; Jan. 1826. A settlement of accounts was filed by Garret P. Heirs and his wife, Jane, late Jane Cottrell who was administrator of the estate of Gershom Cottrell, dec'd.

CONOVER –pg. 207; April 1826. Heirs of Peter H. Conover, dec'd., petitioned for a division of said deceased's real estate. Peter H. Conover died intestate leaving real estate then held as tenants in common by Hendrick P. Conover, Garret P. Conover, Ann P. Conover, Margaret P. Conover, Peter P. Conover, and Mary P. Conover. Note: The division of the real estate in Book G, pgs. 255 – 260, July 1826, named Patience Conover as the widow of Peter H. Conover, dec'd.

CONOVER –pg. 208; April 1826. Cornelia Ann Conover, a minor over 14yrs., dau. of Samuel Conover, chose William J. Conover as her guardian.

SLOCUM –pg. 209; April 1826. Ruth W. Slocum, a minor over 14yrs., dau. of Thomas Slocum, chose Job West and Josiah Holmes as her guardians.

VANKIRK –pg. 209; April 1826. Sarah Jane VanKirk and Schenck VanKirk, minors over 14yrs., children of Peter VanKirk, elected John R. Schenck as their guardian. Note: two separate entries on the same page.

VANKIRK –pg. 210; April 1826. James VanKirk, a minor over 14yrs., son of Peter VanKirk, chose John R. Schenck as his guardian.

VANKIRK –pg. 210; April 1826. Catharine VanKirk requested guardianship of Eleanor VanKirk, Julia Ann VanKirk, Mary VanKirk, and Catharine VanKirk, minors under 14yrs., children of Peter VanKirk, dec'd.

LITTLE –pg. 215; April 1826. Joseph Doty and his wife, Lydia, requested guardianship of Thomas Little, Jane Amanda Little, John Little, Arthur Little, and Robert Little, minors under 14yrs., children of John Little, dec'd.

CONKLING –pg. 247; July 1826. James Arnold requested guardianship of Stephen Inman Conkling, a minor under 14yrs., son of Benjamin Conkling, dec'd.

HALL –pg. 248; July 1826. Mary Ann Hall and Samuel Hall, minors over 14yrs., requested John M. Hall as their guardian.

CRAWFORD –pg. 253; July 1826. John Crawford, a minor over 14yrs., son of Andrew Crawford, chose Richard Smith as his guardian.

HENDRICKSON –pg. 253; July 1826. Harriet Hendrickson and Mary Hendrickson, minors over 14yrs., children of David Hendrickson, chose Samuel Middleton as their guardian. Note: two separate entries on the same page.

HENDRICKSON –pg. 254; July 1826. Nathan Hendrickson, a minor over 14yrs., son of David Hendrickson, chose Samuel Middleton as his guardian.

HENDRICKSON –pg. 254; July 1826. Hannah Hendrickson requested guardianship of Susan Hendrickson and Margaret Hendrickson, minors under 14yrs., children of David Hendrickson, dec'd.

SPRAGG –pg. 254; July 1826. Martha Spragg requested guardianship of Benjamin Spragg, Charlotte Spragg, Jonathan Spragg, Matilda Ann Spragg, Mary Ann Spragg, and Keziah Spragg, minors under 14yrs., children of Joel Spragg, dec'd.

BORDEN –pg. 273; Oct. 1826. Mary Borden, a minor over 14yrs., dau. of William Borden, chose Rachel Borden as her guardian.

CRAWFORD –pg. 273; Oct. 1826. John Crawford, a minor over 14yrs., son of Andrew Crawford, elected Rachel Smith as his guardian.

CLAYTON –pg. 295; Jan. 1827. Corlies Lloyd and his wife, Sarah, late Sarah Clayton who was administrator of the estate of John Clayton, dec'd., were named in a citation.

NOE –pg. 298; Jan. 1827. Susannah Noe and Richard Noe, minors over 14yrs., children of Mary Noe, chose Frances Noe as their guardian. Note: two separate entries on the same page.

HENDRICKSON –pg. 298; Jan. 1827. Jacob Hendrickson, a minor over 14yrs., son of Samuel M. Hendrickson, elected Forman Hendrickson as his guardian.

SHUMAR –pg. 298; Jan. 1827. William Shumar, a minor over 14yrs., son of John Shumar, chose William Holeman and Henry D. Perrine as his guardians.

SHUMAR –pg. 299; Jan. 1827. Lydia Shumar, a minor over 14yrs., dau. of John Shumar, chose William Holeman and Henry D. Perrine as her guardians.

CHUMAR –pg. 299; Jan. 1827. William Holeman and Henry D. Perrine requested guardianship of Rebecca Chumar, John Chumar, and Harriet Chumar, minors under 14yrs., children of John Chumar, dec'd.

LITTLE –pg. 299; Jan. 1827. Margaret Little requested guardianship of Sarah Jane Little and Fanny Little, minors under 14yrs., children of Robert Little, dec'd.

OAKERSON –pg. 302; Jan. 1827. Uriah White and his wife, Nancy, late Nancy Oakerson who was executor of the estate of David Oakerson, dec'd., and John Errickson, also executor of said estate, filed a record of their accounts.

CLAYTON –pg. 306; Jan. 1827. John C. Ely and his wife, Ann, late Ann Clayton, were complainants against Corlies Lloyd and his wife, Sarah, and against Addi Mount, co-administrators of the estate of John Clayton, dec'd.

SMOCK –pg. 317; April 1827. John W. Holmes and Gilbert VanMater, trustees of Micah Clark, late Micah Polhemus, were complainants against Aaron Smock, John H. Smock, and Garret Smock, executors of the estate of Hendrick Smock, dec'd.

HERBERT –pg. 318; April 1827. Wade Little and Ann Herbert, widow of Henry Herbert, dec'd., petitioned to have Ann's dower set off from her late husband's real estate. Wade Little purchased a house and real estate in Howell Tshp. belonging to Henry Herbert, dec'd., at a sheriff's sale.

TAYLOR –pg. 321; April 1827. John Cooper was guardian of William C. Cooper, George W. Cooper, and James G. Cooper, only children of Ida Cooper, dec'd., late Ida Taylor. For his wards, he petitioned for a division of the real estate owned by William Taylor, dec'd. William Taylor, dec'd., died intestate owning real estate in Middletown Tshp. and leaving heirs: Hetty Rowland, late Hetty Taylor; Ann Taylor; Phebe Luffburrow, late Phebe Taylor; Eliza Applegate, late Eliza Taylor; James G. Taylor; Fanny Taylor; and the children of Ida Cooper, dec'd.

EDWARDS –pg. 322; April 1827. The siblings of Deborah Fisher, dec'd., petitioned for a division of the real estate owned by the deceased that was situated in the county of Monmouth. Deborah Fisher, late Deborah Edwards, late of New York City, died intestate owning a house and lot in Shrewsbury Tshp. They and the children of Daniel Edwards, dec'd., were her heirs. Her brothers: Abigail Edwards, Joseph Edwards, James Edwards, Stephen Edwards, and John Edwards.
Her sisters: Sarah Cook, wife of Samuel Cook; and Abigail Cook, wife of William Cook.
Children of Daniel Edwards, dec'd.: William T. Edwards, Joseph Edwards, Stephen Edwards, Henry Edwards, Eliza Edwards, and James H. L. H. Edwards.
Note: There was no explanation for listing Abigail Edwards as a brother and Abigail Cook as a sister.

MATTHEWS –pg. 323; April 1827. Thomas DeBow along with James Hendrickson and his wife, Hannah, late Hannah Matthews, administrators of the estate of Charles Mathews, dec'd., reported on the sale of the said deceased's real estate.

APPLEGATE –pg. 324; April 1827. Sarah Applegate, late Sarah Vanderveer, a minor over 14yrs., dau. of Garret G. Vanderveer, elected her husband, Obediah Applegate, as her guardian.

CRAMMER –pg. 324; April 1827. John C. Crammer requested guardianship of Nancy Crammer, Charity Crammer, and Stephen Crammer, minors under 14yrs., children of Timothy Crammer, dec'd.

BELL –pg. 339; June 1827. Thomas Singleton requested guardianship of Margaret Bell, John Bell, Hugh Bell, Samuel T. Bell, and Sarah Ann Bell, minors under 14yrs.

LEFFERSON –pg. 339; June 1827. Benjamin Lefferson, a minor over 14yrs., son of Benjamin Lefferson, elected William I. Conover as his guardian.

WOOLLEY –pg. 354; July 1827. Herbert C. Pearce in behalf of himself and his wife, Margaret, late Margaret Woolley, and John Howland in behalf of himself and his wife, Caroline, late Caroline Woolley, applied for a division of the real estate owned by Abraham Woolley, Esq., dec'd. Margaret and Caroline were daus. of Abraham Woolley, Esq., dec'd., who died intestate.
Children and heirs entitled to a share of the estate of Abraham Woolley, Esq., dec'd.: Margaret Pearce, Caroline Howland, Reuben Woolley, Lloyd Woolley, Lydia Woolley, Clark Woolley, and Jane Ann Woolley. Only Margaret and Caroline were adults.

MIDDLETON –pg. 356; July 1827. Apollo H. Woodward and his wife, Maria, who was a dau. of Abel Middleton, dec'd., petitioned for a division of her father's real estate. Abel Middleton, dec'd., late of Nottingham Tshp., Burlington Co., died intestate owning real estate in Upper Freehold Tshp., Monmouth Co.
Heirs of Abel Middleton, dec'd.: Maria Woodward, wife of Apollo H. Woodward; Elizabeth Pitts, wife of John Pitts; and the infant children of Lydia Woodward, dec'd, late wife of Henry Woodward. Note: Book H, pg. 77, Oct. 1828 – children of Lydia Woodward, dec'd., lived in another country.

WOOLLEY –pg. 358; July 1827. Reuben Woolley, a minor over 14yrs., son of Abraham Woolley, elected Herbert C. Pearce as his guardian.

THOMPSON –pg. 358; July 1827. Mary Ann Thompson, a minor over 14yrs., dau. of Cornelius Thompson, elected Thomas Robbins as her guardian.

THOMPSON –pg. 359; July 1827. Caroline Thompson, a minor over 14yrs., dau. of Cornelius Thompson, elected Thomas Robbins as her guardian.

DENISE –pg. 359; July 1827. Mary Ann Denise and Benjamin D. Denise, minors over 14yrs., children of Daniel Denise, chose their brother Daniel Denise as their guardian. Note: two separate entries on the same page.

ENGLISH –pg. 359; July 1827. Mary English, a minor over 14yrs., dau. of James R. English, chose Jeremiah Smith English as her guardian.

ENGLISH –pg. 360; July 1827. James T. English, a minor over 14yrs., son of James R. English, chose Jeremiah Smith English as his guardian.

DRUMMOND –pg. 360; July 1827. Taber Chadwick requested guardianship of Gavine Drummond, a minor under 14yrs., son of John Drummond, dec'd.

PEACOCK –pg. 360; July 1827. Sarah Peacock requested guardianship of Ann Peacock and Daniel Peacock, minors under 14yrs., children of John Peacock, dec'd.

NEWELL –pg. 361; July 1827. James English requested guardianship of Lydia Newell, Hugh Newell, and Mary Ann Newell, minors under 14yrs., children of William Newell, dec'd.

WOOLLEY –pg. 361; July 1827. Herbert C. Pearce requested guardianship of Lloyd Woolley and Lydia Woolley, minors under 14yrs., children of Abraham Woolley, dec'd.

HORNER –pg. 362; July 1827. An account for the estate of Isaiah Horner, dec'd., was filed by the executors of his estate, John Horner, James Moore and his wife, Elizabeth, late Elizabeth Horner.

BOOK H

1828 – 1833

SMITH –pg. 4; Jan. 1828. Sarah Smith, Robert Perrine and his wife, Ann Eliza, late Ann Eliza Smith, and the guardians of Louisa Smith and Alfred Smith petitioned for a division of the real estate owned by Edward Smith, dec'd., who died intestate owning real estate in Shrewsbury Tshp.
Children and heirs of Edward Smith, dec'd.: Sarah Smith, Ann Eliza Perrine, Louisa Smith, and Alfred Smith.

LAFETRA –pg. 4; Jan. 1828. Joseph Smith petitioned to set off the dower of Hannah Lafetra, widow of John Lafetra, dec'd. He purchased real estate in Shrewsbury Tshp. owned by John Lafetra, dec'd., at a sheriff's sale.

BELL –pg. 6; Jan. 1828. Thomas Singleton, guardian of Margaret Bell, William T. Bell, John Bell, Hugh Bell, Samuel Bell, and Sarah Ann Bell, children of Hugh Bell, dec'd., petitioned for a division of the real estate owned by Hugh Bell, dec'd. Hugh Bell died intestate owning real estate in Upper Freehold that had descended to James Bell, Robert Bell, and Thomas Singleton's previously named wards.

THOMPSON –pg. 8; Jan. 1828. William C. Thompson, a minor over 14yrs., son of Thomas D. Thompson, elected James Craig as his guardian.

BOGART –pg. 9; Jan. 1828. John Bogart, a minor over 14yrs., son of John Bogart, chose Joseph Bogart as his guardian.

CLAYTON –pg. 9; Jan. 1828. James H. Clayton requested guardianship of Cornelia Ann Clayton, a minor under 14yrs., dau. of James H. Clayton, dec'd. Note: Although the record specified Cornelia's father was deceased, the header stated she was the petitioner's dau.

CONOVER –pg. 9 – 14; Jan. 1828. The real estate of Theodorus Conover and William P. Conover, both dec'd., late of Freehold, was divided amongst the heirs of Samuel Conover, dec'd., who were identified as William S. Conover, Letty Abraham, Kenneth A. Conover, Cornelia Ammerman, and Cornelia Clayton (grandchild of the deceased). Note: The original petition in Book G, pg. 378, Oct. 1827, identified William S., Letty, Kenneth A. and Cornelia only as legatees of both Theodorus and William P. Conover. It also named Stephen Abraham, husband of Letty Abraham and Abraham Ammerman, husband of Cornelia Ammerman.

WOLCOTT –pg. 33; April 1828. James VanNote and his wife, Clementine, who was an heir of Lydia Wolcott, dec'd., were complainants against Henry Wolcott, administrator of the estate of Lydia Wolcott, dec'd.

WHITE –pg. 33; April 1828. Jacob Butcher and his wife, Harriet, late Harriet White and dau. of Esek White, dec'd., petitioned for a division of her father's real estate. Esek White died intestate owning a half share of a piece of property near Red Bank, Shrewsbury Tshp. James Morford owned the other half. Esek White, dec'd., left children: Harriet, wife of Jacob Butcher; Caroline White; Henry B. White; Isaac P. White; and Esek T. White, a minor.

BRAY –pg. 34; April 1828. Rachel Bent, late Rachel Bray, applied for assignment of her dower from the real estate of James Bray, dec'd., late of Middletown Tshp. Half of the real estate was owned by her eldest son David Bray. Samuel Bray and Laura Bray, both children of said Rachel Bent, possessed the other half, consisting of a house and about 160 acres of land. Note: Book H, pg. 160, July 1829, a settlement of accounts named Samuel Bent as the husband of Rachel Bent, late Rachel Bray.

CONOVER –pg. 35; April 1828. Hendrick P. Conover, son of Peter H. Conover, dec'd., petitioned

for a division of his father's real estate. Peter H. Conover died intestate owning real estate in Freehold Tshp. and elsewhere.
Children and heirs of Peter H. Conover, dec'd.: Hendrick P. Conover, Garret P. Conover, Ann P. Conover, Margaret P. Conover, Peter P. Conover, and Mary P. Conover.

GANT –pg. 36; April 1828. John S. VanNote and his wife, Mary, dau. of Richard Gant, dec'd., petitioned for a division of her father's real estate. Richard Gant, dec'd., late of Dover Tshp., died intestate owning real estate. The land had descended to Mary VanNote, wife of John S. VanNote, Richard Gant, Lydia Gant, Zacharia Gant, Clarissa Gant, James Gant, Catharine Gant, and John Gant.

GREEN –pg. 36; April 1828. Henrietta Green, a minor over 14yrs., dau. of Henry Green, elected William W. Forman as her guardian.

HALL –pg. 37; April 1828. John Hall requested guardianship of Caroline Hall, Harriet Hall, Elizabeth Hall, and Washington Hall, minors under 14yrs., children of Samuel Hall, dec'd.

BREWER –pg. 37; April 1828. Robert Walker petitioned for a division of the real estate owned by Hendrick Brewer, dec'd., who died intestate leaving no heirs.
Heirs of Hendrick Brewer, dec'd.: Sylvanus Brewer and Aaron Brewer who sold their shares to the petitioner, Robert Walker; Lena Walker, late Lena Brewer, wife of Robert Walker, the petitioner; Hendrick Brewer who sold his share to Joseph VanNote; William Brewer; Abigail Bowne, late Abigail Brewer, wife of Elisha Bowne; and John Brewer who died after the demise of said Hendrick Brewer, dec'd., and left children, viz., Hendrick Brewer, Catherine Brewer, Lydia Brewer, Garret Brewer, and Abigail Paulding, dec'd., late wife of George Paulding.

BARCALOW –pg. 57; July 1828. Deborah Ann Barcalow and John Jeffrey Barcalow, minors over 14yrs., children of Matthias Barcalow, chose Elizabeth Barcalow as their guardian. Note: two separate entries on the same page.

WOOLLEY –pg. 58; July 1828. William W. Woolley, a minor over 14yrs., son of Adam Woolley Jr., chose Herbert C. Pearce as his guardian.

BARCALOW –pg. 58; July 1828. Elizabeth Barcalow requested guardianship of Job S. Barcalow, Milton Pitts Barcalow, and Sarah Conover Barcalow, minors under 14yrs., children of Matthias Barcalow, dec'd.

TENBROOK –pg. 78; Oct. 1828. Jane G. Tenbrook, dau. of Samuel W. Tenbrook, dec'd., petitioned for a division of her father's real estate. Samuel W. Tenbrook died leaving a will to dispose of his real estate amongst his widow and children.
Widow: Mary Tenbrook, dec'd., who died before said testator.
Children: petitioner, Jane G. Tenbrook; Mary Mayell, wife of William Mayell; Elizabeth Corlies, dec'd., late wife of John P. Corlies, who predeceased her father; and Edmund W. Tenbrook.
Jane G. Tenbrook, Mary Mayall, and Edmund W. Tenbrook were also joint heirs to property owned by their deceased mother, Mary Tenbrook, that was bequeathed to her by her father, Edmund Williams, dec'd., late of Monmouth Co.

TENBROOK –pg. 82; Oct. 1828. Edmund W. Tenbrook, a minor over 14yrs., son of Doctor Samuel W. Tenbrook, elected Seth Lippincott as his guardian.

KEARNEY –pg. 82; Oct. 1828. Joseph Taylor, Esq., requested guardianship of Catherine Kearney and Ann Kearney, minors under 14yrs., children of Edward Kearney, dec'd.

HORNER –pg. 83; Oct. 1828. Isaac N. Woodward requested guardianship of Jemina Horner, Catherine Pawnsine Horner, and Margaret Horner, minors under 14yrs., children of Isaiah Horner, dec'd.

PARKER –pg. 95; Dec. 1828. George J. Parker, a minor over 14yrs., son of Thomas Parker, elected Joseph T. Parker as his guardian.

McCHESNEY –pg. 100; Jan. 1829. Elizabeth McChesney, widow of John McChesney, dec'd., petitioned to have her dower set aside. Notice of the application was served on Dr. James English, current owner of said real estate.

BELL –pg. 100; Jan. 1829. Sarah Bell, widow of Hugh Bell, dec'd., petitioned to have her dower set off. Hugh Bell died intestate owning land in New Egypt, Upper Freehold Tshp.

CLAYTON –pg. 101; Jan. 1829. Mary Clayton, widow of Jonathan Clayton, dec'd., petitioned to have her dower set off. Jonathan Clayton, dec'd., owned a farm and meadow in Freehold Tshp.

VANDERVEER –pg. 102; Jan. 1829. Benjamin S. Vanderveer, a minor over 14yrs., son of Garret G. Vanderveer, chose Disbrow Carson as his guardian.

PARKER –pg. 102; Jan. 1829. Mary Ann Parker and Lydia Ann Parker, minors over 14yrs., children of Thomas Parker, chose Hiram Mount as their guardian. Note: two separate entries on the same page.

STOUT –pg. 103; Jan. 1829. Sarah Stout requested guardianship of Peter Stout, Ann Stout, Tenbrook Stout, Thomas Stout, and Edward Stout, minors under 14yrs., children of Richard Stout, dec'd.

CRANE –pg. 103; Jan. 1829. Nathan Haywood requested guardianship of Ann M. Crane, a minor under 14yrs., dau. of William H. Crane, dec'd. Note: Book H, pg. 222, April 1830 – A statement of accounts gave her full name as Ann Marie Crane.

KEARNEY –pg. 119; April 1829. Daniel Holmes, Esq., petitioned for a division of the real estate owned by Edmund Kearney, dec'd. Daniel Holmes, Esq., and John W. Holmes purchased real estate from James P. Kearney, dec'd., prior to his death, described as 1/7 part of the lands of Edmund Kearney, dec'd. The petition stated that James P. Kearney, Horatio Kearney, Thomas Kearney, Anastatia Kearney, Catherine Kearney, Ann Kearney, and Mary Eliza Kearney were the only children and heirs of said Edmund Kearney, dec'd., who died intestate owning real estate in Middletown Tshp.

KEARNEY –pg. 121; April 1829. Anastatia Kearney, a minor over 14yrs., dau. of Edmund Kearney, elected Joseph Taylor as her guardian.

HORSFULL –pg. 121 – 123; April 1829. A report on the sale of the real estate owned by Richard Horsfull, dec'd., identified his widow as Margaret Horsfull.

BEATY –pg. 123; April 1829. John W. Davison, Esq., administrator of the estate of William Beaty, dec'd., reported the real estate of William Beaty, dec'd., was sold to Ann Bailey, widow of said deceased.

SOPER –pg. 156; July 1829. Reuben Soper, son of Timothy Soper, dec'd., applied for a division of his father's real estate. Timothy Soper died intestate owning real estate in Stafford Tshp. and elsewhere.
Children and heirs of Timothy Soper, dec'd.: Reuben Soper; Charity Brown, wife of Abraham Brown; Joel Soper; Mary Tucker, wife of Jacob Tucker; Lydia Clevenger, wife of Elias Clevenger; Sarah Stiles, wife of Martin Stiles; Timothy Soper; Hannah Soper; Theodosia Soper; Fanny Soper; Rebecca Soper; Rhoda Soper; Samuel Soper; and Thomas Soper.

WOLCOTT –pg. 158; July 1829. John Wolcott and Elizabeth Wolcott, minors over 14yrs., children of John Wolcott, chose Ann Wolcott as their guardian. Note: two separate entries on the same page.

ROGERS –pg. 158; July 1829. Elihu Rogers, a minor over 14yrs., son of Brittain Rogers, elected Samuel Rogers as his guardian.

WOLCOTT –pg. 158; July 1829. Ann Wolcott requested guardianship of Robinson Wolcott, Lewis Wolcott, and David Wolcott, minors under 14yrs., children of John Wolcott, dec'd.

ROGERS –pg. 159; July 1829. Sarah Rogers requested guardianship of Sarah Rogers, Rebecca Rogers, and Jeremiah Rogers, minors under 14yrs., children of Brittain Rogers, dec'd.

ROBINSON –pg. 164; July 1829. Elijah Combs, guardian of Sarah Robinson, late Sarah Lefferson, filed a statement of accounts.

SOPER –pg. 178; Oct. 1829. Theodosia Soper, a minor over 14yrs., dau. of Timothy Soper, elected Amos Birdsall as her guardian.

SOPER –pg. 179; Oct. 1829. Fanny Soper, a minor over 14yrs., dau. of Timothy Soper, elected Amos Birdsall as her guardian.

WHITE –pg. 179; Oct. 1829. George White, a minor over 14yrs., son of Thomas White, chose Samuel Haggerty as his guardian.

SOPER –pg. 179; Oct. 1829. Amos Birdsall requested guardianship of Rebecca Soper, Rhoda Soper, Samuel Soper, and Thomas Soper, minors under 14yrs., children of Timothy Soper, dec'd.

REMSON –pg. 197; Jan. 1830. James T. Bartine, guardian of Eliza Remson, Deborah Remson, Julia Ann Remson, Maria Remson, and Henrietta Remson, children of Henry Remson, dec'd., petitioned for a division of the children's father's real estate. Henry Remson died intestate owning real estate in Stafford Tshp., and the children held the real estate as tenants in common, subject to the widow's dower.

ROGERS –pg. 198; Jan. 1830. William Rogers applied for a division of the real estate owned by Brittan Rogers, dec'd., who died intestate owning real estate in Howell Tshp.
Children and heirs of Brittan Rogers, dec'd.: William Rogers, Elizabeth Rogers, Lucretia Rogers, Brittan Rogers, Elihu Rogers, Sarah Rogers, Rebecca Rogers, and Jeremiah Newman Rogers. Note: Book H, pg. 236 – 240, April 1830 – The actual division of the real estate gave married names for two of the children named above. A share went to Lucretia Carpenter, late Lucretia Rogers and another went to Elizabeth Longstreet, late Elizabeth Rogers, wife of Garret Longstreet.

HERBERT –pg. 199; Jan. 1830. Abraham Herbert petitioned for a division of the real estate owned by Jacob Herbert, dec'd., who died intestate owing real estate in Howell Tshp.
Widow: Margaret Herbert.
Children and heirs of Jacob Herbert, dec'd.: Abraham Herbert, Mercy Little, Isaac Herbert, and Hannah Herbert. One of the heirs was a minor.

THROCKMORTON –pg. 201; Jan. 1830. William Throckmorton and Sarah Throckmorton, minors over 14yrs., children of Furman Throckmorton, chose Elizabeth Throckmorton as their guardian. Note: two separate entries on the same page.

THROCKMORTON –pg. 201; Jan. 1830. Elizabeth Throckmorton requested guardianship of Ann Matilda Throckmorton, Susan Throckmorton, Furman Throckmorton, and John Throckmorton, minors under 14yrs., children of Furman Throckmorton, dec'd.

REMSON –pg. 201; Jan. 1830. James T. Bartine requested guardianship of Eliza Remson, Deborah Remson, Julia Ann Remson, Maria Remson, and Henrietta Remson, minors under 14yrs., children of Henry Remson, dec'd.

THROCKMORTON –pg. 207; Jan. 1830. William Smith, guardian of Mary Willson, late Mary Throckmorton, filed a statement of accounts.

LITTLE –pg. 217; April 1830. Joseph Doty and his wife, Lydia, guardian of Thomas Little, Amanda Little, John Little, and Arthur Little, minor children of John T. Little, dec'd., petitioned to sell their wards' real estate to offset the expenses of maintaining and educating the children.

OLIPHANT –pg. 217 and pg. 218; April 1830. David S. Haywood petitioned for a division of the real estate owned by David Oliphant, dec'd. David S. Haywood was the husband of Hope Haywood, dau. of said deceased.
Children and heirs of David Oliphant, dec'd.: Hope Haywood, William Oliphant, Celia Oliphant, James Oliphant, Jane Oliphant, Mahle Oliphant, George Oliphant, Caroline Oliphant, Ann Eliza Oliphant, and David Oliphant. Note: On the pages indicated, there were two separate applications for the same division.

ROBBINS –pg. 219; April 1830. An application for letters of administration on the estate of John Robbins, dec'd., revealed Rebecca Robbins, widow of John Robbins, dec'd., declined in favor of her son Ezekiel Robbins, and her son-in-law Rice Hadsell.

NEWELL –pg. 219; April 1830. James T. Newell, a minor over 14yrs., son of William Newell, chose Mary Newell as his guardian.

CURTIS –pg. 220; April 1830. Joseph Curtis, a minor over 14yrs., son of Joseph Curtis, elected David Curtis as his guardian.

HERBERT –pg. 220; April 1830. Elizabeth L. Herbert, a minor over 14yrs., dau. of James G. Herbert, Esq., chose Samuel Laird as her guardian.

HERBERT –pg. 220; April 1830. John C. Herbert, a minor over 14yrs., son of James G. Herbert, Esq., chose Dr. Gilbert S. Woodhull as his guardian.

HORSFULL –pg. 220; April 1830. Sarah Horsfull, a minor over 14yrs., dau. of Richard Horsfull, elected Samuel Craft as her guardian.

HORSFULL –pg. 221; April 1830. Margaret Horsfull, a minor over 14yrs., dau. of Richard Horsfull, chose Samuel Craft as her guardian.

HERBERT –pg. 221; April 1830. David Laird Jr. and Daniel Laird requested guardianship of Ann Herbert, Mary Herbert, Sarah Herbert, and James A. Herbert, minors under 14yrs., children of James G. Herbert, dec'd.

CONOVER –pg. 221; April 1830. Sarah Conover requested guardianship of Ira Conover, Gilbert Conover, and Mary Louisa Conover, minors under 14yrs., children of Garret J. Conover, dec'd.

DENISE –pg. 243; April 1830. Daniel Denise, guardian of Mary Ann Denise, then Mary Ann Hunt, filed a settlement of accounts.

HALL –pg. 255; July 1830. John M. Hall, guardian of the children of Samuel Hall, dec'd., petitioned for a division of the real estate owned by said Samuel Hall, dec'd., who died leaving a will and owning real estate in Howell Tshp. He was guardian of the following children of Samuel Hall, dec'd.: Mary Ann Platues, late Hall, wife of Randolph Platues; Samuel Hall; Caroline Wolston, late Hall, wife of Charles Wolston; Harriet Hall; Elizabeth Hall; and George Washington Hall.

BROWN –pg. 256; July 1830. David Brown, a minor over 14yrs., son of Isaac Brown, chose Merrick Burdge as his guardian.

BROWN –pg. 257; July 1830. Robert Brown, a minor over 14yrs., son of Isaac Brown, chose Merrick Burdge as his guardian.

HERBERT –pg. 257; July 1830. Margaret Herbert requested guardianship of Hannah Herbert, a minor under 14yrs., dau. of Jacob Herbert, dec'd.

CAMPBELL –pg. 257; July 1830. Martha Campbell requested guardianship of Jane Haviland Campbell, Sarah Winans Campbell, Martha Campbell, and Catharine Campbell, minors under 14yrs., children of Richard B. Campbell, dec'd.

POLHEMUS –pg. 271; Oct. 1830. Mary Kelly, late Mary Polhemus, and Tabor Chadwick, executors of the estate of William Polhemus, dec'd., petitioned to sell the real estate of William Polhemus, dec'd., to pay the debts of said deceased.

CLAYTON –pg. 273; Oct. 1830. Mary Clayton requested guardianship of Ann Eliza Clayton, a minor under 14yrs., dau. of Joseph Riggs Clayton, dec'd.

DRUMMOND –pg. 285 - 286; Jan. 1831. Taber Chadwick, guardian of Gavin Drummond, son of Gavin Drummond, dec'd. (see note), late of Shrewsbury Tshp. petitioned for a division of real estate. Gavin Drummond, dec'd., left a will dated April 20, 1810 in which he bequeathed land to his son John Drummond, and at the demise of this son, the land would pass to the male heirs of said son John Drummond. Since the death of Gavin Drummond, his son and legatee John Drummond had died leaving two sons, viz., Gavin Drummond, the petitioner's ward, and Peter Drummond who was an adult. Taber Chadwick petitioned to have the described real estate divided. Note: Gavin Drummond, ward of Taber Chadwick, was first noted as the son of Gavin Drummond. Further on and throughout he was noted as the son of John Drummond.

BOICE –pg. 287; Jan. 1831. Mary Boice, a minor over 14yrs., dau. of William Boice, elected Sarah Boice as her guardian.

COMBS –pg. 287; Jan. 1831. Elizabeth R. Combs, a minor over 14yrs., dau. of Elijah Combs, chose Rulif R. Schenck as her guardian.

BOICE –pg. 287; Jan. 1831. Cornelius Boice, a minor over 14yrs., son of William Boice, elected Benjamin Griggs as his guardian.

BOICE –pg. 287; Jan. 1831. Sarah Boice requested guardianship of Margaret Ann Boice and Sarah Boice, minors under 14yrs., children of William Boice, dec'd.

LONGSTREET –pg. 288; Jan. 1831. Richard Longstreet requested guardianship of John M. Longstreet and Hannah Longstreet, minors under 14yrs., children of Aaron Longstreet, dec'd.

COMBS –pg. 288; Jan. 1831. William T. Sutphen requested guardianship of Gilbert Combs, a minor under 14yrs., son of Elijah Combs, dec'd.

LANE –pg. 301; April 1831. Sarah Lane, a minor over 14yrs., dau. of John Lane, elected Jane Lane as her guardian.

FLEMING –pg. 302; April 1831. Charles T. Fleming, a minor over 14yrs., son of Joseph Fleming, chose Gabriel West as his guardian.

HERBERT –pg. 302; April 1831. John C. Herbert, a minor over 14yrs., son of James G. Herbert, Esq., elected John Suydam as his guardian.

CHAMBERLAIN –pg. 302; April 1831. Benjamin Pridmore requested guardianship of Thomas B. Chamberlain, Samuel B. Chamberlain, and Mary B. Chamberlain, minors under 14yrs., children of Jesse Chamberlain, dec'd.

LANE –pg. 302; April 1831. Jane Lane requested guardianship of Cornelius Lane, Alice Lane, and Rebecca Lane, minors under 14yrs., children of John Lane, dec'd.

DORSETT –pg. 303; Aril 1831. Oliver Sproule requested guardianship of Joseph Dorsett, a minor under 14yrs., son of Joseph I. Dorsett, dec'd.

COMBS –pg. 303; April 1831. William Sutphen and Rulif R. Schenck petitioned for the division of the real estate owned by Elijah Combs, dec'd. William Sutphen was the husband of Nancy Sutphen, late Nancy Combs, and Rulif R. Schenck was the husband of Esther Schenck, late Esther Combs.
Children and heirs of Elijah Combs, dec'd.: Nancy Sutphen, Esther Schenck, Thomas E. Combs, Aaron R. Combs, Joseph Combs, Elizabeth Combs, and Gilbert Combs. Some of the heirs were minors.

THROCKMORTON –pg. 327 – 328; July 1831. William A. Nivison and his wife, Sarah, late Sarah Throckmorton who was over 14yrs., were complainants against Charles H. Baxter and his wife, Elizabeth, late Elizabeth Throckmorton who was the guardian of the minor children of Furman Throckmorton, dec'd., viz., William Throckmorton, Ann Throckmorton, Susan Throckmorton, Furman Throckmorton, John Throckmorton, and Sarah (Throckmorton) Nivison.

HERBERT –pg. 328; July 1831. Lewis H. Johnston and his wife, Pauline, late Pauline Herbert, petitioned for a division of the real estate owned by Jacob Herbert, dec'd., who died intestate owning land in Howell Tshp.
Children and heirs of Jacob Herbert, dec'd.: Pauline (Herbert) Johnston, Ann Herbert, James Herbert, Isaac Herbert, Mary Herbert, and Lydia Herbert.

WOOLLEY –pg. 343; Oct. 1831. Ann Cook, late Ann Woolley, guardian of Elizabeth Woolley, William W. Woolley, Hannah Woolley, and Ann Woolley, children of Adam Woolley, dec'd., petitioned to sell real estate for support of the children.

CONOVER –pg. 347; Oct. 1831. David S. Conover, a minor over 14yrs., son of Col. Robert Conover, elected William I. Conover as his guardian.

CONOVER –pg. 348; Oct. 1831. Joshua S. Conover, a minor over 14yrs., son of Col. Robert Conover, elected William I. Conover as his guardian.

DORSETT –pg. 350; Oct. 1831. Joseph Taylor petitioned for a division of the real estate owned by

Joseph Dorsett, dec'd., who died intestate owning real estate in Middletown Tshp. Joseph Taylor was the husband of Martha Taylor, formerly Martha Dorsett. Martha (Dorsett) Taylor, Mary Conover (late Mary Dorsett), Elizabeth Dorsett, Ann Dorsett, Hannah Bedle (wife of Thomas Bedle), and Joseph Dorsett were "children of Joseph Dorsett Jr., dec'd., and the only children and heirs of Joseph Dorsett, dec'd.," whose lands were the subject of this petition. This record was poorly worded, and omitted the relationship between Joseph Dorsett and Joseph Dorsett Jr. The phrase in quotes was taken directly from the record.

ELY –pg. 351; Oct. 1831. Lucy Ely's name appeared in a citation as the guardian of Elizabeth Tantum, late Elizabeth Ely, wife of Samuel Tantum.

CLAYTON –pg. 355; Oct. 1831. A settlement of accounts was filed by Corlies Lloyd and his wife, Sarah, guardian of Lucy Drake, late Lucy Clayton.

LONGSTREET –pg. 364; Jan. 1832. Robert James Jr., petitioned for a division of the real estate owned by William G. Longstreet, dec'd. Robert James Jr. was the husband of Alice, late Alice Longstreet, dau. of William G. Longstreet, dec'd., who died intestate owning real estate in Howell Tshp.
Widow: Deborah Longstreet.
Children and heirs of William G. Longstreet, dec'd.: Mary Longstreet, Alice (Longstreet) James, Elizabeth Longstreet, Kenneth Longstreet, Moses Longstreet, Joseph Longstreet, John Longstreet, Taber C. Longstreet, Carhart S. Longstreet, and William T. Longstreet. Note: Book H, pg. 427, July 1832 - The division of the real estate provided middle initials for two of the children. Moses was Moses H. Longstreet, and Joseph was Joseph B. Longstreet.

ELY –pg. 365; Jan. 1832. The commissioners could not fairly divide the real estate of Isaac Ely, dec'd. and declared it must be sold. Isaac's widow was identified as Lucy Ely.

CURTIS –pg. 367; Jan. 1832. Elizabeth Curtis, a minor over 14yrs., dau. of John Curtis, chose John Corlies Curtis as her guardian.

HERBERT –pg. 367; Jan. 1832. John G. Bartholph requested guardianship of Margaret Herbert, Mary Ann Herbert, Alletta Herbert, and Jacob Brucker Herbert, minors under 14yrs., children of Isaac Herbert, dec'd.

LONGSTREET –pg. 367; Jan. 1832. Deborah Longstreet requested guardianship of Elizabeth Longstreet, Taber C. Longstreet, Carhart S. Longstreet, and William T. Longstreet, minors under 14yrs., children of William G. Longstreet, dec'd.

CURTIS –pg. 367; Jan. 1832. John C. Curtis requested guardianship of Susan Curtis and Thomas Curtis, minors under 14yrs.

WHITE –pg. 368; Jan. 1832. Joseph L. White requested guardianship of Cynus Jones White, a minor under 14yrs., son of Charles White, dec'd.

WOOD –pg. 379; Feb. 1832. Samuel Wood, a minor over 14yrs., son of Robert Wood, elected John B. Hartshorne as his guardian.

WILLIAMS –pg. 385; April 1832. Robert Jobs Jr. and his wife, Sarah, who was the dau. of Samuel Williams, dec'd., petitioned for a division of her father's real estate. Samuel Williams, dec'd., was a "man of color" who died intestate owning a small lot in Shrewsbury Tshp.
Widow: Mary Williams who had remarried and was then Mary Kearney, wife of Joseph Kearney.
Heirs of Samuel Williams, dec'd.: Sarah (Williams) Jobs, Peter Williams, Samuel Williams, Ann Williams, Eliza Williams, Elizabeth Williams, and Deborah (Williams) Holmes who was the wife of Joseph Holmes.

ARROWSMITH –pg. 388; April 1832. Thomas Arrowsmith, a minor over 14yrs., son of Joseph Arrowsmith, chose Stephen VanBrackle as his guardian.

COWARD –pg. 388; April 1832. Cleminor L. Coward, a minor over 14yrs., dau. of Enoch Coward, elected her brother Enoch Coward as her guardian.

WOODWARD –pg. 389; April 1832. James W. Woodward requested guardianship of William Allen Woodward, Henry Wheelock Woodward, and Lydia Woodward, minors under 14yrs., children of Lydia Woodward, dec'd.

GORDON –pg. 389; April 1832. John E. Gordon requested guardianship of William J. Gordon and
Elizabeth Gordon, minors under 14yrs., children of Jonathan R. Gordon, dec'd.

IVINS –pg. 389; April 1832. James Ivins requested guardianship of his son Robert Ivins, a minor
under 14yrs.

BUTCHER –pg. 389; April 1832. Isaac P. White requested guardianship of Margaret Butcher and
Elizabeth Butcher, minors under 14yrs., children of Harriet Butcher, dec'd.

TAYLOR –pg. 390; April 1832. John A. Taylor requested guardianship of his children David
Taylor, Ann W. Taylor, and Meribah W. Taylor, minors under 14yrs.

ROGERS –pg. 394 - 400; April 1832. Ann Rogers, widow of Samuel Rogers, dec'd., late of Upper
Freehold Tshp., petitioned to have her dau. Mary Ann Rogers declared mentally incompetent.
Samuel Rogers, dec'd., died intestate around Sept. 1831 owning considerable real estate. He
left two children, viz., Mary Ann Rogers and Hannah Rogers. Hannah Rogers married
Francis Burden (also spelled Borden in the record). Mary Ann Rogers was about 23yrs. old
and had been weak and mentally incapacitated from birth. Joseph Rogers, about 56yrs. of
age, brother of Samuel Rogers, dec'd., testified. Investigators reported Mary Ann Rogers was
about 25yrs of age, and her sister Hannah Borden was about 23yrs. of age. Mary Ann Rogers
was declared mentally incompetent.

HOLMES –pg. 414; July 1832. Richard Holmes petitioned for a division of the real estate owned by
Charles Holmes, dec'd., "a man of color" who died intestate owning considerable real estate
in Middletown Tshp.
Widow: Dinah Holmes.
Children and heirs: Richard Holmes, Judah Holmes, Abraham Holmes, William Holmes, and
Oliver Holmes. One unspecified heir was a minor.

HENDRICKSON –pg. 417; July 1832. William H. Hendrickson, Sarah Ann Hendrickson, and
Charles D. Hendrickson, minors over 14yrs., children of William Hendrickson, chose Eleanor
D. Hendrickson as their guardian. Note: three separate entries on the same page.

ROY –pg. 418; July 1832. Sarah T. Roy requested guardianship of Jane Ann Roy, a minor under
14yrs., dau. of John Roy, dec'd.

MOORE –pg. 418; July 1832. Caroline Moore requested guardianship of Sarah Moore and Ann
Maria Moore, minors under 14yrs., children of Samuel Moore, dec'd.

HENDRICKSON –pg. 418; July 1832. Eleanor D. Hendrickson requested guardianship of
Francinka Hendrickson and Mary Hendrickson, minors under 14yrs., children of William
Hendrickson, dec'd.

MOUNT –pg. 418; July 1832. Ann Mount requested guardianship of Isabella Mount, Samuel
Mount, Nisbet Mount, Caroline Mount, and Elizabeth Mount, minors under 14yrs., children
of Brittain Mount, dec'd.

ROUZE –pg. 425; July 1832. A settlement of accounts was filed by William Crawford and his wife,
Mary, late Mary Rouze, late acting executor of the estate of Theodore Rouze, dec'd.

IRETON –pg. 440; Oct. 1832. Vashta Ireton, a minor over 14yrs., chose Elizabeth Ireton as her
guardian.

LLOYD –pg. 440; Oct. 1832. Maria Lloyd petitioned for a division of the real estate owned by
Caleb Lloyd, dec'd., who died intestate.
Children and heirs of Caleb Lloyd, dec'd.: Maria Lloyd; Rachel B. Ryall, late Rachel Lloyd,
wife of Daniel B. Ryall, Esq.; Elizabeth Ann Bartleson, late Elizabeth Lloyd, wife of Enos
Bartleson; Henrietta Lloyd; and Louisa Matilda Lloyd.
Rachel B. Ryall had died leaving a son, Caleb L. Ryall, and Elizabeth Ann Bartleson had died
leaving a son, Charles P. Bartleson.

JOHNSON –pg. 441; Oct. 1832. Joseph D. Thompson and his wife, Nancy, petitioned for a division
of the real estate owned by Thomas Johnson, dec'd., who died intestate.
Children of Thomas Johnson, dec'd.: William Johnson; Samuel Johnson; Benjamin Johnson;
Nancy Thompson, the petitioner, wife of Joseph D. Thompson; Timothy Johnson; Mary
Anderson, wife of John Anderson; Alice Johnson; Edith Johnson; Thomas Johnson; Sarah

Johnson; James Johnson; Rebecca Johnson; and George Washington Johnson.
Elizabeth Leming, dec'd., late wife of Lewis Leming, was a dau. of Thomas Johnson, dec'd.,
who predeceased her father and left several children.

JOHNSON –pg. 455; Nov. 1832. Martha Johnson requested guardianship of Thomas Johnson,
Sarah Johnson, James Johnson, Rebecca Johnson, and George Washington Johnson, minors
under 14yrs., children of Thomas Johnson, dec'd.

PACKER –pg. 455; Nov. 1832. Mary W. Packer requested guardianship of Mary Jane Packer, a
minor under 14yrs., dau. of Charles Packer, dec'd.

REMSEN –pg. 464; Jan. 1833. Eliza Bartine, a minor over 14yrs., dau. of Henry Remsen, requested
James T. Bartine as her guardian.

LLOYD –pg. 464; Jan. 1833. Louisa Matilda Lloyd, a minor over 14yrs., dau. of Caleb Lloyd,
chose Enos R. Bartleson as her guardian.

THOMPSON –pg. 464; Jan. 1833. Hannah Thompson, a minor over 14yrs., dau. of Thomas
Thompson, elected Miriam Thompson as her guardian.

THOMPSON –pg. 465; Jan. 1833. Mary Thompson, a minor over 14yrs., dau. of Thomas
Thompson, elected Miriam Thompson as her guardian.

VANMATER –pg. 465; Jan. 1833. Eliza Jane VanMater, a minor over 14yrs. and a legatee of
Joseph VanMater, dec'd., elected Joseph H. VanMater and Holmes VanMater as her
guardians.

KNOTT –pg. 465; Jan. 1833. Elisha Lippincott requested guardianship of Elizabeth Knott and Ann
Maria Knott, minors under 14yrs., children of Jacob Knott, dec'd.

BARTLESON –pg. 466; Jan. 1833. Enos R. Bartleson requested guardianship of his son Charles P.
Bartleson, a minor under 14yrs.

LAWSON –pg. 466; Jan. 1833. Catherine Lawson requested guardianship of Henry Lawson,
Benjamin Lawson, Solomon Lawson, Aaron Lawson, and Mary Lawson, minors under 14yrs.,
children of Edward Lawson, dec'd.

THOMPSON –pg. 466; Jan. 1833. Miriam Thompson requested guardianship of Acsah Thompson,
Ten Brook Thompson, Jane Thompson, Thomas Thompson, and Elizabeth Thompson, minors
under 14yrs., children of Thomas Thompson, dec'd.

HAZLETON –pg. 466; Jan. 1833. Samuel Lawson requested guardianship of Mary Ann Lawson, a
minor under 14yrs., dau. of Thomas Hazleton, dec'd.

BOOK I
1833 – 1838

CLAYTON –pg. 3; April 1833. Addi Mount and his wife, Hetty, late Hetty Clayton and dau. of
John Clayton, dec'd., petitioned for a division of her father's real estate. John Clayton,
dec'd., owned real estate in Upper Freehold Tshp. and died intestate.
Children and heirs of John Clayton, dec'd.: Hetty Mount, the petitioner; Nancy Ely, late
Nancy Clayton, wife of John C. Ely; Lucy Drake, late Lucy Clayton, wife of Charles S.
Drake; Matilda Rue, late Matilda Clayton, wife of Edmund Rue; Elizabeth Clayton; and
Moses Clayton. Some of the heirs were minors.

CRAWFORD –pg. 19; July 1833. Joseph Clark and his wife, Filey, petitioned for a division of real
estate. On Dec. 4, 1824 John Crawford transferred real estate to Faliska, otherwise called
Filey, who had since married Joseph Clark, and to her sister Sarah Sands Smith, a minor
otherwise known as Sarah Gent.

JOHNSTON –pg. 19; July 1833. Luke Johnston, son of George Johnston, dec'd., petitioned for a
division of his father's real estate. George Johnston, dec'd., owned real estate in Howell
Tshp. and died intestate.
Children and heirs of George Johnston, dec'd.: Luke Johnston; William G. Johnston; Joanna
Johnston; Elizabeth Johnston; George Johnston; James Johnston; Catharine Johnston; Sarah
Johnston; Charles Johnston; and Mary Truax, dec'd., late dau. of George Johnston, dec'd.,
and late wife of Samuel Truax.
Grandchildren who were children of his previously mentioned dau. Mary Truax, dec'd.:
Wesley Truax, Leonard Truax, Samuel Jones Truax, and Forman Truax.

ANTRIM –pg. 21; July 1833. Samuel M. Antrim, a minor over 14yrs., chose Thomas E. Antrim as
his guardian.

HEADLEY –pg. 21; July 1833. Phebe Headley, late Phebe Lawson, a minor over 14yrs., chose John
M. Headley as her guardian.

LAMBERSON –pg. 21; July 1833. William C. Lamberson requested guardianship of his children
Eliza Lamberson, William Lamberson, Ellenor Lamberson, and Daniel Lamberson, minors
under 14yrs.

LEFFERSON –pg. 35; July 1833. A settlement of accounts was filed by William I. Conover as
guardian of Lydia Clayton, late Lydia Lefferson, wife of Ellison Clayton.

ALLEN –pg. 41; Oct. 1833. William W. Allen, son of James S. Allen, dec'd., applied for a division
of his father's real estate. James S. Allen, dec'd., owned real estate in Howell and Dover
Tshps. and died intestate.
Children and heirs of said deceased: William W. Allen; Catharine Saxton, wife of Isaac
Saxton; Lydia Tilton, wife of James Tilton; Elizabeth Ann Allen; James Allen; and Deborah
Allen. Some of the heirs were minors.

MORRIS –pg. 42; Oct. 1833. Joseph Morris and Henry Morris requested guardianship of William
R. Morris and Forman Morris, minors under 14yrs.

NEWBERRY –pg. 59; Jan. 1834. Charles M. Newberry, a minor over 14yrs., chose William H.
Newberry as his guardian.

ROGERS –pg. 60; Jan. 1834. Deliverance Rogers requested guardianship of Andrew T. Rogers,
Sarah Rogers, John M. Rogers, and Eleanor Rogers, minors under 14yrs., children of William
A. Rogers, dec'd.

MURRAY –pg. 60; Jan. 1834. William W. Murray, son of William Murray, dec'd., petitioned for a
division of his father's real estate. William Murray, dec'd., died intestate owning real estate
in Middletown Tshp.
Children and heirs of the deceased: William W. Murray; James Murray; Eliza Layton, wife of
James Layton; and Sisera Ann Frost, dec'd., late Sisera Murray, late wife of Joseph Frost.
Grandchildren who were children of his dau. Sisera Ann Frost, dec'd.: William Frost, James
Frost, and Lydia Ann Frost.

HERBERT –pg. 77; Jan. 1834. The court required Thomas Curby and his wife, Margaret, to provide
additional sureties on her bond or they would revoke her guardianship of Hannah Herbert, a
minor under 14yrs., dau. of Jacob Herbert, dec'd.

HERBERT –pg. 79; Jan. 1834. Henry H. Bennett and his wife, Eliz. L., late Eliz. L. Herbert, were
complainants against James Herbert, administrator of the estate of James G. Herbert, dec'd.

AUMACK –pg. 80; Jan. 1834. John P. White and his wife, Mary, late widow of David Aumack,
dec'd., petitioned to have her dower set off from her late husband's estate in Howell Tshp.

MILLER –pg. 87; March 1834. Nancy Miller, Rachel H. Miller, and John V. Miller, minors over
14yrs., chose Robert W. Miller as their guardian. Note: three separate entries on the same
page.

COX –pg. 88; March 1834. Elizabeth H. Cox, a minor over 14yrs., elected Leah Cox as her
guardian.

DEY –pg. 88; March 1834. Randle R. Dey, a minor over 14yrs., chose Jane Dey as his guardian.

COX –pg. 89; March 1834. Sarah Ann Meirs, late Sarah Ann Cox, a minor over 14yrs., requested
her husband, Charles Meirs, be appointed her guardian.

MILLER –pg. 89; March 1834. Robert W. Miller requested guardianship of Sarah T. Miller, a
minor under 14yrs.

COX –pg. 89; March 1834. Leah Cox requested guardianship of Maria Louisa Cox, a minor under
14yrs.

DEY –pg. 89; March 1834. Jane Dey requested guardianship of Sarah M. Dey, Gilbert W. Dey, and
William H. W. Dey, minors under 14yrs.

PATTERSON –pg. 90; March 1834. Tylee Patterson applied for a division of the real estate owned
by Ellenor VanDyke, dec'd., who died intestate owning real estate in Freehold. The
following were named as her heirs without establishing their relationship to her: David
Cooper Sr.; David Cooper Jr.; Mary McDormott, widow, late Mary Cooper; Tylee Patterson,
the petitioner; Benjamin Patterson; Stephen Patterson; John Patterson; William Patterson;
Ann Williamson, late Ann Patterson, wife of William Williamson; Susan Patterson; Sarah
Patterson; Edward Patterson; and James Patterson. The word "and" was placed between those
with Cooper and Patterson surnames.

GORDON –pg. 95 – 96; April 1834. Lewis J. Gordon, son of Jonathan R. Gordon, dec'd.,
petitioned for a division of his father's real estate. Jonathan R. Gordon died intestate owning
real estate in Freehold Tshp.
Children and heirs of Jonathan R. Gordon, dec'd.: Lewis J. Gordon; Sarah Foot, late Sarah
Gordon; Jane Gordon; Mary Gordon; John J. Gordon; William J. Gordon; and Elizabeth
Gordon.

HOLMAN –pg. 96; April 1834. George Field and his wife, Maria, late Maria Holman, William
Griggs and his wife, Lydia Ann, late Lydia Ann Holman and Aaron Armstrong and his wife,
Eleanor, late Eleanor Holman, were complainants against Abraham Johnston and John
Johnston, administrators of the estate of Jacob Johnston, dec'd., and against David Craig and
Archibald Craig, executors of the estate of David Craig, dec'd., where Jacob Johnston, dec'd.,
and David Craig, dec'd., were executors of the estate of Robert Holman, dec'd. Maria Field,
Lydia Ann Griggs and Eleanor Armstrong were children and legatees of Robert Holman,
dec'd.

GORDON –pg. 97; April 1834. John J. Gordon, a minor over 14yrs., chose John E. Gordon as his
guardian.

FROST –pg. 97; April 1834. Joseph Frost requested guardianship of William M. Frost, James Frost, and Lydia Ann Frost, minors under 14yrs.

HOLMES –pg. 98; April 1834. Dinah Holmes, "a woman of color," requested guardianship of Oliver Holmes, a minor under 14yrs.

REMSEN –pg. 109; April 1834. A settlement of accounts was filed by John Collins Jr., Joseph T. Martin, and his wife, Sarah, late Sarah Remsen, where Sarah Martin and John Collins were administrators of the estate of Henry Remsen, dec'd.

MORRIS –pg. 117; July 1834. Charles Borden and his wife, Mary Ann, late Mary Ann Morris, dau. of Joseph Morris, dec'd., applied for a division of her father's real estate. Joseph Morris died intestate owning real estate in Shrewsbury Tshp.
Children and heirs of Joseph Morris, dec'd.: Mary Ann Borden, Joseph Morris, Henry Morris, Elleanor Morris, Eliza Jane Morris, Forman Morris, and William Ryer Morris. Note: William Ryer Morris' name was also spelled William Rye Morris within the same record.

JOHNSTON –pg. 118; July 1834. Lyttleton Herbert and his wife, Mary, who was the widow of George Johnston, dec'd., applied to have her dower set off from her late husband's estate.

COOK –pg. 118; July 1834. Mary Cook requested guardianship of Thomas Cook, a minor under 14yrs.

COOK –pg. 118; July 1834. John Cook requested guardianship of Jane Cook and Deborah Cook, minors under 14yrs.

CONOVER –pg. 122; July 1834. William T. Burtis, guardian of Richard Conover, was a complainant against Samuel Bunting and his wife, Rebecca, late Rebecca Conover who was the mother of said Richard Conover.

CLAYTON –pg. 124 – 125; July 1834. Regarding the distribution of the real estate owned by John Clayton, dec'd.: Lucy Drake, dau. of John Clayton, dec'd., and her husband, Charles S. Drake, were "absent from the state of New Jersey."

MITTEN –pg. 137; Oct. 1834. Jesse Test and Ann Test, late Ann Mitten who was administrator of the estate of William Mitten, dec'd., applied to sell the deceased's real estate for payment of his debts.

OLIPHANT –pg. 139; Oct. 1834. Selah Oliphant, son of David Oliphant, dec'd., petitioned for a division of his father's real estate. David Oliphant died intestate owning real estate in Stafford Tshp.
Children and heirs of David Oliphant, dec'd.: William D. Oliphant; Selah Oliphant who sold his rights to David S. Haywood; James Oliphant; Jane Ann Oliphant; Molly Ann Oliphant, also spelled Maly Ann Oliphant within the record; George Oliphant; Caroline Oliphant; Ann Eliza Oliphant; David Oliphant; and Hope Haywood, late Hope Oliphant, wife of David S. Haywood.

COOK –pg. 140; Oct. 1834. Taber Chadwick, guardian of Rebecca Cook, dau. of Aaron Cook, dec'd., petitioned for a division of the real estate belonging to the deceased father of his ward. Children of Aaron Cook, dec'd.: Rebecca Cook, Charles Cook, Lydia Cook, and William Henry Cook.

INMAN –pg. 141; Oct. 1834. Job Inman, heir of both Esther Inman, dec'd., and Mary Conklin, dec'd., late Mary Inman, petitioned for a division of the real estate belonging to both deceased women who died intestate.
Heirs of Esther Inman and Mary Conklin, both dec'd.: Job Inman; Hannah Inman, wife of Michael Inman; Nancy Mills, late Nancy Inman, wife of Thomas Mills; and Stephen Inman Conklin, son of Benjamin Conklin and his wife, Sarah, late Sarah Inman.

JONES –pg. 148; Oct. 1834. Clarkson Crammer requested guardianship of Harriet Jones, Juli Ann Jones, and Lloyd Jones, minors under 14yrs. Note: Book I, pg. 275, Jan. 1836, they were children of Lloyd Jones, dec'd.

COOK –pg. 149; Oct. 1834. John Cook requested guardianship of William Henry Cook, a minor under 14yrs.

ALLEN –pg. 149; Oct. 1834. Anna Allen requested guardianship of Deborah Allen, a minor under 14yrs.

ALLEN –pg. 149; Oct. 1834. Elizabeth Ann Allen, a minor over 14yrs., chose Anna Allen as her guardian.

ALLEN –pg. 150; Oct. 1834. James Allen, a minor over 14yrs., chose William W. Allen as his guardian.

VOORHEES –pg. 162; Jan. 1835. Richard H. Applegate and his wife, Elizabeth D., late Elizabeth D. Voorhees, dau. of James Voorhees, dec'd., petitioned for a division of her father's real estate. James Voorhees died intestate owning real estate in Freehold.
Children and heirs of James Voorhees, dec'd.: Elizabeth D. Applegate, Ellenor Voorhees, John Voorhees, Mary Voorhees, and James E. Voorhees.

LANE –pg. 163 – 164; Jan. 1835. To cover maintenance costs, Tunis Lane petitioned to sell real estate belonging to his wards, Mary Lane and Sarah Lane. Alice Lane, dec'd., late Alice Norris, died owning real estate in Freehold Tshp. that she inherited from her grandmother Mary Norris, dec'd. Mary Lane and Sarah Lane were Alice Lane's only children.

SCHANCK –pg. 173; Jan. 1835. Cryneonce Schanck, guardian, was a complainant against John S. Watters and his wife, Anna, late Anna Schanck and late ward of the complainant.

HERBERT –pg. 176; Jan. 1835. Samuel Laird, guardian of Elizabeth L. Bennett, late Elizabeth L. Herbert, filed a settlement of accounts.

AUMACK –pg. 177; Jan. 1835. A record of accounts was filed by John P. White and his wife, Mary, who was the guardian of Elizabeth Newman, late Elizabeth Aumack.

PATTERSON –pg. 182; Feb. 1835. Susan Patterson, a minor over 14yrs., chose Mary Patterson as her guardian.

PATTERSON –pg. 182; Feb. 1835. Mary Patterson requested guardianship of Sarah Patterson, Forman Patterson, James Patterson, and William Patterson, minors under 14yrs.

WHITE –pg. 188; April 1835. Joseph T. White, son of Amos White, dec'd., petitioned for a division of his father's real estate. Amos White died intestate owning real estate in Shrewsbury.
Children and heirs of Amos White, dec'd.: Joseph T. White, the petitioner; James White; Jeremiah White; Hartshorne White; Mary Ann White; Amos White; and Deborah Tilton, late Deborah White, wife of Corlies Tilton.

CRAIG –pg. 194; April 1835. David Craig, a minor over 14yrs., elected Ellenor Craig as his guardian.

SHINN –pg. 195; April 1835. Adelaide Shinn and Caroline Shinn, minors over 14yrs., chose James Shinn as their guardian.

LEE –pg. 195; April 1835. Elizabeth Lee and Lydia Ann Lee, minors over 14yrs., elected Thomas Lee as their guardian.

PALMER –pg. 195; April 1835. Lydia W. Palmer, a minor over 14yrs., elected John Palmer as her guardian.

PALMER –pg. 196; April 1835. John Palmer requested guardianship of Aaron S. Palmer, a minor under 14yrs.

LEE –pg. 196; April 1835. Thomas Lee requested guardianship of Hannah Lee, Harriet Lee, Rachel Lee, and Charles Lee, minors under 14yrs.

SHINN –pg. 197; April 1835. James Shinn requested guardianship of George Shinn and James Shinn, minors under 14yrs.

TILTON –pg. 202; April 1835. Gideon M. Tilton, son of Amos Tilton, dec'd., petitioned for a division of his father's real estate. Amos Tilton died intestate owning real estate in Shrewsbury and Middletown Tshps.
Children and heirs of Amos Tilton, dec'd.: Gideon M. Tilton, the petitioner; William W.

Tilton; Caroline W. Lippincott, wife of Isaac K. Lippincott; Mary W. Stateser, wife of John Stateser; Ann Stateser, wife of Isaac Stateser; and Benjamin W. Tilton.

HALL –pg. 207; April 1835. John M. Hall as guardian of Mary Ann Hall, Samuel Hall, Caroline Hall, Harriet Hall, Elizabeth Hall, and George W. Hall, filed a record of his accounts. The record showed J. M. Hartshorne was the attorney for Samuel Hall, William Simpson, and his wife, Harriet, late Harriet Hall, where Samuel Hall and Harriet (Hall) Simpson were two of the named wards.

WOOLLEY –pg. 217; July 1835. William Doudney represented William Woolley, son of Adam Woolley, dec'd., in a petition for a division of the real estate owned by Adam Woolley, dec'd., who died intestate owning real estate in Dover Tshp.
Children and heirs of Adam Woolley, dec'd.: Elizabeth Woolley; Hannah Woolley; William Woolley who had sold his share to William Doudney; and Ann Doudney, late Ann Woolley, wife of William Doudney.

BRITTON –pg. 219; July 1835. Mary Britton, a minor over 14yrs., chose Ann Britton as her guardian.

WHITE –pg. 219; July 1835. Amos S. White, a minor over 14yrs., elected James White as his guardian.

THROCKMORTON –pg. 220; July 1835. James Throckmorton, a minor over 14yrs., chose Abigail Throckmorton as his guardian.

SHINN –pg. 220; July 1835. Benjamin Shinn and Job Shinn, minors over 14yrs., chose James Cowpertwaite as their guardian. Note: two separate entries on the same page.

SHINN –pg. 221; July 1835. The executors of the estate of Benjamin Shinn, dec'd., requested James Cowpertwaite be appointed guardian of William Shinn and George Shinn, minors under 14yrs.

THROCKMORTON –pg. 221; July 1835. Abigail Throckmorton requested guardianship of Mary Throckmorton, Lydia Throckmorton, and Susan Amanda Throckmorton, minors under 14yrs.

WOOLLEY –pg. 247; Oct. 1835. William Doudney and his wife, Ann, dau. of Adam Woolley, dec'd., petitioned to have the dower for the widow of Adam Woolley, dec'd., set off. His widow, Ann Woolley, had remarried and was then Ann Cook.

WOLCOTT –pg. 249; Oct. 1835. Job Wolcott, son of Henry Wolcott, dec'd., petitioned to have the widow's dower set aside from his father's real estate. Abigail Wolcott was named as the widow.

WOLCOTT –pg. 249; Oct. 1835. Job Wolcott, Jacob Wolcott, and Thomas Howland and his wife, Elizabeth, late Elizabeth Wolcott, petitioned for a division of the real estate owned by Henry Wolcott, dec'd., who died intestate owning real estate in Shrewsbury Tshp.
Children and heirs of Henry Wolcott, dec'd.: John Wolcott; Henry Wolcott; Jacob Wolcott; Job Wolcott; Elizabeth Howland, late Elizabeth Wolcott, wife of Thomas Howland; and the three minor children of Ezek Wolcott, dec'd., viz., Henry Wolcott, Samuel Wolcott, and Mary Wolcott.

NEWBERRY –pg. 251; Oct. 1835. Jonathan Johnston, Timothy Hurley, and his wife, Hannah, late Hannah Newberry, requested Jonathan Johnston be assigned guardianship of William Newberry, Miles Newberry, and John Newberry, minors under 14yrs.

ELY –pg. 251; Oct. 1835. John G. Ely requested guardianship of George Ely, Samuel G. W. Ely, and Amos Ely, minors under 14yrs.

OLIPHANT –pg. 252; Oct. 1835. William D. Oliphant requested guardianship of George Oliphant, Caroline Oliphant, Ann Eliza Oliphant, and David Oliphant, minors under 14yrs.

HOOPER –pg. 272; Jan. 1836. Edward Hooper, a minor over 14yrs., elected Ursula Hooper as his guardian.

HOOPER –pg. 272; Jan. 1836. Ursula Hooper requested guardianship of William Hooper, Deborah Hooper, and Samuel Hooper, minors under 14yrs.

HORNER –pg. 273; Jan. 1836. Sarah B. Horner requested guardianship of Hiram Horner and Delia Horner, minors under 14yrs.

SCHANCK –pg. 280; Jan. 1836. Chreneyonce Schanck, guardian of Ann Walters, late Ann Schanck, filed a record of his accounts.

HILYER –pg. 287; April 1836. John Taylor and his wife, Sally, late Sally Hilyer who was the administrator of the estate of Benjamin Hillyer, dec'd., requested permission to sell the real estate of Benjamin Hillyer, dec'd., to pay his debts. Within the record, Hillyer was spelled with both one and two 'l's."

WOOLLEY –pg. 288 – 291; April 1836. The division of the real estate of Adam Woolley, dec'd., showed Hannah Woolley was then Hannah Kennedy.

VANCLEAF –pg. 299; April 1836. Sarah VanCleaf and Garret VanCleaf, minors over 14yrs., chose Ann VanCleaf as their guardian. Note: two separate entries on the same page.

TAYLOR –pg. 299; April 1836. Elizabeth Taylor, a minor over 14yrs., elected Ann B. Taylor as her guardian.

SMOCK –pg. 300; April 1836. Aaron A. Smock, a minor over 14yrs., elected Garret S. Smock as his guardian.

CONOVER –pg. 300; April 1836. Peter F. Conover and Daniel Conover, minors over 14yrs., chose Garret Conover as their guardian. Note: two separate entries on the same page.

TAYLOR –pg. 300; April 1836. John I. Taylor, a minor over 14yrs., elected John G. Taylor as his guardian.

TAYLOR –pg. 301; April 1836. Ann B. Taylor requested guardianship of James Taylor, a minor under 14yrs.

HAVENS –pg. 301; April 1836. Steven Frazer and Mary Frazer requested guardianship of Newberry Havens. Record written that guardianship would continue until he attained the age of 21yrs., and the under/over qualifier for age was crossed out, leaving the petition stating he was 14yrs. of age.

SMOCK –pg. 302; April 1836. Daniel P. Smock requested guardianship of John A. Smock, a minor under 14yrs.

NORRIS –pg. 302; April 1836. Tunis Lane applied to sell his ward's real estate to offset the cost of their maintenance. His wards were Joseph Norris, Augustus Norris, and Charles Norris, children of John Norris, dec'd., late of Freehold Tshp.

NEWMAN –pg. 303; April 1836. Jeremiah Newman Jr., son of John Newman Sr., dec'd., petitioned for a division of his father's real estate. John Newman died intestate owning real estate in Howell Tshp.
Children and heirs of John Newman, dec'd.: Jeremiah Newman Jr.; Joseph Newman; Abagail Trowbridge, late Abigail Newman; John Saplin Newman; Jesse Newman; Jane Brown, late Jane Newman, wife of Abraham Brown; Aaron Newman; Mary Shibla, late Mary Newman, wife of Theophilus Shibla; Francis Newman; Benjamin Newman; Matthias Newman; Ferdinand Newman; Stephen Newman; Amy Newman; and Hannah Newman.

SCHANCK –pg. 308; April 1836. Chrineyonce Schanck, late guardian of Ann McLean, late Ann Schanck, filed a report of his accounts.

TILTON –pg. 318; July 1836. Abraham Antonides and his wife, Lydia, dau. of Reuben Tilton, dec'd., petitioned for a division of her father's real estate. Reuben Tilton died intestate owning real estate in Middletown Tshp.
Children and heirs of Reuben Tilton, dec'd.: Lydia Antonides, late Lydia Tilton; Jeremiah Tilton; Joseph Tilton; Charles Tilton; Tylee Tilton; Eliza Ann Tilton; Mary Tilton; Obediah Tilton; and William Tilton.

WOODHULL –pg. 319; July 1836. Amanda Woodhull requested guardianship of William W. Woodhull, Spafford Woodhull, and Nelson Woodhull, minors under 14yrs.

BAIRD –pg. 319; July 1836. Sarah Baird requested guardianship of Catharine Baird, Jacob Baird, Mary Baird, and Sarah Matilda Baird, minors under 14yrs.

HERBERT –pg. 320; July 1836. Hannah Herbert requested guardianship of John Herbert and David Herbert, minors under 14yrs.

HERBERT –pg. 320; July 1836. Hannah Herbert, a minor over 14yrs., elected Hannah Herbert as her guardian.

APPLEGATE –pg. 332; July 1836. Samuel Applegate, Reuben Stilwell and his wife, Esther, who had a caveat against proving the last will and testament of Daniel Applegate, dec'd., were complainants against Elizabeth Applegate, John P. Applegate, Reuben Haines and his wife, Mary, Lewis James and his wife, Lucretia, David Clayton and his wife, Rachel, Hiram Poinsett and his wife, Lucy Ann, Joseph Cook and his wife, Elizabeth, William P. Applegate and Daniel Applegate.

STOUT –pg. 346; Oct. 1836. Elizabeth W. Stout, Mary Stout, and Anna L. Stout, minors over 14yrs., elected Richard M. Stout as their guardian.

STOUT –pg. 346; Oct. 1836. Richard M. Stout requested guardianship of Caroline H. Stout, Wisel T. Stout, Peter W. Stout, and John W. Stout, minors under 14yrs.

WIKOFF –pg. 347; Oct. 1836. Garret R. Wikoff requested guardianship of James H. Wikoff, a minor under 14yrs.

CRAWFORD –pg. 347; Oct. 1836. William C. Lamberson, guardian of Elizabeth Lamberson, William Lamberson, Ellenor Lamberson, and Daniel Lamberson who were grandchildren of Stephen Crawford, dec'd., petitioned for a division of the real estate belonging to the said Stephen Crawford, dec'd., who died intestate owning real estate in Middletown Tshp. Heirs of Stephen Crawford, dec'd.: petitioners Elizabeth Lamberson, William Lamberson, Ellenor Lamberson, and Daniel Lamberson in right of their deceased mother, Maria Lamberson, late Maria Crawford; Gideon Crawford; David Crawford; John Crawford; Johanna Crawford; Catharine Ann Lamberson, late Catharine Ann Crawford, wife of James Lamberson; and Amey VanNuys, late Amey Crawford, wife of John VanNuys.

KIRBY –pg. 348; Oct. 1836. Maria Kirby, dau. of Nathaniel Kirby, dec'd., petitioned for a division of her father's real estate. Nathaniel Kirby died intestate owning real estate in Upper Freehold Tshp. Children and heirs of Nathaniel Kirby, dec'd.: Maria Kirby, Thomas Kirby, William Kirby, Sarah Ann Kirby, Leberny L. Kirby, and George Kirby.

CLEMENT –pg. 352; Oct. 1836. A settlement of accounts was filed by James Prince and his wife, Caroline, late Caroline Clement who was administrator for the estate of John Clement, dec'd.

LANE –pg. 362; Jan. 1837. David Letts and his wife, Sarah, late Sarah Lane and dau. of John Lane, dec'd., petitioned for a division of her father's real estate. John Lane died intestate owning real estate in Dover Tshp. Children and heirs of John Lane, dec'd.: Sarah (Lane) Letts, Cornelius Lane, Alice Lane, and Rebecca Lane.

LANE –pg. 362; Jan. 1837. David Letts and his wife, Sarah, petitioned to have the dower for Jane Lane, widow of John Lane, dec'd., set off.

LONGSTREET –pg. 364; Jan. 1837. John M. Longstreet and Richard Longstreet, minors over 14yrs., elected Richard Longstreet as their guardian. Note: two separate entries on the same page.

TILTON –pg. 364; Jan. 1837. Obediah Tilton, a minor over 14yrs., chose Mary Tilton as his guardian.

COX –pg. 365; Jan. 1837. Elizabeth L. Cox requested guardianship of Lewis Cox, a minor under 14yrs.

TILTON –pg. 365; Jan. 1837. Mary Tilton requested guardianship of William Tilton, a minor under 14yrs.

KNOTT –pg. 365 - 366; Jan. 1837. Elisha Lippincott, guardian of Elizabeth Knott and Ann Maria
   Knott, children of Jacob Knott, dec'd., petitioned for a division of the real estate belonging to
   the father of his wards. Jacob Knott died intestate owning real estate in Shrewsbury and
   Dover Tshps.
   Children of Jacob Knott, dec'd.: Elizabeth Knott and Ann Maria Knott.

LIPPINCOTT –pg. 366; Jan. 1837. Esek H. Williams and his wife, Amelia L., late Amelia L.
   Lippincott, a dau. of William L. Lippincott, dec'd., petitioned for a division of her father's
   real estate. William L. Lippincott died intestate owning real estate in Shrewsbury Tshp.
   Children and heirs of William L. Lippincott, dec'd.: Amelia L. Williams, Benjamin S.
   Lippincott, Clemence S. Lippincott, William I. Lippincott, Shepherd T. Lippincott, John M.
   Lippincott, Charles A. Lippincott, Rachel E. Lippincott, and Harriet Lippincott.

HERBERT –pg. 380; April 1837. Jonathan Tilton and his wife, Lydia Ann, late Lydia Ann Herbert,
   a dau. of Isaac Herbert, dec'd., petitioned for a division of her father's real estate. Isaac
   Herbert died intestate owning real estate in Howell Tshp.
   Children and heirs of Isaac Herbert, dec'd.: Lydia Ann (Herbert) Tilton, Abigail Herbert,
   Elizabeth Herbert, Ettialinda Herbert, Obediah Herbert, John Herbert, Isaac Herbert,
   Benjamin Herbert, Sarah Herbert, Hance Herbert, Sidney Herbert, and Joseph Herbert.

WOOLLEY –pg. 384; April 1837. Richard Wikoff Woolley, a minor over 14yrs., chose Benjamin
   Woolley as his guardian.

HALL –pg. 384; April 1837. Joanna B. Hall and Rhuhania Hall, minors over 14yrs., elected Britta
   Hall as their guardian. Note: two separate entries on the same page.

CONOVER –pg. 384; April 1837. Mary Conover, a minor over 14yrs., chose Arintha Conover as
   her guardian.

CONOVER –pg. 385; April 1837. Arintha Conover requested guardianship of Margaret Conover,
   Garret Conover, and William Conover, minors under 14yrs.

HALL –pg. 385; April 1837. Britta Hall requested guardianship of John Hall, Silas B. Hall, and
   Albert Hall, minors under 14yrs.

WOODHULL –pg. 386; April 1837. Levi S. Beebee and his wife, Charlotte, late Charlotte
   Woodhull who was the administrator of the estate of Dr. Gilbert S. Woodhull, dec'd., were
   complainants against John T. Woodhull and Nathaniel S. Wikoff, administrators of the estate
   of Dr. Gilbert S. Woodhull, dec'd.

MORRIS –pg 407 - 413; July 1837. The record was an inquiry into the mental health of Obediah
   Morris, believed mentally incompetent for two years, who was confined to the Poor House
   because of his aggressive behavior. Obediah Morris, son of Benjamin Morris, dec'd., had no
   wife, children, or living parents, but he did have siblings.
   Siblings of Obediah Morris: Deborah Johnson of Ohio, wife of Ezekiel Johnson, was 50yrs.
   old and the oldest sister of Obediah; Adam B. Morris of Ohio was 48yrs. old and the eldest
   brother of Obediah; Sarah Herbert of Howell Tshp., wife of Isaac Herbert, dec'd., was 45yrs.
   old; Anne Lippincott, wife of John M. Lippincott of Howell Tshp., was 44yrs. old; and
   Katuriah Miller, wife of Gilbert Miller of Howell Tshp., was 42yrs. old.

LONGSTREET –pg. 414; July 1837. James Longstreet, grandson of Richard Longstreet, dec'd.,
   petitioned for division of his father's estate. The will of Richard Longstreet, dec'd., dated
   July 11, 1826, did, among other things, devise land to his son Samuel and on his demise, to
   Samuel's heirs. Samuel Longstreet had died intestate leaving children.
   Children of Samuel Longstreet, dec'd.: Elizabeth, wife of James W. Osborn; Prudence, wife
   of Jesse Chamberlain; Richard Longstreet; Jacob Longstreet; Stephen Longstreet, dec'd., who
   died intestate after his father; Mary Ann, wife of William E. Johnson; Saithia Longstreet;
   Hannah Longstreet; Bloomfield Longstreet; Sarah Longstreet; and petitioner, James
   Longstreet.

SNYDER –pg. 424; Oct. 1837. Mary Snyder, a minor over 14yrs., requested Hendrick Snyder as
   her guardian.

SNYDER –pg. 424; Oct. 1837. Hendrick Snyder requested guardianship of Margaret Snyder, Lucy
   Ann Snyder, and Ellenor Snyder, minors under 14yrs.

LANE –pg. 451; Jan. 1838. William Lane, son of Jacob Lane, dec'd., applied for a division of his father's real estate. The heirs of Jacob Lane, dec'd. were children and grandchildren. Children: William Lane and Catharine Lane.
Grandchildren (parents not identified): Tunis Lane; Stephen Lane; Mary Ann Lane, wife of Isaiah Lane; Sarah Letts, dec'd., late Sarah Lane, late wife of David Letts; Cornelius Lane; Alice Lane; Rebecca Lane; Randolph Lane; Alice Lane; Mary Lane; Catharine Lane; Jacob Lane; Anna Lane; Bloomfield Lane; and Washington Lane. Note: There were two grandchildren named Alice Lane.

QUACKENBUSH –pg. 452; Jan. 1838. Hendrick Snyder, guardian of Mary Snyder, Margaret Snyder, Lucy Ann Snyder, and Ellenor Snyder, heirs of John Quackenbush, dec'd., petitioned for a division of real estate belonging to John Quackenbush, dec'd., who died intestate owning real estate in Freehold Tshp.
Heirs of John Quackenbush, dec'd.: the minors petitioning, in right of their mother, Mary Snyder, dec'd., late Mary Quackenbush; Catharine Lockerman, late Catharine Quackenbush, wife of James Lockerman; William Quackenbush; Elizabeth Williams, late Elizabeth Quackenbush, wife of Isaac Williams; Peter Quackenbush; Jacob Quackenbush; Ruliff Quackenbush; Ellenor Boice, late Ellenor Quackenbush, wife of John A. Boice; and Elizabeth Bailey, late Elizabeth Snyder, wife of Joseph Bailey.

SCHANCK –pg. 458; Jan. 1838. Ann Eliza Schanck, a minor over 14yrs., chose Elisha Schanck as her guardian.

WOODHULL –pg. 471; April 1838. Henry W. B. Woodhull and Sarah S. Woodhull, minors over 14yrs., chose Rev. Levi S. Beebee as their guardian. Note: two separate entries on the same page.

WOODHULL –pg. 471; April 1838. Rev. Levi S. Beebee and his wife, Charlotte, late Charlotte Woodhull, requested guardianship of Anna Matilda Woodhull and Charlotte Woodhull, minors under 14yrs.

MORTON –pg. 471; April 1838. Alexander Forbes and his wife, Deborah, late Deborah Morton, requested George Rankin be appointed guardian of Elizabeth Morton and Thomas Morton, minors under 14yrs. Petitioner Deborah Forbes was the mother of the children.

COOK –pg. 472; April 1838. John Cook was leaving the state of New Jersey. Charles C. Cook petitioned to take over guardianship of his ward, William Henry Cook, a minor under 14yrs.

SCHENCK –pg. 474 - 475; April 1838. Daniel Schanck petitioned for a division of real estate that belonged to Peter Schenck, dec'd. Peter Schenck, late of Middletown Tshp., died around June of 1837, leaving a will devising land to his four daughters and one granddaughter, to wit, Maria Dorsett, Ann Conover, Nelle Schenck, Catharine Golden, and Ann Eliza Schanck (the granddaughter). His will did not dispose of a 60 acre tract of land in Freehold Tshp. then held by Joseph Dorsett and his wife, Maria, Mathias W. Conover and his wife, Ann, John Golden and his wife, Catharine, Ann Eliza Schenck, and the petitioner, Daniel Schanck, who had purchased the rights of John R. Smock and his wife, Nelle, late Nelle Schenck.

LIPPINCOTT –pg. 477; April 1838. A commissioners' report correcting errors they previously made in dispersing proceeds from the sale of the real estate owned by William L. Lippincott, dec'd., revealed new information on the family. Hannah Ann Lippincott was named the widow of the said William L. Lippincott, dec'd., and Amelia Lippincott was named widow of William Lippincott, dec'd. William I. Lippincott, Shepherd T. Lippincott, John M. Lippincott, Charles H. Lippincott, Rachel E. Lippincott, and Harriet L. Lippincott all resided outside the state of New Jersey. Charles A. Lippincott from the original petition was referred to as Charles H. Lippincott. Note: See commissioners' report in Book I, pg. 443, Oct. 1837.

VANMATER –pg. 483; April 1838. Joseph H. VanMater and Holmes VanMater, guardians of Eliza Jane VanDorn, late Eliza VanMater, filed a settlement of accounts.

BOOK K

1838 – 1842

BURTIS –pg. 6; July 1838. Alice H. Burtis requested guardianship of Catharine Ann Burtis and Josephine C. Burtis, minors under 14yrs.

HORNER –pg. 14; July 1838. A settlement of accounts was filed by Isaac N. Woodward, guardian of Catharine P. Harker, late Catharine P. Horner who married Benjamin Harker Jr.

JACKSON –pg. 15; July 1838. A settlement of accounts was filed by Benjamin Matthews and his wife, Ann, late Ann Jackson who was administrator of the estate of Hugh Jackson, dec'd.

KIRBY –pg. 38; Jan. 1839. Elizabeth Kirby and Harriet Kirby, minors over 14yrs., chose Ellenor Kirby as their guardian. Note: two separate entries on the same page.

KIRBY –pg. 39; Jan. 1839. Ellenor Kirby requested guardianship of Rachel Kirby, a minor under 14yrs.

RUSSELL –pg. 42; Jan. 1839. James Bunnell, grandson of John Russell, dec'd., petitioned for a division of his grandfather's estate. John Russell died intestate owning real estate in Dover Tshp. and leaving children, grandchildren, and great-grandchildren.
Children: Edward Russell, James Russell, and Abraham Russell.
Grandchildren: James Russell; James Bunnell; Mary Bunnell; Lydia Price, late Lydia Bunnell, wife of William Price; Taylor Phillips; Maria Woolley, late Maria Phillips, wife of Levi Woolley.
Great-grandchildren: Ake Bennett and _____. Note: The surnames of great-grandchildren Ake and the unknown child were also spelled Bunnell in the same record.

DEY –pg. 45; Jan. 1839. Gilbert S. Reid petitioned for a division of the real estate owned by John Dey, dec'd., who died intestate owning real estate in Upper Freehold Tshp.
Children and heirs of John Dey, dec'd.: Delilah Campbell, late Delilah Dey, wife of Lewis Campbell; Lydia Ann Campbell, late Lydia Ann Dey, wife of Joshua Campbell; Joseph Dey; John Dey; Selah Dey; Randle R. Dey; Sarah M. Dey; Gilbert W. Dey; and William H. W. Dey. Delilah Campbell and Lydia Ann Campbell had sold their shares to Gilbert S. Reid, the petitioner. Note: Book K, pg. 44, Jan. 1839, Jane Dey named as widow of John Dey, dec'd.

HERBERT –pg. 52; Jan. 1839. Thomas Kirby and his wife, Margaret, late Margaret Herbert who was guardian of Hannah Herbert, a minor now dec'd., filed a settlement of accounts.

KIRBY –pg. 59; April 1839. George W. Davison and his wife, Rebecca, late Rebecca Kirby who was a dau. of Joseph Kirby, dec'd., petitioned for a division of her father's real estate. Joseph Kirby died intestate owning real estate in Upper Freehold Tshp.
Children and heirs of Joseph Kirby, dec'd.: Mary Ann Chamberlain, late Mary Ann Kirby; Rebecca Davison, late Rebecca Kirby; Elizabeth Kirby; Harriet Kirby; and Rachel Kirby.

KIRBY –pg. 68; April 1839. Elizabeth Kirby requested guardianship of George Kirby, a minor under 14yrs.

KIRBY –pg. 68; April 1839. Lebrus L. Kirby, a minor over 14yrs., chose Elizabeth Kirby as his guardian.

KIRBY –pg. 69; April 1839. Sarah Ann Kirby, a minor over 14yrs., chose Elizabeth Kirby as her guardian.

COOK –pg. 71; April 1839. A settlement of accounts was filed by William W. Croxsan, guardian of Lydia Edwards, late Lydia Cook who had married Henry Edwards.

COMBS –pg. 72; April 1839. A settlement of acounts was filed by Rulif R. Schenck, guardian of Elizabeth Thompson, late Elizabeth Combs who was then the wife of Dr. Joseph C. Thompson.

THROCKMORTON –pg. 81; July 1839. Jacob Throckmorton and Ann Throckmorton, children of James Throckmorton, dec'd., petitioned for a division of their father's real estate. James Throckmorton died intestate owning real estate in Shrewsbury Tshp.
Children and heirs of James Throckmorton, dec'd.: Jacob Throckmorton; Ann Throckmorton; Alice Webster, late Alice Throckmorton, wife of John Webster, now dec'd.; Elizabeth Williams, late Elizabeth Throckmorton, wife of Isaiah Williams; Mary Throckmorton; Lydia Throckmorton; Susan Amanda Throckmorton; and James Throckmorton.

BARCALOW –pg. 82; July 1839. James S. Morris and his wife, Deborah Ann, late Deborah Ann Barcalow, petitioned for a division of real estate. Derick Barcalow, dec'd., left a will devising real estate in Freehold Tshp. to his son Mathias Barcalow who had since died and left children.
Children and heirs of Mathias Barcalow, dec'd.: Deborah Ann (Barcalow) Morris, the petitioner; John J. Barcalow; Job S. Barcalow; Milton P. Barcalow; and Sarah C. Barcalow.

DENNIS –pg. 83; July 1839. Charles A. Dennis, son of Jesse Dennis, dec'd., petitioned for a division of his father's real estate. Jesse Dennis died intestate owning real estate in Shrewsbury Tshp.
Children and heirs of Jesse Dennis, dec'd.: Charles A. Dennis, Hester L. Dennis, Emma E. Dennis, Samuel R. Dennis, and Julia M. Dennis.

NORTON –pg. 85; July 1839. Joshua Norton requested guardianship of Mary Ann Norton, Harriet Norton, Joshua Norton, and John Norton, minors under 14yrs.

SCHENCK –pg. 85; July 1839. Peter W. Schenck requested guardianship of Henry Schenck, a minor under 14yrs.

SAUNDERS –pg. 86; July 1839. Mary Ann Saunders, a minor over 14yr., elected Henry Saunders as her guardian.

HAVENS –pg. 88 – 94; July 1839. Jesse Havens of Howell Tshp. requested the court declare his mother, Jemmina Havens, mentally incompetent. Jemmina Havens, widow of Aron Havens, dec'd., lived in Howell Tshp. and had been deprived of her senses for several years. David Havens, nephew of Jemmina Havens, supported his cousin's petition. The court decided she had been mentally unsound for 10yrs.
Children of Jemmina Havens: Jesse Havens, 31yrs.old; Zebulon Havens, 29yrs. old; Aaron Havens, 27yrs. old, resided in the western country; Benjamin Havens, 23yrs. old, lived in Indiana; Newbury Havens, 14yrs. old; Mary Frazee, 40yrs. old, wife of Stephen Frazee; Jane Havens, 20yrs. old; and Charlotte Havens, 18yrs. old.

COWARD –pg. 98; July 1839. James Osborn and his wife, Hannah, late Hannah Coward who was the administrator of the estate of Thomas Coward, dec'd., filed a settlement of accounts.

VANDERHOEF –pg. 108; Oct. 1839. Catharine Vanderhoef requested guardianship of her dau. Elenora Vanderhoef, a minor under 14yrs.

MOUNT –pg. 109; Oct. 1839. Jane Sanford, late Jane Mount, a minor over 14yrs. who was now the wife of Enoch Sanford, requested her husband be appointed her guardian.

WEST –pg. 109 – 115; Oct. 1839. The siblings of William West requested Samuel Cooper petition the court to have their brother William West declared mentally incompetent. William West of Shrewsbury Tshp., about 33yrs. old, had been mentally incapacitated for several years. Lately, his condition had deteriorated, he exhibited intemperate drinking habits, and he was considered dangerous by some who knew him. The parents of William West were deceased. Siblings of William West: Elias West, 40yrs. old, of Shrewsbury Tshp.; Eleanor Lockwood, 38yrs. old, wife of Benjamin Lockwood of New York City; and Mary Woolley, 36yrs. old, wife of Elisha Woolley of Shrewsbury Tshp.

HORNER –pg. 118; Oct. 1839. A settlement of accounts was filed by Isaac N. Woodward, guardian of Jemima Moore, late Jemima Horner.

MOORE –pg. 118; Oct. 1839. William Clark and his wife, Sarah, late Sarah Moore who was a dau.

of Samuel Moore, dec'd., applied to have the widow's dower assigned from her father's estate. Caroline Pearce, late Caroline Moore and widow of Samuel Moore, dec'd., had remarried and was then the wife of Benjamin D. Pearce. Sarah Clark, the petitioner, and Maria Moore, dec'd., were the only children of Samuel Moore, dec'd., and Maria had died intestate.

IRONS –pg. 127; Jan. 1840. Aaron B. Irons, son of Garret Irons, dec'd., petitioned for a division of his father's real estate. Garret Irons died intestate owning real estate in Dover Tshp.
Surviving children of Garret Irons, dec'd.: Ellen (Irons) Jeffrey; James A. Irons; Benjamin L. Irons; Ann Irons; Garret L. Irons; and petitioner, Aaron B. Irons.
Grandchildren of Garret Irons, dec'd.: Ellen Jackson, Mary Jackson, and Sarah Ann Jackson.
Note: See Book K, pg. 163, April 1840 – the grandchildren were children of his dau. Mary (Irons) Jackson.

BROWN –pg. 127; Jan. 1840. Job Falkingburgh petitioned for a division of the real estate owned by Rebecca Brown, dec'd., who died intestate owning real estate in Stafford Tshp.
Children of Rebecca Brown, dec'd.: Abner Brown; Samuel Brown; Jacob Brown; William Brown; Isaac Brown; Caleb Brown; Abraham Brown; and Mihala Clevinger, late Mihala Brown, wife of Elias Clevinger.
Grandchildren, all minors, who were children of her son John Wesley Brown, dec'd.: Rebecca Brown, Eliza Ann Brown, Rachel Brown, Joshua Brown, Caleb Brown, and John Wesley Brown.
Job Falkingburgh had purchased the shares of Abner Brown and Samuel Brown.

HULSHART –pg. 129; Jan. 1840. Warren Stilwagon and his wife, Margaret, late Margaret Hulshart who was a dau. of Peter M. Hulshart, dec'd., petitioned for a division of her father's real estate. Peter M. Hulshart died intestate owning real estate in Middletown and Freehold.
Children and heirs of Peter M. Hulshart, dec'd.: Margaret Stilwagon, late Margaret Hulshart; Eliza Ann Vaile, late Eliza Ann Hulshart, wife of James Vaile; Catharine Cooper, late Catharine Hulshart, wife of Jacob W. Cooper; Mathias Hulshart; Cornelius Hulshart; William Hulshart; Peter Hulshart; Michael Hulshart; and Rulif Hulshart. Note: In Book K, pg. 156, April 1840, Rulif Hulshart, Michael Hulshart, Peter Hulshart, William Hulshart, Cornelius Hulshart, and Mathias Hulshart were described as minors. Also, Robert Matthews then owned half the property and the heirs the other half.

GREEN –pg. 131; Jan. 1840. Samuel D. Green, a minor over 14yrs., son of Samuel R. Green, dec'd., late of Philadelphia, Pa., chose Henry Bennett of Monmouth Co. as his guardian.

ANTONIDES –pg. 131; Jan. 1840. Gertrude Antonides, requested guardianship of her children Elizabeth Antonides, Charles Antonides, William Antonides, and John Antonides, minors under 14yrs.

JOHNSON –pg. 131; Jan. 1840. Mary Johnson requested guardianship of her children William Johnson and Lydia Johnson, minors under 14yrs.

HULSHART –pg. 132; Jan. 1840. Jacob W. Cooper requested guardianship of his brother-in-law Michael Hulshart, a minor under 14yrs.

CONOVER –pg. 137; Jan. 1840. A settlement of accounts was filed by James S. Lawrence, guardian of Ann B. Belden, late Ann B. Conover, who had died.

MAXSON –pg. 151; April 1840. John Maxson applied for a division of the real estate belonging to Abigail Maxson, dec'd., who died intestate owning real estate in Howell Tshp. and Dover Tshp.
Heirs of Abigail Maxson, dec'd.: John Maxson, the petitioner; Britton Maxson; Elizabeth Boude, late Elizabeth Maxson, wife of James Boude; and Sarah Ann Maxson, a minor, dau. of George Maxson, dec'd.

BIRDSALL –pg. 152; April 1840. Andrew J. Birdsall petitioned for a division of the real estate owned by Amos Birdsall, Esq., dec'd., who died intestate owning real estate in Dover Tshp. and Stafford Tshp.
Children and heirs of Amos Birdsall, Esq., dec'd.: Andrew J. Birdsall, the petitioner; Samuel Birdsall; Jacob Birdsall; William Birdsall; Ezekiel Birdsall; Mary Ann Falkingburgh, late Mary Ann Birdsall, wife of Job Falkingburgh; Martha Jane Newberry, late Martha Jane Birdsall, wife of Taylor Newberry; and Desire Birdsall, a minor.

BAIRD –pg. 153; April 1840. Thomas Baird applied for a division of the real estate owned by David Baird Sr., dec'd., and John Baird, dec'd., that was devised to the heirs of Capt. David Baird, dec'd. David Baird Sr., dec'd., grandfather of the petitioner, left a last will and testament in which he devised, among other things, land in Upper Freehold Tshp. to his son Capt. David Baird, father of the petitioner. Also, John Baird, dec'd., died leaving a will in which he bequeathed his homestead farm to his brother Capt. David Baird, dec'd.
Surviving children of Capt. David Baird, dec'd.: Thomas Baird, the petitioner; Rebecca Ely; Sarah Applegate; Mary McLane, wife of ___ McClane (two spellings in record); John Baird; Lydia Johnson; Phebe Perrine, wife of David Perrine; David Baird; Elizabeth Wikoff, wife of Peter Wikoff; Eveline Forman, wife of William P. Forman; Ann Tantum, wife of Hartshorne Tantum; James Baird; Zebulon Baird; Rachel Riggs, wife of Elias Riggs; and Ellen Sutphen, wife of George W. Sutphen.
Grandchildren who were children of his deceased son Rei Baird: Catharine Eliza Baird, Jacob Baird, Mary Baird, and Sarah Matilda Baird. All the grandchildren were minors except Jacob Baird.

COLLINS –pg. 155; April 1840. John Collins and Eli Collins petitioned for a division of the real estate owned by their father, John Collins, dec'd., described in the will of said deceased.
Children of John Collins, dec'd.: John Collins, Eli Collins, James Collins, Phebe Pharo, Deliverance Butler, and Anne Pharo, dec'd.
Anne Pharo, dec'd., left three children, viz., Allen Pharo, Charlotte Tilton, and Ann Pharo. Phebe Pharo died after the demise of her father and left seven children: Mary, wife of John Ellison; Hannah, wife of Henry Leeds; Robert Pharo; Phebe Ann Pharo; Matilda Pharo; Orrin Pharo; and Ann Pharo. Note: See Book K, pg. 338, Jan. 1842.

LITTLE –pg. 157; April 1840. Jane A. Little petitioned for a division of the real estate owned by John T. Little, dec'd., who died intestate owning real estate in Shrewsbury Tshp.
Children and heirs of John T. Little, dec'd.: Jane A. Little, the petitioner; Arthur W. Little; Thomas Little; and John Little, a minor.

CAFFERTY –pg. 158; April 1840. William I. Cafferty, a minor over 14yrs., elected Abel Cafferty as his guardian.

ROBBINS –pg. 158; April 1840. Maria Robbins, a minor over 14yrs., chose Angeline Robbins as her guardian.

PEASE –pg. 158; April 1840. Rhoda Pease, a minor over 14yrs., chose Adam D. Pease as her guardian.

PEASE –pg. 159; April 1840. John Nelson Pease and Harriet Pease, minors over 14yrs., elected Adam D. Pease as their guardian. Note: two separate entries on the same page.

CONOVER –pg. 159; April 1840. Margaret Ann Conover requested guardianship of her children Stephen D. Conover, William S. Conover, Amanda Conover, and John Conover, minors under 14yrs. Note: See Book L, pg. 398, 399, 406, 407, Nov. 1846.

ROBBINS –pg. 160; April 1840. Angeline Robbins requested guardianship of her children Sarah Robbins, Charles Robbins, and Clayton Robbins, minors under 14yrs.

BURDGE –pg. 160; April 1840. Asher Burdge requested guardianship of his children Anna Rosa Burdge, Mary Matilda Burdge, William Burdge, Catharine Burdge, and John Burdge, minors under 14yrs.

PEASE –pg. 160; April 1840. Adam D. Pease requested guardianship of his brother Cornelius Pease, a minor under 14yrs.

SANSBURY –pg. 161; April 1840. Dunbar Sansbury and his wife, Mary, late Mary Throckmorton who was the mother of James Stevenson Throckmorton, a minor under 14yrs., requested Dunbar Sansbury be appointed guardian of said minor.

MOUNT –pg. 161; April 1840. The final distribution of the estate of William Mount, dec'd., identified his widow and six children.
Widow: Catharine Mount.
Children: Jessie Mount, Rachel Mount, Enoch Mount, Elizabeth Mount, Richard Mount, and Hannah Mount.

WOODWARD –pg. 193; July 1840. Caroline Woodward requested guardianship of her children Keziah Woodward, Elizabeth Woodward, Hannah Ann Woodward, William Woodward, and Anthony Woodward, minors under 14yrs.

TYSON –pg. 215; Oct. 1840. Lydia Tyson requested guardianship of her children Henry Tyson, Mary Jane Tyson, and Caroline Tyson, minors under 14yrs.

WALLING –pg. 215; Oct. 1840. Rebecca Walling requested guardianship of her son Benjamin Walling, a minor under 14yrs.

COOK –pg. 222; Oct. 1840. A settlement of accounts was filed by William R. Maps, guardian of Deborah Corlies, late Deborah Cook.

McCLEES –pg. 229; Jan. 1841. Peter McClees, son of Ann McClees, dec'd., petitioned for a division of his mother's real estate. Ann McClees died intestate leaving children and grandchildren.
Children of Ann McClees, dec'd.: Peter McClees, the petitioner; Catharine McClees; Phoebe McClees; and Prudence Brown, late Prudence McClees, wife of Andrew Brown.
Grandchildren who were children of her dau. Ann Moreau, dec'd.: John B. Moreau, Joseph Moreau, and Peter Moreau.
Grandchildren who were children of her son James McClees, dec'd.: Tyler McClees, Ann McClees, and James McClees.

BRINLEY –pg. 233; Jan. 1841. William Brinley of Freehold Tshp., a minor over 14yrs., elected Hannah Brinley as his guardian.

BRINLEY –pg. 234; Jan. 1841. Louisa Brinley of Freehold Tshp., a minor over 14yrs., elected Hannah Brinley as her guardian.

BRINLEY –pg. 235; Jan. 1841. Hannah Brinley requested guardianship of her children John Brinley and Cornelia Brinley, minors under 14yrs.

VANDERBECK –pg. 235; Jan. 1841. Margaret R. Vanderbeck requested guardianship of her children Adeline Vanderbeck, Josephine Vanderbeck, and Sarah Elizabeth Vanderbeck, minors under 14yrs.

HULSHART –pg. 235; Jan. 1841. Thomas J. Smith and Jane Smith who was the mother of Ruliff S. Hulshart, a minor under 14yrs., requested Thomas J. Smith be appointed guardian of said minor.

McCLEES –pg. 236; Jan. 1841. Rebecca McClees, mother of Tylee McClees, James McClees, and Ann McClees, minors under 14 yrs., asked that Joseph Bowne be appointed guardian of the children. Note: See Book K, pg. 229, Jan. 1841 - Tylee was spelled Tyler in Peter McClees' application for a division of real estate.

COX –pg. 252; Jan. 1841. A settlement of accounts was filed by Leah Griggs, late Leah Cox, and Charles Meirs, administrators of the estate of Thomas H. Cox, dec'd.

BOICE –pg. 253; Jan. 1841. Oliver Cox and his wife, Sarah, late Sarah Boice who was guardian of Mary Boice, Margaret Ann Boice, and Sarah Boice, filed a settlement of accounts.

PRESTON –pg. 257; March 1841. Clayton Preston, Samuel Bennett, Susannah Bennett (late Susannah Preston), Samuel Brinley, Sally Brinley (late Sally Preston), and Margaret Preston, all heirs of Samuel Preston, dec'd., petitioned for the assignment of the dower of Maria Preston, widow of said deceased. Maria Preston had remarried and was then Maria Wilson, wife of Alfred Wilson. Some heirs of Samuel Preston, dec'd., resided outside New Jersey.

CLAYTON –pg. 267; April 1841. Thomas Clayton of Freehold Tshp., a minor over 14yrs., chose Ellenor Clayton as his guardian.

VANSCHOICK –pg. 269; April 1841. Elizabeth S. VanSchoick and John H. VanSchoick of Freehold Tshp., minors over 14yrs., chose Juliann VanSchoick as their guardian. Note: two separate entries on the same page.

LAYTON –pg. 269; April 1841. George W. Layton of Freehold Tshp., a minor over 14yrs., chose Eliza Layton as his guardian.

LAYTON –pg. 270; April 1841. Job Layton, a minor over 14yrs., chose Eliza Layton as his guardian.

CLAYTON –pg. 270; April 1841. Ellen Clayton requested guardianship of her children William Clayton, Gertrude Clayton, Jane Clayton, Polhemus Clayton, Ellenor Clayton, Taylor Clayton, John Clayton, and Mary Elizabeth Clayton, minors under 14yrs.

VANSCHOICK –pg. 270; April 1841. Julia Ann VanSchoick requested guardianship of her children George W. VanSchoick, David VanSchoick, and Juliann VanSchoick, minors under 14yrs.

LAYTON –pg. 271; April 1841. Eliza Layton requested guardianship of her children Andrew J. Layton, John Layton, and Lydiann Layton, minors under 14yrs.

ROBBINS –pg. 271; April 1841. Samuel C. Dunham and his wife, Angeline, petitioned to sell some real estate near Toms River to cover the living and educational expenses of Angeline's wards, viz., Maria Robbins, Sarah Robbins, Charles Robbins, and Clayton Robbins.

REMSEN –pg. 292; July 1841. Selah H. Oliphant and his wife, Eliza, late Eliza Remsen a dau. of Henry Remsen, dec'd., petitioned for a division of her father's real estate. Henry Remsen died intestate leaving five children and owning real estate in Dover Tshp. and Stafford Tshp. Children of Henry Remsen, dec'd.: Eliza Oliphant, the petitioner; Deborah Remsen; Julia Remsen; Ann Maria Remsen; and Henrietta Remsen.

MOUNT –pg. 293; July 1841. Thomas Tilton and his wife, Isabelle, late Isabelle Mount a dau. of Britton Mount, dec'd., petitioned for assignment of the dower for Ann Chadwick, late Ann Mount and the widow of Britton Mount, dec'd., who had since married Taber Chadwick.

MOUNT –pg. 293; July 1841. Taber Chadwick and his wife, Ann, late Ann Mount, petitioned for a division of the real estate belonging to Britton Mount, dec'd., who died intestate owning real estate.
Children of Britton Mount, dec'd.: Isabelle, wife of Thomas Tilton; Samuel Mount; Nisbet Mount; Caroline Mount; and Elizabeth Mount who was born after the death of her father. Ann Chadwick, the petitioner, was the guardian of all the children, except Isabelle.

HENDRICKSON –pg. 294; July 1841. Ellen Hendrickson, a minor over 14yrs., elected her mother, Elizabeth Hendrickson, as her guardian.

CONOVER –pg. 294; July 1841. William F. Conover, a minor over 14yrs., chose Mary Messler as his guardian.

MESSLER –pg. 295; July 1841. Achsah Messler and Lewis G. Messler, minors over 14yrs., chose Mary Messler as their guardian. Note: two separate entries on the same page.

MESLER –pg. 296; July 1841. Hiram M. Mesler, a minor over 14yrs., chose Mary Mesler as his guardian.

MESLER –pg. 296; July 1841. Mary Mesler requested guardianship of her children William W. Mesler, Holmes Mesler, Charles W. Mesler, and Cornelius Mesler, minors under 14yrs.

BAIRD –pg. 296; July 1841. Sarah Mushon, late Sarah Baird, former guardian and mother of Sarah Matilda Baird and Mary Baird, both minors under 14yrs., requested William P. Forman be appointed guardian of said children.

HERBERT –pg. 300; July 1841. David Laird Jr. and Daniel H. Laird, guardians of Mary Nivison, late Mary Herbert, filed a settlement of accounts.

BAIRD –pg. 300; July 1841. William W. Mushon and his wife, Sarah, late Sarah Baird who was guardian of Sarah Matilda Baird, filed a settlement of accounts.

STEWART –pg. 311; Oct. 1841. James Stewart petitioned for a division of the real estate owned by John Stewart, dec'd., who owned real estate in Middletown Tshp.
Children of John Stewart, dec'd.: William H. Stewart; Samuel Stewart; Lawrence H. Stewart; James Stewart, the petitioner; and Caroline Stewart, under 21yrs., wife of William P. Patterson.

HIERS –pg. 329; Jan. 1842. Garret Hiers petitioned for a division of real estate. Neither the original property owner, nor family relationships were identified.
Entitled to 1/5 share each: Garret Hiers, Nancy Norris, Ellenor Hiers, and Sarah West.
Entitled to 1/5 share total: Cornelia Hiers, Deborah Hiers, John Hiers, Sarah Hiers, and Hendrick Hiers, all minors under 21yrs. of age.

BRAY –pg. 334; Jan. 1842. Ann Maria Bray requested guardianship of her child Ann Rebecca Bray, a minor under 14yrs.

WALN –pg. 334; Jan. 1842. Richard Waln requested guardianship of his children Nicholas Waln and Elizabeth Waln, minors under 14yrs.

ALLEN –pg. 334; Jan. 1842. Nancy Allen petitioned for guardianship of her children Elizabeth Allen, Arthur Allen, and Carolina Ann Allen, minors under 14yrs.

COLLINS –pg. 338 – 358; Jan. 1842. The actual division of the real estate owned by John Collins, dec'd., provided more information on him and his children. John Collins, dec'd., a brother of Thomas Collins, was of Barneget in Stafford Tshp. He wrote his will Dec. 23, 1836 and it was proven Sept. 9, 1837. Deliverance Butler was the wife of Charles Butler, Charlotte Tilton was the wife of John Tilton, Mary Ellison was the wife of John Ellison, and Hannah Leeds was the wife of Henry Leeds. Note: See Book K, pg. 155, April 1840.

COOK –pg. 361; Jan. 1842. John Cook, guardian of Jane Cropsey, late Jane Cook, filed a settlement of accounts.

THROCKMORTON –pg. 361; Jan. 1842. Abigail Throckmorton, guardian of Mary Gardiner, late Mary Throckmorton, filed a settlement of accounts.

CROXSON –pg. 368; April 1842. William W. Croxson applied for the assignment of the dower for Elizabeth Croxson, widow of Jacob Croxson, dec'd. He had purchased the real estate of Jacob Croxson, dec'd., subject to the dower being set aside.

BRINLEY –pg. 369; April 1842. Joseph Brinley applied for a division of the real estate owned by Jacob Brinley, dec'd, who owned real estate near Shark River in Howell Tshp. The heirs of Jacob Brinley, dec'd., were identified by shares.
Entitled to 1/3 share each: Jacob Brinley and Joseph Brinley.
Entitled to 1/6 share each: Elizabeth Yard, late Elizabeth Brinley, and Mary Jane Shafto, a minor under 21yrs. of age.

BRAY –pg. 369; April 1842. Francis Murphy, guardian of James Bray, Joseph Warren Bray, Charles Douglass Bray, David Watson Bray, Ann Eliza Bray, Rachel Bray, Mary Bray, Catharine Bray, and Cordelia Bray, all children of David S. Bray, dec'd., petitioned to sell his wards' real estate to offset costs of education and maintenance.

BROWN –pg. 372; April 1842. Mark Brown requested guardianship of his sister-in-law Catharine C. Rogers, a minor under 14yrs.

WALLING –pg. 372; April 1842. Thomas B. Stout requested guardianship of Adaline Walling and Catharine Walling, minors under 14yrs.

WALLING –pg. 373; April 1842. Leonard Walling and Jacob A. Walling of Middletown, minors over 14yrs., chose Richard D. Walling as their guardian. Note: two separate entries on the same page.

HARTSHORNE –pg. 373; April 1842. Tyler W. Hartshorne, a minor over 14yrs., chose Ann Hartshorne as his guardian.

LANE –pg. 437; July 1842. The heirs of Gilbert Lane, dec'd., petitioned for a division of his real estate. Gilbert Lane died intestate leaving children and grandchildren.
Children of Gilbert Lane, dec'd.: Hannah Chasey, wife of William Chasey; Sarah VanBrunt, wife of Daniel VanBrunt; Margaret Hampton, wife of Moses Hampton; Eleanor Brown, wife of Thomas Brown; Mary Price, wife of John Price; Ann Jackson, wife of Benjamin Jackson; John Lane; and Abraham Lane.
Grandchildren who were the children of his dau. Susan White, dec'd.: Phillip White; Gilbert White; John White; and Susan Mead, wife of Alfred Mead.
Grandchildren who were the children of his son James Lane, dec'd.: James Henry Lane,

Adaline Lane, and Matilda Lane.

PEASE –pg. 438; July 1842. Samuel Mairs petitioned for a division of the real estate devised to the heirs of David Pease, dec'd., by the last will and testament, dated Jan. 3, 1811, of Cornelius Pease, dec'd., and also for a division of two tracts of land purchased by Jonathan C. Pease. By purchasing some of the shares, Samuel Mairs was entitled to 1/3 of the real estate. Entitled to 1/9 share each: Mary Smith, wife of Peter Smith; Rebecca Hunsinger, wife of George Hunsinger; Elizabeth Morlatt, wife of Joseph Morlatt; Keziah Bush, wife of George Bush; Melinda Smith, wife of Jacob Smith; and Charlotte Pease, a minor.

SHEARMAN –pg. 460; Oct. 1842. Hester Shearman, a minor over 14yrs., chose Catharine Shearman as her guardian.

SHEARMAN –pg. 460; Oct. 1842. Catharine Shearman requested guardianship of her children Deborah Shearman, Phebe Shearman, and Mary Shearman, minors under 14yrs.

BOOK L

1843 – 1847

COX –pg. 8; Jan. 1843. Peter Wikoff and his wife, Harriet, late Harriet Cox, petitioned for a
division of real estate owned by Joshua Cox, dec'd., late of Upper Freehold Tshp., who died
intestate leaving two children and four grandchildren.
Children: Harriet Wikoff, the petitioner, and Catherine Cox.
Grandchildren who were children, all under 21yrs., of his dau. Sarah Norton, dec'd.: Mary
Ann Norton, Harriet Norton, Joshua Norton, and John Norton.

ELY –pg. 10; Jan. 1843. John B. Ely petitioned for division of land belonging to Phebe Ely, dec'd.,
who died intestate.
Siblings of Phebe Ely, dec'd.: Richard Ely; and Mary Perrine, dec'd., late wife of John
Perrine.
Children of her brother William W. Ely, dec'd.: Phebe Robbins, wife of Richard C. Robbins
now deceased; Elizabeth Shepherd, wife of David Shepherd; Lucy Britton, wife of Abraham
Britton; Mary Ely; John B. Ely, the petitioner; William Ely; David Ely; Isaac Ely; Sarah Ely;
James H. Ely; Joseph Ely; and George A. Ely.
Children of her brother Joseph Ely, dec'd.: William Ely, John Ely, James Ely, Mary Ely, and
Sarah Ely.
Children of her brother John Ely, dec'd.: Mary Shafto, wife of John Shafto; Sarah Tilton, wife
of John P. L. Tilton; Milton Ely; Rolin Ely, then deceased; Racine Ely; Wellington Ely;
Caroline Ely; and Rhoda Ely.
Children of her brother Isaac Ely, dec'd.: John L. Ely; Joseph Ely; William Ely; Mary
Vaughn, wife of Samuel Vaughn; Elizabeth Tantum, wife of Samuel Tantum; and Lucy Ely.

EDWARDS –pg. 12; Jan. 1843. Thursa Edwards requested guardianship of her children Samuel
Edwards, Thomas Edwards, and Phoebe Ann Edwards, minors under 14yrs.

SMITH –pg. 12; Jan. 1843. Joseph S. Smith, father of Charles Smith , Emma Smith, and Palmer W.
Smith, minors under 14yrs., requested appointment as their guardian.

ERRICKSON –pg. 21; Feb. 1843. Francis V. Errickson, a minor over 14yrs., chose Hannah
Errickson as his guardian.

ERRICKSON –pg. 22; Feb. 1843. Hannah Errickson requested guardianship of her dau. Hannah C.
Errickson, a minor under 14yrs.

PITTENGER –pg. 29; April 1843. Mary Pittenger requested guardianship of her dau. Ellenor Jane
Pittenger, a minor under 14yrs.

VANCLEAF –pg. 29; April 1843. Elijah C. VanCleaf applied for a division of real estate, a house
and 2 acres of land in Freehold Tshp. that he held as tenants in common with several others.
Entitled to 1/10 each: Tunis VanCleaf, Ann Carmen, Hannah Clayton, Jane VanPelt, David
VanCleaf, John I. VanCleaf, Joseph P. VanCleaf, Samuel H. VanCleaf, and petitioner Elijah
C. VanCleaf.
Entitled to 1/80 each, all minors under 21 yrs. of age: Carche Walling, John VanCleaf,
William VanCleaf, Maria VanCleaf, Septenius Stephen VanCleaf, Elizabeth Ann VanCleaf,
James VanCleaf, and Hannah Jane VanCleaf. Note: Book L, pg. 72, Oct. 1843, identified the
previous property owner as Carche VanCleaf, dec'd.

COLLINS –pg. 30; April 1843. Teresea Collins petitioned for guardianship of her children Arthur
Collins, Job Collins, Ann Eliza Collins, and Cornelia Collins, all minors under 14yrs.

HOLLOWAY –pg. 30; April 1843. Nelson Newman and Jane Newman requested guardianship of
Deborah Holloway and Ferdinand S. Holloway, minors under 14yrs. Jane Newman was the

mother of the children.

HOLLOWAY –pg. 30; April 1843. John Holloway, a minor over 14yrs., son of James Holloway, dec'd., chose Nelson Newman and Jane Newman as his guardians.

PITTENGER –pg. 31; April 1843. William Pittenger, a minor over 14yrs., son of John Pittenger, dec'd., chose Mary Pittenger as his guardian.

CRAWFORD –pg. 37 - 44; April 1843. John Lloyd Hendrickson petitioned the court to hold proceedings on the mental capabilities of Eleanor Crawford of Middletown Tshp., mother of his wife. Said Eleanor Crawford, aged about 80yrs. old, was the widow of George Crawford, dec'd., and was living with Jacob T. B. Beekman and William W. Murray. Petitioner claimed Eleanor Crawford possessed a sizable amount of real estate that would pass to the petitioner's wife if Eleanor died intestate. Petitioner claimed she'd been mentally unfit to handle her affairs for the last 7 to 8 years. Murray and Beekman were charged with the care of Eleanor Crawford by the will of her husband, and were owed for her care.
Children of Eleanor Crawford: Mary Murray, about 43yrs. old, wife of William W. Murray; Ann Beekman, about 40yrs. old, wife of Jacob T. B. Beekman; and Adaline Hendrickson, 39yrs. old, wife of John L. Hendrickson.

NEWMAN –pg. 47; June 1843. Jesse B. Newman requested assignment of a dower for Lydia Newman, widow of Joseph P. Newman, dec'd. The land was in Howell Tshp.
Heirs of Joseph P. Newman, dec'd., who resided in N.J.: Jesse B. Newman; Phebe Romaine, wife of Theophilus Romaine; and Blessing Newman, wife of Samuel Newman.
Heirs of Joseph P. Newman, dec'd. who resided in Ohio: Jane Stout, wife of Robert Stout; Jedidah Morris wife of George Morris; and Uriah Newman.

BOUDE –pg. 52; July 1843. John Boude, father of John Boude, Henry Boude, and Mary Boude, minors under 14yrs., asked to have Gilbert Breese appointed their guardian.

ARNOLD –pg. 56; July 1843. Charles Arnold requested assignment of a dower for Elizabeth Arnold, widow of James Arnold, dec'd.
Heirs of James Arnold, dec'd.: Charles Arnold, the petitioner; Rachel Headly, late Rachel Arnold; Mary Weaver, late Mary Arnold; Charlotte Craft, late Charlotte Arnold; Hester Weber, late Hester Arnold; and the children of Job Arnold, dec'd., who were noted as having no guardian, but weren't identified by name.

BAIRD –pg. 57; July 1843. John B. Ely requested a division of the real estate owned by John Baird, dec'd. John Baird died leaving a will devising a farm of 450 acres where William and Rebecca Ely then lived, whereby use of the land was given to said Rebecca Ely and her husband, William Ely, during their natural lives. At their death, which had occurred, the farm was devised to their children, to be divided equally.
Children of William and Rebecca Ely, entitled to 1/12 share each: Phebe Robbins, then deceased, late wife of Richard Robbins; Mary Ely; William W. Ely; Sarah Ely; John B. Ely; David B. Ely; Isaac Ely; James H. Ely; Elizabeth Shepherd, wife of David Shepherd; Lucy Britton, wife of Abraham Britton; Joseph Ely; and George Ely.
Grandchildren of William and Rebecca Ely who were children of their dau. Phebe Robbins, dec'd.: John Robbins; Benjamin Robbins; Rebecca Ann Robbins, now wife of William West; William Robbins; Wikoff Robbins; Ezekiel Robbins; Mary Robbins, under 21yrs.; Sarah Robbins, under 21yrs.; Samuel Robbins, under 21yrs.; Elizabeth Robbins, under 21yrs.; Clayton Robbins, under 21yrs.; Jacob Robbins, under 21yrs.; and Clark Robbins, under 21yrs.
Note: See Book L, pg. 161, July 1844 where Clayton Robbins is referred to as Richard C. Robbins.

EMMONS –pg. 58; July 1843. Distribution of the estate of John B. Emmons, dec'd., who died intestate, identified his children and grandchildren and showed he left no widow.
Child: Benjamin B. Emmons.
Grandchildren who were children of his dau. Lydia Boude, dec'd.: John Henry Boude and Mary Boude.

DAVISON –pg. 62; July 1843. Within 'Exceptions and Report of Auditor,' they noted John Davison, dec'd., died intestate leaving children.
Children of John Davison, dec'd.: John Davison; Peter Davison; Ann Havens, wife of Abraham O. S. Havens; Deborah Davison; Sarah C. Davison; Richard Davison; and Emeline Davison.

SHEARMAN –pg. 76; Oct. 1843. John Shearman applied for a division of real estate. The original
    owner was not identified, but the property was located in Howell Tshp. The land was held as
    tenants in common by several people.
    Those entitled to 1/11 share each: John Shearman, the petitioner; Theophilus Shearman;
    Hester Shearman; Deborah Shearman; Mary Shearman; and Phebe Shearman.
    Children of David Shearman, dec'd., entitled to 1/11 share total: Elizabeth Shearman, Lydia
    Shearman, Thomas Shearman, Emeline Shearman, David Shearman, and Margaret Shearman.
    Children of Catherine Newman, dec'd., late Catherine Shearman, entitled 1/11 share total:
    Esther Newman, Gilbert Newman, Eden Newman, Morris Newman, and Benjamin Newman.
    Children of Thomas Shearman, dec'd., entitled to 1/11 share total: Ann Shearman, Melvinia
    Shearman, Elisha Shearman, Elizabeth Shearman, and Elijah Shearman.
    Children of Mary Ann Brand, dec'd., late Mary Ann Shearman, entitled 1/11 share total:
    Esther Brand and Elizabeth Brand.
    Children of an unidentified heir entitled to 1/11 share total: Ann Bigling, late Ann Shearman;
    Samuel Shearman; Charles Shearman; Hannah Shearman; Thomas Shearman; Joseph
    Shearman; and Catherine Shearman.

VANCLEAF –pg. 77; Oct. 1843. John VanCleaf, a minor over 14yrs., chose his mother, Mary
    VanCleaf, as his guardian.

VANCLEAF –pg. 77; Oct. 1843. Mary VanCleaf asked for guardianship of her children William
    VanCleaf, Marie VanCleaf, Septinius Steven VanCleaf, Elizabeth Ann VanCleaf, James
    VanCleaf, and Hannah Jane VanCleaf, all minors under 14yrs.

LAYTON –pg. 87 - 88; Dec. 1843. William Murray Layton placed two separate applications before
    the court, asking the court to set aside the dower for the widow of James W. Layton, dec'd.,
    and divide the real estate for the heirs of the said deceased.
    Widow of James W. Layton, dec'd.: Eliza Layton.
    Children of James W. Layton, dec'd.: William Murray Layton; James W. Layton; Job Layton
    George W. Layton; Andrew J. Layton; John Layton; Lydia Ann Layton; and Eliza Applebee,
    late Eliza Layton, wife of James Applebee. All children except Eliza Applebee and William
    M. Layton were minors under 21yrs. of age. Eliza (Layton) Applebee sold her share to her
    widowed mother, Eliza Layton.

LONGSTREET –pg. 100; Jan. 1844. Hendrick H. Longstreet, requested guardianship of his son
    John Edward Longstreet, a minor under 14yrs.

MURRAY –pg. 101 - 106; Jan. 1844. Susan Murray of Middletown Tshp. petitioned the court to
    declare her husband, James Murray, mentally incompetent. He had been without a sense of
    reason for three years. James Murray was declared incompetent. He owned two plantations
    in Middletown Tshp.
    Children of James Murray, all unmarried and under 21yrs. old: Ann Murray, Susan Murray,
    William Murray, Cecelia Murray, Edward Murray, and 3 other younger children not named.

BORDEN –pg. 107; Jan. 1844. Joseph W. Borden petitioned for a division of land, specifically a
    shop and lot in Red Bank, Shrewsbury Tshp. Joseph W. Borden was entitled to 1/2 share.
    Frances Jane Borden, Sarah Elizabeth Borden, William Borden, and Richard Borden, all
    under 21yrs. of age, were entitled to 1/8 share each. Note: See Book L, pg. 156, July 1844 for
    father of the minors.

ELY –pg. 116; March 1844. Caroline Ely and Rolinda Ely, minors over 14yrs., requested Milton
    Ely as their guardian. Note: two separate entries on the same page.

HALL –pg. 116; March 1844. Isaac B. Patterson and his wife, Rubamah, late Rubamah Hall,
    petitioned for a division of the real estate owned by Samuel Hall, dec'd., who died intestate.
    Children of Samuel Hall, dec'd.: Rubamah Patterson, wife of Isaac B. Patterson; Joanna B.
    Patterson, late Joanna Hall, wife of George L. Patterson; John Hall, under 21yrs.; Silas B.
    Hall, under 21yrs.; and Albert Hall, under 21yrs.

THOMPSON –pg. 118; March 1844. Ezekiel Perrine and his wife, Lydia, late Lydia Thompson,
    applied for a division of real estate owned by Lydia's father, William Thompson, dec'd.,
    described as four contiguous tracts of about 57 acres in Upper Freehold Tshp. where William
    Thompson and his wife, Nancy, then lived.
    Heirs entitled to 1/8 share each: Joseph Thompson; Nathan Thompson; William Thompson;
    Ann Tilton, late Ann Thompson, wife of Asher C. Tilton; Sarah Webb, late Sarah Thompson,
    wife of Samuel Webb; Nancy Thompson, widow of William Thompson, dec'd.; Lydia

Perrine, late Lydia Thompson, wife of Ezekiel Perrine; and John Gant who was the infant son of Margaret Gant, dec'd., late Margaret Thompson, late wife of Charles Gant.

BRINLEY –pg. 123-124; April 1844. Joseph West and wife, Henrietta, late Henrietta Brinley, petitioned for division of land owned by Sylvester Brinley, dec'd., who died intestate owning land in Shrewsbury Tshp.
Children and heirs of Sylvester Brinley, dec'd.: Henrietta West, wife of Joseph West; Rebecca VanDyke, late Rebecca Brinley, wife of Michael VanDyke; Louisa Brinley; William Brinley; John Brinley; and Cornelia Brinley.

STOUT –pg. 129; April 1844. David I. C. Rogers and his wife, Sarah, late Sarah Stout who was the dau. of Daniel Stout, dec'd., petitioned for a division of her father's real estate. Daniel Stout, late of Dover Tshp., died intestate leaving eight children and four grandchildren.
Children of Daniel Stout, dec'd.: Elizabeth Stout; Hannah Rogers, wife of William C. Rogers; Caroline Henderson, wife of John Henderson; Rachel Williams, wife of John Williams; Ann Holmes, wife of Joseph Holmes; Alice Stout; Margaret Applegate, wife of John Applegate; and Sarah Rogers, wife of David I. C. Rogers.
Grandchildren who were children of his dau. Catherine Holmes, dec'd., late wife of William Holmes: Matilda Holmes, Daniel Holmes, Charles Holmes, and Hannah E. Holmes.
Note: "Alice" Stout of this entry was referred to as "Allen" Stout in the actual division of the real estate.

TILTON –pg. 140; April 1844. Jane Tilton, mother of Catherine Alice Tilton and Lydia Maria Tilton, minors under 14yrs., requested Benjamin Stout be appointed guardian of her children.

ALLEN –pg. 141; April 1844. Charlotte Allen, mother of Joseph F. Allen and Sarah Ann Allen, minors under 14yrs., asked that Joseph I. Allen be appointed guardian of her children.

IRONS –pg. 142; April 1844. Anthony Irons and John W. Irons petitioned for a division of the land owned by John W. Irons, dec'd., who died intestate.
Heirs of John W. Irons, dec'd.: Anthony Irons, John W. Irons, Mary Irons, Borden Irons, Emeline Irons, Sally Irons, Hannah Ann Irons, and Jacob Irons. All except John W. and Mary were under 21yrs. of age.

MIDDLETON –pg. 155; July 1844. Henry Middleton and wife, Elizabeth Ann, along with Emily N. Applegate, late Emily N. Middleton, petitioned for division of real estate owned by Chamless Middleton, dec'd., who died intestate leaving six children as his heirs.
Children of Chamless Middleton, dec'd.: Elizabeth Ann Middleton; Emily N. Applegate; Hannah W. Middleton, under 21yrs.; Granville W. Middleton, under 21yrs.; Edwin Middleton, under 21yrs.; and Charles H. Middleton, under 21yrs.

BORDEN –pg. 156; July 1844. John Borden, administrator of the estate of Richard Borden, dec'd., stated Richard Borden died on the 4th day of December 1843 leaving four minor children and co-owning land in Red Bank with Joseph Borden. Joseph Borden had applied for a division of the deceased's estate. Note: See Book L, pg. 107, Jan. 1844.

BAILEY –pg. 157; July 1844. Thomas Bailey petitioned for a division of real estate previously owned by Joseph W. Bailey, described as 21 acres west of the road from Holmdel to Keport.
Entitled to 1/7 share each: Thomas Bailey, James Bailey, Samuel Bailey, and Mary Collins.
Entitled to 1/56 share each: William P. Bailey; Joseph P. Bailey; James P. Bailey; Edward P. Bailey; Samuel P. Bailey, under 21yrs.; Richard P. Bailey, under 21yrs.; Mary Bailey; and Eliza Roberts, late Eliza Bailey.
Entitled to 1/70 share each: Joseph J. Bailey, Stephen J. Bailey, John Bailey Jr., Lewis Bailey, Mary Vanderbilt, Nancy Place, Elizabeth Dow, Catherine Dow, Sarah Fenton, and Margaret Ford.
Entitled to 1/35 share each: William Griffin, Joseph Griffin, Charles Griffin, Mary Griffin, and Gloriana Griffin.
Note: In this record Eliza (Bailey) Roberts was also recorded as Eliza (Bailey) Robbins. In Book L, pg. 186, Oct. 1844, the land was identified as belonging to the heirs of Joseph W. Bailey, dec'd.

MIDDLETON –pg. 160; July 1844. Hannah W. Middleton, Granville W. Middleton, and Edwin Middleton, minors over 14yrs., children of Chamless Middleton, dec'd., late of Upper Freehold, elected their mother, Rachel W. Middleton, as their guardian. Note: three separate entries on the same page.

MIDDLETON –pg. 161; July 1844. Rachel W. Middleton requested guardianship of her son Charles H. Middleton, a minor under 14yrs.

ROGERS –pg. 161; July 1844. Rebecca Rogers of New York City, mother of Ann Rogers, John Rogers, and Michael Rogers, all minors under 14yrs., requested Joseph Combs, Esq., be appointed the children's guardian.

ROBBINS –pg. 161; July 1844. Richard C. Robbins requested guardianship of his children Richard C. Robbins, Jacob B. Robbins, and Clark Robbins, all minors under 14yrs. Note: See Book L, pg. 57, July 1843, where the son Richard C. Robbins was referred to as Clayton Robbins.

ROBBINS –pg. 161; July 1844. Mary E. Robbins, Sarah E. Robbins, Samuel C. Robbins, and Elizabeth E. Robbins, minors over 14yrs. of age, asked that their father, Richard C. Robbins, be appointed their guardian. Note: See Book L, pg. 57, July 1843.

IRONS –pg. 172; Aug. 1844. James L. Giberson and Hester his wife, late Hester Irons who was the widow of John W. Irons, dec'd., applied for the dower she was entitled to from her late husband's estate. Notice was served on the heirs of John W. Irons, dec'd., viz., Anthony Irons, John W. Irons, Mary Irons, Borden Irons, Emeline Irons, Sally Irons, Hannah Ann Irons, and Jacob Irons.

BENNETT –pg. 173-179; July 1844. Moses G. Bennett of Jackson Tshp. petitioned the court to have his father, Moses Bennett, also of Jackson Tshp., declared mentally incompetent. He had been without reason for several years. Moses Bennett was declared incompetent. Children of Moses Bennett: Sarah Lucretia Bennett, about 33yrs. old; Margaret Myers, late Margaret Bennett, about 31yrs. old; Abigail Strickland, late Abigail Bennett, about 29yrs. old; Mary Ann Andrews, late Mary Ann Bennett, about 27yrs. old; Moses G. Bennett, about 25yrs. old; Patience Bennett, 20yrs. old; Charles Bennett, 18yrs. old; William Henry Bennett, 12yrs. old; Sarah Elizabeth Bennett, 10yrs. old; and Caroline Bennett, 4yrs. old.

VANCLEAF –pg. 184; Oct. 1844. Samuel A. V. VanCleaf, a minor over 14yrs., elected his mother, Alice VanCleaf, as his guardian.

VANCLEAF –pg. 185; Oct. 1844. Lydia VanCleaf and Garret C. VanCleaf, minors over 14yrs., elected Alice VanCleaf as their guardian. Note: two separate entries on the same page.

VANCLEAF –pg. 185; Oct. 1844. Alice VanCleaf requested guardianship of her children Joseph VanCleaf and Charles VanCleaf, both minors under 14yrs.

ELDRIDGE –pg. 188; Oct. 1844. Rebecca Eldridge, widow of John Eldridge, dec'd., applied for the assignment of her dower. Notice was served on the heirs of John Eldridge, dec'd.
Heirs who were residents of N.J.: George Eldridge; Samuel Eldridge; Ann Marie Hurley, wife of Wesley Hurley; and Joseph Lafetra.
Heirs who were not residents of N.J.: Maria Humphreys, Elias Eldridge, John Eldridge, and the heirs of Elizabeth McBityre, dec'd.

ALLEN –pg. 193 - 194; Oct. 1844. Distribution of the estate of Samuel W. Allen, dec'd., revealed no widow, child, or parent survived him. He was survived by three brothers and one sister, along with three half-brothers and one half-sister. His full siblings were John Allen, Abraham Allen, Isaac Allen, and Catherine Miller, wife of Joseph Miller. His half-siblings were Joseph Allen, James Allen, William Allen, and Mary Lewis, wife of Joseph B. Lewis.

SPRINGSTEEN –pg. 197; Dec. 1844. Caroline Springsteen, a minor over 14yrs., requested her mother, Mary Springsteen, be appointed her guardian.

SPRINGSTEEN –pg. 198; Dec. 1844. Mary Springsteen requested guardianship of her children Ellenor Springsteen and Mariette Springsteen, minors under 14yrs.

CURTIS –pg. 210; Jan. 1845. Taber C. Longstreet and Charlotte, his wife, applied for a division of the real estate owned by Charlotte's father, Jacob Curtis, dec'd., who died intestate leaving five children.
Children of Jacob Curtis, dec'd., all under 21 years of age: Pitney Curtis, Christina Curtis, Hiram Curtis, Eliza Jane Curtis, and Charlotte Longstreet, wife of Taber C. Longstreet.

CONOVER –pg. 213; Jan. 1845. Sarah Conover, Peter Conover, and Asher Conover, all minors over 14yrs., requested their father, Hendrick P. Conover, be appointed their guardian.

CONOVER –pg. 213; Jan. 1845. Hendrick P. Conover requested guardianship of his sons John W. Conover and Charles Conover, minors under 14yrs.

HARTSHORNE –pg. 213; Jan. 1845. Jane Ann Hartshorne requested guardianship of her children James M. Hartshorne, Jane Hartshorne, Richard S. Hartshorne, and Sidney G. Hartshorne, all minors under 14yrs.

CONOVER –pg. 220; Jan. 1845. A settlement of accounts was filed by Elisha Holmes and his wife, Arintha, late Arintha Conover, who were guardians of Margaret Luyster, late Margaret Conover.

CURTIS –pg. 229; April 1845. Prudence Curtis, widow of Jacob Curtis, dec'd., applied to have her dower set aside. Notice was served on the heirs of Jacob Curtis, dec'd., viz., Pitney Curtis, Christina Curtis, Hiram Curtis, Eliza Jane Curtis, and Charlotte Longstreet, late Charlotte Curtis, wife of Taber C. Longstreet.

CONOVER –pg. 232; April 1845. John Hall petitioned for a division of real estate. The land was held by the following nine people as tenants in common: Alice Noble, late Alice Conover, wife of Andrew Noble; Caroline Corlies, late Caroline Conover, wife of John L. Corlies; Ann Eliza Pittenger, late Ann Eliza Conover, wife of Richard Pittenger; Rebecca Bearmore, late Rebecca Conover, wife of David Bearmore; Elias Conover; David Conover; Mary Matilda Conover; Garret Wikoff Conover; and John Hall, the petitioner. Prior owner from whom they inherited the land was not named. Only John Hall was over 21yrs. of age.

ALLEN –pg. 233; April 1845. Andrew J. Allen petitioned for a division of the real estate owned by Riley Allen, dec.d., who died intestate survived by a widow, five children, and two grandchildren.
Widow: Sarah W. Allen.
Children: Rachel H. Allen; Harriet S. Newbold, wife of Alexander Newbold; Margaret Brick, wife of Joseph W. Brick; Andrew J. Allen; and John W. Allen.
Grandchildren, both under 21yrs. of age, who were children of his dau. Mary Ann Waln, dec'd., late wife of Richard Waln: Elizabeth Waln and Nicholas Waln.

BROWER –pg. 234; April 1845. Annamiah Gifford and his wife, Elizabeth, petitioned for division of real estate devised by the will of David Brower, dec'd., to his children, some of whom had since married or died. His son Isaac Brower was deceased, survived by sons David Brower and Robert D. Brower. His other children Robert Brower, Elizabeth Brower, Rebecca Brower, Hannah Brower, John Brower, and Lydia Brower were to receive the rest of the land after the death of their mother who had also died. His sons Robert Brower and John Brower were still alive. His dau. Rebecca was deceased and left six children, viz., John Bullock, Amos Bullock, Thomas Bullock, Margaret Bullock, Ann Bullock, and Elizabeth Bullock. His dau. Hannah had married Benjamin Davis. His dau. Lydia was the widow of David Harker, dec'd. His dau. Elizabeth had married Annamiah Gifford. Thomas Bullock was under 21yrs. of age.

SMOCK –pg. 235; April 1845. Emeline Smock requested guardianship of her dau. Lydia Ann Smock, a minor under 14yrs.

WOOLLEY –pg. 235; April 1845. George Woolley, Rebecca Woolley, and Julia Ann Woolley, minors over 14yrs., elected their brother William M. Woolley as their guardian.

WOOLLEY –pg. 236; April 1845. William M. Woolley, brother to Adam Woolley, Charles Woolley, and David Woolley, minors under 14yrs., requested guardianship of his siblings. The mother of the minors gave her consent.

MORRIS –pg. 237 - 245; April 1845. Charles I. Morris petitioned to have his father, Isaac Z. Morris, declared mentally incompetent. Isaac Z. Morris had exhibited signs of dementia since an overnight exposure to extreme cold in 1836. The court declared him mentally incompetent.
Wife: Ann Morris.
Children of Isaac Z. Morris: Charles I. Morris, about53yrs. old; Mary Cook, wife of John Cook, about 57yrs. old; Elizabeth Earle, wife of Lawrence Earle, about 40yrs. old; Harriet Hay, wife of George Hay, about 43yrs. old; Cornelius Morris, about 38yrs. old; Lydia Ann Emmons, wife of Ashbury Emmons, about 33yrs. old; and John Morris, about 31yrs. old. Harriet Hay was also referred to as Margaret Hay in one document.

APPLEGATE –pg. 259; Aug. 1845. Gilbert B. Lawrence and Alice L., his wife, late Alice L.
Applegate a dau. of Bartholemew Applegate, dec'd., petitioned for a division of her father's
real estate. Bartholemew Applegate died intestate leaving eleven children.
Children: John B. Applegate; Jacob Applegate; Margaret Applegate, wife of Joseph
Applegate; Alice L. Lawrence, wife of Gilbert B. Lawrence; Hester Thompson, wife of
Cornelius Thompson; Mehala Warner, wife of Solomon Warner; Mary Woodmansee, wife of
Isaac Woodmansee; Charity Williams, wife of John Williams; Catherine Hogan, wife of John
Hogan; Sarah Fifer, wife of John Fifer; and Harriet Wainwright, wife of Edward Wainwright.
Grandchild who was a child of his dau. Lucretia Bowker, dec'd.: Samuel Bowker.
Grandchildren who were children of his son Bartholemew Applegate, dec'd.: John Applegate
and Mary Ann Applegate, both under 21yrs. of age.

RIDGEWAY –pg. 263; Aug. 1845. Joseph Waln and Eliza Ridgeway who was the mother of Susan
Ridgeway, Rebecca Ridgeway, and John Andrew Ridgeway, minors under 14yrs., requested
Joseph Waln be appointed guardian of the children.

SUYDAM –pg. 263; Aug. 1845. Jacob Suydam requested guardianship of his children William
Suydam, George Suydam, Augustus Suydam, and Thompson Suydam, minors under 14yrs.

COMPTON –pg. 302; Nov. 1845. John Compton petitioned for a division of the real estate owned
by Job Compton, dec'd., who died intestate leaving nine living children and four
grandchildren.
Children of Job Compton, dec'd.: John Compton; Joseph Compton; Cornelius Compton;
Lydia Myers, wife of Isaac Myers; Phebe Stout; Eliza Willett; Julia Willett; Catherine Palmer,
wife of John Palmer; Janette Morris, wife of Lewis Morris.
Grandchildren who were children of his dau. Mary Jane Walling, dec'd.: Benjamin Walling,
William Henry Walling, Charles Walling, and Lucinda Walling, all under 21yrs. of age.

LANE –pg. 320; Jan. 1846. Eleanor Lane requested guardianship of her children Mary Elizabeth
Lane, and Adden Colwell Lane, minors under 14yrs.

CONOVER –pg. 320; Jan. 1846. Eliza Schanck, late Eliza Conover, requested guardianship of her
sons Joseph L. Conover, and Gorden Conover, minors under 14yrs. of age.

CONOVER –pg. 321; Jan. 1846. Jonathan Conover and William S. Conover, minors over the age of
14yrs., chose their mother, Eliza Schanck, late Eliza Conover, as their guardian. Note: two
separate entries on the same page.

SWAN –pg. 328; Feb. 1846. John R. Conover petitioned for a division of the real estate owned by
Gabriel Swan, dec'd. The real estate consisted of several lots in Red Bank, and was held as
tenants in common by several people.
Entitled to 1/2 share: John R. Conover.
Entitled to 1/6 share each: Elizabeth Parker, late Elizabeth Swan, wife of John Parker; David
Swan; and Charles Mortimer Swan, under 21yrs. of age.

IRONS –pg. 329; Feb. 1846. John H. Irons petitioned for a division of the property that belonged to
Edward W. Irons, dec'd., who died intestate leaving thirteen children.
Children of Edward W. Irons, dec'd.: Hannah Ashton, late Hannah Irons; Judidah Johnson,
late Judidah Irons; Edward Irons; Elizabeth Ann Hagerman, late Elizabeth Ann Irons; Sarah
Hagerman, late Sarah Irons; Charles Irons, under 21yrs.; Gilbert Irons, under 21yrs.; Taylor
Irons, under 21yrs.; Walter Irons, under 21yrs.; Richmond Irons, under 21yrs.; Caroline Irons,
under 21yrs.; Ivins Irons, under 21yrs.; and John H. Irons, the petitioner.

HOLMES –pg. 335; Feb. 1846. William Holmes petitioned for guardianship of his children Matilda
Holmes, Daniel S. Holmes, Charles P. Holmes, and Hannah E. Holmes, minors under 14yrs.

ELLISON –pg. 335; Feb. 1846. Johannah Ellison requested guardianship of her son Parker Ellison,
a minor under 14yrs.

JAMES –pg. 336; Feb. 1846. Joseph James petitioned for guardianship of Thomas James and Susan
James, minors under 14yrs. He was their uncle. Notice was served on their mother who had
married Aaron Reid.

BORDEN –pg. 352; May 1846. Samuel H. Horner and Ann Rogers who was the grandmother of
Samuel R. Borden, Ann R. Borden, Caroline Borden, and William Henry Borden, all minors
under 14yrs., asked the court to appoint Samuel H. Horner guardian of the said minors.

JAMES –pg. 353; May 1846. Joseph James, their uncle, requested guardianship of William James, Henry James, and Charles James, minors under 14yrs. old. Their mother had married Aaron Reed.

WRIGHT –pg. 353; May 1846. Ann Wright asked to be appointed guardian of her son Milton Wright, a minor child under 14yrs.

WRIGHT –pg. 353; May 1846. William Wright, a minor over 14yrs., son of Thomas Wright, dec'd., asked that his mother, Ann Wright, be appointed his guardian.

CORLIES –pg. 354 - 359; May 1846. John Corlies petitioned the court to declare his brother Edward Pennington Corlies of Shrewsbury Tshp. mentally incompetent. Edward, an unwed man over 40yrs. old, had been afflicted since infancy. The court decided he had been mentally incompetent for about 30yrs. Edward P. Corlies, son of Peter Corlies Sr., dec'd., owned no real estate. He was due money from his father's estate and from the estate of a deceased brother Peter Corlies Jr. He had no living parent, but did have living siblings. Siblings: John Corlies, aged about 70yrs.; Phebe Corlies, aged about 67yrs.; Leah Corlies, aged about 64yrs.; and Sarah Corlies, aged about 60yrs. Benjamin W. Corlies was appointed his guardian.

WOOLLEY –pg. 365; May 1846. David Miller and his wife, Elizabeth, late Elizabeth Woolley who was administrator of estate of William Woolley, dec'd., filed a settlement of accounts.

JOHNSTON –pg. 375; Aug. 1846. William Johnston applied for a division of the real estate owned by Peter Johnston, dec'd., who owned 139 acres in Millstone Tshp.
Heirs entitled to 1/4 share each: William Johnston, petitioner; Michael Johnston; and Euphamana Johnston.
Heirs entitled to 1/8 share each: William Johnston, under 21yrs.; and Lydia Johnston, under 21yrs. of age.

TUNIS –pg. 379; Aug. 1846. Henry Tunis, Charles Tunis, and Lauriet Tunis, children of Abraham Tunis, dec'd., minors over 14yrs., selected Lydia Tunis as their guardian. Note: three separate entries on the same page.

SHAW –pg. 380; Aug. 1846. Josephine Shaw, Eugene Shaw, and Wallace Shaw, children of Aaron D. Shaw, minors over 14yrs. old, asked that Ellenor Shaw be appointed their guardian.

SHAW –pg. 380; Aug. 1846. Ellenor Shaw requested guardianship of her children Melinda Shaw, Livingston Shaw, Ross Shaw, and Aaron Shaw, minors under 14yrs.

SUMMERBELL –pg. 380; Aug. 1846. Mary Summerbell requested guardianship of her children Mary Catherine Summerbell, Ann Matilda Summerbell, and Eliza Summerbell, minors under 14yrs.

FISHER –pg. 381; Aug. 1846. Elizabeth Fisher requested guardianship of her son William Augustus Fisher, a minor under 14yrs.

MCKEAN –pg. 381; Aug. 1846. Isaac Rogers and his wife, Martha W. Rogers, late Martha W. McKean, requested Isaac Rogers be appointed guardian of Letetia S. McKean and Washington McKean, minors under 14yrs.

LAYTON –pg. 382; Aug. 1846. Anne Layton, mother of Grandin Layton, a minor under 14yrs., asked that guardianship of her son be granted to Bennington F. Randolph, Esq.

LAYTON –pg. 382; Aug. 1846. Jonathan Layton, a minor over 14yrs., son of Safety Layton, dec'd., chose Bennington F. Randolph, Esq., as his guardian.

JEFFREY –pg. 398; Nov. 1846. Mary Elizabeth Jeffrey, a minor over 14yrs., chose her mother, Elizabeth Jeffrey, as her guardian.

CONOVER –pg. 398; Nov. 1846. Stephen D. Conover and William S. Conover, minors over 14yrs., requested Rev. Charles F. Worrell as their guardian. Note: See Book K, pg. 159, April 1840 and Book L, pg. 399, 406, 407, Nov. 1846.

JEFFREY –pg. 399; Nov. 1846. Elizabeth Jeffrey requested guardianship of her son William Stewart Jeffrey, a minor under 14yrs.

CONOVER –pg. 399; Nov. 1846. Rev. Charles F. Worrell and Margaret Ann Johnson who was the mother of Amanda Conover and John Conover, minors under 14yrs., requested Rev. Charles F. Worrell be appointed guardian of said Amanda and John Conover. Note: See Book K, pg. 159, April 1840 and Book L, pg. 398, 406, 407, Nov. 1846.

BURTIS –pg. 399; Nov. 1846. Richard W. Burtis requested guardianship of his son Charles R. Burtis, a minor under 14yrs.

JOHNS –pg. 401; Nov. 1846. Elizabeth Johns requested guardianship of her children Samuel Johns and Walter Johns, minors under 14yrs.

ALLEN –pg. 402; Nov. 1846. Joseph Mount and Charlotte, his wife, the late Charlotte Allen, applied for the assignment of her dower from the property of Richard L. Allen, dec'd. Charlotte Allen, the widow of Richard L. Allen of Howell Tshp., had remarried to Joseph Mount. Notice of the application was served on Joseph I. Allen, guardian of Joseph F. Allen and Sarah Ann Allen, minors and the only known children of Richard L. Allen, dec'd.

CONOVER –pg. 406 - 407; Nov. 1846. A settlement of accounts was filed by Jacob Johnson and his wife, Margaret Ann, late Margaret Ann Conover, guardians of Stephen D. Conover and William S. Conover, minors over 14yrs., and John Conover and Amanda Conover, minors under 14yrs. Note: This represents four separate entries on two pages. See Book K, pg. 159, April 1840 and Book L, pg. 398, 399, Nov. 1846.

BOOK M

1847 – 1850

IRONS –pg. 8; Feb. 1847. John H. Irons, oldest brother of Wallace Irons, Richmond Irons, Caroline Irons, and Ivins Irons, all minors under 14yrs., asked to be appointed their guardian. The minors had no mother, and John H. Irons was the only brother of legal age.

ROGERS –pg. 8; Feb. 1847. Eliza Rogers, widow of Britton Rogers (late of the state of Indiana), dec'd., and mother of William Rogers, Charles Rogers, John Rogers, and George Rogers, minors under 14yrs., sons of Britton Rogers, dec'd., asked that Peter Davison, Esq., be appointed guardian of her children.

AKINS –pg. 21; April 1847. William Akins requested a division of the property of William Akins and wife, both deceased. Their heirs were described by share allotments.
Entitled to 1/7 share each: William Akins; Mary Jeffrey, late Mary Akins, wife of Lewis Jeffrey; Hannah Chatlier, late Hannah Akins, wife of John Chatlier; Lydia Ellean, late Lydia Akins, wife of Augustus Ellean; and Sarah Badly, late Sarah Akins, wife of Joseph J. Badly.
Entitled to 1/35 share each: Sarah Rogers, late Sarah Akins, wife of David Rogers; Lydia Wyckoff, late Lydia Akins, wife of Charles Wyckoff; Alice Akins; Rebecca Akins; and Joseph Akins.
Entitled to 1/21 share each, all minors under 21yrs.: William Pochea, John Pochea, and Benjamin Leming.

LEMING –pg. 22; April 1847. Henry Leming, a minor over 14yrs., son of James Leming, dec'd., elected John Calon of Middlesex Co. as his guardian.

CORTELYOU –pg. 31; May 1847. Timothy T. Cortelyou applied for a division of real estate that belonged to Timothy T. Cortelyou, dec'd., late of Kings Co., N.Y., and was held by his heirs as tenants in common.
Children and heirs of Timothy T. Cortelyou, dec'd., entitled to 1/8 share each: Sarah T. Cortelyou, widow of Isaac Cortelyou, dec'd.; Johanna Berque, late Johanna Cortelyou, widow of Simon Berque, dec'd.; Ann Mariah VanPelt, late Ann Mariah Cortelyou, wife of John E. VanPelt; Freelow Jane Cortelyou; Ida Cortelyou; William K. Cortelyou; Timothy T. Cortelyou; and Mary E. Cortelyou who was under 21yrs.

JOHNSTON –pg. 35; May 1847. Lydia Johnston and William Johnston, minors over 14yrs., children of John Johnston, dec'd., asked that Charles Parker, Esq., of Freehold be appointed their guardian. Note: two separate entries on the same page.

IRONS –pg. 36; May 1847. Taylor Irons, a minor over 14yrs., son of Edward Irons, dec'd., requested Aaron B. Irons be appointed his guardian.

CORLIES –pg. 36; May 1847. Chandler Corlies requested guardianship of his children William P. Corlies, Mary P. Corlies, Elizabeth A. Corlies, John Corlies, and David Corlies, all minors under 14yrs.

VAN PELT –pg. 36; May 1847. Eliza Hanson, late Eliza VanPelt, mother of Charles R. VanPelt and Martha Jane VanPelt, minors under 14yrs., requested Thomas I. Beedle be appointed guardian of said children.

COOK –pg. 37; May 1847. William C. Jones, great uncle of Mary Hannah Cook, Sarah Ann Cook, John Cook, and William Cook, minors under 14yrs. who had no mother or siblings of age to care for them, asked to be appointed guardian of the minors.

BRUERE –pg. 57; Aug. 1847. Stephen H. Bruere, Asa Hunt and his wife, Susan, late Susan Bruere, petitioned the court for a division of the real estate owned by John H. Bruere, dec'd. John H.

Bruere made his last will and testament on May 22, 1826 in which he disposed of all the land he then owned. He later purchased two tracts of land in Upper Freehold Tshp. John H. Bruere died without disposing of these two pieces of land and leaving heirs, all his children. Children of John H. Bruere, dec'd.: Susan Hunt, late Susan Bruere, wife of Asa Hunt; Stephen H. Bruere; Ruth Tilton, late Ruth Bruere, wife of William Tilton; Price Bruere; Napoleon B. Bruere; Joseph B. Bruere; George W. Bruere; and John Bruere. Susan, John, and Stephen were the only children over 21yrs. of age.
Note: In Book M, pg. 77, Nov. 1847, John H. Bruere's land was sold, and his widow, Ann Bruere, relinquished her right of dower.

AKINS –pg. 60; Aug. 1847. David Rogers and his wife, Sarah R., late Sarah R. Akins, and Alice P. Akins applied for a division of the property owned by Benjamin S. Akins, dec'd., who died intestate.
Children of Benjamin S. Akins, dec'd.: Sarah R. Rogers, late Sarah R. Akins, wife of David Rogers; Alice P. Akins; Lydia Wikoff, late Lydia Akins, wife of Charles Wikoff; Rebecca P. W. Akins, under 21yrs.; and Joseph F. Akins, under 21yrs.

VAN PELT –pg. 85; Nov. 1847. Jacob Van Pelt applied for division of a house and lot in Middletown Point belonging to Christopher Van Pelt, dec'd. The land was held as tenants in common by his heirs who were brothers and children of a deceased brother.
Brothers entitled to 1/4 share each: James Van Pelt, David Van Pelt, and Henry Van Pelt.
Children of his brother Jacob VanPelt, dec'd., entitled to 1/4 share total: Jacob Van Pelt, the petitioner; David Van Pelt; Charles R. Van Pelt, under 21yrs.; and Martha Jane VanPelt, under 21yrs.

CONOVER –pg. 86; Nov. 1847. John S. Conover, a minor over 14yrs., chose his father, Barnes S. Conover, as his guardian.

WEST –pg. 86; Nov. 1847. Almirah West, a minor over 14yrs., dau. of Josiah West, dec'd., elected Peter S. West as her guardian.

LAYTON –pg. 86; Nov. 1847. John Layton, a minor over 14yrs., son of James W. Layton, dec'd., selected William W. Murray as his guardian.

CONOVER –pg. 95; Dec. 1847. Garret S. Conover, a minor over 14yrs., son of Tylee Conover, dec'd., chose Daniel Conover and William V. Conover as his guardians.

HOLMES –pg. 95; Dec. 1847. William T. Holmes, a minor over 14yrs., son of Josiah Holmes, dec'd., chose John A. Morford as his guardian.

HOLMES –pg. 96; Dec. 1847. Deborah Holmes, mother of Peter T. Holmes, a minor under 14yrs., asked the court to appoint John A. Morford as Peter's guardian.

ANTONIDES –pg. 102; Jan. 1848. Charles Antonides and Elizabeth H. Antonides, minors over 14yrs., requested Amzi C. McLean, Esq., be appointed their guardian. Note: two separate entries on the same page.

ANTONIDES –pg. 109 - 115; Feb. 1848. Amzi C. McLean as guardian of Elizabeth Antonides and Charles Antonides, minors and heirs of William Antonides, dec'd., applied to have the dower for the widow of William Antonides, dec'd., set aside. Notice of the application was sent to Gertrude Sanford, widow of William Antonides, dec'd., and guardian of John Antonides and William Antonides who were also heirs of William Antonides, dec'd. William Antonides was of Freehold Tshp. Gertrude had remarried and was then the wife of Gordon Sanford.

NEWMAN –pg. 118; Feb. 1848. Elijah Newman and Nelson Newman applied for a division of the real estate owned by Joseph I. Newman, dec'd., who died intestate. The heirs held his lands in Howell Tshp. as tenants in common since April 16, 1846.
Heirs entitled to 1/6 share each: Samuel Morris Jr.; Rhoda Allen, wife of John Allen; Lummus W. Newman; Elijah Newman; and Nelson Newman.
Heirs entitled to 1/42 share each: Barzilla Brand; Vincent W. Brand; Lydia Cooper, under 21yrs., wife of John Cooper; John M. Brand, under 21yrs.; Sarah Brand, under 21yrs.; Nelson Brand, under 21yrs.; and James Brand, under 21yrs.

JOHNSON –pg. 124; Feb. 1848. Mary Johnson petitioned for guardianship of her children Catherine Johnson, Robert Johnson, and Mary Cyrenia Johnson, all minors under 14yrs.

HOLMES pg. 133; March 1848. Deborah Holmes, widow of Josiah Holmes, dec'd., requested her dower be set off.

ESTILL –pg. 134; March 1848. Benjamin B. Estill petitioned for guardianship of his children Sarah Elizabeth Estill, Benjamin H. Estill, and John W. Estill, all minors under 14yrs. old.

ESTILL –pg. 134; March 1848. Thomas H. Estill, a minor over 14yrs., chose Benjamin B. Estill as his guardian.

PIERCE –pg. 137; April 1848. John G. Hall and Phebe A. Hall, late Phebe A. Pierce who was administrator of the estate of William W. Pierce, dec'd., submitted a settlement of accounts.

PERRINE –pg. 146; May 1848. James W. Perrine and William R. Perrine petitioned for a division of the real estate belonging to their father, William I. Perrine, dec'd.
Heirs entitled to 1/7 share each: William R. Perrine; James W. Perrine; John H. Perrine; Thomas Perrine; Mary Forman, late Mary Perrine, wife of William Forman; Martha Robinson, late Martha Perrine, wife of James Robinson; and Alfred Perrine, under 21yrs.

RUSSELL –pg. 149; May 1848. John Russell petitioned the court for a division of the real estate owned by Edward Russell, dec'd., located in Union Tshp., Monmouth Co.
Heirs entitled to 1/8 share each: John Russell; Jane Platt, late Jane Russell, wife of Jacob Platt; Lydia Ann Crawford, late Lydia Ann Russell, wife of John Crawford; James Russell; Forman Russell; Holmes W. Russell, under 21yrs.; William T. Russell, under 21yrs.; and Charles F. Russell, under 21yrs.

LIPPINCOTT –pg. 150; May 1848. Maria Louisa Lippincott, a minor over 14yrs., dau. of Manley Lippincott, dec'd., requested Maria Lippincott as her guardian.

VANBRACKLE –pg. 151; May 1848. Emma VanBrackle and James VanBrackle, children of Stephen VanBrackle, dec'd., minors over 14yrs., chose Ann VanBrackle as their guardian.

STRICKLAND –pg. 151; May 1848. Kasiah Strickland, Adolphus Strickland, and William Henry Strickland, minors over 14yrs., children of Jonathan Strickland, dec'd., chose Nancy Strickland as their guardian.

ROBINSON –pg. 151; May 1848. Edward Robinson, a minor over 14yrs., son of John Robinson, dec'd., chose Maria Robinson as his guardian.

LIPPINCOTT –pg. 152; May 1848. Maria Lippincott asked for guardianship of her children Garret Lippincott, William Lippincott, and Catherine Amelia Lippincott, minors under 14yrs.

VANBRACKLE –pg. 152; May 1848. Ann VanBrackle petitioned for guardianship of her children Thomas VanBrackle, Stephen Henry VanBrackle, and George VanBrackle, minors under 14yrs.

WATSON –pg. 153; May 1848. Margaret Watson, mother of Margaret Jane Watson and John W. Watson, minors under 14yrs., asked to be appointed their guardian.

STRICKLAND –pg. 153; May 1848. Nancy Strickland, mother of Cornelius Strickland, Mary Strickland, and Susan Strickland, minors under 14yrs., asked to be appointed their guardian.

ROBINSON –pg. 153; May 1848. Maria Robinson, mother of Joseph C. Robinson, John Henry Robinson, and Catherine Maria Robinson, minors under 14yrs., asked to be appointed their guardian.

SWAN –pg. 178 - 179; Aug. 1848. Joseph G. Mount petitioned for a division of the real estate owned by Morgan Swan, dec'd., described as about 4 acres on the north side of Claypit Creek in Middletown Tshp. Joseph G. Mount had purchased three heirs' shares in the property prior to this. Note: The next entry reported a Joseph E. Mount and included the same heirs, but this definitely read "G." for a middle initial.
Entitled to 1/2 share: Joseph G. Mount because he bought out the interests of three heirs, viz., Clarissa A. Truax, late Clarissa A. Swan, wife of John Truax, Mary Elizabeth Mount, late Mary E. Swan, wife of John H. Mount, and John B. Swan.
Entitled to 1/6 share: David B. Swan.
Entitled to 1/6 share total, all children of Sally L. Van Gorx, dec'd., late Sally L. Swan, late wife of Mathew Van Gorx: James Van Gorx; Addison Van Gorx; and Abby Ann Tompkins,

late Abby Van Gorx, wife of Elijah Tompkins.
Entitled to 1/6 share total, all heirs of Francis V. Swan, dec'd.: Eleanor L. Swan, John Swan, and Sidney Swan.

SWAN –pg. 180; Aug. 1848. Application for a division of real estate was made by Joseph E. Mount. Gabriel Swan and Morgan Swan died owning land as tenants in common, described as about 10 acres of woodland in the Navesink Highlands, Middletown Tshp. By purchasing the shares of certain heirs Joseph E. Mount held ownership as tenants in common with the following named heirs.
Children and surviving heirs of Gabriel Swan, entitled to 1/4 share each: David Burdge Swan; and Elizabeth Parker, late Elizabeth Swan, wife of John Parker.
Children and surviving heirs of Morgan Swan collectively entitled to 1/4 share total are listed below.
David B. Swan, entitled to 1/12 share.
Children of Sally L. Van Gorx, dec'd., late Sally Swan, entitled to 1/36 share each: Abby Ann Tomkins, late Abby Van Gorx, wife of Elijah Tompkins; James Van Gorx; and Addison Van Gorx.
Children of Francis V. Swan, dec'd., entitled to 1/36 share each: Eleanor L. Swan, John Swan, and Sidney Swan.
Heirs of Morgan Swan from whom Joseph E. Mount purchased shares, entitling him to 1/4 share: Clarissa A. Truax, late Clarissa Swan, wife of John Truax; John B. Swan; and Mary Elizabeth Mount, late Mary E. Swan, wife of John H. Mount.

TILTON –pg. 181; Aug. 1848. Edwin Tilton and Harriet Tilton, minors over 14yrs., children of Amos Tilton, dec'd., chose Joseph W. Borden as their guardian.

GREIG –pg. 181; Aug. 1848. Catherine M. Greig and George Greig, minors over 14yrs., children of George Greig, dec'd., chose William C. Greig as their guardian.

GREIG –pg. 181; Aug. 1848. William C. Greig of N.Y. asked for guardianship of Harriet M. Greig, a minor under 14yrs.

ERRICKSON –pg. 181; Aug. 1848. Samuel Conover asked for guardianship of Matilda C. Errickson, a minor under 14yrs.

KERR –pg. 187; Aug. 1848. A statement of accounts was filed by Thomas Kerr as administrator of the estate of David Kerr, dec'd., who was administrator of the estate of Sarah Roberts, late Sarah Kerr, dec'd., and also of the estate of Margaret Stopes, late Margaret Kerr, dec'd. Note: two separate entries on the same page.

ANTONIDES –pg. 193; Sept. 1848. For the benefit of his wards, Amzi C. McLean petitioned for a division of the land belonging to William Antonides, dec'd. Amzi C. McLean was the guardian of Elizabeth Antonides and Charles Antonides. His wards, along with John Antonides and William Antonides, two other minors and heirs of William Antonides, dec'd., owned as tenants in common a dwelling house and farm where Gordon Sanford then lived. The four children were entitled to 1/4 share each. Notice had been served on Gertrude Sanford, late Gertrude Antonides, guardian of John Antonides and William Antonides, and on her husband, Gordon Sanford.

CHAMBERS –pg. 203; Nov. 1848. John Chambers petitioned for a division of the real estate owned by James Chambers, dec'd., who died intestate owning land in Freehold, Jackson, and Millstone Townships. The real estate was held by his heirs as tenants-in-common.
Entitled to 1/9 share each: John Chambers, the petitioner; Phebe Stevens, wife of John Stevens; Joseph Chambers; Hannah Moore; and Margaret Reynolds, wife of Enoch Reynolds.
Children of Job Chambers, dec'd., entitled to 1/54 share each: James Chambers; Ezekial Chambers; Robert Chambers; Job Chambers, under 21yrs.; Jane Chambers, under 21yrs.; and Sarah Chambers, under 21yrs.
Children of Solomon Chambers, dec'd., entitled to 1/81 share each: Caleb Chambers; Ann Chambers; Augustus Chambers; George Chambers; Margaret Chambers; Maria Chambers; Emley Chambers; Louisa Chambers; and Rachel Chambers, under 21yrs.
Children of Abby Gravat, dec'd., late Abby Chambers, entitled to 1/27 share each: Jane Gravat; Edith Gravat, under 21yrs.; and Julia Gravat, under 21yrs.
Child of Sarah Headly, dec'd., late Sarah Chambers, entitled to 1/9 share: Mary Headly, under 21yrs.

ROGERS –pg. 214; Nov. 1848. Jacob A. Oakerson and his wife, Mary Jane Oakerson, late Mary

Jane Rogers, applied for division of the real estate belonging to Daniel Rogers, dec'd., who died intestate leaving eleven children.
Children of Daniel Rogers, dec'd.: Mary Jane Oakerson, late Mary Jane Rogers, wife of Jacob A. Oakerson; John Rogers; Adaline Lyons, late Adaline Rogers, wife of Adam C. Lyons; Margaret Rogers; Rebecca Rogers, under 21yrs.; Jesse Rogers; Lydia Rogers, under 21yrs.; Forman Rogers, under 21yrs.; Althea Rogers, under 21yrs.; Elvira Rogers, under 21yrs.; and Asenath Rogers, under 21yrs.

JOHNSON –pg. 216; Nov. 1848. Joseph Johnson, a minor over 14yrs., son of Joseph Johnson, dec'd., chose Elijah Walling as his guardian.

JOHNSON –pg. 217; Nov. 1848. William H. Johnson requested guardianship of Alfred M. Johnson, James H. Johnson, and Johannah M. Johnson, minors under 14yrs.

BROWER –pg. 217; Nov. 1848. Deborah T. Brower, mother of Jacob Brower and Gilbert Henry Brower, minors under 14yrs., asked to be appointed their guardian.

HUGHES –pg. 244; Feb. 1849. Elias Hughes requested a division of the real estate owned by Mary Hughes, dec'd., late of Allentown, who died intestate.
Children and heirs entitled to 1/12 share each: Elias Hughes, the petitioner; Joseph Hughes; Aaron Hughes; John Hughes; James P. Hughes; Henry Hughes; Enoch Hughes; Elizabeth Horner, late Elizabeth Hughes; Margaret Knowles, late Margaret Hughes; Ann Nutt, late Ann Hughes; Maria Borden, late Maria Hughes.
Children of Sarah Norton, dec'd., late Sarah Hughes, entitled to 1/12 share total: Elizabeth Norton and Lydia Norton.

DEBOW –pg. 247; Feb. 1849. Richard DeBow, a minor over 14yrs., son of Richard DeBow, dec'd., chose Richard I. Francis as his guardian.

PERRINE –pg. 247; Feb. 1849. Mary Matilda Perrine, a minor over 14yrs., dau. of John Perrine, dec'd., chose Robert E. Craig as her guardian.

BROWN –pg. 247; Feb. 1849. William W. Brown, a minor over 14yrs., son of Gilbert Brown, dec'd., chose Samuel C. Morris as his guardian.

TILTON –pg. 248; Feb. 1849. Mary Tilton, mother of Alpheus Tilton, Martha Tilton, Adelaid Tilton, and Olivia Tilton, minors under 14yrs., asked to be guardian of her children.

PERRINE –pg. 248; Feb. 1849. Robert E. Craig requested guardianship of Catharine Henry Perrine, a minor under 14yrs.

LARISON –pg. 248; Feb. 1849. Rebecca Ann Larison, mother of Emeline Larison and William Henry Larison, minors under 14yrs., asked to be their guardian.

SOPER –pg. 255; March 1849. Stephen C. Rulon and his wife, Lydia, late Lydia Collins, petitioned for a division of the real estate owned by Hezekiah Soper, dec'd., who died intestate. The heirs were his children and grandchildren.
Children, entitled to 1/9 share each: Anthony Soper; Harriet Cambern, wife of William Cambern; Mary Letts, wife of James Letts; and Eliza Bowker, now widow, formerly wife of William Bowker, dec'd.
Grandchildren who were children of his son James Soper, dec'd., entitled to 1/9 share total: Hannah Soper, DeWitt Clinton Soper, Charles Soper, and Selah O. Soper.
Grandchildren who were children of his dau. Kesiah Thomas, dec'd., late wife of Benjamin Thomas, entitled to 1/9 share total: Mary Thomas, Jane Thomas, Naomi Thomas, and Harriet Thomas.
Grandchildren who were children of his son Charles Soper, dec'd., entitled to 1/9 share total: Mary Ann Soper, Hezekiah Soper, and Edward Soper.
Grandchildren who were children of his dau. Rachel Collins, dec'd., late wife of Eli Collins, entitled to 1/9 share total: Charles Collins, Thomas E. Collins, Eliza Collins, Maria Collins, and Lydia Rulon, late Lydia Collins, wife of Stephen C. Rulon.
Grandchildren who were children of his dau. Nancy Rulon, dec'd., late wife of petitioner Stephen C. Rulon, entitled to 1/9 share total: Elmira Rulon, Emeline Rulon, Roxana Rulon, and Stephen D. Rulon.

ANTONIDES –pg. 257; March 1849. Richard Davis asked to be appointed guardian of William Antonides and John Antonides, minors under 14yrs.

BRUERE –pg. 259; April 1849. Napoleon B. Bruere and Joseph B. Bruere, minors over 14yrs., son of John H. Bruere, dec'd., chose John Bruere as their guardian.

PERRRINE –pg. 259; April 1849. Alfred Perrine, a minor over 14yrs., son of William I. Perrine, dec'd., chose William W. Furman as his guardian.

LINDSAY –pg. 268; May 1849. Maria Lindsay petitioned for a division of the land owned by George Harper, dec'd. George Harper, dec'd., devised his estate to his widow, and after her death, to his brothers and sisters as tenants-in-common. Siblings and heirs of George Harper, dec'd. were identified.
His sister, entitled to 1/4 share: Maria Lindsay.
Daughter of his deceased sister Ann Harper, entitled to 1/4 share: Maria H. Watres.
Daughter his deceased sister Sarah Harper, entitled to 1/4 share: Mary Ann Craig, wife of Thomas H. Craig.
Children of his deceased brother Charles A. Harper, entitled to 1/4 share total: Mary J. Bridges, wife of William C. Bridges; Caroline English, wife of Charles English; Harriet Harvey, wife of Henry D. Harvey; Anna Smith, wife of Hancock Smith; Ellen Watters, wife of William T. Watters; Elizabeth W. Harper; Henry I. Harper; Charles A. Harper; and Virginia Harper, under 21yrs.

REYNOLDS –pg. 272; May 1849. Mary Reynolds, late Mary Williams, wife of Israel Reynolds, petitioned for a division of the real estate that belonged to Daniel Williams, dec'd. Daniel Williams died intestate owning land in Howell township.
Heirs of Daniel Williams, dec'd., entitled to 1/9 share each: Mary Reynolds, wife of Israel Reynolds; Rebecca Williams; Thomas Williams; Catherine Williams; Josephine Williams; Lucinda Williams; Daniel Williams; Ann Williams; and William H. Williams. Only Mary Reynolds was over 21yrs. of age.

CLEMENTS –pg. 273; May 1849. William Clements petitioned for a division of the land belonging to John Clements, dec'd., who died intestate.
Entitled to 1/3 share each: William Clements, John D. Forman, and Isaac Clements who was under 21yrs. of age.

BUCKELEW –pg. 274; May 1849. John P. Buckelew, Andrew L. Buckelew, and Enoch D. Buckelew, all sons of Sarah Buckelew, dec'd., and minors over 14yrs., chose Andrew Perrine as their guardian. Note: three separate entries on the same page.

TALLMAN –pg. 274; May 1849. Cordelia M. Tallman, a minor over 14yrs., dau. of William Tallman Jr., dec'd., chose George T. Brown as her guardian.

TALLMAN –pg. 275; May 1849. Mary E. Tallman, a minor over 14yrs., dau. of William Tallman Jr., dec'd., chose George T. Brown as her guardian.

SEAMAN –pg. 275; May 1849. Hannah Seaman asked for guardianship of her children William W. Seaman, Susan L. Seaman, Jane Ann Seaman, and Jeremiah C. Seaman, minors under 14yrs.

CLAYTON –pg. 284; May 1849. Lydia Osborn (late Lydia Clayton), Isaac Osborn, Didamah Osborn (late Didamah Clayton), and John Osborn petitioned for a division of the real estate belonging to John Clayton, dec'd., who died intestate owning land in Dover Tshp. The heirs of John Clayton, dec'd., were identified by shares.
Entitled to 1/13 share each: Lydia Osborn, wife of Isaac Osborn, petitioners; Didamah Osborn, wife of John Osborn, petitioners; Rebecca Tilton, wife of Jacob Tilton; Cornelius Clayton; Sarah Pierce, wife of Elisha Pierce; David Clayton; John Clayton; George Clayton; Deborah Ann Gant, wife of Ezek Gant; Joseph Clayton; Rachel Leming, wife of Isaiah Leming; Hannah Britton, wife of William Britton.
Children of Catherine Mount, a deceased dau. of John Clayton, dec'd., entitled to 1/91 share each: Ann Fish, late Ann Mount, wife of James Fish; Rebecca Butler, late Rebecca Mount, wife of James Butler; Zachariah Mount; Elizabeth Mount; David Bloomfield Mount; Joseph Mount; and William Mount. All of Catherine's children were under 21yrs. except Zachariah Mount.

ROGERS –pg. 296; Aug. 1849. Althea E. Rogers, Forman D. Rogers, and Rebecca Ann Rogers, minors over 14yrs. and children of Daniel Rogers, dec'd., selected Azenath Rogers as their guardian. Note: three separate entries on the same page.

DANSER –pg. 297; Aug. 1849. Elias J. Danser, a minor over 14yrs., chose David C. Danser as his guardian.

ROGERS –pg. 297; Aug. 1849. Azenath Rogers asked for appointment as guardian of her children Elvira C. Rogers and Azenath O. Rogers, minors under 14yrs.

SHEBLY –pg. 307; Aug. 1849. A settlement of accounts was filed by James L. Wilson and Peter Davidson who were administrators of the estate of Deborah Ely, late D. Shebly, dec'd.

POLIN –pg. 320; Nov. 1849. Cornelia Ann Polin, a minor over 14yrs., dau. of Richard Polin, dec'd., chose Andrew Pette as her guardian.

ROBBINS –pg. 320; Nov. 1849. John B. Robbins asked to be appointed guardian of Sarah Jane Robbins and William Henry Robbins, minors under 14yrs.

FIELDS –pg. 329; Nov. 1849. Brittian Fields applied for a division of the real estate owned by John Fields, dec'd. The heirs of John Fields were identified by share.
Entitled to 1/10 share: Brittian Fields; Mary Campbell, late Mary Fields, wife of William Campbell; Catherine Clayton, late Catherine Fields, wife of Joel Clayton; Deborah Cook, late Deborah Fields, wife of Allen Cook; Margaret Wilson, late Margaret Fields, wife of Edward Wilson; Edmund Fields; and Jacob Fields.
Anthony Dennis was entitled to 1/10 by right of deceased wife Hannah Dennis, late Hannah Fields. After his death, his shares would pass to Anna Margaret Dennis and Lora Dennis, children of his late wife, Hannah Dennis, dec'd.
Abigail Fields and William Albert Fields shared 1/10 share under conditions: Under the will of James Fields, Abigail Fields was due 1/10 share during her widowhood, and on her death or at the end of her widowhood, her 1/10 share passed to William Albert Fields.
Entitled to 1/30 share each: John Fields, Caroline Fields, and Edwa Fields who were all minors.

CHAMBERLAIN –pg. 332; Nov. 1849. Order to discharge of any liabilities John Hall, executor of the estate of Aaron Chamberlain, dec'd., on his passing over money of said estate. Mary Chamberlain of Hamilton Co., Ohio, guardian of Cornelia Chamberlain, a minor living in Hamilton Co., Ohio, had applied to receive the money owed her ward from the estate of Aaron Chamberlain, dec'd.

COLLINS –pg. 338; Nov. 1849. Ezekiel C. Cramner and his wife, Theresa, late Theresa Collins, guardians to Job Collins and Ann Eliza Collins, filed settlements of their accounts. Note: two separate entries on the same page.

PERRINE –pg. 338; Nov. 1849. A settlement of accounts was filed by James Bearmore and Hannah Bearmore, late Hannah Perrine, administrators of estate of Benjamin Perrine, dec'd.

GREEN –pg. 340; Nov. 1849. Charles H. Green, Elevyn S. Green, and Lois C. Green, minors over 14yrs., children of James and Elizabeth Green, requested their father, James Green, be appointed their guardian.

GREEN –pg. 341; Nov. 1849. James Green requested guardianship of his children Walter S. Green, Hannah Elizabeth Green, and James Oscar Green, minors under 14yrs.

HOFFMIRE –pg. 343; Jan. 1850. Distribution of the estate of James Hoffmire, dec'd., revealed he died intestate and left no widow or children. His heirs were his siblings and their children.
Siblings: William Hoffmire; Richard Salter Hoffmire; and Mary Banks, late Mary Hoffmire, wife of Bartholomew Banks.
Children of his deceased brother Jacob Hoffmire, dec'd.: James Hoffmire, John B. Hoffmire, Samuel E. Hoffmire, William B. Hoffmire, and George E. Hoffmire.

CHAMBERS –pg. 344; Jan. 1850. Thomas Bedell of Clay Co., Indiana was guardian to Isabella Oliver Bedell, Job Bedell, and Thomas Jefferson Bedell, all minors in Clay Co., Indiana and heirs of Job Chambers. Charles Allen, administrator of the estate of James Chambers, dec'd., was ordered to pay to Thomas Bedell the amount due to said minors from the estate of James Chambers, dec'd., who was the father of Job Chambers.

VANDERVEER –pg. 345 - 352; Jan. 1850. John Vanderveer of Manalapan Tshp. declared his brother Henry Vanderveer of Marlborough Tshp. had, for the past 20yrs., been deprived of reasoning and unable to manage his affairs. He asked the court to declare Henry mentally incompetent. Henry Vanderveer was entitled to 1/12 share of the property previously owned

by David G. Vanderveer, dec'd. Henry was about 33yrs. old with no lawful issue.
Siblings of Henry Vanderveer: Eliza VanDorn, wife of Peter VanDorn, aged about 47yrs.;
Garret D. Vanderveer, aged about 45yrs.; Phebe Ann Vanderveer, aged about 43yrs.; Sarah
Jane Lefferson, wife of Joseph Lefferson, aged about 43yrs.; Joseph D. Vanderveer, aged
about 41yrs.; Tunis D. Vanderveer, aged about 39yrs.; Benjamin D. Vanderveer, aged about
37yrs.; Sophia Hebart, wife of Addison N. Hebart, aged about 31yrs.; John Vanderveer, aged
about 27yrs.; Margaret Vanderveer, aged about 25yrs.; and Catherine Amanda Quackenbush,
wife of Isaac Quackenbush, aged about 21yrs.

JOHNSON –pg. 363 –364; Feb. 1850. Elijah Walling applied for a division of the real estate owned
by Joseph Johnson, dec'd., who died intestate owning 36 acres of land in Middletown Tshp.
The land was held as tenants in common by heirs: Mary Ann Walling, late Mary Ann
Johnson, wife of Elijah Walling; Stephen Johnson; William H. Johnson; John Johnson;
Lucinda Walling, late Lucinda Johnson, wife of John Walling; Joseph Johnson, under 21yrs.;
Alfred Johnson, under 21yrs.; James Johnson, under 21yrs.; and Johanna Johnson, under
21yrs. Note: See Book N, pg. 21, Nov. 1850.

GORDEN –pg. 368; Feb. 1850. Mary Matilda Gorden, a minor over 14yrs., dau. of John E. Gorden,
dec'd., chose John M. Brair as her guardian.

ELLIOT – pg. 368; Feb. 1850. Holmes Elliot, a minor over 14yrs., son of Robert Elliot, dec'd.,
asked that Johnathan C. Raner be appointed his guardian.

HOLMES –pg. 371-372; Feb. 1850. Peter S. Conover, executor of the estate of Catherine Holmes,
dec'd., was ordered to pay the rightful share of the minors Huldah H. Hubbard, Harmanies B.
Hubbard, Maria S. Hubbard, and Ida E. Hubbard, legatees of Catherine Holmes, dec'd., to
their guardian Ida Hubbard of Brooklyn, Kings Co., N.Y. The children resided in Brooklyn.

BROWN –pg. 386; May 1850. Elizabeth Brown, mother and guardian of Ellen Ann Brown, James
Lewis Brown, Mary Emily Brown, Ann Elizabeth Brown, and Margaret Brown, all children
of Thomas Brown, dec'd., must sell property now owned by her children to support the
children. Note: In the first paragraph of the record, Margaret Brown's name was omitted, but
appeared later when the names of Thomas Brown's children were repeated.

FORSYTH –pg. 390; May 1850. Emma Agustus Forsyth, a minor over 14yrs., dau. of William R.
Forsyth, dec'd., chose her mother, Helen Forsyth, as her guardian.

COOPER –pg. 390; May 1850. Alfred Cooper, a minor over 14yrs., chose Miles Cooper as his
guardian.

FORSYTH –pg. 390-391; May 1850. Helen Forsyth asked to be appointed guardian of Mary
Elizabeth Forsyth, Ellen S. Forsyth, Samuel Forsyth, William R. Forsyth, and Adelaide
Forsyth, minors under 14yrs.

BROWN –pg. 391; May 1850. Elizabeth Brown asked to be appointed guardian of Ellen Ann
Brown, James Lewis Brown, Mary Emily Brown, Margaret Brown, and Elizabeth Brown,
minors under 14yrs.

McDOWELL –pg. 400; May 1850. Distribution of the estate of David McDowell, dec'd., revealed
he died intestate leaving neither wife nor children. His heirs were his siblings and their
children.
Siblings, entitled to 1/5 share each: John McDowell, Marie McDowell, Helen McDowell, and
Jane McDowell.
Children of his brother James McDowell, dec'd., entitled to 1/10 share each: John McDowell
and Walter Lawrence McDowell.

SMITH –pg. 413; Aug. 1850. Samuel D. Smith, a minor over 14yrs., son of Samuel Smith, dec'd.,
elected William M. McChesney as his guardian.

LIPPINCOTT –pg. 414; Aug. 1850. Ann B. Lippincott and Edmund C. Lippincott, minors over
14yrs., children of David Lippincott, dec'd., chose their mother, Mary Lippincott, as their
guardian. Note: two separate entries on the same page.

LIPPINCOTT –pg. 415; Aug. 1850. Abigail P. Lippincott, a minor over 14yrs., dau. of David
Lippincott, dec'd., chose her mother, Mary Lippincott, as her guardian.

ELY –pg. 415; Aug. 1850. Mary Ellenor Ely, a minor over 14yrs., child of Joshua A. Ely, dec'd., of Monmouth Co., chose Thomas Ely of Middlesex Co. as her guardian.

LIPPINCOTT –pg. 415; Aug. 1850. Mary Lippincott requested appointment as guardian of her children William F. Lippincott, David C. Lippincott, and Mary E. Lippincott, minors under 14yrs.

ELY –pg. 415; Aug. 1850. Thomas Ely of Middlesex Co. asked appointment as guardian of Joshua Ely and Allison Ely, minors under 14yrs., children of Joshua A. Ely, dec'd.

LAYTON –pg. 419; Aug. 1850. Hannah Layton, widow of Henry Layton, dec'd., asked for assignment of her dower.
Children of Henry Layton, dec'd.: James Layton; Francis Borden, late Francis Layton, wife of Amos Borden; Nathaniel Layton; and Henry Layton.

BOOK N

1850 – 1854

ROBBINS –pg. 4; Sept. 1850. Mary Ann Robbins, a minor over 14yrs., dau. of George Robbins, dec'd., chose her mother, Charlotte Ann Robbins, as her guardian.

JOHNSON –pg. 10; Nov. 1850. Aaron Johnson applied for a division of the real estate owned by Samuel Johnson, dec'd., who died intestate leaving children, grandchildren, and great grandchildren as heirs.
Children entitled to 1/7 share each: Aaron Johnson; Joseph Johnson; Ellenor Cliver, wife of Samuel Cliver; Phoebe Assy, wife of Isaac Assy; and John Johnson.
Grandchildren who were children of his son Amos Johnson, dec'd., entitled to 1/49 share each: Richard Johnson; William A. Johnson; Hendrick Johnson; Ann Hancock, wife of Stewart Hancock; Susan Lincoln, wife of Samuel Lincoln; and Emma Gibbs, wife of Amos Gibbs.
Grandchildren who were children of his dau. Mary Sager, dec'd., entitled to 1/35 share each: Caleb Sager; Ellenor Sager, wife of John Sager; Elizabeth Warren, wife of Joseph Warren; and Mary Sager.
Great grandchildren who were children of Louisa Carr, dec'd., late wife of James Carr and deceased dau. of Amos Johnson, dec'd., entitled to 1/245 share each: William Carr, Burroughs Carr, Amos Carr, James Carr, and John A. Carr.
Great grandchildren who were children of Ann Caulkite, dec'd., late wife of Joseph Caulkite and deceased dau. of Mary Sager, dec'd., entitled to 1/105 share each: Sarah Caulkite, Samuel Caulkite, Joanna Caulkite. Note: the last paragraph of this petition contradicts the first part by stating Sarah, Samuel, and Joanna Caulkite were children of Amos Caulkite, son of Mary Sager, dec'd.

JOHNSON –pg. 17; Nov. 1850. Elmira West requested a division of the real estate owned by William Johnson, dec'd.
Entitled to 2/3 share: Elmira West, by law and will of William Johnson, dec'd.
Children of Peter G. West were entitled to 1/9 share each: Caroline West, under 21yrs.; Alice West, under 21yrs.; and John West, under 21yrs.

JOHNSON –pg. 21 – 22; Nov. 1850. A report on the sale of the real estate belonging to Joseph Johnson, dec'd., stated that Maria Johnson, widow of Joseph Johnson, dec'd., relinquished her right to dower in lieu of cash. Note: See Book M, pg. 363, Feb. 1850.

POLING –pg. 22; Nov. 1850. William Poling, a minor over 14yrs., son of Elihu Poling, dec'd., requested Daniel Scott be appointed his guardian.

BILLS –pg. 22; Nov. 1850. Mary Bills and Samuel Bills, minors over 14yrs., requested James Bills be appointed their guardian. Note: two separate entries on the same page.

CROXSON –pg. 23; Nov. 1850. Elizabeth S. Croxson requested appointment as guardian of William H. Croxson, Mary Croxson, and Samuel Croxson, all minors under 14yrs.

DENNIS –pg. 24; Nov. 1850. Anthony Dennis asked to be appointed guardian of Anna Margaret Dennis and Laura Dennis, both minors under 14yrs.

LEMING –pg. 35 – 36; Feb. 1851. Peter Tilton requested a division of the real estate owned by William Leming, dec'd., who died intestate leaving seven children plus the heirs-at-law of four of his children who predeceased him.
Children of William Leming, dec'd.: William Leming; Idah Leming, now wife of William Bearmore; Job Leming; Isaac Leming; Jane Leming, now wife of Peter Tilton; Deliverance Leming, now wife of Joseph Flood; and John Leming.
Grandchildren who were children of his dau. Anna Leming, dec'd., late wife of Maxson

Brand: Joel Brand, William Brand, Richard H. Brand, Margaretta Brand, Rebecca Brand, Taylor Brand, and Idah Brand.

Grandchildren who were children of his son Jacob Leming, dec'd.: David Leming, William Leming, Charlotte Leming, Freeman Leming, Isaac Leming, Jacob Leming, Abraham Leming, and Washington Leming.

Grandchildren who were children of his dau. Mary Leming, dec'd., late wife of Jonathan Brown: Rebecca Brown, Idah Brown, Morris Brown, Rachel Brown, William Brown, Mariah Brown, Jonathan Brown, Deborah Brown, and Allen Brown.

Grandchildren who were children of his dau. Rebecca Ann Leming, dec'd., late wife of Peter Tilton: John Tilton and William Tilton.

MORTON –pg. 52 – 53; Feb. 1851. Thomas Morton, a minor over 14yrs., son of Theophilus Morton, dec'd., requested Clark Newman be appointed his guardian.

PERRINE –pg. 53; Feb. 1851. Edwin A. Perrine and Margaret E. C. Perrine, minors over 14yrs., children of David Perrine, dec'd., requested David C. Perrine be appointed their guardian. Note: two separate entries on the same page.

VANCLIEF –pg. 54; Feb. 1851. Jane Ann VanClief and Tunis VanClief, minors over 14yrs., children of William I. VanClief, dec'd., elected Jane VanClief for their guardian. Note: two separate entries on same page.

VANCLIEF –pg. 56; Feb. 1851. Jane VanClief requested appointment as guardian of her children Cornelius W. VanClief and Elizabeth VanClief, minors under 14yrs.

SCHENCK –pg. 56; Feb. 1851. Sarah Ann Schenck requested appointment as guardian of her children Sarah Elizabeth Schenck, De Lafayett T. Schenck, Daniel I. Schenck, and Ann Schenck, minors under 14yrs. Note: Daniel's and Ann's names appeared in the petition title, but not in the body of the petition.

HOWLAND –pg. 56; Feb. 1851. John Howland asked to be appointed guardian of his son George Howland, a minor under 14yrs.

BURROWS –pg. 74; May 1851. Thomas Burrows and Joseph T. Burrows, minors over 14yrs., sons of Richard C. Burrows, dec'd., requested Mary Burrows be appointed their guardian. Note: two separate entries on the same page.

TILTON –pg. 75; May 1851. John E. Tilton and William Tilton, minors over 14yrs., sons of Peter Tilton, dec'd., asked that Peter Tilton be appointed their guardian. Note: two separate entries on the same page.

BURROWS –pg. 75 – 76; May 1851. Mary Burrows requested guardianship of her son Edward T. Burrows, a minor under 14yrs., son of Richard C. Burrows.

SLOCUM –pg. 76; May 1851. Mary Slocum requested guardianship of her children Augustus Slocum and Emma Slocum, minors under 14yrs. of age. Note: See Book N, pg. 104, Sept. 1851.

BRINLEY –pg. 76; May 1851. Maria Brinley requested guardianship of her children Howard Brinley, Hannah Brinley, and Jane Brinley, minors under 14yrs. Note: A record in Book N, pg. 402, Sept. 1854, provided a middle initial for one child—Howard A. Brinley.

TUNIS –pg. 77 – 78; May 1851. John B. Tunis requested a division of the real estate owned by Abraham Tunis, dec'd. The property was held as tenants in common by the following people: John B. Tunis, the petitioner; Elizabeth Wyckoff, late Elizabeth Tunis, wife of Holmes Wyckoff; Adaline Tunis; Lawvelle (in later records spelled Lawrette) Tunis; Charles Tunis; and Henry Tunis who was under 21yrs.

BRINLEY –pg. 78 – 79; May 1851. Henry R. Brinley and others petitioned for a division of the real estate belonging to Henry R. Brinley, dec'd. [In the record's heading the middle initial "R" was inserted in the deceased's name with a caret; however, subsequent references to him did not use the middle initial.]

Entitled to 1/6 share each: Henry R. Brinley, Rachel Flimin, Mary Ann Brinley, Deborah Brinley, and John W. Brinley.

Grandchildren, all under 21yrs., who were children of his son James Brinley, dec'd., entitled to 1/18 share each: Howard Brinley, Jane Brinley, and Hannah Brinley.

POLAND –pg. 81 – 82; May 1851. Cornelius Poland applied for a division of the real estate owned by Peter B. Poland, dec'd., who died intestate leaving eight children.
Children: John Poland; Sarah Ann Brown, wife of Daniel Brown; Allen Poland; William Poland; Cornelius Poland; Catherine Halloway, wife of John Halloway; Mary Louisa Poland; and Barnes B. Poland, under 21yrs.

LAYTON –pg. 83 - 87; May 1851. Application of Hannah Layton, widow of Henry Layton, for assignment of her dower. Notice was served on the children and devisees of Henry Layton, dec'd., identified as follows: James Layton; Francis Borden, late Francis Layton, wife of Amos Borden; Nathaniel Layton; and Henry Layton.

WALLING –pg. 101 – 102; Sept. 1851. Richard D. Walling applied for a division of the real estate owned by Daniel Walling, dec'd., who died intestate. Heirs were children and grandchildren of Daniel Walling, dec'd.
Children: Richard D. Walling; Elizabeth Walling; George D. Walling; Gersham D. Walling; and Adaline Wilson, late Adaline Walling, wife of James L. Wilson.
Grandchildren who were children of his son John D. Walling, dec'd.: Sarah Rider, late Sarah Walling, wife of Henry Rider; Eleanor Bedle, late Eleanor Walling, wife of Leonard Bedle; Elizabeth Holmes, late Elizabeth Walling, wife of Asher Holmes; and Jonathan Walling.
Grandchildren who were children of his son Leonard Walling, dec'd.: George Washington Walling; Theresa Walling; Jacob A. Walling; Leonard Walling; and Adaline Walling, under 21yrs.
Grandchild who was the child of his son Daniel D. Walling, dec'd.: George Wilson Walling.

SLOCUM –pg. 104; Sept. 1851. Mary Slocum, guardian of Agustus F. Slocum and Emma L. Slocum, reported on the sale of her wards' property. Note: See Book N, pg. 76, May 1851.

HOLMES –pg. 104 – 106; Sept. 1851. Garret P. Conover and his wife, Sarah H. Conover, requested a division of the real estate owned by John W. Holmes, dec'd.
Entitled to 1/2 share: Sarah Holmes.
Entitled to 1/16 share each: Sarah H. Conover, wife of Garret P. Conover; Ellen VanBrunt, wife of Nicholas VanBrunt; Mary Bergen, wife of Garret Bergen; Margaret Conover, wife of Peter P. Conover; James Hubbard; John H. Hubbard; and Asher B. Hubbard.
Entitled to 1/64 share each: Huldah Hubbard, a minor under 21yrs.; Hannanns Hubbard, a minor under 21yrs.; Marie Hubbard, a minor under 21yrs.; and Elizabeth Hubbard, a minor under 21yrs.

BROWN –pg. 129; Sept. 1851. A settlement of accounts was filed on the estate of Daniel Brown, dec'd. by the administrators, Daniel Rouze and Elizabeth Rouze, late Elizabeth Brown.

ROBBINS –pg. 130 – 131; Sept. 1851. Settlements of accounts were filed by Samuel C. Dunham and Angeline Dunham, late Angeline Robbins, as guardians of Clayton Robbins, Charles S. Robbins, Sarah Heyers, late Sarah Robbins, and Maria K. Messinger, late Maria Robbins.

FIELDS –pg. 132 – 133; Sept. 1851. Britton Fields, Margaret Fields, Jacob White Jr., Eliza A. White, and John Kelly placed a caveat against the last will and testament of William Kelly, dec'd., claiming he was not of sound mind, and the will was not duly executed. The will of William Kelly, dec'd., was not allowed to enter probate.

HIGGINS –pg. 135 – 136; Oct. 1851. Caveat by Morris Higgins against the last will and testament of Ellen Higgins, dec'd. Evidence included an article of separation between Ellen Higgins and her husband Morris Higgins, and the will of Ellen Higgins, dec'd. The court decreed she was of sound mind when she wrote her will and she had a perfect right to make and execute her will. The will was allowed to stand and enter probate.

FROST –pg. 147; Dec. 1851. William M. Taylor and his wife, Lydia Ann Taylor, late Lydia Ann Frost, requested her guardian, Joseph Frost, render an account of Lydia Ann's estate.

APPLEGATE –pg. 151; Dec. 1851. Gilbert Applegate, a minor over 14yrs., son of John W. Applegate, asked that his father be appointed his guardian.

APPLEGATE –pg. 151; Dec. 1851. John W. Applegate requested appointment as guardian of his children Ann Eliza Applegate and Sarah Applegate, both minors under 14yrs.

HAIGHT –pg. 161; Dec. 1851. Ann Haight and Charles Haight, minors over 14yrs., children of Thomas G. Haight, dec'd., requested William Haight be appointed their guardian. Note: two separate entries on the same page.

HAIGHT –pg. 162; Dec. 1851. William Haight was appointed guardian of Furonian Haight, John T. Haight, Elizabeth Haight, and Sarah Haight, minors under 14yrs., all children of Thomas G. Haight, dec'd.

HOLMES –pg. 165 – 171; Dec. 1851. Louisa Vanderveer of Raritan Tshp. petitioned the court to declare her son Nathaniel Weed Holmes mentally incompetent. He had been deprived of reasoning since infancy. Nathaniel owned no real estate, but was entitled to about $1400.00 bequeathed to him by his grandmother and held by N. Weed of N.Y. His nearest heirs were his brother Jonathan Jarvis Holmes, 24yrs. old, and his mother, Louisa Vanderveer.

VANCLEAF –pg. 183 – 184; April 1852. John VanCleaf applied for a division of the real estate owned by Daniel VanCleaf, dec'd., who died intestate owning land near Middletown Point in Raritan Tshp.
Widow: Mary VanCleaf, now Mary Smith wife of William Smith.
Children: Catherine Walling, wife of Thomas Walling; John VanCleaf, the petitioner; William VanCleaf; Maria VanPelt, wife of Alexander VanPelt; Septimus Steven VanCleaf, under 21yrs.; Elizabeth Ann VanCleaf, under 21yrs.; James VanCleaf, under 21yrs.; and Hannah Jane VanCleaf, under 21yrs.

HAYS –pg. 184; April 1852. William Hays, a minor over 14yrs., son of William Hays, dec'd., elected Gordon Sanford as his guardian.

BRUER –pg. 185; April 1852. George W. Bruer, a minor over 14yrs., child of Stephen H. Bruer, dec'd., requested Stephen H. Bruer be appointed his guardian.

DRUMMOND –pg. 185; April 1852. Jane Elizabeth Drummond, a minor over 14yrs., requested Bloomfield Drummond be appointed her guardian.

TILTON –pg. 185; April 1852. George Tilton, a minor over 14yrs., elected Lydia Tilton as his guardian.

TILTON –pg. 186; April 1852. Lydia Tilton requested guardianship of her children John Tilton and Edmund Tilton, minors under 14yrs.

ELY –pg. 186; April 1852. George A. Ely requested guardianship of his son George A. Ely, a minor under 14yrs.

HOFFMAN –pg. 186 – 187; April 1852. Elizabeth Hoffman requested guardianship of her son Polhemus DeBow Hoffman, a minor under 14yrs.

HAVENS –pg. 187; April 1852. Elizabeth Margaret Havens requested guardianship of her children Mary Ellen Havens, Judson Havens, and Sarah Elizabeth Havens, minors under 14yrs.

HAMPTON –pg. 187; April 1852. Julia Hampton requested guardianship of her son Robert F. Hampton, a minor under 14yrs.

GREEN –pg. 187; April 1852. John Green requested guardianship of his children William Green, Ann Green, and Conover Green, all minors under 14yrs.

PATTERSON –pg. 188 – 189; April 1852. Jacob Conover, guardian of John Jacob TenBrook Patterson, requested division of the 50 acres of land the minor owned on the south side of the road from Middletown to Highlands of Navesink. He held it as tenants in common with John M. Stout and Abraham Stout, heirs of James F. Stout, dec'd., who were both minors under the guardianship of Richard W. Stout. John Jacob TenBrook Patterson was entitled to one half. John M. Stout and Abraham Stout, together, were entitled to the other half. Note: See Book N, pg. 193, April 1852.

UPDIKE –pg. 192 - 193; April 1852. Record noted exception to the accounts of David H. Schenck, guardian of Emeline Updike, late Emeline Hutchinson, wife of Lewis I. Updike, and other children of Clark Hutchinson, dec'd. Maria Hutchinson, widow, was mentioned.

STOUT –pg. 193; April 1852. Rachel Stout, widow of James F. Stout, dec'd., requested assignment of her dower. Note: See Book N, pg. 188 – 189, April 1852.

LAYTON –pg. 203 - 204; April 1852. Joseph H. Smith and his wife, Julia, late Julia Layton, applied for a division of real estate located in Middletown Tshp. and described in a deed from Job Layton and wife, and James Layton and wife to Elizabeth Layton and others dated Feb. 4, 1823.

Entitled to 2/10 share: Joseph H. Smith, the petitioner, by virtue of purchase from Martina Layton and Deborah Patterson, late Deborah Layton, wife of John M. Patterson.

Entitled to 1/10 share each: Julia Smith, wife of Joseph H. Smith, petitioner; Elizabeth Dayton, late Elizabeth Layton, wife of Cyrus Dayton; Hannah McDougal, late Hannah Layton, wife of Joseph McDougal; Anthony Layton; Andrew Layton; and Noah Layton.

Entitled to 1/10 share total: The heirs of Thomas Layton, dec'd., all minors under 21yrs.

Entitled to 1/10 share total: The heirs of Isaac Layton, dec'd.

NEWMAN –pg. 208; Sept. 1852. Application of Jeremiah Newman to set off the dower of Abigail Newman, widow of Abbot Newman, dec'd., who died intestate owning property near Shark River, Wall Tshp. and leaving a widow and several children. His land was sold, for payment of debts, to William Allgor who then sold it to the petitioner.

WHITE –pg. 217; Sept. 1852. Amy White, a minor over 14yrs., dau. of William White, dec'd., requested Benjamin W. Corlies be appointed her guardian.

WHITE –pg. 218; Sept. 1852. Phebe White and Clarence White, minors over 14yrs., children of William White, dec'd., chose Benjamin W. Corlies as their guardian. Note: two separate entries on the same page.

CURTIS –pg. 218; Sept. 1852. Eliza Jane Curtis, a minor over 14yrs., requested her mother, Prudence Curtis, be appointed her guardian.

CURTIS –pg. 219; Sept. 1852. Christiana Curtis, a minor over 14yrs., requested her mother, Prudence Curtis, be appointed her guardian.

STILLWELL –pg. 219; Sept. 1852. Ann Stillwell, a minor over 14yrs., dau. of Elisha Stillwell, dec'd., requested Archibald Antonides be appointed her guardian.

VANKIRK –pg. 220; Sept. 1852. John D. VanKirk, a minor over 14yrs., chose his mother, Elizabeth VanKirk, as his guardian.

WILLIAMS –pg. 220; Sept. 1852. Martha Williams requested guardianship of her children Charles E. Williams and Daniel Williams, minors under 14yrs.

HAMPTON –pg. 220; Sept. 1852. James Hampton requested guardianship of his son Richard Hampton, a minor under 14yrs.

LITTLE –pg. 221; Sept. 1852. Arthur W. Little requested guardianship of Joseph D. Little, a minor under 14yrs., son of Thomas Little, dec'd.

LITTLE –pg. 221; Sept. 1852. Theodosia D. Little requested guardianship of her dau. Sarah A. Little, a minor under 14yrs.

CONOVER –pg. 225; Sept. 1852. Edward T. Hopping and John J. Hopping applied for the assignment of the dower of Hannah Conover, widow of Daniel G. Conover, dec'd. Petitioners had purchased the property from the heirs.

BRINLEY –pg. 243; Dec. 1852. A sale of property belonging to James Brinley, dec'd., identified his widow as Maria Brinley.

STILWELL –pg. 243; Dec. 1852. David F. Stilwell, a minor over 14yrs., son of George W. Stilwell, chose George W. Stilwell as his guardian.

STILWELL –pg. 244; Dec. 1852. Anna Theodosia Stilwell, a minor over 14yrs., dau. of George W. Stilwell, requested George W. Stilwell be appointed her guardian..

MARTIN –pg. 244; Dec. 1852. Hannah Martin and Deborah Martin, minors over 14yrs., daus. of Jesse Martin, asked that Jesse Martin be appointed their guardian. Note: two separate entries on the same page.

PATTERSON –pg. 245: Dec. 1852. William Patterson, a minor over 14yrs., son of William

Patterson, requested Robert Allen as his guardian.

HOFF –pg. 245; Dec. 1852. John V. Hoff, a minor over 14yrs., child of Thomas T. Hoff, requested Jeremiah Hoff as his guardian.

STILWELL –pg. 246; Dec. 1852. George W. Stilwell requested guardianship of Mary Elenor Stilwell, Joseph H. Stilwell, and Charles Stilwell, minors under 14yrs.

HUFFMAN –pg. 248; Dec. 1852. Daniel Stephens, Mary A. Stephens, Henry P. Huffman, John W. Thomas, William Hill, Rebecca Hill, and Elizabeth Huffman (as guardian of Polhemus D. Huffman) requested a division of the real estate they inherited from John Huffman, dec'd. Entitled to 1/5 share each: Mary A. Stephens, Henry P. Huffman, John W. Thomas, Rebecca Hill, and Polhemus D. Huffman.

GRAVATS –pg. 255; Dec. 1852. Enoch Reynolds applied for a division of the real estate owned by Elizabeth Gravats, dec'd., who died intestate owning land in Millstone Tshp.
Entitled to 1/6 share each: Enoch Reynolds; Mary Ann VanClief, late Mary Ann Smith, wife of Levi VanClief; Hiram B. Reynolds; Abraham Gravats; and Charity Hall, late Charity Gravats, wife of Edward Hall. Abraham Gravats had conveyed his share to Ezekiel Thomas. Entitled to 1/6 share total or 1/24 share each: Mary E. Thomas, William Henry Thomas, Rachel Thomas, and Maria Thomas. All four were under 21yrs. old.
Note: On pg. 323, Sept. 1853, Enoch Reynolds was referred to as Enoch D. Reynolds.

BURTIS –pg. 267; March 1853. Lucy Ann Burtis requested guardianship of her children Zilpha Ann Burtis, Louisa A. Burtis, and Sarah L. Burtis, minors under 14yrs.

LLOYD –pg. 267; March 1853. James Lloyd, a minor over 14yrs., son of Zera Curtis Lloyd, requested William R. Maps as his guardian.

SUTPHEN –pg. 272; April 1853. John V. Sutphen petitioned for a division of the land belonging to William D. Sutphen, dec'd., who died intestate leaving children and grandchildren.
Children: Thomas T. Sutphen; Maria Conover, wife of Charles Conover; Richard Sutphen; Lydia Meyers, wife of Amos Meyers; Ann Reid, wife of Charles Reid; and John V. Sutphen. Grandchildren, all under 21yrs., who were children of his dau. Elizabeth Havens, dec'd., late wife of Charles Havens: Milford Havens, Amos Havens, and Holmes Havens.

MORRIS –pg. 278; April 1853. Edwin L. Rogers and his wife, Deborah Ann Rogers, requested a division of the real estate in Ocean Tshp. owned by Benjamin Morris, dec'd., who died intestate leaving children and grandchildren.
Children: Deborah Ann Rogers, wife of Edwin L. Rogers; William Morris; Benjamin Morris; Rebecca White, wife of Jesse White Jr.; Mary Elizabeth Hathaway, wife of Isaac Hathaway; George H. Morris; John L. Morris; and Hannah P. VanPelt, wife of Winard VanPelt. Grandchildren who were children of his dau. Catherine Mitten, dec'd., late wife of Garret Mitten, dec'd.: James F. Mitten and Ezekiel Mitten.

WARDELL –pg. 278 1/2; April 1853. Eliza L. Wardell, a minor over 14yrs., dau. of Henry Wardell, dec'd., requested Elizabeth Wardell as her guardian.

WARDELL –pg. 279; April 1853. Jacob H. Wardell, a minor over 14yrs., son of Henry Wardell, dec'd., requested Elizabeth Wardell be appointed his guardian.

MITTEN –pg. 279; April 1853. Obediah L. Mitten, a minor over 14yrs., son of Ezekiel C. Mitten, dec'd., requested Pecci Mitten as his guardian. Note: Pecci was referred to as a female.

MITTEN –pg. 280; April 1853. Ann Martha Mitten, a minor over 14yrs., dau. of Ezekiel C. Mitten, dec'd., requested Pecci Mitten as her guardian.

APPLEGATE –pg. 280; April 1853. Henry Applegate, a minor over 14yrs., son of Reuben Applegate, dec'd., requested Pearson Hendrickson be appointed his guardian.

APPLEGATE –pg. 281; April 1853. Eli Applegate and Mary E. Applegate, minors over 14yrs., children of Reuben Applegate, dec'd., chose Pearson Hendrickson as their guardian. Note: two separate entries on the same page.

JEMISON –pg. 282; April 1853. Martin V. Jemison, a minor over 14yrs., son of Jacob J. Jemison, dec'd., requested the appointment of Abel R. Taylor as his guardian.

HURLEY –pg. 282; April 1853. John Hurley, a minor over 14yrs., son of Lewis Hurley, elected
    Lewis Hurley as his guardian.

LONGSTREET –pg. 283; April 1853. William M. Longstreet requested guardianship of Cornelius
    B. Longstreet, a minor under 14yrs.

WARDELL –pg. 283; April 1853. Elizabeth Wardell requested guardianship of her dau. Josephine
    D. Wardell, a minor under 14yrs.

APPLEGATE –pg. 284; April 1853. Pearson Hendrickson requested appointment as guardian to
    Sarah Applegate, Daniel Applegate, and Reuben Applegate, children of Reuben Applegate,
    dec'd., all minors under 14yrs.

BROWN –pg. 284; April 1853. Jeremiah Brown of Kings Co., N.Y. requested guardianship of
    Jeremiah Brown and Robert Brown, minors under 14yrs., children of Anthony Brown, dec'd.

HURLEY –pg. 285; April 1853. Lewis Hurley requested guardianship of Sarah Ann Hurley, a
    minor under 14yrs.

PRICE –pg. 285; April 1853. Mary Price requested guardianship of her children Elizabeth Price,
    Caroline Price, Agnes Price, and Hartsanna Price, minors under 14yrs., children of Hartshorne
    Price, dec'd.

MASON –pg. 306; Sept. 1853. John Mason requested a division of the 10 acres of land owned by
    Phoebe Mason, dec'd.
    Entitled to 1/4 share each: John Mason, the petitioner; Wesley Mason, under 21yrs.; Thomas
    Mason, under 21yrs.; and Adaline Polin, late Adaline Mason, wife of William Polin.

MORRIS –pg. 315; Sept. 1853. Caroline Morris, a minor over 14yrs., dau. of Charles Morris,
    dec'd., chose James Seely as her guardian.

VANDORN –pg. 315; Sept. 1853. Jonathan C. Vandorn, a minor over 14yrs., son of Luther H.
    Vandorn, dec'd., chose Luther H. Vandorn as his guardian.

BRINLEY –pg. 316; Sept. 1853. Rebecca Brinley, a minor over 14yrs., dau. of Henry R. Brinley,
    dec'd., selected her mother, Jane Brinley, as her guardian.

SMITH –pg. 317; Sept. 1853. Elizabeth Smith requested guardianship of her son William C. Smith,
    a minor under 14yrs., son of John R. Smith, dec'd.

BRINLEY –pg. 318; Sept. 1853. Jane Brinley requested guardianship of her children Emily Brinley,
    George H. Brinley, Walter Brinley, Mary Jane Brinley, and Loiza A. Brinley, all minors
    under 14yrs. and children of Henry R. Brinley, dec'd.

WILLIAMS –pg. 318; Sept. 1853. Thomas T. Williams requested guardianship of Charles E.
    Williams, Daniel Williams, and Mary D. Williams, all minors under 14yrs.

WILLIAMS –pg. 319; Sept. 1853. Martha S. Williams stated that on Sept. 11, 1852 guardianship of
    Charles E. Williams and Daniel Williams, minors under 14yrs., children of herself and Israel
    Williams, dec'd., was granted to her. After her husband's death, a third child, Mary D.
    Williams, was born. She requested release from the bonds of guardianship, and asked that
    Thomas T. Williams be appointed guardian of her children.

SMITH –pg. 328 - 330; Sept. 1853. William Hathaway and wife, Jane, late Jane Smith, petitioned
    for a division of lands owned by Lewis Smith, dec'd., late of Brooklyn, N.Y., who died about
    Dec. 1852 leaving a will that disposed of his Monmouth County real estate.
    Children of Lewis Smith, dec'd.: Hannah R. Smith, William B. Smith, and Jane Hathaway,
    the petitioner.
    Children of Jane Hathaway, petitioner: Benjamin Hathaway; John C. Hathaway; William
    Hathaway; Eliza Hathaway, under 21yrs.; Mary Hathaway, under 21yrs.; and Anna
    Hathaway, under 21 yrs. Note: See Book N, pg. 434, Dec. 1854.

STOUT –pg. 339; Sept. 1853. Marti Brown, guardian of Caroline Stout, late Caroline Rogers, filed
    a settlement of accounts.

NEWMAN –pg. 356; Dec. 1853. Ann Newman, widow of John S. Newman, dec'd., petitioned for assignment of her dower.

GARDNER –pg. 382; April 1854. Ann Gardner, a minor over 14yrs., dau. of Richard Gardner, elected James S. Lawrence as her guardian.

MELVIN –pg. 382; April 1854. George Melvin, a minor over 14yrs., son of George Melvin of Scotland, requested John N. Disbrow of Monmouth Co., N.J. as his guardian.

STOUT –pg. 383; April 1854. Tenbrook Stout and John C. Stout, minors over 14yrs., chose Elijah Stout as their guardian. Note: two separate entries on the same page.

VANDERVEER –pg. 383; April 1854. Abraham T. Vanderveer asked to be appointed guardian of his dau. Mary Elizabeth Vanderveer, a minor under 14yrs. whose mother was deceased.

STOUT –pg. 384; April 1854. Elijah Stout requested appointment as guardian of his children James C. Stout, Julia C. Stout, and Edward G. Stout, all minors under 14yrs. Their mother was deceased.

SCHENCK –pg. 406; Sept. 1854. Sarah C. Schenck, a minor over 14yrs., asked that Eleanor Schenck be appointed her guardian.

CONOVER –pg. 407; Sept. 1854. Charlotte Conover, a minor over 14yrs., selected Elizabeth Conover as her guardian.

HAIGHT –pg. 408; Sept. 1854. Eliza Ann Haight requested guardianship her children John T. Haight and Sarah Haight, minors under 14yrs.

PARKER –pg. 408; Sept. 1854. Catherine Havens requested guardianship of her dau. Hester Parker, a minor under 14yrs.

CONOVER –pg. 408; Sept. 1854. Elizabeth Conover asked for appointment as guardian of her children Cornelia Conover, Julia Conover, and Sydney Conover, minors under 14yrs.

BEDLE –pg. 416 - 417; Sept. 1854. Thomas Stout applied for a division of the real estate owned by Elizabeth Bedle, dec'd., who died intestate leaving several heirs.
Siblings entitled to 1/12 share each: Mary Vanderbelt; James Bedle; Catherine Hendrickson, wife of Daniel D. Hendrickson; Joseph Bedle; and Lydia Burrows.
Child of her sister Nancy Dye, dec'd., entitled to 1/12 share: Catherine Dye.
Children of her sister Martha Stout, dec'd., entitled to 1/13 of 1/12 share each: Richard B. Stout, Thomas B. Stout, Elijah Stout, Joel Stout, Garret Stout, Sarah Ann Sproul, Maria Stout, and Lucy Stout, wife of Peter Stout.
Children of Douglas Stout, dec'd., a son of her sister Martha Stout, dec'd., entitled to 1/2 of 1/13 of 1/12 share each: Elmira Stout and Charles Stout.
Children of Joseph Stout, dec'd., a son of her sister Martha Stout, dec'd., entitled to 1/3 of 1/13 of 1/12 share each: John W. Stout, William W. Stout, and James Stout.
Children of John Stout, dec'd., a son of her sister Martha Stout, dec'd., entitled to 1/3 of 1/13 of 1/12 share each: Maria Stephens, Elijah B. Stout, and Desire Storms, wife of John G. Storms.
Children of Catherine Stricker, dec'd., a dau. of her sister Martha Stout, dec'd., entitled to 1/6 of 1/13 of 1/12 share each: Susan P. Stricker, David Stricker, Daniel Stricker Jr., Maria Stricker, James Stricker, and Elizabeth H. Stricker. Susan, David, Daniel, and Elizabeth were under 21yrs. of age.
Children of Elizabeth Walling, dec'd., a dau. of her sister Martha Stout, dec'd., entitled to 1/3 of 1/13 of 1/12 share each: Matilda Walling, Eusibius Walling, and Alfred Walling Jr. All three under 21yrs. of age.
Children of Sarah Stout, dec'd., each entitled to 1/3 of 1/12 share: Peter Stout; Thomas Stout, the petitioner; and Ann Crawford, wife of Stephen J. Crawford. Relationship of Sarah Stout, dec'd., not specified in document, but share allotment was for a sibling.
Children of her brother Richard Bedle, dec'd., entitled to 1/7 of 1/12 share each: Hendrick Bedle, Jeremiah Bedle, Daniel Bedle, Timothy Bedle, Sarah Bedle, Edith Bedle, and Lydia Bedle, wife of John A. Bedle.
Children of her brother Joel Bedle, dec'd., entitled to 1/4 of 1/12 share each: Thomas J. Bedle, Maria Green, and Ann Eliza Arrowsmith, wife of Thomas H. Arrowsmith.
Children of Amy Shepherd, dec'd., a dau. of her bro. Joel Bedle, dec'd., entitled to 1/2 of 1/4 of 1/12 share each: Thomas Edgar Shepherd and Louisa Warters, wife of David Warters.
Children of her brother Thomas Bedle, dec'd., entitled to 1/10 of 1/12 share each: Mary Hoff;

William Bedle; Richard Bedle; Leonard Bedle; James Bedle; Elizabeth Vandine, wife of
William Vandine; Susan Wharton, wife of George S. Wharton; Ann VanBrackle; and Elmira
Holmes, wife of Daniel W. Holmes.
Children of Sarah Carhart, dec'd., a dau. of her bro. Thomas Bedle, dec'd., entitled to 1/4 of
1/10 of 1/12 share each: Timothy Carhart, Samuel Carhart Jr., Joel Carhart Jr., and Emiline
Carhart. Joel and Emiline were under 21yrs. of age.
Children of her brother Elijah Bedle, entitled to 1/5 of 1/12 share each: Mary Collins, wife of
Asher Collins; Phiatta Hoff; Amy Johnson, wife of Gilbert Johnson; Aaron Bedle; and Louisa
Stoney, wife of Stephen Stoney. Elijah Bedle was not noted as deceased although the share
allotment indicated he was.

PARKER –pg. 429; Dec. 1854. Jacob C. Parker requested a division of the real estate that belonged
     to Michael Parker, dec'd.
     Entitled to 1/6 share each: Jacob C. Parker, the petitioner; Josiah Parker; Samuel Parker;
     William Parker; and Robert W. Parker.
     Entitled to 1/24 share each: Ann Amanda Hammond and her three children who were all
     under 21yrs. of age, viz., Samuel P. Hammond, Jane Hammond, and George Hammond.

HAVENS –pg. 431; Dec. 1854. Charles Havens requested guardianship of his children Milford S.
     Havens, Amos M. Havens, and William W. Havens, minors under 14yrs.

HOFF –pg. 431; Dec. 1854. Pheatta Hoff requested guardianship of her children Lucy Ann Hoff
     and Aaron Hoff, minors under 14yrs.

SMITH –pg. 434 – 437; Dec. 1854. A report on a sale of the property owned by Lewis Smith,
     dec'd., stated, his heir William B. Smith died around Feb. 7, 1854, leaving Robert E. Smith as
     a devisee of his will. Note: See Book N, pg. 328, Sept. 1853.

ROLPH –pg. 438 – 445; Dec. 1854. Richard A. Sickles petitioned the court to declare Hannah
     Rolph of Shrewsbury Tshp. mentally incompetent. She had been deprived of reason for two
     months. Hannah was about 55yrs. old, never married, and had no children. Her nearest heir
     was her brother Joseph Rolph who was about 60yrs. old.

BOOK O
1854 – 1857

LECOMPTE –pg. 27; April 1855. John Lecompte petitioned for a division of the real estate owned
by William Lecompte, dec'd., who died intestate owning real estate in Howell Tshp. and
leaving children and grandchildren.
Children: Rachel Grant, wife of William Grant; Mary Parker, widow of Esek Parker, dec'd.;
Hannah Layton, wife of David L. Layton; John Lecompte, petitioner; Sarah Ann Lecompte;
Phebe Stiles, wife of John Stiles; William Lecompte; George Lecompte; and Garret I.
Lecompte.
Grandchildren who were children of his son Joseph Lecompte, dec'd.: Mary Hannah
Lecompte, William Henry Lecompte, and Elizabeth Lecompte. All the grandchildren were
under 21yrs. of age.

BENT –pg. 29; April 1855. James Bray petitioned for a division of the real estate owned by Rachel
Bent, dec'd., who died intestate owning real estate in the village of Middletown Point in
Raritan Tshp.
Entitled to 1/4 share each: Ann Murphy, wife of Francis Murphy; Samuel O. Bray; and Laura
Bell, wife of George Bell.
Entitled to 1/4 share total: James Bray; David W. Bray; Joseph W. Bray; Charles D. Bray;
Ann E. Bray; Rachel Bray, under 21yrs.; Mary C. Bray, under 21yrs.; and Cordelia Bray,
under 21yrs.

FIELDS –pg. 30; April 1855. Theodore Fields, a minor over 14yrs., chose Thomas S. Fields as his
guardian.

JOHNSON –pg. 31; April 1855. Thomas S. Fields petitioned for the guardianship of James N.
Johnson and Jacob S. Johnson, minors under 14yrs., children of James Johnson, dec'd.

STIERS –pg. 31; April 1855. Thomas S. Fields requested guardianship of Mary Eliza Stiers, a
minor under 14yrs., dau. of Thomas Stiers, dec'd.

GRANT –pg. 32; April 1855. Jacob W. Morris requested guardianship of Noah Grant, Rhoda Grant,
William Grant, Hannah Grant, and Catherine Grant, minors under 14yrs., children of John
Grant, dec'd.

VANPELT –pg. 37; April 1855. Alexander VanPelt petitioned for a division of the real estate in
Raritan Tshp. owned by Alexander VanPelt, dec'd. His heirs held the land as tenants in
common.
Entitled to 1/14 share each: Catherine Lecor, wife of John Lecor; Samuel VanPelt; Mary Jane
VanCleaf, wife of William VanCleaf; John VanPelt; Thomas VanPelt; and Alexander
VanPelt.
Children of his dau. Ann VanCleaf, dec'd., late wife of the said William VanCleaf, entitled to
1/14 share total: Joseph VanCleaf and Sarah VanCleaf.
Heirs of John VanPelt, dec'd., entitled to 1/2 share total: William VanPelt; John I. VanPelt;
Catherine Smith, wife of Holmes Smith; Walter VanPelt; David VanPelt; Elijah VanPelt;
Ellen Walling, wife of Stephen Walling; Joel VanPelt; Nancy VanPelt; Jane VanPelt; and
Alexander VanPelt, the petitioner.

WIKOFF –pg. 39; April 1855. The final distribution of the estate of Joshua B. Wikoff, dec'd.,
revealed he died unwed and intestate, leaving his siblings and their children as his heirs.
Siblings: William G. Wikoff, Henry Wikoff, Garret Wikoff, John F. Wikoff, and Ezekiel
Wikoff.
Children of his sister Ann Denise, dec'd.: Alice Buck, wife of Henry Buck; Mary Buck, wife
of Sylvester Buck; Catherine Dubois, wife of John Dubois; and Sarah Ann Baird, wife of John
Baird.

Children of Jane Maria Buck, dec'd., who was a dau. of his sister Ann Denise, dec'd.: James
Monroe Buck and David Buck.
Child of his brother Samuel Wikoff, dec'd.: Jacob Wikoff.

WEST –pg. 42; April 1855. Daniel West petitioned for a division of the real estate in Shrewsbury
Tshp., now Ocean Tshp., that Benjamin West, dec'd., bequeathed in his will, dated Jan. 28,
1829, to his son James West. Upon James' death, which had occurred, the property passed to
the heirs of said James West.
Children of James West, dec'd.: Deborah Ann Williams, wife of James Williams; Matilda
Woolley, wife of Charles Woolley; Sarah Huver, wife of William Huver; Daniel West, the
petitioner; Nicholas West, under 21yrs.; Elisha West, under 21yrs.; Abner West, under 21yrs.;
Ann E. West, under 21yrs.; James B. West, under 21yrs.; George E. West, under 21yrs.; and
Theodore West, under 21yrs.

CARMAN –pg. 52; Sept. 1855. Sarah Ann Jenings petitioned for a division of the real estate held
by Eden B. Carman, dec'd., who died intestate owning about 115 acres in Middletown Tshp.
Entitled to 1/6 share each: Sarah Ann Jenings, the petitioner; Joseph Carman; and Eleanor
Carman, under 21yrs.
Entitled to 1/4 share each: Caroline D. Garham, wife of William R. Garham; and Charles
Martin.

SHAFTO –pg. 59 – 62; Sept. 1855. Distribution of the estate of Robert Shafto Sr., dec'd., revealed
he died intestate leaving seven children, no widow, and none of his children had died and left
children.
Children: John Shafto; Robert R. Shafto; Jane White, late Jane Shafto, wife of Peter White;
William C. Shafto; George W. Shafto; Samuel G. Shafto; and Thomas Shafto.

FORMAN –pg. 62 - 63; Sept. 1855. Final distribution of the estate of John B. Forman, dec'd.,
identified his heirs by shares.
Entitled to 1/3 share each: Mary Ann Forman; Jonathan Forman; and Eliza F. Randolph, late
Eliza Forman, wife of Bennington F. Randolph. Only Eliza Randolph was specifically
identified as his daughter.

WILBUR –pg. 66; Sept. 1855. A settlement of accounts was filed for the estate of Wesley Wilbur,
dec'd.
Widow: Sarah A. Burtis, late Sarah A. Wilbur who since married Richard W. Burtis.
Sons and only children: Howard Wilbur, Emley Wilbur, and Wesley Wilbur.

HONCE –pg. 70 – 80; Sept. 1855. The children of David Honce of Marlboro Tshp. petitioned the
court to declare their father mentally incompetent. He had been without reason for a year.
Children of David Honce: Jane Prest, 56yrs. old, wife of William Prest of Ontario, Wayne
Co., N.Y.; Alice Cottrell, 54yrs. old, wife of James Cottrell of South Amboy, Middlesex Co.,
N.J.; Elizabeth Tilton, 39yrs. old, wife of William Tilton of Atlantic Tshp., Monmouth Co.,
N.J.; Cornelia Robinson, 52yrs. old, wife of Peter Robinson of Middletown, Monmouth Co.,
N.J.; David D. Honce, 47yrs. old, of Marlboro Tshp., Monmouth Co., N.J.; Phebe Ann
VanPelt, 45yrs. old, wife of Henry VanPelt of Raritan Tshp., Monmouth Co., N.J.; and James
Honce, 41yrs. old.

HANCE –pg. 80; Sept. 1855. John Hance and Joseph Hance, minors over 14yrs., elected their
father, Edward Hance, as their guardian. Note: two separate entries on same page.

HANCE –pg. 81; Sept. 1855. Francis Hance, a minor over 14yrs., elected his father, Edward Hance,
as his guardian.

HANCE –pg. 81; Sept. 1855. Edward Hance requested guardianship of Ann Hance and Martha
Hance, minors under 14yrs.

THOMPSON –pg. 83; Sept. 1855. Isaac N. Woodward petitioned for a division of the real estate
owned by John F. Thompson, dec'd., who died intestate leaving children and grandchildren.
Children: Angeline Hamilton, wife of William B. Hamilton; John L. Thompson; Jane Wikoff,
wife of Richard Wikoff; Rosha Thompson; Elizabeth A. Woodward, wife of Isaac N.
Woodward; Alice Woodward, wife of Tilton Woodward; Ellen D. Probasco, wife of Abraham
Probasco; Margaret Burtis, wife of Peter W. Burtis; Mary Woodward, wife of Anthony
Woodward; and Samuel R. Thompson.
Grandchildren who were the children of Luke D. Thompson, dec'd.: not named.

MARKS –pg. 100; Dec. 1855. George Morris petitioned for a division of real estate. He purchased a 3/4 share in some real estate in Middletown Tshp. from the administrator of the estate of Abraham Marks, dec'd. Theodore Agustus Marks and Lydia Francis Marks held the other 1/4 share.

MACKEY –pg. 102 – 109; Dec. 1855. Sarah Mackey of Raritan Tshp. petitioned to have her husband, George Mackey, declared mentally incompetent. He had been without reason for a little over one year, and confined to an asylum for several months. Because there was no hope of curing him, he was discharged around April 10, 1855. George Mackey was declared mentally incompetent.
Children: Peter Mackey, 20yrs. old; George Mackey, 17yrs. old; Frederick Mackey, 13yrs. old; and Malissa Mackey, 11yrs. old.

WEST –pg. 110; Dec. 1855. Nicholas West, Elisha West, and Abner West, minors over 14yrs., sons of James West, dec'd., elected Jordan Woolley as their guardian. Note: three separate entries on the same page.

WEST –pg. 118; Dec. 1855. Jordan Woolley requested guardianship of Ann West, George West, James West, and Theodore West, minors under 14yrs., children of James West, dec'd.

MORRIS –pg. 118; Dec. 1855. Lydia W. Morris requested guardianship of Henry J. Morris, Olevice Morris, and Henrietta Morris, minors under 14yrs., children of William H. Morris, dec'd.

FLINN –pg. 119; Dec. 1855. E. B. Goldtra and his wife, Harriet, late Harriet Flinn who was the mother of Susan A. Flinn and Sarah T. Flinn, minors under 14yrs., children of John W. Flinn, dec'd., requested guardianship of said minors.

SEABROOK –pg. 119; Dec. 1855. Elias Seabrook petitioned for a division of the real estate owned by John Seabrook, dec'd., who died intestate owning real estate in Raritan Tshp.
Children: Stephen Seabrook; Ann Rogers, wife of Josiah B. Rogers; and Elias Seabrook, the petitioner.
Grandchild who was the son of his dau. Mary Clark, dec'd., late Mary Seabrook, late wife of Thomas L. Clark: Thomas Clark, under 21yrs.

WALL –pg. 120; Dec. 1855. Proof of the death of John Wall was found in an order to distribute an estate. Deborah Pintard, dec'd., left a will dated Sept. 2, 1836 that bequeathed a portion of her estate to her nephew John Wall, the son of her brother Dr. Elisha Wall. Upon the death of John Wall, the estate was to be divided between her grandnephew Bloomfield Wall and grandniece Deborah A. Wall. Mary Wall, widow of the said John Wall, declared that Deborah A. Wall and Bloomfield Wall were still living. Her husband, their father, left the states of Pa. and N.J., and she believed he had been dead for more than 20yrs. She had not seen or heard from him in 30yrs. The court accepted her statement as proof of the death of John Wall and ordered the shares allotted to the children.

ALLGOR –pg. 128; Jan. 1856. Elizabeth Allgor requested guardianship of her children Thomas Allgor, William W. Allgor, and David Allgor, minors under 14yrs., children of Cornelius Allgor.

VANDOREN –pg. 128 – 129; Jan. 1856. Rev. Luther Halsey Vandoren was appointed guardian of his wife, Lydia Ann Vandoren.

BRUERE –pg. 129 – 131; Jan. 1856. Distribution of the estate of James Bruere, dec'd., revealed he died intestate leaving no widow, children, parents, or lineal heirs.
Siblings: Jonathan Bruere; and Ruth Sennickson, late Ruth Bruere, wife of Senica Sennickson.
Children of his brother Peter Bruere, dec'd.: John Hankins Bruere and Hannah R. Worth, widow of Josiah S. Worth, dec'd.
Children of his brother John Hornfield Bruere, dec'd.: John Bruere; Stephen H. Bruere; Susan Chamberlain, late Susan Bruere, wife of Abijah Chamberlain; Price Bruere; Ruth Tilton, late Ruth Bruere, wife of William Tilton; Napoleon B. Bruere; Joseph B. Bruere; and George W. Bruere.
Children of his brother Price Bruere, dec'd.: Ruth Ann Bruere, James H. Bruere, Sarah J. Bruere, and Peter H. Bruere.
Children of Price Bruere's dau. Mary Hale, dec'd.: Mary O. Hale and Henry E. Hale. Hannah H. Worth was guardian of the Hale children.

Children of his sister Mary Holmes, dec'd., late Mary Bruere, late wife of Joseph Holmes, dec'd.: Alice Davis, wife of Dr. William Davis; and Joseph Holmes.
Child of Mary Holmes' son James Holmes, dec'd.: Edward S̲. Holmes. Edward's middle initial later given as 'T.'
Children of Mary Holmes' dau. Sarah Bruere, dec'd., late wife of John Hankins Bruere: Peter Bruere and Joseph H. Bruere.

BRUERE –pg. 131 – 133; Jan. 1856. The distribution of the estate of Richard Bruere, dec'd., revealed he left no widow, children, or lineal descendants.
Siblings: Jonathan Bruere; and Ruth Sennickson, late Ruth Bruere, wife of Senica Sennickson.
Children of his brother Peter Bruere, dec'd.: John Hankins Bruere and Hannah R. Worth, widow of Josiah S. Worth, dec'd.
Children of his sister Mary Holmes, dec'd., late Mary Bruere, late wife of Joseph Holmes, dec'd.: Alice Davis, wife of Dr. William Davis; and Joseph Holmes.
Child of Mary Holmes' son James Holmes, dec'd.: Edward T̲. Holmes. Edward's middle initial previously given as 'S.'
Children of Mary Holmes' dau. Sarah Bruere, dec'd., late wife of John Hankins Bruere: Peter Bruere and Joseph H. Bruere.
Children of his brother John H̲orsefield Bruere, dec'd. (middle name previously given as Hornfield): John Bruere; Stephen H. Bruere; Susan Chamberlain, late Susan Bruere, wife of Abijah Chamberlain; Price Bruere; Ruth Tilton, late Ruth Bruere, wife of William Tilton; Napoleon B. Bruere; Joseph B. Bruere; and George W. Bruere.
Children of his brother Price Bruere, dec'd.: Ruth Ann Bruere, James H. Bruere, Sarah J. Bruere, and Peter H. Bruere.
Children of Price Bruere's dau. Mary Hale, dec'd.: Mary O. Hale and Henry E. Hale. Hannah H. Worth was guardian of the Hale children.

HAIGHT –pg. 133; Jan. 1856. The distribution of the estate of William Haight, dec'd., showed he died intestate leaving a widow, Mary W. Haight, and no children. His father, Thomas G. Haight, died several years earlier and his mother, Mrs. Eliza Ann Haight, was still alive. His surviving siblings were Ann Haight, Charles Haight, Trevonian Haight, Sarah Haight, and John Tyler Haight, all under 21yrs. of age, except Ann. His uncle Charles Haight was deceased, as was his sister Elizabeth Haight who died at 8 or 9 years of age.

VANDOREN –pg. 174 – 179; April 1856. James Carnaham of Princeton, Mercer Co., petitioned to have his dau. Lydia Ann VanDoren declared mentally incompetent. She had been deprived of reason for several years, and confined to an asylum for the past 18 months. Hannah M. McDonald, 42yrs. old, wife of William K. McDonald, was her nearest heir. The proceedings were held in Mercer Co., but Monmouth Co. was the legal residence of Lydia Ann VanDoren who was declared mentally incompetent.

BREWER –pg. 180; April 1856. Elizabeth Brewer, a minor over 14yrs., elected Harriet Brewer as her guardian.

LAFETRA –pg. 180; April 1856. Ruth Ann Lafetra, a minor over 14yrs., chose Mary D. Lafetra as her guardian.

LAFETRA –pg. 181; April 1856. Josephine Lafetra and Charles E. Lafetra, minors over 14yrs., chose Mary D. Lafetra as their guardian. Note: two separate entries on the same page.

HONCE –pg. 182; April 1856. Rachel Honce, a minor over 14yrs., elected David Honce as her guardian.

BREWER –pg. 183; April 1856. Harriet Brewer requested guardianship of Mary Brewer, Ellen Brewer, Rachel A. Brewer, and Rebecca Brewer, minors under 14yrs.

WOOLLEY –pg. 183; April 1856. Eliza Jane Woolley requested guardianship of William Edward Woolley, Jane Ann Woolley, Ellen Woolley, Lydia Woolley, and Alfred Woolley, minors under 14yrs.

BUTLER –pg. 184; April 1856. Charles K̲. Butler requested guardianship of Mary Butler and Isabella Butler, minors under 14yrs.

LAFETRA –pg. 184; April 1856. Mary D. Lafetra requested guardianship of Priscilla Lafetra, Caroline Lafetra, and Harriet Lafetra, minors under 14yrs.

ALLGOR –pg. 185; April 1856. Nancy Allgor requested guardianship of Israel Allgor, James Monroe Allgor, Mary E. Allgor, and Sarah Jane Allgor, minors under 14yrs.

COOPER –pg. 185; April 1856. Mary Cooper requested guardianship of Prudence Cooper and Henrietta Cooper, minors under 14yrs.

HOWLAND –pg. 185; April 1856. Hannah Howland requested guardianship of Henry T. Howland, Peter W. Howland, Thomas F. Howland, and Susan Ann Howland, minors under 14yrs.

LAYTON –pg. 186; April 1856. Rebecca Ann Layton requested guardianship of Mary S. Layton, Alice Layton, Charlotte Layton, and Elizabeth Ann Layton, minors under 14yrs.

DOWNS –pg. 186; April 1856. John H. Buck requested guardianship of George Downs and Ephraim Downs, minors under 14yrs.

PEARCE –pg. 190; April 1856. The final distribution of the estate of Abraham Pearce, dec'd., named Alice Pearce, ward of Pitney Curtis, as his only daughter and sole next of kin. His wife predeceased him.

CARMAN –pg. 191; April 1856. Fanny Carman, 60yrs. old, widow of Eden B. Carman, dec'd., agreed to accept cash for her dower.

CLARK –pg. 194; April 1856. Thomas Clark, a minor over 14yrs., son of Thomas S. Clark, elected Thomas S. Clark as his guardian.

ALLEN –pg. 209; Sept. 1856. Joseph F. Allen, son of Richard L. Allen, dec'd., petitioned for a division of his father's real estate in Wall Tshp. He owned the land as tenants in common with Sarah Ann Allen who was under 21yrs. of age. Dower for Charlotte Mount, late Charlotte Allen, widow of Richard L. Allen, dec'd., had been set off. Note: Richard's middle initial was difficult to interpret and appeared to vary within the record.

BROWER –pg. 210; Sept. 1856. Deborah T. Brower, guardian of Gilbert H. Brower and Jacob M. Brower minors who were children of Gilbert Brower, dec'd., petitioned to sell her wards' real estate. Note: The record opened referring to Deborah as Deborah T. Allen, but later identified her as Deborah T. Brower, as do other records.

MORRIS –pg. 211; Sept. 1856. Mary Cook along with Lawrence Earle and his wife, Elizabeth, petitioned for a division of the real estate in Shrewsbury Tshp. owned by Isaac Z. Morris, dec'd.
Entitled to 1/7 share each: Mary Cook; Elizabeth Earle, wife of Lawrence Earle; Harriet Hay, wife of George Hay; Cornelius Morris; Lydia Ann Emmons, wife of Asbury Emmons; and John Morris.
Entitled to 1/9 of 1/7 share each: William H. Morris; Susan Mary Johnson, wife of Peter Johnson; Ann VanCleaf, wife of Garret VanCleaf; Joseph E. Morris; Louisa Morrell, wife of John Morrell; Borden Morris; John Morris; and Jane Morris, a minor under 21yrs. Note: The name of the ninth child was missing in this allotment. A subsequent report, ordering the sale of the real estate, in Book O, pg. 228, Oct. 1856, added the name of George Morris, under 21yrs., to the list of those to receive 1/9 of 1/7 share

MARKS –pg. 216; Sept. 1856. Arintha Smith requested guardianship of Theodore A. Marks and Lydia F. Marks, minors under 14yrs., children of Abraham Marks, dec'd.

JONES –pg. 216; Sept. 1856. William A. Newell requested guardianship of Martha Jones, a minor under 14yrs., child of Daniel C. Jones.

JOHNSON –pg. 217; Sept. 1856. Thomas V. Arrowsmith requested guardianship of Robert Johnson and Mary Johnson, minors under 14yrs., children of John Johnson.

CHESNEY –pg. 217; Sept. 1856. Charles C. M. Chesney requested guardianship of Samuel M. M. Chesney and Charles E. M. Chesney, minors under 14yrs., children of Mary M. Chesney.

THOMPSON –pg. 217; Sept. 1856. Sarah Ann Thompson and John B. Robbins requested guardianship of Winfield S. Thompson, Charles Thompson, Mary Ellen Thompson, and Perrine G. Thompson, minors under 14yrs., children of Samuel Thompson.

JOHNSON –pg. 218; Sept. 1856. Catherine Johnson, a minor over 14yrs., dau. of John Johnson, dec'd., chose Thomas V. Arrowsmith as her guardian.

JONES –pg. 218; Sept. 1856. Anna Elizabeth Jones, a minor over 14yrs., dau. of Daniel C. Jones, dec'd., elected William A. Newell as her guardian.

CONOVER –pg. 229; Oct. 1856. The final distribution of the estate of John C. Conover, dec'd., who died intestate, showed he left a widow, children, and grandchildren.
Widow: Elizabeth Conover.
Children: Mary Schenck, late Mary Conover, wife of Daniel P. Schenck; Simpson Conover; John V. Conover; Charlotte Conover, bet. 14yrs. and 21yrs. of age; Cornelia Conover, about 14yrs. old; Julia Conover, under 14yrs. of age; and Sidney Conover, under 14yrs. of age.
Grandchildren who were children of his dau. Emily Butler, dec'd., late wife of Charles K. Butler: Mary Butler, 3yrs. old; and Isabel Butler, 2yrs. old. Emily Butler, late Emily Conover died about Feb. 14, 1856.

LONGSTREET –pg. 232; Oct. 1856. Final distribution of the estate of intestate William Longstreet dec'd., divided the estate by shares.
Entitled to 1/8 share each: Gilbert S. Reid, in right of his late wife, Catherine, dec'd.; Samuel Longstreet; Margaret Dey, wife of Ezekiel Dey; Caroline Dey, wife of John C. Dey; Archebald C. Longstreet; Aaron R. Longstreet; and John R. Longstreet.
Children of William Longstreet, dec'd., entitled to 1/8 share total: William L. Longstreet and Sarah Longstreet.

CLAYTON –pg. 244; Dec. 1856. Alice Clayton, guardian of Ezekiel D. Clayton, Henry D. Clayton and Jane M. Clayton, petitioned to sell her wards' real estate in Howell Tshp. Alice Clayton was the mother of her wards and the widow of John M. Clayton, dec'd., father of her wards.

BILLS –pg. 245; Dec. 1856. Mary A. Bills, a minor over 14yrs., dau. of David W. Bills, dec'd., chose Washington McKean as her guardian.

BILLS –pg. 246; Dec. 1856. Sarah A. Bills, a minor over 14yrs., dau. of David W. Bills, dec'd., chose Washington McKean as her guardian.

HANKINS –pg. 246; Dec. 1856. William Hankins, a minor over 14yrs., son of Joseph Hankins, dec'd., chose his mother, Emily S. Hankins, as his guardian.

HANKINS –pg. 247; Dec. 1856. Susan L. Hankins, a minor over 14yrs., dau. of Joseph Hankins, dec'd., elected her mother, Emily S. Hankins, as her guardian.

MCMINN –pg. 247; Dec. 1856. William McMinn, a minor over 14yrs., son of Samuel McMinn who had been absent from N.J. for over 2yrs., elected Daniel I. Sanford as his guardian.

BILLS –pg. 247; Dec. 1856. Washington McKean requested guardianship of Francis Bills, Daniel W. Bills, Edward I. Bills, and Emma Bills, minors under 14yrs., children of Daniel W. Bills, dec'd.

HANKINS –pg. 248; Dec. 1856. Emily S. Hankins requested guardianship of her dau. Julia H. S. Hankins, a minor under 14yrs., dau. of Joseph Hankins, dec'd.

MCMINN –pg. 249; Dec. 1856. Daniel I. Sanford requested guardianship of Jane McMinn, a minor under 14yrs., dau. of Samuel McMinn who left the state two years ago.

CLAYTON –pg. 249; Dec. 1856. Alice Clayton petitioned for guardianship of her children Ezekiel D. Clayton, Henry D. Clayton, and Jane M. Clayton, minors under 14yrs.

ELY –pg. 261; Dec. 1856. The final distribution of the estate of intestate Joseph I. Ely, dec'd., identified his heirs.
Mother: Lucy Ely.
Widow: Eliza Ann Ely, guardian of their children who were all under 21yrs. of age.
Children: James Nelson Ely, Mary Lavinia Ely, Charles Herbert Ely, Leasen English Ely, John Atlantic Ely, and Josephine Ely who was born after her father's death and died as an infant.

BRAY –pg. 277; April 1857. Mary Catherine Bray, a minor over 14yrs., chose James Bray as her guardian.

VANCLIEF –pg. 280; April 1857. William VanClief requested guardianship of Joseph Alexander VanClief, a minor under 14yrs.

WINANT –pg. 280; April 1857. Gilbert W. Winant requested guardianship of Sarah Ellen Winant and Mary Eliza Winant, minors under 14yrs.

LONGSTREET –pg. 281; April 1857. Huldah Longstreet requested guardianship of Rhoda H. Longstreet and Lydia Anna Longstreet, minors under 14yrs.

BARR –pg. 281; April 1857. George C. Barr requested guardianship of Georgianna Barr, a minor under 14yrs.

QUACKENBUSH –pg. 295; April 1857. Isaac Quackenbush petitioned for a division of his father's real estate. Isaac Quackenbush, dec'd., his father, died leaving a widow, children, and grandchildren.
Widow: Eleanor Quackenbush.
Children: Mary Johnson, wife of John A. Johnson; Ellen Smith, wife of Joshua Smith; and Isaac Quackenbush, the petitioner.
Grandchild who was the only child of his son Jacob Quackenbush, dec'd.: Jacob Quackenbush, under 21yrs.

LIPPINCOTT –pg. 317; Sept. 1857. James M. Lippincott, a minor over 14yrs., elected his mother, Rachel Lippincott, as his guardian.

MAPS –pg. 318; Sept. 1857. Deborah Maps, a minor over 14yrs., dau. of Charles Maps, dec'd., chose her mother, Julia A. Maps, as her guardian.

BRINLEY –pg. 318; Sept. 1857. George H. Brinley and Emily Brinley, minors over 14yrs., children of Henry Brinley, dec'd., elected Jordan Woolley as their guardian. Note: two separate entries on same page.

BRINLEY –pg. 319; Sept. 1857. Rebecca Brinley, a minor over 14yrs., dau. of Henry Brinley, dec'd., chose Jordan Woolley as her guardian.

MCDERMOTT –pg. 319; Sept. 1857. Martha H. McDermott, a minor over 14yrs., dau. of William McDermott, dec'd., chose her mother, Esther H. McDermott, as her guardian.

BOOK P

1857 – 1860

MCDERMOTT –pg. 1; Sept. 1857. Mary M. McDermott, a minor over 14yrs., dau. of William McDermott, chose her mother, Esther H. McDermott, as her guardian.

SHERMAN –pg. 1; Sept. 1857. James Sherman, a minor over 14yrs., son of Thomas Sherman, elected his mother, Lucretia Sherman, as his guardian. Note: See Book P, pg. 208, April 1859.

HOPPING –pg. 1; Sept. 1857. Francis Hopping, a minor over 14yrs., son of James Hopping, dec'd., chose Primrose Hopping as his guardian. Note: Primrose Hopping was referred to as a male person.

HOPPING –pg. 2; Sept. 1857. Nancy Hopping, a minor over 14yrs., dau of James Hopping, chose Primrose Hopping as her guardian.

BEERS –pg. 2; Sept. 1857. Elizabeth Beers and William Beers, minors over 14yrs., children of John N. Beers, elected their mother, Huldah Beers, as their guardian. Note: two separate entries on the same page.

BEERS –pg. 3; Sept. 1857. John I. Beers, a minor over 14yrs., son of John N. Beers, chose his mother, Huldah Beers, as his guardian.

BRINLEY –pg. 3; Sept. 1857. Jordan Woolley requested guardianship of Walter Brinley, Mary Jane Brinley, and Lora Agnes Brinley, minors under 14yrs., children of Henry Brinley.

MAPS –pg. 4; Sept. 1857. Julia Maps requested guardianship of her children Julia Maps, Clara Maps, and Michael Howard Maps, minors under 14yrs., children of Charles Maps.

MCDERMOTT –pg. 4; Sept. 1857. Esther Ann McDermott requested guardianship of her children Ellen McDermott and Emily McDermott, minors under 14yrs., children of William McDermott.

SHERMAN –pg. 4; Sept. 1857. Lucretia Sherman requested guardianship of her children John Sherman, Ellenor Jane Sherman, and Thomas Sherman, minors under 14yrs., children of Thomas Sherman. Note: See Book P, pg. 208, April 1859.

BARR –pg. 5; Sept. 1857. George H. Barr requested guardianship of Georgianna Barr, a minor under 14yrs., dau. of George H. Barr.

PARKER –pg. 5; Sept. 1857. James H. Parker petitioned for a division of the real estate owned by Hyde Parker, dec'd., in Shrewsbury Tshp.
Entitled to 1/8 share each: Susan Parker, wife of Hyde Parker; James H. Parker; Lydia B. Parker; Mary Clark, wife of George Clark; Ann Wolcott, wife of Joseph Wolcott; Charles Parker; Deborah L. Keyser, wife of William Keyser.
Entitled to 1/8 share total: Charles Bowne and Amanda Bowne, minors under 21yrs., children of Elizabeth Bowne, dec'd., late wife of Edward Bowne.

MORRIS –pg. 17; Sept. 1857. Lydia W. Morris, guardian of Henry Judson Morris, filed a settlement of accounts.

ELY –pg. 21; Sept. 1857. Final distribution of the estate of intestate Allison Ely, dec'd., identified his mother and siblings who were his only heirs.
Mother: Ann Ely.
Siblings: Achsah Thomas, wife of Peter Thomas; Elizabeth Ann Dey, wife of Lewis Dey;

Mary Ellen Anderson, wife of John Anderson; and Joshua Ely, a minor under 21yrs.

ACKERMAN –pg. 22 – 30; Sept. 1857. Caroline Ackerman of Howell Tshp., widow of Abram
(also given as Abraham) Ackerman, dec'd., who died Feb. 17, 1854, petitioned the court to
have their son Garline Ackerman declared mentally incompetent. Garline was about 26yrs.
old, suffered convulsions at an early age, and had been deprived of reason for the past 20yrs.
Garline was unmarried and lived with his mother. The court decided Garline turned 28yrs.
old on Dec. 4, 1856.
Siblings: George S. Ackerman, 31yrs. old; Elizabeth R. Ackerman, 25yrs. old; and Catherine
A. Ackerman, 14yrs. old.

MAIRS –pg. 31; Sept. 1857. Joseph H. Chapman, guardian of Samuel W. Mairs who was the sole
heir of Samuel Mairs, dec'd., requested the administrators of the estate of Samuel Mairs,
dec'd., turn over the assets due his ward. Note: Book P, pg. 31, Sept. 1857, a guardianship
record gave the ward's full name as Samuel Wykoff Mairs.

MORRIS –pg. 37; Dec. 1857. Jacob H. Morris petitioned for a division of the real estate owned by
Charles Morris, dec'd.
Heirs entitled to 1/7 share each: Jacob H. Morris; William L. Morris; Gertrude Stout, wife of
William W. Stout; Catherine Morris; James L. Morris; Mary Morris, under 21yrs.; and
Matilda Morris, under 21yrs.

MORRIS –pg. 38; Dec. 1857. Jacob H. Morris petitioned to have the dower set off from the estate
of Charles Morris, dec'd., for his widow, Ann Eliza Morris. Ann Eliza Morris was specified
as the mother of Mary Morris and Matilda Morris, minors with no legal guardian.

KELLY –pg. 41 - 43; Dec. 1857. Final distribution of the estate of William Kelly, dec'd., identified
his children and grandchildren. Shares allotments in this record were unbalanced.
Children: Peter B. Kelly; Ruth Davison, wife of John E. Davison; William Kelly; George B.
Kelly; John B. Kelly; and Margaret Fields, wife of Britton Fields. Peter, Ruth, William,
George and Margaret sold their shares to James R. Keeler.
Grandchildren who were children of his dau. Sarah Hendren, dec'd., late wife of Michael
Hendren of Virginia: Samuel H. Hendren; Silas Hendren; Virginia Hendren; Henry R.
Henderson (should probably read Hendren); Gertrude Holmes, wife of William I. Holmes;
Margaret Cruser, wife of Cornelius C. Cruser; Sarah J. Simpson or Simpkins, wife of John
Simpson or Simpkins; and Francis Hendren. Both surnames given for Sarah J.
Grandchildren who were children of his dau. Eliza Ann White, dec'd., late wife of Jacob
White, were all deceased prior to her death, leaving her husband as her heir.

LITTLE –pg. 51; Dec. 1857. Theodosia Finch, late Theodosia Little, guardian of Sarah A. Little,
filed a settlement of accounts.

COTTRELL –pg. 52; Dec. 1857. John A. Heiser petitioned for guardianship of Hannah Ann
Cottrell and Angeline Cottrell, minors under 14yrs., children of Alfred C. Cottrell, dec'd.

WYCKOFF –pg. 53; Jan. 1858. Hendrick Wyckoff requested guardianship of Nicholas Wyckoff, a
minor under 14yrs., son of David H. Wyckoff.

BERGEN –pg. 74; April 1858. H. Virginia Bergen and Edward Bergen of Millstone Tshp., minors
over 14yrs., chose their mother, Hannah Bergen, as their guardian. Note: two separate entries
on the same page.

THOMPSON –pg. 75; April 1858. Jackson H. Thompson of Raritan Tshp., a minor over 14yrs.,
chose his mother, Letitia Thompson, as his guardian.

SMITH –pg. 75; April 1858. Ellen V. D. Smith of Manalapan Tshp., a minor over 14yrs., elected
her father, Thomas Smith, as her guardian.

SMITH –pg. 76; April 1858. Lydia M. Smith of Manalapan Tshp., a minor over 14yrs., elected her
father, Thomas Smith, as her guardian.

THOMPSON –pg. 76; April 1858. Letitia Thompson requested guardianship of her son Charles E.
Thompson, a minor under 14yrs., son of Elisha W. Thompson, dec'd.

ACKERMAN –pg. 77; April 1858. Petition notified the court Caroline Ackerman, mother and
guardian of Garline Ackerman, had died. James Craig was appointed his guardian.

WINTER –pg. 77 – 93; April 1858. Joseph Shepherd and his wife, Elizabeth, petitioned the court to declare her sister Ann Winter of Raritan Tshp. mentally incompetent. She had been deprived of reason for four to six months. Her only heirs were her siblings.
Siblings: Samuel Dorn, 52yrs. old; John Dorn, 45yrs. old; Sarah Johnson, wife of Lambert Johnson, 58yrs. old; Catherine Dorn, 54yrs. old; Charity Sweeny, wife of Dennis Sweeny, 50yrs. old; Mary Willet, wife of James Willet, 47yrs. old; and Elizabeth Shepherd, wife of Joseph Shepherd, 43yrs. old.

MURRAY –pg. 104; April 1858. Mary Murray and Martha Murray, minors over 14yrs., chose their mother, Susan Murray, as their guardian.

MIDDLETON –pg. 105 – 115; April 1858. Lydia Tilton of Middletown Tshp. petitioned the court to declare her nephew George Middleton mentally incompetent. George Middleton, about 35yrs. old, son of Gideon and Abigail Middleton, had been deprived of reason for 35yrs. or more. His mother, Abigail Middleton, was the sister of Lydia Tilton, the petitioner. Both of George's parents had been dead for years. Others testified George Middleton lived with his aunts Lydia and Catherine Tilton for many years, and Catherine Tilton was now dead. George Middleton possessed an estate he inherited from Catherine Tilton, dec'd., and from Thomas Tilton, dec'd. Sarah Ann Middleton, 41yrs. old, was his sister and only heir.

HERBERT –pg. 122; May 1858. Mary Louisa Herbert, a minor over 14yrs., chose William Hudson Heyer as her guardian.

HERBERT –pg. 123; May 1858. Obediah C. Herbert requested guardianship of his siblings Evelina E. Herbert and John W. Herbert, minors under 14yrs., children of Conover Herbert, dec'd. Their mother was also deceased. Note: two separate entries on the same page.

HERBERT –pg. 124; May 1858. Obediah C. Herbert requested guardianship of his brother William C. Herbert, a minor under 14yrs., son of Conover Herbert, dec'd. Their mother was also deceased.

BROWN –pg. 124; May 1858. William H. Brown requested guardianship of his children Amelia Brown and Lucretia Brown, minors under 14yrs.

BOWNE –pg. 131; Sept. 1858. Charles P. Bowne, a minor over 14yrs., chose his father, Edward Bowne, as his guardian.

BOWNE –pg. 132; Sept. 1858. Mary A. Bowne, a minor over 14yrs., chose her father, Edward Bowne, as her guardian.

TAYLOR –pg. 132; Sept. 1858. Henry C. Taylor, a minor over 14yrs., chose his brother James J. Taylor as his guardian.

BREWER –pg. 132; Sept. 1858. Mary C. Brewer, a minor over 14yrs., elected her mother, Harriet Brewer, as her guardian.

VANKIRK –pg. 133; Sept. 1858. Sarah C. VanKirk, a minor over 14yrs., chose her mother, Eleanor S. VanKirk, as her guardian.

WHITE –pg. 133; Sept. 1858. Lydia White requested guardianship of her children Deborah A. White, Hubbard White, Catherine White, and Mary White, minors under 14yrs.

VANKIRK –pg. 134; Sept. 1858. Eleanor S. VanKirk requested guardianship of her children Schanck VanKirk and John VanKirk, minors under 14yrs.

NEWMAN –pg. 138; Sept. 1858. Correll Newman petitioned for a division of the real estate owned by John H. Newman, dec'd., who owned property in Wall Tshp.
Entitled to 1/2 share: Correll Newman.
Entitled to 1/4 share each, daus. of Abbot H. Newman, dec'd.: Hannah M. Newman and Sarah E. Newman, minors under 21yrs.

TILTON –pg. 148; Sept. 1858. A settlement of accounts was filed by Garret Stout as guardian of Catherine A. Tilton who was then Catherine A. Grant, wife of Joel Grant.

LANE –pg. 153; Sept. 1858. Phebe Lane requested guardianship of her children Anna A. Lane, Phebe E. Lane, William H. Lane, and Charles E. Lane, minors under 14yrs.

BERGEN –pg. 153; Sept. 1858. John P. Bergen petitioned for a division of the real estate owned by Peter C. Bergen, dec'd.
Entitled to her dower: his widow, Hannah Bergen.
Entitled to 1/11 share each: John P. Bergen; Ann C. Lake, wife of John I. Lake; James A. Bergen; Helen Conover, wife of Joshua S. Conover; Lydia A. Wilson, wife of Anthony A. Wilson; Matilda Perrine, wife of Peter F. Perrine; Emma Smith, wife of William M. Smith; Cornelia Perrine, wife of Matthew Perrine; Hannah Virginia Bergen, under 21yrs.; and Edward Bergen, under 21yrs.
Entitled to 1/22 share each: Lydia M. Smith, under 21yrs.; and Ellen V. D. Smith, under 21yrs. Note: The final distribution of the estate, Book P, pg. 358, April 1860, identified Lydia M. Smith and Ellen V. D. Smith as children of Elizabeth Smith, dec'd., late wife of Thomas Smith.

WINTER –pg. 169; Dec. 1858. Letters of administration to Joseph Shepherd on the estate of Ann Winter, dec'd., were revoked and turned over to Samuel Dorn her oldest brother.

SCHENCK –pg. 170; Dec. 1858. Chrineyonce Schenck and Eleanore Schenck of Holmdel Tshp., minors over 14yrs., elected their mother, Margaret Schenck, as their guardian. Note: two separate entries on the same page.

SCHENCK –pg. 171; Dec. 1858. Margaret Schenck requested guardianship of her dau. Sarah Schenck, a minor under 14yrs.

NEWMAN –pg. 171; Dec. 1858. Correll Newman requested guardianship of his niece Sarah E. Newman, a minor under 14yrs.

WOOLLEY –pg. 178; Dec. 1858. The report on Asher Woolley's petition for a division of the real estate owned by William Woolley, dec'd., named Asher Woolley, William Woolley, William Edward Woolley, and Alfred Woolley as the heirs entitled to shares.

WALLING –pg. 183 – 191; Dec. 1858. Amos Walling of Raritan Tshp. petitioned to have his brother Isaac Walling of Keyport, Raritan Tshp. declared incompetent. Isaac Walling had been addicted to alcohol for six years and it left him deprived of reason. The petition identified his wife and children.
Wife: Mary Walling, 60yrs. old and still living.
Children: Elizabeth Force, 30yrs. old, wife of William Force; Mary Jane Taylor, 28yrs. old, wife of Richard Taylor; William Walling, 26yrs. old; Lydia Wolcott, 24yrs. old, wife of George Wolcott; Isaac Walling Jr., 22yrs. old; Cecilia Walling, 18yrs. old; and Andrew Jackson Walling, 16yrs. old.

PERRINE –pg. 193; Dec. 1858. Lewis Perrine of Millstone Tshp., a minor over 14yrs., elected his mother, Caroline Perrine, as his guardian.

PERRINE –pg. 194; Dec. 1858. Caroline Perrine requested guardianship of her children Albert Perrine and Margaret Ann Perrine, minors under 14yrs. Note: two separate entries on the same page.

HERBERT –pg. 200; April 1859. Gordon D. Herbert and Charles E. Herbert, minors over 14yrs., chose their mother, Abigail Herbert, as their guardian. Note: two separate entries on the same page.

HERBERT –pg. 201; April 1859. David L. Herbert, a minor over 14yrs., chose his mother, Abigail Herbert, as his guardian.

COX –pg. 201; April 1859. Elizabeth E. Cox of Millstone Tshp., a minor over 14yrs., elected her mother, Matilda Cox, as her guardian.

JEMISON –pg. 203; April 1859. Alfred Jemison requested guardianship of his son Alfred J. Jemison, a minor under 14yrs.

SHEARMAN –pg. 208; April 1859. William G. Shearman petitioned for a division of the real estate owned by Samuel Shearman, dec'd., late of Howell Tshp., who died in June of 1856. The real estate was occupied by his widow.
Children: William G. Shearman, Samuel Shearman, John Shearman, and Ellen Shearman.
Grandchildren who were children of his dau., Mary Reynolds, dec'd., late wife of Samuel Reynolds: Mary Cramer, wife of Josiah Cramer; Rebecca Cramer, wife of Eli Cramer; Eliza

Hilliard, wife of David Hilliard; and Samuel Reynolds.
Grandchildren who were children of his son James Shearman, dec'd.: Abraham M. Shearman; James H. Shearman; Hannah Allen, wife of Reily Allen; Sarah Shearman, under 21yrs. of age; William Shearman, under 21yrs. of age; and Thomas Shearman, under 21yrs. of age.
Grandchildren who were children of his son Thomas Shearman, dec'd.: James Shearman, under 21yrs. of age; John Shearman, under 21yrs. of age; Ellen Jane Shearman, under 21yrs. of age; and Thomas Shearman, under 21yrs. of age.

SHEARMAN –pg. 209; April 1859. Reported a name change to the heirs of Samuel Shearman, dec'd. as reported by William G. Shearman. Ellen Shearman, dau. of Samuel Shearman, dec'd., had married Thomas C. Hilliard and was known as Ellen Hilliard.

CROMER –pg. 215 – 216; April 1859. The record was a petition to change the guardians of Sophia Cromer, over 14yrs., and Mary Louisa Cromer, under 14yrs. Current guardians Cornelius Lane, their step-father, and Lucinda Lane, their mother, would shortly move to New York City, and the minors preferred to remain in N.J. Henry Styles was appointed guardian of both children.

WINTER –pg. 228; April 1859. Joseph Winter, a minor over 14yrs., chose his father, Timothy M. Winter, as his guardian.

WINTER –pg. 228; April 1859. Timothy M. Winter requested guardianship of his children Martha Winter and Timothy M. Winter, minors under 14yrs.

PERRINE –pg. 231; April 1859. Joseph Perrine and James R. Laird and his wife, Mary Ann, petitioned for a division of real estate. Enoch Perrine Sr., dec'd., conveyed land to his sons Lewis Perrine and Enoch Perrine Jr., and after their deaths, to their heirs forever. Enoch Perrine Sr. died in 1853. Ann Perrine, widow of Enoch Perrine Sr., was still alive. Enoch Perrine Jr. died intestate about Nov. of 1850, leaving a widow and children, all under 21yrs. Lewis Perrine died in Jan. of 1859 and left a will leaving his estate to his siblings who were then living.
Widow of Enoch Perrine Jr., dec'd.: Caroline Perrine.
Children of Enoch Perrine Jr., dec'd.: Lewis Perrine, Margaret Ann Perrine, and Albert Perrine.
Siblings of Lewis Perrine, dec'd.: Joseph Perrine, petitioner; Rebecca Miller, wife of James P. Miller; Sarah Ely, widow of Joseph Ely, dec'd.; Mary Ann Laird, wife of James R. Laird, petitioner; Hannah Forman, wife of Reevey R. Forman of Mercer Co., N.J.; and Elizabeth Grover, wife of John D. Grover of Middlesex Co., N.J.

FOUNTAIN –pg. 246; Sept. 1859. Theodore Fountain of Matawan Tshp. requested guardianship of his dau. Sarah C. Fountain, a minor under 14yrs.

LAYTON –pg. 246; Sept. 1859. James Hampton requested guardianship of his grandchildren Mary L. Layton, Alice Layton, and Charlotte Layton, minors of Howell Tshp. under 14yrs.

HERBERT –pg. 258; Sept. 1859. Obediah C. Herbert petitioned for a division of the real estate owned by Conover Herbert, dec'd.
Entitled to 1/8 share each: Obediah C. Herbert; Cornelia Hyer, wife of William H. Hyer; David P. Herbert, under 21yrs.; Ella G. Herbert, under 21yrs.; Mary L. Herbert, under 21yrs.; John W. Herbert, under 21yrs.; Evelina E. Herbert, under 21yrs.; and William C. Herbert, under 21yrs.

HARRIS –pg. 261; Sept. 1859. William L. S. Harrison petitioned for a division of real estate in Matawan Tshp. that he owned as tenants in common with several others. The property was divided into 20 shares because some heirs of Amelia Harris, dec'd., sold their shares. All shares were subject to a curtesy for life to widower Jeremiah Harris, late husband of Amelia Harris, dec'd.
Children of Amelia Harris, dec'd., entitled to 1/20 share: Russell Harris, under 21yrs.; Henrietta Harris, under 21yrs.; Maria Louisa Stillwell, wife of John Stillwell; Catherine Chadwick, under 21yrs., wife of Jackson Chadwick.
Entitled to 1/20 share by a deed from Henry S. Little: William L. S. Harrison, petitioner.
Entitled to 15/20 share: Henry S. Little.
Heirs of Amelia Harris, dec'd., who sold their shares to Henry S. Little: Reuben P. Harris; Charles Harris; Henry W. R. Harris; John W. Harris; William S. Harris; and Mary Matilda Wood, wife of William Wood.

FORMAN –pg. 265; Sept. 1859. Sarah Ann Forman and Richard T. Forman of Freehold Tshp., minors over 14yrs., elected their mother, Elizabeth Forman, as their guardian.

FORMAN –pg. 265; Sept. 1859. Elizabeth Forman, guardian of Sarah Ann Forman and Richard T. Forman, only children of Richard T. Forman, petitioned to sell the real estate belonging to her wards.

MACKEY –pg. 268; Sept. 1859. Sarah Mackey of Raritan Tshp. requested guardianship of her dau. Malissa Mackey, a minor under 14yrs.

MACKEY –pg. 268; Sept. 1859. Frederick Mackey, a minor over 14yrs. residing in the state of Conn., petitioned the court in the Waterburg District of New Haven Co., Conn. to appoint Sarah Mackey of Monmouth Co., N.J. his guardian.

LAIRD –pg. 274 – 277; Sept. 1859. Joseph T. Laird and Robert Laird petitioned for a division of their father's real estate. Their father, Samuel Laird, dec'd., late of Colts Neck, died intestate in July of 1859. His wife predeceased him.
Children: Joseph T. Laird; James Laird; Robert Laird; and Mary S. Laird, under 21yrs. Grandchildren, all under 21yrs., who were children of his dau. Sarah W. Bennett, dec'd., late wife of Garret S. Bennett: Jane L. Bennett, Samuel L. Bennett, and Eleanor L. Bennett.

SPROUL –pg. 285; Dec. 1859. James Sproul petitioned for a division of the real estate belonging to his father, Oliver Sproul, dec'd.
Entitled to 1/5 share each: James Sproul, petitioner; Joseph Sproul; Samuel Sproul; and Alice Walling, widow of John D. Walling.
Children of his son John Sproul, dec'd., entitled to 1/5 share total: Edgar Sproul, John Sproul, and Sarah Sproul, under 21yrs.

SPADER –pg. 286; Dec. 1859. William Spader of Marlboro requested guardianship of his dau. Anna Denton Spader, a minor under 14yrs.

HIERS –pg. 293; Dec. 1859. Final distribution of the estate of Garret Hiers, dec'd., late of Middletown Point, who died intestate, showed he left a widow, Mary F. Hiers, and six children. His widow had since died.
Children: Mary F. Abbott, wife of Henry W. Abbott; Susan N. Mulford, wife of Joseph L. Mulford; Henry A. Hiers, a minor; William F. Hiers, a minor; Samuel M. Hiers, a minor; and Louisa Hiers.

HENDRICKSON –pg. 294; Dec. 1859. William B. Hendrickson petitioned for a division of the real estate owned by Daniel D. Hendrickson, dec'd., who left a widow, Catherine Hendrickson, and several heirs.
Entitled to 1/11 share each: William B. Hendrickson, the petitioner; Eliza Applegate, wife of Samuel Applegate; Ann Willett, wife of Thomas Willett; Catherine Robinson, wife of George Robinson; Mary Morris, widow of Joseph Morris; Sarah L. Thorne, wife of William H. Thorne; Louisa Winter, wife of Timothy M. Winter; Henrietta Wilson, wife of Daniel Wilson; and Emma Hillyer, wife of John Hillyer.
Children of Martha Winter, dec'd., all under 21yrs. of age, were entitled to 1/11 share total: Mary Elizabeth Winter, Joseph Winter, Martha Winter, and Timothy Winter.
Children of Daniel B. Hendrickson, dec'd., all under 21yrs. of age, were entitled to 1/11 share total: Joseph Hendrickson, Eleanor Hendrickson, Henry Hendrickson, Annie Hendrickson, and Elizabeth Hendrickson.
Note: Book P, pg. 298, Dec. 1859, reports the death of the widow Catherine Hendrickson.

CONOVER –pg. 308; Dec. 1859. David R. Vanderveer, guardian of Mary Anna Conover, now Mary Anna Scudder, wife of Silas D. Scudder, filed a settlement of accounts.

PROBASCO –pg. 327; Jan. 1860. The sale of real estate owned by Abraham Probasco, dec'd., named Ellen D. Probasco his widow.

COMBS –pg. 332 – 333; Jan. 1860. The sale of real estate owned by Thomas E. Combs, dec'd., named Jemima Combs as his widow.

JOBES –pg. 334; Jan. 1860. Charles Jobes petitioned for a division of the real estate belonging to Robert Jobes, dec'd. Robert Jobes, late of Shrewsbury Tshp., died leaving a will dividing his real estate into seven equal shares for his children Robert Jobes, Charles Jobes, Hager Jobes, Rosanna Jobes, Jane Jobes, Mary Jobes, and Elizabeth Jobes. The property was left to them and their heirs living when his wife, Euphemia, died. Robert Jobes died before his mother

and left children. Rosanna Jobes married Joseph Pervis and died after her father, leaving two children. Her husband, Joseph Pervis, was also deceased. Hager Jobes married Charles Holmes.
Children of Robert Jobes, dec'd.: Shepherd Jobes; Mary Elizabeth Jimison, dec'd., late Mary Elizabeth Jobes, late wife of Alfred Jimison; and Euphemia Brown, late Euphemia Jobes, wife of Jacob Brown.
Children of Rosanna Pervis, dec'd.: Charles Pervis and Sarah Jane Pervis, a minor under 21yrs.
Child of Mary Elizabeth Jimison, dec'd.: Alfred Jimison.
In listing share size, no mention was made of the dau. Mary Jobes who was entitled to 1/7 share. Instead, a 1/7 share went to Sarah Nelson, wife of William Nelson, who was described as a dau. of the testator.

ZEPP –pg. 348; April 1860. A report on the estate of Henry Zepp, dec'd., showed his widow Tirzah Zepp bought the property.

CONOVER –pg. 350; April 1860. Daniel Conover requested guardianship of his dau. Lydia W. Conover, a minor under 14yrs.

PROBASCO –pg. 351; April 1860. Ellen Probasco requested guardianship of her son Abraham Probasco, a minor under 14yrs.

CONOVER –pg. 351; April 1860. Elisha Holmes requested William Statesir be appointed guardian of Sidney Conover, a minor under 14yrs. who was Elisha's stepson.

BROWN –pg. 352; April 1860. Thomas S. R. Brown of Raritan Tshp. requested guardianship of his children Caroline Brown and Thomas S. Brown, minors under 14yrs.

MOUNT –pg. 357; April 1860. A settlement of accounts was filed by John M. Conover and Lydia C. Bergen, late Lydia C. Mount, both administrators of the estate of Richard R. Mount, dec'd.

LONGSTREET –pg. 357; April 1860. Final distribution of the estate of Joseph H. Longstreet, dec'd., named a widow and two children.
Widow: Huldah Longstreet,
Children: Rodah H. Longstreet and Lydia Ann Longstreet.

SCHANCK –pg. 363; April 1860. Final distribution of the estate of Jonathan G. Schanck, dec'd., who died intestate, named his widow and children.
Widow: Cornelia Schanck.
Children: Gitty S. Herbert, wife of William W. Herbert; and Matilda V. Holmes, wife of Jonathan S. Holmes.

COOK –pg. 364; April 1860. Distribution of the estate of Ann Cook, dec'd., as instructed by her last will, named children and grandchildren.
Children: Daniel Edwards; Henry D. Edwards; Joseph Edwards; Stephen Edwards; and Ann Chamberlain, wife of William I. Chamberlain.
Grandson: James H. Lane.

COTTRELL –pg. 371; April 1860. Gordon H. Cottrell petitioned for a division of the real estate belonging to Tylee Cottrell, dec'd., late of Freehold Tshp. Jane Cottrell was the widow of said Tylee Cottrell, dec'd.
Heirs of Tylee Cottrell, dec'd., entitled to 1/8 share each: Gordon H. Cottrell; Sarah Burk, wife of Abraham Burk; Joseph S. Cottrell; John T. Cottrell; Nelson L. Cottrell, under 21yrs.; Grandin L. Cottrell, under 21yrs.; and Frank Cottrell, under 21yrs.
Abraham Burk purchased another 1/8 share from heir William H. Cottrell. The actual property description also mentioned Catherine Cottrell was the widow of Enoch Cottrell, dec'd.

TILTON –pg. 379 - 381; April 1860. A petition for the final distribution of the estate of Catherine Tilton, dec'd., who died intestate, named her heirs.
Sister: Lydia Tilton.
Children of her brother William Tilton, dec'd.: Amos Tilton; Catherine L. Tilton; Ann Eliza Forman, wife of Richard W. Forman; Thomas B. Tilton; and Useba Tilton, wife of Silas Tilton.
Children of her brother Edward Tilton, dec'd.: John Tilton; Caroline S. Hurlbutt, dec'd., late wife of Warren P. Hurlbutt; and Edmund Tilton.

Children of her sister Abigail Tilton Middleton, dec'd., late wife of Gideon Middleton: Sarah
Ann Middleton and George Middleton.
Children of Caroline S. Hurlbutt, dec'd., a dau. of Edward Tilton dec'd.: George J. Hurlbutt
and Harriett C. Hurlbutt, minors. The Probate Court of the Stanford District of Conn.
appointed them wards of their father.

ANDERSON –pg. 390; April 1860. Margaret A. Anderson of Manalapan Tshp., a minor over 14,
chose Anne Anderson as her guardian.

ANDERSON –pg. 390; April 1860. Anne Anderson of Manalapan Tshp. requested guardianship of
her children Lydia M. Anderson, John R. Anderson, Stephen P. Anderson, Fransinkey R.
Anderson, and Hellen W. Anderson, all minors under 14yrs.

BENNETT –pg. 393 – 401; April 1860. Ann Bennett of Holmdel Tshp. petitioned to have her son
Ruliff S. Bennett declared mentally incompetent. Ruliff S. Bennett, about 26yrs. old, lived
with his mother, suffered convulsions during infancy, and for the past 23yrs. was deprived of
reason. He was declared mentally incompetent.
Mother: Ann Bennett, 57yrs. old.
Siblings: John W. Bennett Jr., 29yrs. old; and Mary Elizabeth McGee, 23yrs. old, wife of
Garret McGee.

PULLEN –pg. 402; April 1860. Rebecca Ann Pullen and Susan J. Pullen, minors over 14yrs., chose
Stockton Pullen as their guardian.

PULLEN –pg. 402; April 1860. Stockton Pullen requested guardianship of Clark Pullen and Isabella
Pullen, minors under 14yrs.

WOOLLEY –pg. 407 – 415; Sept. 1860. Edwin Woolley of Ocean Tshp. petitioned to have his
brother-in-law Nelson Woolley of Ocean Tshp. declared a habitual drunkard. Nelson
Woolley, 45yrs. old, had been an alcoholic for the last 3yrs. He had a wife and children.
Wife: Mary Woolley, 37yrs. old.
Children: Elizabeth Woolley, 15yrs.; Emeline Woolley, 13yrs.; Charles Edward Woolley,
10yrs.; Mary Ann Woolley, 8yrs.; Jane Woolley, 6yrs.; and Francis Woolley, 2yrs.

VANBRAKLE –pg. 417; Sept. 1860. James M. VanBrakle petitioned for a division of the real
estate owned by his father, Stephen VanBrakle, dec'd. Ann VanBrakle was named as widow
of the deceased.
Entitled to 1/6 share each: Thomas E. VanBrakle; George W. VanBrakle, under 21yrs.; and
Charles F. Wyckoff, under 21yrs., son of Emma Wyckoff and her husband, David H.
Wyckoff.
James M. VanBrakle was entitled to 1/2 share total by the following means: 1/6 share
descended to him from his father, Stephen VanBrakle, dec'd.; 1/6 share was sold to him by
his brother Stephen H. VanBrakle; and 1/6 share was sold to him by his sister Emma
Wyckoff, wife of David H. Wyckoff.

SUTPHIN –pg. 437; Sept. 1860. Eleanor Sutphin of Manalapan Tshp. requested guardianship of her
children Harriet E. Sutphin, Hellen Sutphin, and George W. Sutphin, all minors under 14yrs.

SUTPHIN –pg. 437; Sept. 1860. Mary J. Sutphin and Evelina F. Sutphin, minors over 14yrs., chose
their mother, Eleanor Sutphin, as their guardian.

ELLIOT –pg. 438; Sept. 1860. Catherine Elliot of Manalapan Tshp. requested guardianship of her
children Ann J. Elliot, John H. Elliot, Christopher Elliot, Catherine M. Elliot, and Mary Eliza
Elliot, all minors under 14yrs.

ELLIOT –pg. 439; Sept. 1860. James Elliot of Manalapan Tshp., a minor over 14yrs., chose his
mother, Catherine Elliot, as his guardian.

ROOP –pg. 440; Sept. 1860. Anna Roop, widow of Jacob Roop, dec'd., applied for the distribution
of her husband's estate not disposed of by his will. Jacob Roop, dec'd., left no children or
living parents. Next of kin couldn't be determined at that time, and the court ordered
someone to investigate.

ROOP –pg. 441 – 445; Sept. 1860. Final distribution of the estate, not disposed of by a will, of
Jacob Roop, dec'd., late of Middletown, who died on April 10, 1856, showed Jacob Roop,
dec'd., left a widow, had no children, no living siblings, no living parents, and no living aunts

and uncles. He did have 28 nephews and nieces, children of his siblings. The report listed his nephews and nieces.

Child of his half-sister Susan Rayner, dec'd., late Susan Roop, wife of David Rayner, also deceased: Margaret Spicer, widow of Henry Spicer. Margaret Spicer died after Jacob Roop, dec'd.

Son of his half-sister Mary Ames, dec'd., late Mary Roop: Jacob Ames of N.Y.

Children of his brother Christopher Roop, dec'd.: Mary, wife of William Morris; Joseph Roop; and William Roop.

Children of his brother George Roop, dec'd.: Solomon Roop; and Elizabeth, wife of Daniel Madden.

Children of his sister Elizabeth Wilson, dec'd., late Elizabeth Roop, wife of Benjamin Wilson, dec'd.: Andrew Wilson; Sarah, wife of John H. Taylor; William C. Wilson; Susan, widow of David Cottrell, dec'd.; and Hester, widow of Zebulon Collins, dec'd. of Jersey City, N.J.

Children of his brother Isaac Roop, dec'd.: Mary Roop of Digby, Nova Scotia; Margaret, widow of Isaac Roop, dec'd. (son of John Roop, dec'd.), of Digby, Nova Scotia; Susanna, widow of Marcellus Edison, dec'd., of Mantorville, Dodge Co., Minn.; James H. Roop of Nova Scotia; Hannah Roop who was said to be in Maryland; Maria, wife of ____ Covert of Granville, Nova Scotia; William Roop of Granville, Nova Scotia; John Roop of St. Johns, New Brunswick; Isaac Roop of East Port, Maine; and Jacob Roop of Hillsburg, Nova Scotia.

Children of his brother John Roop, dec'd.: John Roop of Clements, Nova Scotia; Margaret, widow of ____ Henderson of Digby, Nova Scotia; Susanna, widow of ____ VanBuren, dec'd., of St. Johns, New Brunswick; Joseph Roop of Digby, Nova Scotia; James M. Roop of Digby, Nova Scotia; and Isaac Roop.

BOOK Q
1860 – 1864

ACKER –pg. 9; Dec. 1860. Rebecca Ann Acker, guardian of Charles Henry Acker, Sidney Acker, Mary Elizabeth Acker, Holmes Acker, and Garret Acker, was allowed to sell a piece of her wards' real estate. Note: A guardianship record in Book Q, pg. 8, Dec. 1860 identified her as the mother of her wards.

PERRINE –pg. 18; Dec. 1860. Margaret Ann Perrine and Lewis Perrine, minors over 14yrs., children of Enoch Perrine Jr., dec'd., chose their uncle Enoch P. Ford of East Winsor Tshp., Mercer Co. as their guardian. Note: two separate entries on the same page.

PERRINE –pg. 19; Dec. 1860. Albert Perrine, a minor over 14yrs., son of Enoch Perrine Jr., dec'd., chose his uncle Enoch P. Ford of East Winsor Tshp., Mercer Co. as his guardian.

LEAVY –pg. 20 – 27; Dec. 1860. Thomas Cook petitioned the court to declare his uncle John Leavy of Ocean Tshp. mentally incompetent. He had been deprived of reason for a few months. Witnesses stated, John Leavy burned over $11,000.00 worth of stocks and bonds on Nov. 9, 1860, and on Nov. 13, 1860 William M. Covert placed him in the state asylum. He was declared mentally incompetent, and Thomas Cook was appointed his guardian. Note: John Leavy was declared sane in Book Q, pg. 115, Dec. 1861.
Wife: Susan Leavy, 58yrs. old.

LONGSTREET –pg. 32; Feb. 1861. Gilbert H. Longstreet of Monmouth Co., a minor over 14yrs., chose William R. Longstreet of Burlington Co. as his guardian.

HARRIS –pg. 32; Feb. 1861. James H. Harris of Wall Tshp. requested guardianship of his children Jane A. Harris and William F. Harris, minors under 14yrs.

WOOLLEY –pg. 36; April 1861. Levi Woolley petitioned for a division of the real estate owned by Thomas Woolley, dec'd., late of Howell Tshp.
Entitled to 1/7 share each: Levi Woolley, petitioner; Adam Woolley; Elizabeth Burdge, wife of John L. Burdge; Herbert Woolley; Mary Lane, wife of Joseph Lane; Abraham Woolley; and Richard Woolley, under 21yrs., son of Thomas P. Woolley, dec'd.

SMITH –pg. 38; April 1861. Henrietta B. Smith of Matawan Tshp., a minor over 14yrs., chose her father, Holmes W. Smith, as her guardian.

SMITH –pg. 39; April 1861. William C. Smith of Raritan Tshp., a minor over 14yrs., elected John Butler of the same township as his guardian.

MACKEY –pg. 42; April 1861. Peter B. Mackey petitioned for a division of the real estate owned by George Mackey, dec'd., late of Keyport, who died intestate.
Heirs entitled to 1/4 share each: George Mackey; Peter B. Mackey, petitioner; Frederic Mackey, under 21yrs.; and Malissa Mackey, under 21yrs.

VANNORKEY –pg. 43; April 1861. Jane Vannorkey requested guardianship of her son Simon Vannorkey, a minor under 14yrs. On the same petition, Sarah Vannorkey and Matilda Vannorkey, minors over 14yrs., petitioned the court to appoint Jane Vannorkey of Philadelphia, Pa. their guardian.

VANNORKEY –pg. 44; April 1861. Jane Vannorkey petitioned to sell her ward's property. She held a right of dower on the property, described as land possessed by Simon Vannorkey Jr. at the time of his death.

WYCKOFF –pg. 48; April 1861. David H. Wyckoff of Matawan Tshp. requested guardianship of his son Charles F. Wyckoff, a minor under 14yrs.

HENDRICKSON –pg. 49; April 1861. Michael M. Hendrickson of Manalapan Tshp. requested
guardianship of his dau. Elizabeth H. Hendrickson, a minor under 14yrs.

WIKOFF –pg. 49; April 1861. Peter Wikoff of Freehold Tshp., a minor over 14yrs., elected Charles
C. Wikoff as his guardian.

CHADWICK –pg. 64; April 1861. William L. Chadwick of Shrewsbury Tshp. requested
guardianship of Samuel L. Chadwick, a minor under 14yrs.

BRADY –pg. 67; April 1861. The court ordered the payment of a dower to 33yr. old Mary Brady,
widow of Edward Brady, dec'd.

HOLMES –pg. 70; April 1861. Final distribution of the estate of Elizabeth Holmes, dec'd., revealed
she left seven children and one grandchild. John C. Conover, dec'd., was the first husband of
said Elizabeth Holmes, dec'd. Elisha Holmes relinquished all rights to said estate.
Children entitled to 1/8 share each: Mary, wife of Daniel Schenck; Simpson Conover; John V.
Conover; Charlotte Conover; Cornelia H. Conover, under 21yrs.; Sidney Conover, under
21yrs.; and Julia Conover, under 21yrs.
Grandchild who was a child of her dau. Emily Conover Butler, dec'd., late wife of Charles K.
Butler, entitled to 1/8 share: Mary C. Butler.
Emily Conover Butler died before her mother. John V. Conover was reported to have died
intestate.

HENDRICKSON –pg. 76; Sept. 1861. William E. Hendrickson of Upper Freehold Tshp., a minor
over 14yrs., chose William J. Hendrickson of the same township as his guardian.

THOMPSON –pg. 76; Sept. 1861. Josephine Thompson of Middletown Tshp., a minor over 14yrs.,
chose George W. Crawford as her guardian.

THOMPSON –pg. 77; Sept. 1861. Ida A. Thompson of Middletown Tshp., mother of Cyrenus
Thompson, Catherine Thompson, and Augustus Thompson, minors under 14yrs., requested
George W. Crawford be appointed guardian of said children.

BAIRD –pg. 78; Sept. 1861. John Baird petitioned for a final distribution of the estate of his brother
James Baird, dec'd., who died intestate. David S. Vanderveer, guardian of said James Baird,
dec'd., settled his accounts in April of 1858, reserving the share due Charles H. Baird until he
could be located. Since Charles H. Baird had not been heard of for seven years, the petitioner
requested he be legally presumed dead, and his share of James Baird's estate be distributed.
Their parents were deceased, leaving the siblings of James Baird, dec'd., his only surviving
heirs.
Surviving siblings of James Baird, dec'd.: John Baird, petitioner; Eleanor Baird, resident of
N.Y. City; and Margaret M. Williams, wife of George Williams.

HARVEY –pg. 79; Sept. 1861. Julia M. Harvey of Raritan Tshp., a minor over 14yrs., elected her
mother, Elizabeth Harvey, as her guardian.

HARVEY –pg. 79; Sept. 1861. Elizabeth Harvey of Raritan Tshp. requested guardianship of her son
George W. Harvey, a minor under 14yrs.

SCHANCK –pg. 88; Sept. 1861. Daniel P. Schanck Jr. petitioned for a division of the real estate
owned by John C. Schanck, dec'd.
Heirs entitled to 1/7 share each: Margaret Schanck; Mary S. Conover, wife of John W.
Conover; Lavinia Jones, wife of George S. Jones; Eleanor Schanck, under 21yrs.; and Sarah
Schanck, under 21yrs.
Heir entitled to 2/7 share: Daniel P. Schanck.

MORRIS –pg. 91; Sept. 1861. William F. Morris of Shrewsbury Tshp., a minor over 14yrs., elected
his mother, Mary Morris, as his guardian.

MORRIS –pg. 92; Sept. 1861. Juliette Morris of Shrewsbury Tshp., a minor over 14yrs., elected her
mother, Mary Morris, as her guardian.

SMITH –pg. 96 – 104; Sept. 1861. Lewis A. Smith petitioned the court to declare his brother
Nelson Smith of Ocean Tshp. mentally incompetent. Both their parents were deceased. Their

father, John Smith, dec'd., late of Ocean Tshp., died Aug. 1860, and left a will appointing
Lewis guardian of Nelson's property. Lewis Smith could not manage Nelson and refused to
accept the guardianship. He wished another appointed guardian of Nelson. Lewis claimed
Nelson was 45yrs. old, suffered seizures since 18yrs. of age, and had been mentally
incompetent for twenty years. The court decided Nelson Smith was about 35yrs. of age.
Siblings: Elizabeth Jackson; Robinson Smith; Cornelius Smith; Catherine Slocum, wife of
Henry Slocum; Lewis Smith; and John H. Smith.
Brothers-in-laws: Benjamin Jackson and Henry Slocum.

GREEN –pg. 109; Dec. 1861. Josephine Green, a minor over 14yrs., dau. of Monmouth H. Green of
Middletown Tshp., chose her mother and step-father, Eliza J. Brainard and James H. Brainard,
as her guardians.

GREEN –pg. 109; Dec. 1861. James H. Brainard and Eliza J. Brainard, step-father and mother of
Orlin H. Green, a minor under 14yrs., son of Monmouth H. Green, dec'd., requested
guardianship of the child.

VANBRUNT –pg. 121; Dec. 1861. Samuel VanBrunt and James VanBrunt, minors over 14yrs.,
sons of Reuben VanBrunt of Ocean Tshp., chose Benjamin King of Ocean Tshp. as their
guardian. Note: two separate entries on the same page.

VANBRUNT –pg. 122; Dec. 1861. Benjamin King requested guardianship of Joseph B. VanBrunt,
a minor under 14yrs., son of Reuben VanBrunt.

BUTLER –pg. 122; Dec. 1861. Thomas Willet petitioned for a division of the real estate in Red
Bank, Shrewsbury Tshp. owned by Rachel Butler, dec'd.
Heirs entitled to 1/8 share each: Thomas Willet; Mary Naylor, wife of Samuel Naylor;
Harriet Grant, wife of Edward W. Grant; Catherine McGee, wife of Jerome McGee; Eleanor
S. McLane, wife of William A. McLane; John Willet; Emma Jane Butler, under 21yrs.; and
Thadius Butler, under 21yrs.

JOHNSON/JOHNSTON –pg. 123; Dec. 1861. William J. VanBrackle petitioned for a division of
the real estate owned by William P. Johnson, dec'd., devised in his will, dated June 10, 1836,
to his sister Mary Smith for her lifetime and then to her children. William P. Johnson was
also referred to as William P. Johnston in the same record.
Heir of Mary Smith, dec'd., entitled to 1/3 share: Ida Conover.
Heirs of Mary Smith, dec'd., entitled to 1/9 share each: John Hankinson; Alice Roberts, wife
of Garret Roberts; and Hannah Ann Hankinson.
Heirs of Mary Smith, dec'd., entitled to 1/18 share each: William J. VanBrackle; Margaret
VanBrackle; Stephen C. VanBrackle; John S. VanBrackle; Mary E. VanBrackle, under
21yrs.; and Charles P. VanBrackle, under 21yrs.

BARTHOLF –pg. 128; March 1862. Ellen A. Bartholf, a minor over 14yrs., dau. of Peter A.
Bartholf of Ocean Tshp., elected Daniel Slocum of the same township as her guardian.

BARTHOLF –pg. 128; March 1862. Daniel Slocum requested guardianship of Mary E. Bartholf, a
minor under 14yrs., dau. of Peter A. Bartholf,

ESTELL –pg. 129; March 1862. Andrew J. Estell, a minor over 14yrs., son of James Estell of
Howell Tshp., chose James Cooper of Howell Tshp. as his guardian.

LITTLE –pg. 132; March 1862. William B. Little petitioned for a division of the real estate owned
by Henry Little, dec'd., late of Shrewsbury Tshp., who died intestate leaving a widow and
several children.
Widow: Jane Little.
Children: William N. Little; Henry Little, under 21yrs.; Harvey Little, under 21yrs.; Mary
Ann Little, under 21yrs.; and Francis A. Little Jr., under 21yrs. William N. Little sold his
share to William B. Little, the petitioner.

VANBRUNT –pg. 155; April 1862. George VanBrunt and John VanBrunt petitioned for a division
of the real estate owned by Reuben VanBrunt, dec'd., late of Ocean Tshp. His wife, Mary
VanBrunt, dec'd., who died after March 12, 1852, was the dau. of Joseph King, dec'd.
Heirs of Reuben VanBrunt, dec'd.: George VanBrunt; John VanBrunt; Samuel VanBrunt,
under 21yrs.; James VanBrunt, under 21yrs.; and Joseph B. VanBrunt, under 21yrs.

VANKIRK –pg. 160; April 1862. Louisa VanBrunt, a minor over 14yrs., dau. of Mahlon VanKirk, late of Monmouth Co., elected William H. Conover Jr. as her guardian.

WEST –pg. 161; April 1862. William West petitioned for a division of the real estate owned by his
father, Elias West, dec'd., late of Ocean Tshp., who died intestate.
Children: William West, petitioner; Edmund West; Catherine Potter, wife of James Potter;
John West; Lydia White, late Lydia West; Owen West; and Borden West.
Grandchildren who were children of his dau. Alice Woolley, dec'd., late wife of Samuel
Woolley: Milton Woolley, Mary M. Woolley, Deborah Woolley, William B. Woolley, Corlies
Woolley, and Indiana Josephine Woolley. Note: See Book Q, pg. 239, Dec. 1862.

PERRINE –pg. 170; Sept. 1862. Richard M. Job of Hightstown, Mercer Co. requested guardianship
of his grandchildren Mary Anna Perrine and Matilda Perrine, minors under 14yrs., children of
Isaac Perrine of Manalapan Tshp., Monmouth Co.

HAMPTON/MCKEAN –pg. 171; Sept. 1862. Robert F. Hampton, a minor over 14yrs., son of
Robert F. McKean, chose William S. Jeffrey as his guardian. Note: The surnames of father
and son were different in the record.

CRAIG –pg. 173; Sept. 1862. A settlement of accounts was filed by Robert E. Craig as executor of
the estate of Abraham Craig (alias A. Hampton), dec'd.

MCCHESNEY –pg. 189; Sept. 1862. Jonathan E. McChesney of East Windsor Tshp., Mercer Co.
petitioned the court to declare his niece Elizabeth McChesney of Manalapan Tshp.,
Monmouth Co., dau. of John C. McChesney, dec'd., mentally incompetent. She was an
orphan, about 23yrs. old, of frail health, could read, but had no sense of money. She had three
siblings, and she was also an heir, entitled to a 1/12 share in the estate of Dr. Charles G.
McChesney, dec'd., who owned real estate in Ca., Iowa, and N.J.
Siblings: Stephen McChesney, 22yrs. old; Samuel McChesney, 18yrs. old; and Charles E.
McChesney, 16yrs. old.

HERBERT –pg. 202; Sept. 1862. Evelina E. Herbert, a minor over 14yrs., dau. of Conover Herbert
of Marlboro Tshp., chose John W. Ely as her guardian.

SCHENCK –pg. 203; Sept. 1862. Tunis V. Schenck of Freehold Tshp. requested guardianship of his
niece Mary A. Schenck and nephew Tunis Schenck, minors under 14yrs., children of Ruliff
V. Schenck of Matawan Tshp.

WEATHERLY –pg. 205; Sept. 1862. William H. Weatherly petitioned for a division of the real
estate owned by Henry Weatherly, dec'd., late of Freehold Tshp.
Entitled to 1/3 share each: William H. Weatherly, Emeline Magee Weatherly, and Thomas
Ogden Weatherly, a minor under 21yrs.

BROWN –pg. 216; Dec. 1862. Elisha Newman and Prudence Newman, the step-father and the
mother of Emma E. Brown, Hannah M. Brown, and Susan A. Brown, minors under 14yrs.,
children of Andrew J. Brown of Wall Tshp., requested guardianship of said minors.

HALLENBAKE –pg. 217; Dec. 1862. Ralph Kirkman of Raritan Tshp. requested guardianship of
Sarah Hallenbake, a minor under 14yrs., dau. of William Hallenbake of Raritan Tshp.

BEERS –pg. 230; Dec. 1862. Thaddeus Beers, son of John N. Beers, dec'd., petitioned for a
division of his father's real estate.
Widow of John N. Beers, dec'd.: Huldah Beers, entitled to her dower.
Entitled to 1/6 share each: Ann Beers; John J. Beers, under 21yrs.; William Beers Jr.;
Elizabeth C. VanBrackle, late Elizabeth C. Beers, wife of Thomas E. VanBrackle; Thaddeus
Beers, the petitioner; and Arthur W. Brown, under 21yrs., in right of his mother who was
deceased.

BRAY –pg. 237; Dec. 1862. A settlement of accounts was filed by Francis Murphy as guardian of
Cordelia Smith, late Cordelia Bray.

WOOD –pg. 238; Dec. 1862. Angelina Wood, mother of Charles E. Wood and Ira E. Wood, minors
under 14yrs., children of Elias H. Wood, requested John W. Griggs be appointed guardian of
her children.

WOOLLEY –pg. 239; Dec. 1862. Samuel Woolley requested guardianship of his children Milton
Woolley, Mary M. Woolley, Deborah Woolley, William B. Woolley, Corlies Woolley, and

Indiana J. Woolley, minors under 14yrs. Note: See Book Q, pg. 161, April 1862.

WOLCOTT –pg. 239; Dec. 1862. William L. Wolcott, Sidney W. Wolcott, and Jacob A. Wolcott, minors over 14yrs., children of Amos Wolcott, dec'd., of Ocean Tshp., elected their aunt Ann Maria Knott as their guardian.

MORFORD –pg. 243; Dec. 1862. Caroline Morford requested guardianship of her children James H. Morford and Emily Morford, minors under 14yrs., children of Thomas Morford, dec'd., late of Middletown Tshp.

TALLMAN –pg. 243; Dec. 1862. Margaret A. Tallman requested guardianship of Shade M. Tallman, William B. Tallman, John E. Tallman, and Clara M. Tallman, minors under 14yrs., children of Joseph Tallman of Ocean Tshp.

LITTLE –pg. 244; Dec. 1862. William B. Little requested the court appoint Robert Allen Jr. of Red Bank guardian of Mary Ann Little and Francis A. Little, minors under 14yrs., children of Henry Little, dec'd.

LITTLE –pg. 244; Dec. 1862. Harvey Little, a minor over 14yrs., son of Henry Little, dec'd., chose Robert Allen Jr. of Red Bank as his guardian.

HOPPING –pg. 246; Dec. 1862. George W. Hopping, a minor over 14yrs., requested Henry H. Seabrook of Raritan Tshp. be appointed his guardian. George's father, James Hopping, left N.J. two years earlier and hadn't returned. He left no provisions for George's education and maintenance.

MCCHESNEY –pg. 246 – 247; Dec. 1862. Amos Haviland, John W. Bartleson, and John R. Haley, sureties of George W. Patterson who was guardian of Samuel Morris McChesney, petitioned for relief from their bonds. Among their reasons, George W. Patterson had enlisted in the 14th Regiment of the NJ Volunteers for three years, and was absent from the state of N.J. Samuel M. McChesney also enlisted in the volunteer militia, deserted the service, and his whereabouts remained unknown. Note: In this report Samuel's middle name appeared to read Morris, but a follow-up report, Book Q, pg. 270, April 1863, showed the middle name clearly as Mairs.

HOFF –pg. 259; April 1863. Jeremiah Hoff petitioned for a division of the real estate owned by Hezekiah Hoff, dec'd., who died intestate.
Entitled to 1/3 share each: Jeremiah Hoff; and Elizabeth Cottrell, wife of Roderic Cottrell. Entitled to 1/9 share each: Catherine Ann Holmes, under 21yrs., wife of John Holmes; Leroy Carhart, under 21yrs.; and Elizabeth Carhart, under 21yrs.

CONOVER –pg. 261; April 1863. William R. Conover requested guardianship of his children Millard F. Conover, Joanna Conover, Adelaide V. Conover, and Frank W. Conover, all minors under 14yrs., children of Eliza Conover.

JEFFERY –pg. 261; April 1863. Clarkson Jeffery, a minor over 14yrs., son of Elisha Jeffery, chose his mother, Ellen Jeffery, as his guardian.

CONK –pg. 263; April 1863. Joseph Shumar of Freehold Tshp. requested guardianship of Matilda Conk, Deborah Conk, Charles Conk, Anthony Conk, and Aaron Conk, minors under 14yrs., children of William Conk, dec'd., late of Freehold Tshp.

BRINLEY –pg. 263; April 1863. Rebecca Brinley petitioned for a division of the real estate owned by Jane Brinley, dec'd., late of Ocean Tshp.
Entitled to 1/5 share each: Rebecca Brinley; Emily Brinley; Walter Brinley, under 21yrs.; Mary Jane Brinley, under 21yrs.; and Laura Brinley, under 21yrs.

ATKINSON –pg. 264; April 1863. Pearson Hendrickson requested guardianship of Ann D. Atkinson and George M. Atkinson, minors under 14yrs., children of Joseph L. Atkinson, dec'd., late of Shrewsbury Tshp.

ATKINSON –pg. 264; April 1863. Joseph S. Atkinson, a minor over 14yrs., son of Joseph L. Atkinson, dec'd., late of Shrewsbury Tshp., elected Scudder Wilson as his guardian.

WOOLLEY –pg. 265; April 1863. Mary L. Woolley requested guardianship of her son James H. Woolley, a minor under 14yrs., son of James H. Woolley, dec'd., late of Ocean Tshp.

VANBRUNT –pg. 267; April 1863. Distribution of the estate of George VanBrunt, dec'd., revealed the names of his children.
Children: George VanBrunt; John VanBrunt; Samuel VanBrunt, under 21yrs.; James VanBrunt, under 21yrs.; and Joseph B. VanBrunt.

SCHANCK –pg. 270; April 1863. Margaret Holmes and her husband, Asher Holmes, petitioned for a division of the real estate owned by Tylee Schanck, dec'd.
Daughter, entitled to 1/2 share: Margaret Holmes, the petitioner, wife of Asher Holmes.
Heir of Sarah Holmes, dec'd., who was an heir of Tylee Schanck, dec'd., entitled to 1/2 share: Tylee S. Holmes, under 21yrs.

WALLING –pg. 282; April 1863. John W. Hoff, administrator of the estate of James Walling, dec'd., filed a settlement of accounts. James Walling, dec'd., never married. He was survived by his mother, siblings, and heirs of deceased siblings.
Mother: Elizabeth Walling.
Siblings: Obediah Walling; John Walling; Benjamin B. Walling; Henrietta Rider; Mary Hoff, wife of John W. Hoff; Rebecca Smith, wife of Mark Smith; Elizabeth Sproul, wife of Joseph Sproul; and Joseph Walling.
Children of his sister Ann Smith, dec'd.: Mary H. Smith; Elizabeth Hyer, wife of James Hyer; Angeline Morrell, wife of John Morrell; and Caroline Smith.
Children of his half-sister Deborah Walling, dec'd.: Permelia Aumack, wife of Thomas Aumack; Eveline Aumack, wife of Daniel Aumack; Sarah Seabrook, wife of Elias Seabrook; Elizabeth Vanderbilt, wife of Edward Vanderbilt; Irenia Walling, wife of John Walling; Timothy Walling; and William Walling.

STOUT –pg. 292; April 1863. John Stout, a minor over 14yrs., son of James Stout, dec'd., late of Middletown Tshp., chose William V. Conover as his guardian.

STOUT –pg. 292; April 1863. William V. Conover requested guardianship of Abraham Stout, a minor under 14yrs., son of James Stout, dec'd., late of Middletown Tshp.

HOWLAND –pg. 297; April 1863. Michael A. Howland, a minor over 14yrs., chose his mother, Merebath Howland of Howell Tshp., as his guardian.

HOWLAND –pg. 298; April 1863. Merebath Howland requested guardianship of her son Charles H. Howland, a minor under 14yrs.

REYNOLDS –pg. 298; April 1863. John B. Robins of Millstone Tshp. requested guardianship of Enoch Reynolds and Paul Reynolds, minors under 14yrs., children of Enoch Reynolds, dec'd., late of Millstone Tshp.

BROWN –pg. 300; April 1863. Solomon G. Brown petitioned for a division of real estate in Ocean Tshp. owned by George Brown, dec'd.
Elizabeth Brown was entitled to her dower.
Elizabeth Havens, widow of William Brown, dec'd., was entitled to her dower.
Entitled to 1/6 share each: Solomon G. Brown, George W. Brown Jr., Phebe Emily Poole, George W. Brown, and Sarah Bennett.
Entitled to 1/24 share each: Ellen Brown, James Brown, Mary Brown, and Margaret Brown.
Hendrick Poole was entitled to 1/6 share as a curtesy of _____.

LACOMPT –pg. 302; April 1863. William Allen and his wife, Mary H. Allen, late Mary H. LaCompt, petitioned for a division of the real estate owned by Joseph LaCompt, dec'd., late of Howell Tshp.
Entitled to 1/3 share each: Mary H. Allen, the petitioner, wife of William Allen; William H. LaCompt, under 21yrs.; and Elizabeth LaCompt, under 21yrs.

CRAIG –pg. 303; April 1863. Mary H. Craig of Manalapan Tshp. requested guardianship of her children Clementine Craig and Robert E. Craig, minors under 14yrs., children of William R. Craig, dec'd.

ABRAHAMS –pg. 304; April 1863. Eliza Abrahams requested guardianship of her dau. Josephine Abrahams, a minor under 14yrs., dau. of John W. Abrahams of Marlboro Tshp.

STEVENS –pg. 305; April 1863. John Morrell and others petitioned for a division of the real estate owned by Mary Stevens, dec'd.
Entitled to 1/5 share each: John Morrell; Jane Bedle, wife of William Bedle; and Mary Smith,

wife of William Smith.
Entitled to 1/25 share each: Mary VanPelt, wife of William VanPelt; Martha Devoe, wife of
Gilbert Devoe; Jane Butler, wife of John Butler; Henrietta Hoffman, wife of William
Hoffman; and Conover Smith.
Entitled to 1/30 share each: Margaret Brown, wife of Alexander Brown; Eleanor Poland, wife
of William Poland; Caroline Allen; Stephen Allen; and Elsida Allen.
Entitled to 1/90 share each: Catherine Allen, William Allen, and Margetta Allen.

BORDEN –pg. 314; Sept. 1863. Catherine T. Borden requested guardianship of Charles E. Borden,
a minor under 14yrs., son of Richard Borden of Shrewsbury Tshp.

BORDEN –pg. 314; Sept. 1863. Daniel W. Borden, a minor over 14yrs., son of Richard Borden of
Shrewsbury Tshp., chose his mother, Catherine T. Borden, as his guardian.

TAYLOR –pg. 315; Sept. 1863. Phebe Ann Taylor, a minor over 14yrs., dau. of David Taylor of
Shrewsbury Tshp., elected her mother, Lavinia Taylor, as her guardian.

TAYLOR –pg. 315; Sept. 1863. Lavinia Taylor requested guardianship of her children Samuel W.
Taylor, John A. Taylor, Daniel H. Taylor, Lavinia Taylor, Cornelia Ann Taylor, and David
Taylor, minors under 14yrs., children of David Taylor, dec'd., late of Shrewsbury Tshp.

MORGAN –pg. 316; Sept. 1863. Agnes Morgan, a minor over 14yrs., dau. of John Morgan Sr.,
dec'd., late of Holmdel Tshp., chose her mother, Eliza J. Morgan, as her guardian.

MORGAN –pg. 317; Sept. 1863. Eliza Jane Morgan requested guardianship of her children Emeline
Morgan and Ann Eliza Morgan, minors under 14yrs., children of John Morgan, dec'd., late of
Holmdel Tshp.

WALLING –pg. 317; Sept. 1863. Taylor Walling of Raritan Tshp. requested guardianship of his
son Joel Walling, a minor under 14yrs.

COTTRELL –pg. 318; Sept. 1863. Rodrick Cottrell of Raritan Tshp. requested guardianship of his
children Thomas Cottrell, Noah Cottrell, and William Cottrell, minors under 14yrs.

BARRICLO –pg. 321; Sept. 1863. Catherine S. Barriclo requested guardianship of her children
William H. Barriclo, John Barriclo, and Catherine G. Barriclo, minors under 14yrs., children
of William J. Barriclo, dec'd., late of Freehold Tshp.

CHERRY –pg. 321; Sept. 1863. Henry Cherry of Raritan Tshp. requested guardianship of his
children John P. Cherry and William H. Cherry, minors under 14yrs.

SMITH –pg. 338; Sept. 1863. Miles Harden and his wife, Phebe Ann, petitioned for a division of
real estate in Marlboro Tshp. owned by Phebe Smith, dec'd., described as land devised to
Phebe Smith by the 1811 will of her father, Cornelius Pease, dec'd.
Children of Phebe Smith, dec'd.: Phebe Ann Harden, wife of Miles Harden; Sarah Meloine
Hinckley, wife of Hiram Hinckley; Cornelius Smith; Josiah Smith; and Pelletia Smith.
Grandchildren who were children of her dau. Elizabeth P. Little, dec'd., late wife of James
Little: Phebe Jane Little; James Henry Little; William Smith Little; John S. Little; and Mary
Elizabeth Potter, wife of Thomas Potter.
Grandchildren who were children of her dau. Olley Maria Hempstead, dec'd., late wife of
Christopher M. Hempstead: John Hempstead; and Phebe Elizabeth Morrell, wife of Adrian
Morrell.
Great grandchildren who were children of Christopher M. Hempstead, dec'd., late son of
Olley Maria Hempstead, dec'd.: Anna Maria Hempstead, Mary Jane Hempstead, and William
Henry Hempstead.
Mary Jane Hempstead was identified as the widow of Christopher M. Hempstead, dec'd.,
grandson of Phebe Smith, dec'd. James Haywood purchased the shares of Cornelius Smith,
Josiah Smith, and Pelletia Smith.

ESTELL –pg. 341; Sept. 1863. Albert S. Larrabe and George Clark petitioned for a division of the
real estate owned by James Estell, dec'd., late of Howell Tshp. He left a widow and several
heirs.
Widow: Mary Estell.
Grandchildren who were children of his son Robert Estell, dec'd.: Elizabeth Clayton, under
21yrs., wife of William Clayton; Robert James Estell, under 21yrs.; Rebecca Estell, under
21yrs.; John Estell, under 21yrs.; Mary Estell, under 21yrs.; Andrew J. Estell, under 21yrs.;

and David Estell, under 21yrs.
Grandchildren who were children of his son Andrew J. Estell, dec'd.: Helena Estell, under 21yrs.; Benjamin Morris Estell, under 21yrs.; Robert James Estell, under 21yrs.; and Andrew Jackson Estell, under 21yrs. Andrew J. Estell, dec'd., left a widow, Matilda Estell.
Children of said James Estell, dec'd., who sold their shares to Albert S. Larrabee and George Clark: Hester Ann Reynolds, wife of John W. Reynolds; Ellen J. Kisner, wife of William H. Kisner; Britton C. Estell; Mary Hannah Cooper, wife of Benjamin M. Cooper; John S. Estell; and James S. Estell.

BREWER –pg. 347; Sept. 1863. A record of accounts was filed by Harriet Brewer as guardian of the following children: Elizabeth S. Slokum, late Elizabeth S. Brewer; Mary C. Boude, late Mary C. Brewer; Ellen H. Brewer, dec'd.; Rachel A. Brewer, dec'd.; Esther Brewer; and Rebecca J. Brewer.

HARTMAN –pg. 359; Dec. 1863. Sarah E. Hartman requested guardianship of her son Walter Hartman, a minor under 14yrs., son of Alexander W. Hartman of Upper Freehold Tshp.

STILLWELL –pg. 360; Dec. 1863. Elisha Stillwell of Howell Tshp. requested guardianship of his dau. Lydia W. C. Stillwell, a minor under 14yrs.

CONOVER –pg. 360; Dec. 1863. Leonard L. Johnson of Brooklyn, N.Y. requested guardianship of Charles E. Conover and William S. Conover, minors under 14yrs., children of John Schuyler Conover, dec'd., of Monmouth Co., N.J.

BRINLEY –pg. 361; Dec. 1863. Rebecca Brinley petitioned for a division of the real estate owned by Henry R. Brinley, dec'd.
Entitled to 1/5 share each: Emily Brinley; Walter Brinley, under 21yrs.; Mary Jane Brinley, under 21yrs.; Laura Brinley, under 21yrs.; and Rebecca Brinley, the petitioner.

DORN –pg. 376; Dec. 1863. James W. Dorn and Hannah C. Dorn, minors over 14yrs., chose their father, Samuel Dorn of Holmdel Tshp., as their guardian. Note: two separate entries on the same page.

DORN –pg. 377; Dec. 1863. John M. Dorn and William P. Dorn, minors over 14yrs., chose their father, Samuel Dorn of Holmdel Tshp., as their guardian. Note: two separate entries on the same page.

BRITTON –pg. 382; Dec. 1863. Dorinda Britton petitioned for a division of the real estate in Millstone Tshp. owned by Lucien Britton, dec'd.
Entitled to 1/6 share each: Clorinda Britton, Isaac Britton, Orson Britton, Ezra Britton, and Dorinda Britton, the petitioner.
Children of Alfred Britton, dec'd., all under 21yrs., entitled to 1/6 share total: Sarah L. Britton, Lucien G. Britton, and Agnes L. Britton.

SLOCUM –pg. 383; Dec. 1863. William B. Slocum, uncle of Lewis Slocum, Alonzo Slocum, Mary Slocum, and Mary M. Slocum, minors under 14yrs., children of Peter E. Slocum, dec'd., late of Ocean Tshp., requested guardianship of said minors.

SCHANCK –pg. 387; Dec. 1863. John V. P. Schanck, P. Austin Schanck, and Aaron P. Schanck petitioned for a division of the real estate owned by their parents Edith Schanck, dec'd., and John D. Schanck, dec'd. The real estate owned by Edith Schanck, dec'd., was bequeathed to her by the will of John P. VanPelt, dec'd.
Children of John D. and Edith Schanck, both dec'd.: John V. P. Schanck, P. Austin Schanck, Aaron P. Schanck, Armenia P. Whitlock, Eleanora M. Schanck, Adeline Schanck, Denise J. Schanck, and Mary G. Schanck, under 21yrs.

ALLEN –pg. 391; Feb. 1864. Caroline Allen, a minor over 14yrs., dau. of Jacob Allen (who was still living), elected her brother-in-law Alexander Brown as her guardian.

PARKER –pg. 398; April 1864. James E. Parker, a minor over 14yrs., son of Samuel Parker of Shrewsbury Tshp., chose Maria L. Parker as his guardian.

FIELDS –pg. 398; April 1864. John Fields, a minor over 14yrs., son of Britton Fields, chose Theodore Fields as his guardian.

BROWN –pg. 399; April 1864. Thomas S. R. Brown of Raritan Tshp. requested guardianship of h son Arthur M. Brown, a minor under 14yrs.

LAYTON –pg. 399; April 1864. Lewis G. Davison requested guardianship of Evelina Eunice Layton and Catherine E. Layton, minors under 14yrs., children of Daniel Layton.

PARKER –pg. 400; April 1864. Maria L. Parker requested guardianship of Maria L. Parker, Samuel Parker, and Elizabeth B. Parker, minors under 14yrs., children of Samuel Parker, late of Monmouth Co.

FIELDS –pg. 400; April 1864. Theodore Fields requested guardianship of Henry Fields, Ruth Anna Fields, and Jacob Fields, minors under 14yrs., children of Britton Fields, late of Monmouth Co.

ESTELL –pg. 401; April 1864. Matilda Estell requested guardianship of Hellena Estell, Benjamin M. Estell, Robert J. Estell, and Andrew J. Estell, minors under 14yrs., children of Andrew J. Estell, late of Monmouth Co., N.J.

ALLEN –pg. 401; April 1864. David F. Wolcott and William T. Corlies requested guardianship of Joseph B. Allen and Edmund Allen, minors under 14yrs., children of William B. Allen of Shrewsbury Tshp. who was still alive.

MITCHELL –pg. 402; April 1864. Amanda M. Mitchell requested guardianship of Elwood Mitchell, a minor under 14yrs., son of Samuel T. Mitchell, dec'd.

SCHENCK –pg. 402; April 1864. Mary Gertrude Schenck, a minor over 14yrs., dau. of John D. Schenck, dec'd., chose Daniel Bray as her guardian.

ANTONIDES –pg. 403; April 1864. James Craig requested guardianship of Daniel J. Antonides, a minor under 14yrs., son of Polhemus Antonides of Freehold Tshp.

SANFORD –pg. 403; April 1864. Henry G. Sanford and Carrie F. Sanford, minors over 14yrs., children of Enoch Sanford, dec'd., elected Jane G. Sanford as their guardian.

WYKOFF –pg. 404; April 1864. Geo. W. Davison requested guardianship of Hettie Wykoff, a minor under 14yrs., dau. of William Wikoff, dec'd. Note: The surnames were spelled differently in the record.

WOOD –pg. 404; April 1864. Amelia Wood, John A. Wood, and Ann M. Wood, minors over 14yrs., children of John Cooper, dec'd., elected Robert Allen as their guardian. Note: The children and father had different surnames.

VANBRACKLE –pg. 405; April 1864. Mary E. VanBrackle, a minor over 14yrs., dau. of John VanBrackle of Matawan Tshp., chose William S. Walling as her guardian.

WOOLLEY –pg. 405; April 1864. Adam M. Pease requested guardianship of Alfred Woolley and Lydia Woolley, minors under 14yrs., children of Alfred Woolley, late of Monmouth Co.

WOOLLEY –pg. 406; April 1864. Mary E. Woolley and Jane Ann Woolley, minors over 14yrs., children of Alfred Woolley, late of Monmouth Co., elected Adam M. Pease as their guardian. Note: two entries on the same page.

WOOLLEY –pg. 407; April 1864. William E. Woolley, a minor over 14yrs., son of Alfred Woolley, late of Monmouth Co., elected Adam M. Pease as his guardian.

ALLEN –pg. 407; April 1864. Stephen Allen of Union Tshp., Miami Co., Ohio requested guardianship of Kate Allen and William Allen, minors under 14yrs., children of William Allen, dec'd., late of Monmouth Co., N.J.

ALLEN –pg. 408; April 1864. Elizabeth Wilson requested guardianship of her dau. Ellanejdia Allen, a minor under 14yrs., dau. of James Allen, dec'd., late of Matawan Tshp.

CLAYTON –pg. 408; April 1864. Ann Amelia Clayton, a minor over 14yrs., dau. of William H. Clayton, dec'd., chose Elias Vanderveer, her step-father, as her guardian.

BENNETT –pg. 430; April 1864. Anne C. Campbell, wife of Richard B. Campbell, petitioned for a division of the real estate owned by Jeremiah Bennett, dec'd., late of Wall Tshp.

Entitled to 1/5 share each: John A. Bennett; Catherine Bennett; and Anne C. Campbell, the petitioner, by purchase.
Entitled to 1/20 share each, all under 21yrs.: Helen B. Copping, Anne B. Copping, Emily Copping, and Charles G. Copping (middle initial for Charles also given as "J" in this record).
Entitled to 1/45 share each, all under 21yrs., all children of Thomas Bennett, dec'd.: Hannah E. Bennett, John H. Bennett, Jeremiah Bennett, Catherine E. Bennett, Delia S. Bennett, Ellen A. Bennett, Theodore H. Bennett, Richard B. Bennett, and Thomas Bennett.
The property of Thomas Bennett, dec'd., was subject to the dower of his widow, Catherine E. Bennett.

POLING –pg. 432; April 1864. William Poling petitioned for a division of the real estate owned by Elihu Poling, dec'd., who owned property in Holmdel Tshp. and Middletown Tshp.
Entitled to 1/4 share each: William Poling, the petitioner; Mary A. Poling; John Poling; and Hannah Poling, under 21yrs. Note: In Book Q, pg. 435, April 1864, a division of this property named Mary Poling as widow of Elihu Poling, dec'd.

WEST –pg. 433; April 1864. Garret H. White and his wife, Elizabeth, petitioned for a division of the real estate owned by Henry West, dec'd.
Entitled to 1/7 share each: Charles West; Margaret L. Fields; Mary Jane West, under 21yrs.; John B. West, under 21yrs.; Loretta M. West, under 21yrs.; Charles H. Cooper, under 21yrs.; and Elizabeth White, wife of Garret H. White. Note: In Book R, pg. 150, Dec. 1864, the sale of this property described Benjamin West, dec'd., as the father of Henry West, dec'd.

SCHROEDER –pg. 434; April 1864. Anthony D. Schroeder petitioned for a division of the real estate owned by Elizabeth Schroeder, dec'd., late wife of Henry C. J. Schroeder of Ocean Tshp.
Children of Elizabeth Schroeder, dec'd.: Ernest Schroeder, under 21yrs.; Henry E. Schroeder, under 21yrs.; John Edmund Schroeder, under 21yrs.; and Anthony D. Schroeder, the petitioner.

BOOK R

1864 – 1866

WEST –pg. 2; April 1864. Pitman West requested guardianship of Mary Rebecca West, a minor under 14yrs., dau. of Albert West, dec'd.

WEST –pg. 2; April 1864. Isaiah S. Lane requested guardianship of Ella West, a minor under 14yrs., dau. of Alfred West, dec'd.

SCHENCK –pg. 3; April 1864. Luke Hance and his wife, Sarah, petitioned for a division of the real estate owned by John P. Schenck, dec'd., late of Shrewsbury Tshp.
Entitled to 1/6 share each: Sarah Hance, wife of Luke Hance; John P. Schenck; Peter Schenck; Daniel I. Schenck; and Eleanor Holmes, wife of Jonathan I. Holmes Jr.
Entitled to 1/18 share each, all under 21yrs.: John P. Tunis, Charles Tunis, and Daniel Tunis. The heir John P. Schenck, and Sarah Jane Schenck, widow of said John P. Schenck, dec'd., sold their shares to Sarah Hance and Eleanor Holmes.

BENNETT –pg. 4; April 1864. William V. Conover and his wife Catherine G. petitioned for a division of the real estate owned by John Bennett, dec'd., late of Middletown Tshp.
Widow of John Bennett, dec'd.: Emma L. Bennett, entitled to her dower.
Entitled to 1/5 share each: Catherine G. Conover, wife of William V. Conover; Elizabeth G. Graff, wife of Peter A. Graff; John H. Bennett; Willie H. Bennett, under 21yrs.; and James Petrie Bennett, under 21yrs.

COOPER –pg. 7; April 1864. Samuel T. Hendrickson and James H. Hendrickson petitioned for a division of the real estate owned by Jacob Cooper, dec'd., late of Howell Tshp.
Entitled to 1/6 share each: Prudence M. Cooper, under 21yrs.; and Hannah Ettie Cooper, under 21yrs.
Benjamin G. Cooper, who was entitled to 1/6 share, purchased another 3/6 shares (heirs not named) and sold all 4/6 to Mary Cooper, the widow of said Jacob Cooper, dec'd. The widow sold the 4/6 shares to Samuel T. and James H. Hendrickson.

CURTIS –pg. 13; April 1864. Samuel P. Curtis petitioned for a division of real estate in Wall Tshp. owned by his parents, Garret Curtis, dec'd., and Sarah Curtis, dec'd.
Entitled to 1/7 share each: Samuel P. Curtis; Mary Morton, wife of Thomas Morton; Eleanor Brown, wife of Sidney Brown; Rebecca Goble, wife of Isaac Goble; Martha White, wife of Charles White; and David M. Curtis.
Children of William Curtis, dec'd., all under 21yrs., entitled to 1/7 share total: Sarah L. Curtis, Hannah E. Curtis, Charlotte A. Curtis, Jane M. Curtis, Henrietta Curtis, William H. Curtis, Catherine M. Curtis, and Eleanor Curtis.
Note: In this record, the share portion for Samuel P. Curtis was reported inaccurately. The error was corrected in Book R, pg. 94 – 95, Sept. 1864, and reported here accurately.

MOUNT –pg. 16; April 1864. Mary A. E. Mount requested guardianship of her son Joseph Mount, a minor under 14yrs., son of Matthias Mount, dec'd., late of N.Y. City.

PARKER –pg. 21; April 1864. A report on a sale of the real estate owned by Hyde Parker, dec'd., late of Monmouth Co., N.J., reported the death of his dau. Deborah A. Kizer, late wife of William Kizer who resided in N.Y. City.

WALLING –pg. 60; Sept. 1864. Matilda Walling requested guardianship of her dau. Lydia Walling, a minor under 14yrs., dau. of John W. Walling, dec'd., late of Raritan Tshp.

WILLIAMS –pg. 60; Sept. 1864. Sidney W. Williams of Upper Freehold requested guardianship of his son Charles L. Williams, a minor under 14yrs.

COOPER –pg. 61; Sept. 1864. Elizabeth Cooper, a minor over 14yrs., dau. of John Cooper, dec'd., chose her step-father, Thomas Jackson, as her guardian.

CARTER –pg. 61; Sept. 1864. Mary Carter requested guardianship of her children Jacob Carter and Marinda Carter, minors under 14yrs., children of Jacob Carter of Middletown Tshp.

PATTERSON –pg. 62; Sept. 1864. Caroline Patterson, a minor over 14yrs., dau. of John T. Patterson, dec'd., late of Freehold Tshp., elected John Hall of Howell Tshp. as her guardian.

CONINE –pg. 62; Sept. 1864. Sarah Ann Conine requested guardianship of her children Matilda Conine, John W. Conine, George Conine, and Sarah Ellen Conine, minors under 14yrs., children of Henry I. Conine, late of Freehold Tshp.

LIPPINCOTT –pg. 63 – 71; Sept. 1864. William Henry Lippincott of N.Y. City petitioned the court to declare his mother mentally incompetent. Ann Lippincott of Ocean Tshp., his mother, had been deprived of reason for seven years. She was the widow of Henry Lippincott, dec'd., and between 66 and 67 years of age. A legacy due her from William Browning, dec'd., was listed in her estate.
Children of Ann Lippincott: Samuel B. Lippincott, dec'd.; Eleanor Williams, 43yrs. old, wife of Charles E. Williams; William Henry Lippincott, 45yrs. old; Benjamin C. Lippincott, 41yrs. old; Edward E. Lippincott, 37yrs. old; Ebenezer W. Lippincott, 34yrs. old; Henry Lippincott, 31yrs. old; Sarah E. Slocum, 28yrs. old, wife of Charles M. Slocum; Alfred B. Lippincott, 26yrs. old; Charles A. Lippincott, 24yrs. old; and Theodore Lippincott, 21yrs. old.

FORD –pg. 71 – 79; Sept. 1864. James Brown of Washington Tshp., Mercer Co. petitioned the court to declare his nephew Zebulon Ford, late of East Windsor Tshp., Mercer Co., then of Millstone Tshp., Monmouth Co., mentally incompetent. Zebulon was an unmarried man, 25yrs. old, whose parents were deceased. His father took care of his finances until his death in Feb. of 1864.
Siblings of Zebulon Ford: Susan Ann Prevo, 22yrs. old, wife of Aaron Prevo; and Henrietta Eldridge, 24yrs. old, wife of Levi Eldridge.

WARDEN –pg. 103; Sept. 1864. Samuel Warden, a minor over 14yrs., son of Benjamin Warden, dec'd., chose William K. Warden of Atlantic Tshp. as his guardian.

BROWN –pg. 107; Sept. 1864. George W. Brown, a minor over 14yrs., son of William Brown, dec'd., late of Mercer Co., elected Solomon G. Brown of Ocean Tshp., Monmouth Co. as his guardian.

RHOADES –pg. 109; Sept. 1864. John B. Wyckoff requested guardianship of Mary Francis Rhoades, a minor under 14yrs., dau. of James H. Rhoades, Co. K, 5 N.J. Vol., dec'd., late of Monmouth Co.

HENDRICKSON –pg. 114; Dec. 1864. Henry H. Hendrickson petitioned for a division of the real estate owned by Gilbert P. Hendrickson, dec'd.
Entitled to 1/3 share each: Henry H. Hendrickson, the petitioner; and William E. Hendrickson, under 21yrs.
Hannah W. Hendrickson, widow of said Gilbert P. Hendrickson, dec'd., was entitled to her dower, plus the 1/3 share she purchased from Anthony W. Hendrickson, another heir of said deceased.

WARDELL –pg. 123; Dec. 1864. Edward H. Price requested guardianship of his niece Marilla Wardell, a minor under 14yrs., dau. of Hance D. Wardell, dec'd., late of Ocean Tshp.

MORTON –pg. 124; Dec. 1864. Fanny A. Morton requested guardianship of her children Thomas A. Morton, Robert M. Morton, and Charlotte E. Morton, minors under 14yrs., children of Joseph A. Morton, dec'd., late of Wall Tshp.

COOPER –pg. 124; Dec. 1864. Francis Corlies requested guardianship of Charles H. Cooper, a minor under 14yrs., son of Jordan Cooper.

BENNETT –pg. 127; Dec. 1864. Emma L. Bennett requested guardianship of her children William H. Bennett and James P. B. Bennett, minors under 14yrs., children of John Bennett, dec'd., late of Middletown Tshp.

CRAWFORD –pg. 127 – 136; Dec. 1864. John H. Rulon of Upper Freehold Tshp. petitioned the

court to declare Theodore N. Crawford mentally incompetent. Theodore had lived with his mother until her death a year ago, and had been deprived of reason for about a year. He had siblings, but no relatives living in N.J.
Siblings: Elizabeth Hand, Susan Herbert, and Anna Coleman, all of Philadelphia, Pa.

COOPER –pg. 144; Dec. 1864. Deborah Jackson, late Deborah Cooper, filed a settlement of accounts as administrator of the estate of John Cooper, dec'd.

GIFFORD –pg. 148; Dec. 1864. Henry Gifford applied for a division of the real estate owned by Amos Gifford, dec'd., late of Wall Tshp.
Children of Amos Gifford, dec'd.: Angeline Allen, wife of Joseph Allen; Mary Herbert, widow of John Herbert, dec'd.; Emily Tilton, wife of Herbert Tilton; Amos Gifford; Henry Gifford, the petitioner; Sarah Tilton, widow of Joseph Tilton, dec'd.; Amy Gifford; Mary Gifford; Joshua Gifford, under 21yrs.; and Rebecca Gifford, under 21yrs.

WHITE –pg. 154; Dec. 1864. Mary H. White, a minor over 14yrs., dau. of Henry White, dec'd., chose William A. Foster as her guardian.

IMLAY –pg. 155; Dec. 1864. Tenbrook S. Imlay, a minor over 14yrs., son of Joseph M. Imlay of Brooklyn, N.Y., elected Oliver H. Wilson of Brooklyn, N.Y. as his guardian.

CURTIS –pg. 162; Dec. 1864. Merrick M. Burdge requested guardianship of Charlotte A. Curtis, Jane M. Curtis, Henrietta Curtis, William H. Curtis, Catherine M. Curtis, and Ellen A. Curtis, minors under 14yrs., children of William H. Curtis, late of Monmouth Co.

CURTIS –pg. 163; Dec. 1864. Sarah L. Curtis and Hannah E. Curtis, minors over 14yrs., children of William H. Curtis, late of Monmouth Co., chose Merrick M. Burdge as their guardian. Note: two separate entries on the same page.

MCCHESNEY –pg. 164; Dec. 1864. William M. McChesney requested guardianship of his son Joseph A. McChesney, a minor under 14yrs.

CONOVER –pg. 170; Feb. 1865. Martha R. Conover requested guardianship of her children Ellis Conover and Lydia Conover, minors under 14yrs., children of Capt. James W. Conover, dec'd.

SMOCK –pg. 190; April 1865. Samuel W. Jones and his wife, Letty Ann, petitioned for a division of the real estate owned by George Smock Sr., dec'd., late of Atlantic Tshp.
Entitled to 1/12 share each: Letty Ann Jones, wife of Samuel W. Jones; Henry Smock; and Mary Smalley.
Entitled to 5/12 share: George G. Smock.
Entitled to 2/12 share: Robert C. Smock.
Children of Sarah Schanck, dec'd., entitled to 1/12 share total: George Schanck, David Schanck, and Mary Schanck.
Children of Eliza Byrn, dec'd., entitled to 1/12 share total: Garret S. Byrn, George P. Byrn, and James T. Byrn, under 21yrs.

RODGERS –pg. 196; April 1865. Eleanor A. Morris, late Eleanor A. Rodgers, administrator of the estate of John M. Rodgers, dec'd., petitioned the court to sell property to pay the debts of the deceased.

ELY –pg. 198; April 1865. Aaron Ely requested guardianship of Edward H. Ely, a minor under 14yrs., son of Richard A. Ely, dec'd.

PARKER –pg. 198; April 1865. Julia A. Parker requested guardianship of her dau. Rebecca B. Parker, a minor under 14yrs., child of Robert F. Parker, dec'd.

TAYLOR –pg. 199; April 1865. Esther Grant requested guardianship of her children Guisbert Taylor, Violetta Taylor, Samuel H. Taylor, James B. Taylor, and Lydia Taylor, minors under 14yrs., children of Samuel Taylor, dec'd.

TAYLOR –pg. 199; April 1865. Morford D. Taylor, a minor over 14yrs., son of Samuel Taylor, dec'd., elected his mother, Esther Grant, as his guardian.

CHAMBERLAIN –pg. 200; April 1865. Elizabeth Chamberlain, a minor over 14yrs., dau. of Daniel J. Chamberlain, dec'd., chose John M. Chamberlain of Middlesex Co. as her guardian.

WOOLLEY –pg. 201; April 1865. Mary Ellen Bergen, a minor over 14yrs., dau. of Alfred Woolley, dec'd., chose her husband, Thomas P. Bergen, as her guardian.

BORDEN –pg. 201; April 1865. Rebecca Borden, a minor over 14yrs., dau. of Amos Borden, dec'd., elected Margaret Ann Brocklebank as her guardian.

CHAMBERLAIN –pg. 202; April 1865. Daniel J. Chamberlain, a minor over 14yrs., son of Daniel I. Chamberlain, dec'd., chose Randal C. Robbins of Mercer Co. as his guardian.

MCCHESNEY –pg. 202; April 1865. William H. VanCleaf requested guardianship of James P. McChesney, a minor under 14yrs., son of George McChesney.

HULSART –pg. 203; April 1865. Susan Hulsart requested guardianship of her children Thomas P. Hulsart and James H. Hulsart, minors under 14yrs., children of William P. Hulsart, dec'd.

CONOVER –pg. 218; April 1865. William T. Conover petitioned for a division of the real estate owned by Charles A. Conover, dec'd., and Alexander Conover, dec'd. At the time of his death, Charles A. Conover, dec'd., owned half the property with the heirs of said Alexander Conover, dec'd., who owned the other half.
Entitled to 1/10 share each: William T. Conover; Juliet Conover; Matilda Appleton, wife of James Appleton; and Louisa Conover.
Heirs of Alexander Conover, dec'd., entitled to 2/10 share each: William L. Conover, Benjamin Dey Conover, and Julia Conover.
Hannah Conover, widow of Alexander Conover, dec'd., was entitled to her dower.

REYNOLDS –pg. 223; April 1865. Joseph T. Laird requested guardianship of Lewis W. Reynolds, Theodore F. Reynolds, and William E. Reynolds, minors under 14yrs., children of William Reynolds, dec'd.

DANGLER –pg. 224; April 1865. Joel Clayton requested guardianship of Ann Joline Dangler, a minor under 14yrs., dau. of John Dangler, dec'd.

PROBASCO –pg. 224; April 1865. Elizabeth Probasco requested guardianship of her children Huldah Probasco, Mary Jane Probasco, Hendrick L. Probasco, and Rynier Probasco, minors under 14yrs., children of Joseph P. Probasco, dec'd.

PROBASCO –pg. 225; April 1865. Joanna Probasco, a minor over 14yrs., dau. of Joseph P. Probasco, dec'd., chose her mother, Elizabeth Probasco, as her guardian.

PROBASCO –pg. 225; April 1865. James K. Probasco, a minor over 14yrs., son of Joseph P. Probasco, dec'd., elected Christopher Probasco as his guardian.

PROBASCO –pg. 226; April 1865. Robert S. Probasco, a minor over 14yrs., son of Joseph P. Probasco, dec'd., elected Christopher Probasco as his guardian.

SHEPHERD –pg. 227; April 1865. Matilda C. Shepherd, a minor over 14yrs., dau. of Joseph Shepherd, dec'd., chose her mother, Lydia B. Shepherd, as her guardian.

BROWER –pg. 237; April 1865. John S. Brower of Raritan Tshp. requested guardianship of his son John Phineas Brower, a minor under 14yrs.

BOWNE –pg. 237; April 1865. Rebecca A. Bowne and John D. Bowne, minors over 14yrs., children of William A. Bowne, dec'd., chose their mother, Maria J. Bowne, as their guardian.

BOWNE –pg. 238; April 1865. Maria J. Bowne requested guardianship of David S. Bowne and Henry Bowne, minors under 14yrs., children of William A. Bowne, dec'd.

STILLWELL –pg. 238; April 1865. Jemima T. Stillwell, a minor over 14yrs., dau. of Joseph Stillwell, dec'd., elected her mother, Lois E. Stillwell, as her guardian.

STILLWELL –pg. 239; April 1865. Lois E. Stillwell requested guardianship of her son Jedidah Stillwell, a minor under 14yrs., son of Joseph Stillwell, dec'd.

STILLWELL –pg. 240; April 1865. Francinia Stillwell requested guardianship of her son John Stillwell, a minor under 14yrs., son of David Stillwell, dec'd.

MCCORMICK –pg. 242; April 1865. Mary A. Dugan petitioned for a division of the real estate
owned by Patrick McCormick, dec'd.
Heirs entitled to 1/3 share each: Mary A. Dugan; Annie E. McCormick, under 21yrs.; and
Catherine M. McCormick, under 21yrs. Note: Sale of this property recorded in Book R, pg.
405, April 1866, named Bridget M. McCormick the widow of the deceased, and referred to
Mary A. as Mary Agnes McCormick.

COOK –pg. 264; Sept. 1865. Caroline C. Cook requested guardianship of her children Bloomfield
Cook and Mary E. Cook, minors under 14yrs.

COOK –pg. 265; Sept. 1865. Charles H. Cook of Ocean Tshp., a minor over 14yrs., chose his
mother, Caroline C. Cook, as his guardian.

HOADLEY –pg. 267; Sept. 1865. Elisa Jane Hoadley of Bramford, Conn., a minor over 14yrs.,
elected her husband, Paschal K. Hoadley of Bramford, Conn., and Jonathan Morgan of
Matawan, Monmouth Co., N.J. as her guardians.

PITTENGER –pg. 268; Sept. 1865. Richard Pittenger of Howell Tshp. requested guardianship of
his children Elmeretta Pittenger, Washington Pittenger, and Christina Pittenger, minors under
14yrs.

PITTENGER –pg. 268; Sept. 1865. Lydia G. Pittenger, a minor over 14yrs., elected Richard
Pittenger as her guardian.

TALLMAN –pg. 271; Sept. 1865. Abram T. Vanderveer, as guardian of Mary E. Vanderveer,
petitioned for a division of the real estate owned by William Tallman, dec'd., also known as
William Tallman Jr. He left a will devising lifetime estates to his four daus. Martha S.
(Tallman) (Williams) Bennett, Emily N. Tallman, Cordelia Tallman, and Mary E. Tallman.
Widow of said William Tallman Jr., dec'd.: Elizabeth Tallman.
Children of his dau. Martha S. Bennett, wife of Harman Bennett, formerly the widow Martha
S. Williams: Charles E. Williams; Daniel Williams, under 21yrs.; Mary A. Williams, under
21yrs.; William Bennett, under 21yrs.; Evelyn Bennett, under 21yrs.; Martha S. Bennett,
under 21yrs.; and Maria Bennett, under 21yrs.
Children of Emily N. Lewis, late Emily N. Tallman, wife of Charles Lewis: James T. Lewis,
under 21yrs.; George Lewis, under 21yrs.; Charles Lewis, under 21yrs.; and Emeline Lewis,
under 21yrs.
Children of Cordelia L. Conover, late Cordelia L. Tallman, wife of Garret S. Conover: Mary
E. Conover, under 21yrs.; Emily L. Conover, under 21yrs.; Charles H. Conover, under 21yrs.;
and Jane A. Conover, under 21yrs.
Child of Mary E. Vanderveer, dec'd., late Mary E. Tallman, late wife of Abram Vanderveer:
Mary E. Vanderveer, 21yrs. old, petitioner.

HOLMES –pg. 292; Sept. 1865. Asher H. Holmes of Marlboro Tshp. requested guardianship of his
step-son Tylee S. Holmes, a minor under 14yrs.

COOK –pg. 298; Sept. 1865. Caroline C. Cook petitioned for a division of the real estate owned by
Albert S. Cook, dec'd.
Widow: Caroline C. Cook, entitled to her dower.
Heirs entitled to 1/3 share each: Charles H. Cook, Bloomfield Cook, and Mary E. Cook.

BROWER –pg. 301; Sept. 1865. Mary Borden petitioned for a division of the real estate owned by
Benjamin Brower, dec'd., who died leaving a will.
Entitled to 1/3 share: Mary Borden, petitioner.
Children of Robert W. Brower, entitled to 1/3 share total: Ambrose Brower, under 21yrs.;
Samuel Brower, under 21yrs.; Andrew Brower, under 21yrs.; and John E. Brower, under
21yrs.
Children of Margaret Sickles, entitled to 1/3 share total: Benjamin Sickles, under 21yrs.;
Tunis Sickles, under 21yrs.; Mary E. Sickles, under 21yrs.; and Robert Sickles, under 21yrs.

ANTONIDES –pg. 307; Dec. 1865. Martha Ann Newell petitioned for a division of the real estate
owned by David Antonides, dec'd. Martha Ann Newell was entitled to 1/2 share. Daniel J.
Antonides, a minor under 21yrs., son of Polhemus Antonides, dec'd., was entitled to 1/2
share. Hetty Antonides, widow of said David Antonides, dec'd., was entitled to her dower.

WILLIAMS –pg. 312; Dec. 1865. Thomas T. Williams petitioned for a division of the real estate
owned by Daniel Williams, dec'd.

Children of Daniel Williams, dec'd.: Catherine T. Borden; Elizabeth Woolley, wife of Eden
Woolley; John Williams; Ann C. Sutherland, wife of John D. Sutherland; Charles E.
Williams; Mary T. Williams; and Thomas T. Williams, the petitioner.
Grandchildren who were children of his son Israel Williams, dec'd.: Charles E. Williams;
Daniel Williams, under 21yrs.; and Mary A. Williams, under 21yrs.

CHAMBERLIN –pg. 317; Dec. 1865. David Johnes petitioned for a division of the real estate
    owned by Daniel J. Chamberlin, dec'd.
    Entitled to 1/3 share each: David Johnes; Elizabeth Chamberlin, under 21yrs.; and Daniel
    Chamberlin, under 21yrs.

ALLEN –pg. 318; Dec. 1865. William Poling and Eleanor Poling petitioned for a division of the
    real estate owned by Ann Allen, dec'd., late wife of Jacob Allen.
    Entitled to 1/5 share each: Margaret Brown, wife of Alexander Brown; Stephen Allen; and
    Eleanor Poling, the petitioner.
    Daughter of James Allen, dec'd., entitled to 1/5 share: Ellenida Allen, under 21yrs.
    Children of William Allen, dec'd., entitled to 1/10 share each: William Allen, under 21yrs.;
    and Catherine Allen, under 21yrs. Margaret Allen, widow of William Allen, dec'd., was
    entitled to her dower from this 1/10 share.

CONOVER –pg. 324; Dec. 1865. Louisa Conover of Freehold Tshp., a minor over 14yrs., chose
    Sarah E. Conover of the same township as her guardian.

CONOVER –pg. 324; Dec. 1865. Hannah Conover of Manalapan Tshp. requested guardianship of
    her dau. Juliet Conover, a minor under 14yrs.

COTTRELL –pg. 343; Dec. 1865. Garret Cottrell petitioned for a division of the real estate co-
    owned by himself and Daniel G. Cottrell, dec'd. Garret Cottrell, as grantee in the original
    deed, was entitled to 1/2 share. Rachel E. Cottrell, under 21yrs., as heir of Daniel G. Cottrell,
    dec'd., was entitled to the other half. Mary Cottrell, widow of Daniel G. Cottrell, dec'd., was
    entitled to her dower.

CONOVER –pg. 351 – 362; Dec. 1865. Sarah E. Conover of Freehold Tshp. asked the court to
    declare her sister Margaret L. Conover of Freehold Tshp. mentally incompetent. Margaret L.
    Conover had been deprived of reason for fourteen months and was placed in an asylum on
    Sept. 13, 1864.
    Father: Daniel Conover, 57yrs. old.
    Siblings: Sarah E. Conover, 31yrs. old; Mary A. Conover, 28yrs. old; Louisa Conover, 18yrs.
    old; and William D. Conover, 23yrs. old.

BARRICLO –pg. 365; Dec. 1865. William H. Barriclo of Holmdel Tshp., a minor over 14yrs.,
    chose Peter S. Golden as his guardian.

BARRICLO –pg. 366; Dec. 1865. Peter S. Golden requested guardianship of his nephew John G.
    Barriclo and niece Catherine G. Barriclo, minors under 14yrs., children of William J. Barriclo,
    dec'd.

ESTELL –pg. 374; March 1866. Elizabeth Estell requested guardianship of her children John Estell,
    Mary Estell, Andrew J. Estell, and David Estell, minors under 14yrs.

ESTELL –pg. 375; March 1866. Sarah E. Clayton, Robert J. Estell, and Rebecca Estell, minors over
    14yrs., elected their mother, Elizabeth Estell of Freehold Tshp., as their guardian.

VAUGHN –pg. 390; April 1866. Samuel Vaughn petitioned for a division of the real estate owned
    by Samuel Vaughn Sr., dec'd., late of Millstone Tshp. who died leaving a will.
    Entitled to 1/7 share each: Mercy Mount, wife of William H. Mount Jr.; Mary E. Gordon,
    wife of Thomas Gordon.
    Entitled to 2/7 share each: Thomas S. Vaughn; and Samuel Vaughn, the petitioner.
    Children of Permelia Ely, dec'd., late wife of John L. Ely, entitled to 1/7 share total: Caroline
    E. Robins, wife of Charles Robins; Abigail A. Ely; John Henry Ely; and Rainbert Ely, under
    21yrs.

BRAILLARD –pg. 392; April 1866. Francis F. Braillard petitioned for a division of the real estate
    owned by Francis Braillard, dec'd., late of Marlboro Tshp.
    Widow: Francis Braillard, entitled to her dower.
    Entitled to 1/5 share each: Julius L. Braillard, under 21yrs.; Adilla Braillard, under 21yrs.;

Emyle Braillard, under 21yrs.; Henry Edward Braillard, under 21yrs.; and Francis F. Braillard, the petitioner.

SECOR –pg. 407; April 1866. Oliveretta C. Secor of Freehold Tshp., a minor over 14yrs., elected her aunt Phebe Ann Lawrence of Freehold Tshp. as her guardian.

EMMONS –pg. 408; April 1866. Mary Annah Emmons and Charles Edward Emmons of Freehold Tshp., minors over 14yrs., elected their mother, Rachel S. Emmons, as their guardian. Note: two separate entries on the same page.

ELY –pg. 409; April 1866. Rainbert Ely of Millstone Tshp., a minor over 14yrs., chose John L. Ely as his guardian.

POOLE –pg. 410; April 1866. Solomon G. Brown of Ocean Tshp. requested guardianship of Phebe E. Poole, a minor under 14yrs., dau. of Hendrick Poole who was still living.

CARHART –pg. 410; April 1866. Eleanor D. Wagner requested guardianship of her children Zephina Carhart and John Carhart, minors under 14yrs., children of Daniel A. Carhart of Holmdel Tshp.

CROXSON –pg. 411; April 1866. Reuhama C. Clayton, a minor over 14yrs., dau. of Jonathan C. Croxson who was still living, chose her husband, Granden L. Clayton, as her guardian.

CROXSON –pg. 411; April 1866. Ann M. Croxson, a minor over 14yrs., chose her father, Jonathan C. Croxson, as her guardain.

COTTRELL –pg. 412; April 1866. Job Cottrell requested guardianship of his children Clark Cottrell, Louisa Cottrell, William Cottrell, and Maggie Cottrell, minors under 14yrs.

COTTRELL –pg. 412: April 1866. Joel P. Cottrell and Gertrude A. Cottrell, minors over 14yrs., chose their father, Job Cottrell, as their guardian.

CROXSON –pg. 413; April 1866. Jonathan C. Croxson requested guardianship of his son Joseph B. Croxson, a minor under 14yrs.

PATTERSON –pg. 414; April 1866. John DuBois requested guardianship of Amos Patterson and Marietta Patterson, minors under 14yrs., children of Albert Patterson, dec'd.

LAYTON –pg. 414; April 1866. Alice Layton, a minor over 14yrs., dau. of William H. Layton, dec'd., elected James Cooper as her guardian.

LAYTON –pg. 415; April 1866. Mary S. Brown, a minor over 14yrs., dau. of William H. Layton, dec'd., chose her husband, Joseph Brown, as her guardian.

LAYTON –pg. 415; April 1866. James Cooper was appointed guardian of Charlotte Layton, a minor under 14yrs., dau. of William H. Layton, dec'd.

SICKLES –pg. 416; April 1866. Eleanor J. Sickles, a minor over 14yrs., dau. of William Sickles, dec'd., chose her mother, Hannah S. Sickles, as her guardian.

SICKLES –pg. 416; April 1866. Hannah S. Sickles requested guardianship of her children Sarah Jane Sickles, Laura Sickles, Irene Sickles, and William J. Sickles, minors under 14yrs., children of William Sickles, dec'd.

BOOK S

1866 – 1868

BRINLEY –pg. 14; April 1866. Mary Jane Brinley, a minor over 14yrs., dau. of Henry R. Brinley, dec'd., elected her brother Walter R. Brinley of Ocean Tshp. as her guardian.

BRINLEY –pg. 15; April 1866. Walter R. Brinley requested guardianship of his sister Laura A. Brinley, a minor under 14yrs., dau. of Henry R. Brinley, dec'd.

COLE –pg. 17; April 1866. John Morris and his wife, Mary Ann, petitioned the court to distribute the estate of Aaron Cole, dec'd.
Entitled to 1/5 share each: Mary Ann Morris, wife of John Morris; Emma Layton, wife of George Layton; Sarah Macole, wife of James Macole; George Harris; and Charles Harris.

COTTRELL –pg. 19; April 1866. George W. Patterson requested guardianship of Silas H. Cottrell, Mary L. Cottrell, and Annie E. Cottrell, minors under 14yrs., children of John L. Cottrell, dec'd.

HARRIS –pg. 20; April 1866. Emlin Satterthwaite requested guardianship of Charles Harris, a minor under 14yrs., son of Tallman Harris, dec'd.

HEYER –pg. 32; Sept. 1866. Koertenius C. Heyer petitioned the court for division of the real estate owned by John V. M. Heyer, dec'd., late of Atlantic Tshp.
Entitled to 1/3 share each: Koertenius C. Heyer and John H. Heyer.
Children of Joseph Heyer, dec'd., entitled to 1/3 share total: Sarah Wikoff, wife of Henry Wikoff; Lydia Wikoff, wife of Koertenius H. Wikoff; and Dewitt Heyer, under 21yrs.

HOLMES –pg. 38; Sept. 1866. Asher Holmes of Raritan Tshp. requested guardianship of his children Franklin P. Holmes, Daniel W. Holmes, Alice W. Holmes, Lydia B. Holmes, Eugene A. Holmes, and Mary E. Holmes, minors under 14yrs.

WOOLLEY –pg. 38; Sept. 1866. Montillion W. Woolley of Ocean Tshp. requested guardianship of John B. Woolley and Charles M. Woolley, minors under 14yrs., children of James T. Woolley, dec'd.

ASAY –pg. 39; Sept. 1866. Lafayett G. Schanck of Atlantic Tshp. requested guardianship of Mary Ellen Asay and James H. Asay, minor under 14yrs., children of John Asay, dec'd.

LAYTON –pg. 39; Sept. 1866. R. Morris Hartshorne of Freehold requested guardianship of William P. Layton, a minor under 14yrs., son of William Layton, dec'd.

MARTIN –pg. 40; Sept. 1866. Cornelius Smith of Ocean Tshp. requested guardianship of Laura J. Martin, a minor under 14yrs., dau. of Benjamin Martin, dec'd.

REID –pg. 59; Sept. 1866. John W. Estell and his wife, Ann M. Estell, petitioned for a division of the real estate owned by Charles T. Reid, dec'd.
Widow: Adaline Reid, entitled to her dower.
Entitled to 1/4 share each: Adaline Hampton, wife of Sidney Hampton; Ann Maria Estell, wife of John W. Estell, the petitioner; William Reid, under 21yrs.; and Charles T. Reid, under 21yrs.

WARD –pg. 60; Sept. 1866. Elizabeth H. Ward of Freehold, a minor over 14yrs., dau. of William V. Ward, dec'd., chose her mother, Catherine K. Ward, as her guardian.

WARD –pg. 61; Sept. 1866. Catherine K. Ward requested guardianship of her children Everett Ward and George F. Ward, minors under 14yrs., children of William V. Ward, dec'd.

VANBUREN –pg. 61; Sept. 1866. Elizabeth Eldridge requested guardianship of Abby A. Vanburen, a minor under 14yrs., dau. of Dr. John H. Vanburen of Hudson, N.Y., dec'd.

MCMINN –pg. 65; Sept. 1866. John W. Parker of Shrewsbury Tshp. requested guardianship of Julia Ann McMinn and David McMinn, minors under 14yrs., children of Samuel McMinn, dec'd.

REED –pg. 68; Sept. 1866. Sara Ann Reed requested guardianship of Jonathan Reed, Margaret Reed, and Catherine Reed, minors under 14yrs., children of Daniel Reed, dec'd.

POLAND –pg. 69; Sept. 1866. William H. Havens and Mary J. Havens requested guardianship of Mary A. Poland, a minor under 14yrs., dau. of Barnes B. Poland, dec'd.

COTTRELL –pg. 70; Sept. 1866. Martha E. Cottrell requested guardianship of Mary Cottrell, a minor under 14yrs., dau. of Nelson L. Cottrell, dec'd.

HOLMES –pg. 74; Sept. 1866. Mary L. Holmes petitioned for a division of the real estate owned by Jonathan L. Holmes, dec'd.
Entitled to 1/6 share each: Mary L. Holmes, the petitioner; Catherine S. Jones, wife of William L. Jones; Rhoda Holmes; Ellen Holmes; and Huldah Holmes.
Entitled to 1/6 share total: Ellen Thorne, under 21yrs.; and Ann Eliza Thorne, under 21yrs.

THOMPSON –pg. 82; Sept. 1866. Gertrude Thompson, a minor over 14yrs., dau. of Joseph Thompson, dec'd., elected Robert Stewart of Bordentown, Burlington Co. as her guardian.

MCGEE –pg. 84; Sept. 1866. Mary E. McGee and John H. McGee, minors over 14yrs., children of John H. McGee, chose Samuel Applegate as their guardian.

SCUDDER –pg. 89; Sept. 1866. William M. Scudder, a minor over 14yrs., chose his father, Henry G. Scudder of Huntington, Suffolk Co., N.Y. as his guardian.

SCUDDER –pg. 89; Sept. 1866. Henry G. Scudder of Huntington, Suffolk Co., N.Y. requested guardianship of his children Nora Scudder and Henry G. Scudder Jr., minors under 14yrs.

JOHNSON –pg. 90; Sept. 1866. Alice Jackson of Monroe Tshp., Middlesex Co. requested guardianship of Ann Amelia Johnson, a minor under 14yrs., dau. of Patience Johnson, dec'd., late of Monmouth Co.

LONGSTREET –pg. 96 – 105; Dec. 1866. Corlies L. Emmons of Howell Tshp. petitioned the court to declare his brother-in-law Mahlon M. Longstreet of Howell Thsp. mentally incompetent. He was the 45yr. old son of Richard Longstreet, dec'd., and had been deprived of reason for years.
Siblings: Thomas W. Longstreet; James Longstreet; David Longstreet; and Hetty Smith, wife of John C. Smith.
His only child: Richard Longstreet, 3yrs. old.

DORN –pg. 106 – 118; Dec. 1866. John Dorn of Holmdel Tshp. petitioned the court to declare William P. Dorn of Holmdel Tshp. mentally incompetent. He was single, about 23yrs. old, and had been deprived of reason for two years. He had lived with his parents until Dec. 28, 1865, when his father, Samuel Dorn, placed him in an asylum. He was still in the asylum, and his father had recently died.
Mother: Hepsibeth E. Dorn, widow of Samuel Dorn, dec'd.
Siblings: John M. Dorn of Holmdel Tshp., 22yrs. old; James W. Dorn, 18yrs. old; and Hannah C. Dorn, 20yrs. old.

PERRINE –pg. 118 – 130; Dec. 1866. Stephen Perrine of Millstone Tshp. petitioned the court to declare his brother Matthew Perrine of Millstone Tshp. mentally incompetent. Matthew Perrine, aged 56yrs., son of Joseph and Elizabeth Perrine, had been deprived of reason since infancy. His father died when Matthew was 11yrs. old and he lived with his mother until she died on April 23, 1866. His living relatives consisted of siblings, nephews, and nieces.
Siblings: Mary Hankinson, 68yrs. old, wife of William Hankinson, resident of N.Y.; Margaret Hendrickson, 64yrs. old, widow of Tobias Hendrickson, dec'd., resident of Monmouth Co., N.J.; Hannah Mount, 48yrs. old, wife of Hezekiah Mount; Caroline E. Baird, 45yrs. old, wife of Zebulon Baird, resident of Ill.; and Stephen Perrine, 54yrs. old.
Children of his brother John Perrine, dec'd.: Mary E. Emley, 35yrs. old, wife of William Emley, resident of Ill.; Joseph Perrine, 34yrs. old, resident of Middlesex Co., N.J.; William

M. Perrine, 30yrs. old, resident of Ill.; and Lydia Smock, 25yrs. old, wife of Henry Smock, resident of Monmouth Co., N.J.
Children of his brother William I. Perrine, dec'd.: Peter F. Perrine, 37yrs. old, resident of Middlesex Co., N.J.; Catherine E. Hendrickson, 35yrs. old, widow of David V. Hendrickson, dec'd.; Joseph W. Perrine, 32yrs. old, resident of Monmouth Co., N.J.; Stephen Perrine, 23yrs. old, resident of Monmouth Co., N.J.; Francis R. Perrine, 21yrs. old, resident of Monmouth Co., N.J.; and Sarah E. Perrine, 19yrs. old, who had no legal guardian.

VANBRACKLE –pg. 132; Dec. 1866. Thomas E. VanBrakle petitioned for a division of the real estate owned by Stephen VanBrakle, dec'd.
Entitled to 1/6 share each: Thomas E. VanBrakle; George W. VanBrakle; and Charles Wyckoff, under 21yrs.
Entitled to 3/6 share: James M. VanBrakle.

FROST –pg. 133; Dec. 1866. Samuel T. Frost petitioned for a division of the real estate owned by Benjamin Frost, dec'd.
Widow: Sarah B. Frost, entitled to her dower.
Entitled to 1/7 share each: Samuel T. Frost, the petitoner; Henry J. Frost; Jane F. Taylor; Lydia T. Frost; Sarah B. Frost; George C. Frost, under 21yrs.; and Kate C. Frost, under 21yrs

HARTMAN –pg. 148; Dec. 1866. Sarah E. Hartman, now Sarah E. Tantum, guardian of Walter Hartman, was ordered to provide more surety on her bond.

ALLEN –pg. 148; Dec. 1866. George Middleton, administrator of the estate of Elizabeth T. Allen, dec'd., was ordered to pay the remaining proceeds of the estate to the available heirs. In Aug of 1845, Emily Hooper, Beulah Ann Pew, Lydia Cafferty, and Joel R. Allen were entitled to, and paid, 1/5 share each. Theodore Coulter and Samuel Coulter, sons of Harriet Coulter, dec'd., late dau. of Elizabeth T. Allen, dec'd., were entitled to 1/5 share total, but George Middleton could not locate Theodore or Samuel Coulter. After 20yrs., their whereabouts remained unknown.

GRIGGS –pg. 150; Dec. 1866. Orsemus Griggs petitioned for a division of the real estate owned by John W. Griggs, dec'd.
Widow: Hannah A. Griggs, entitled to her dower.
Heirs entitled to 1/5 share each: Orsemus Griggs; Catherine A. Griggs; Mary A. Griggs; Benjamin F. Griggs; and Lydia C. Griggs, under 21yrs.

HOWLAND –pg. 151; Dec. 1866. Maribath Howland, guardian of Charles H. Howland and Michael A. Howland, petitioned for a division of the real estate owned by Michael Howland, dec'd.
Widow: Maribath Howland, the petitioner, entitled to her dower.
Heirs entitled to 1/4 share each: Elihu Howland; James W. Howland; Charles H. Howland, under 21yrs.; and Michael Howland, under 21yrs.

DORN –pg. 154; Dec. 1866. Hannah C. Dorn, a minor over 14yrs., dau. of Samuel Dorn, dec'd., elected John Dorn as her guardian.

DORN –pg. 155; Dec. 1866. James W. Dorn, a minor over 14yrs., son of Samuel Dorn, dec'd., elected John Dorn as his guardian.

RAVATT –pg. 155; Dec. 1866. Daniel W. Ravatt, a minor over 14yrs., son of William S. Ravatt, dec'd., chose Edmund M. Throckmorton as his guardian.

RAVATT –pg. 156; Dec. 1866. George M. Ravatt, a minor over 14yrs., son of William S. Ravatt, dec'd., chose Edmund M. Throckmorton as his guardian. Note: George's middle initial was given as an 'M,' but in subsequent records it was 'W.' See Book S, pg. 288 and pg. 318.

RAVATT –pg. 156; Dec. 1866. William V. Conover requested guardianship of Euretta Ravatt, Catherine S. Ravatt, and William Ravatt, minors under 14yrs., children of William Ravatt, dec'd.

POLHEMUS –pg. 157; Dec. 1866. Ann Polhemus requested guardianship of her children Charles Polhemus, DeWitt Polhemus, John H. Polhemus, and Ann M. Polhemus, minors under 14yrs. children of William Polhemus, dec'd.

MATTHEWS –pg. 158; Dec. 1866. Joseph B. Bailey of Raritan Tshp. requested guardianship of

John S. Matthews, a minor under 14yrs., son of Joseph Matthews who was in the insane asylum.

WOLCOTT –pg. 158; Dec. 1866. Nathan P. Teed of Ocean Tshp. requested guardianship of Ann Wolcott and Hannah Wolcott, minors under 14yrs., children of Gordon Wolcott, dec'd.

DAVIS –pg. 159; Dec. 1866. Annie E. Davis, a minor over 14yrs., elected her father, Thomas Davis, as her guardian.

BRUERE –pg. 176; Dec. 1866. Lafayette S. Schanck requested guardianship of Ann Bruere, Forman Bruere, Henry Bruere, and Willie Bruere, minors under 14yrs., children of William Bruere, dec'd.

REED –pg. 177; Dec. 1866. Antoinette Reed, a minor over 14yrs., dau. of Jonathan F. Reed, dec'd., chose Catherine Reed as her guardian.

POPE –pg. 177; Dec. 1866. Albert Pope, a minor over 14yrs., son of Amos Pope, dec'd., elected James M. Atkins as his guardian.

CASE –pg. 189; Dec. 1866. William H. Case of Freehold Tshp. requested guardianship of his children Evilina Case and Florence Case, minors under 14yrs.

YOUNG –pg. 197; Dec. 1866. Sarah S. Young, a minor over 14yrs., dau. of John Young who was still alive but resided outside N.J., chose James S. Yard as her guardian.

THOMPSON –pg. 198; Dec. 1866. Carrie Thompson, a minor over 14yrs., dau. of Joseph Thompson, dec'd., chose her mother, Malvina Thompson, as her guardian.

PATTERSON –pg. 198; Dec. 1866. Hannah J. Patterson, a minor over 14yrs., child of Daniel T. Hendrickson, dec'd., chose her mother, Deborah A. Hendrickson, as her guardian.

HENDRICKSON –pg. 199; Dec. 1866. Fannie M. Hendrickson and George M. Hendrickson, minors over 14yrs., children of Daniel T. Hendrickson, elected their mother, Deborah A. Hendrickson, as their guardian. Note: two separate entries on the same page.

HENDRICKSON –pg. 200; Dec. 1866. Deborah A. Hendrickson requested guardianship of her children Daniel C. Hendrickson and Charles T. Hendrickson, minors under 14yrs., children of Daniel T. Hendrickson, dec'd.

RUE –pg. 201; Dec. 1866. Daniel J. Rue and Forman M. Rue, minors over 14yrs., children of Daniel J. Rue, dec'd., elected Ellen Rue of Mercer Co., N.J. and Jacob Wycoff of Middlesex Co., N.J. as their guardians.

REID –pg. 201; Dec. 1866. Adaline C. Reid requested guardianship of her son Charles Reid, a minor under 14yrs., son of Charles T. Reid, dec'd.

CONOVER –pg. 202; Dec. 1866. Maria Louisa Conover and Eliza Ann Conover, minors over 14yrs., children of John P. Conover, dec'd., chose George Schenck as their guardian. Note: two separate entries on the same page.

CONOVER –pg. 203; Dec. 1866. George Schenck requested guardianship of Henrietta Conover Jr., a minor under 14yrs., dau. of John P. Conover, dec'd.

SCHENCK –pg. 207 – 208; Dec. 1866. The court ordered payment of money from the estate of John R. Schenck, dec'd. to his great grandson's guardian. John R. Schenck, dec'd., left a legacy to his granddaughter Eliza Jane Honce who later married Paschal K. Hoadley of Conn. Eliza Jane Hoadley died leaving a son, James Morgan Hoadley, who was entitled to his mother's legacy.

REID –pg. 210; Dec. 1866. William D. Reid, a minor over 14yrs., son of Charles T. Reid, dec'd., late of Howell Tshp., chose Sidney T. Hampton as his guardian.

LAYTON –pg. 211; Dec. 1866. Sarah A. Newman requested guardianship of Joseph H. Layton, a minor under 14yrs., son of Josiah Layton, dec'd.

REED –pg. 212; Dec. 1866. Harriet Reed, a minor over 14yrs., dau. of Daniel Reed, dec'd., elected her mother, Sarah A. Reed, as her guardian.

GRIGGS –pg. 212; Dec. 1866. Lydia C. Griggs, a minor over 14yrs., dau. of John W. Griggs, dec'd., chose her mother, Hannah A. Griggs, as her guardian.

SPINNING –pg. 236; April 1867. Thomas W. Spinning petitioned for a division of the real estate owned by Daniel Spinning, dec'd.
Entitled to 1/6 share each: Thomas W. Spinning, the petitioner; Ansel Spinning; Matilda A. Layton; Elvira Chadwic; and Daniel Spinning.
Entitled to 1/6 share total: Emeline Wimple; Elizabeth Tabor; John Wolcott; Daniel Wolcott; Charles H. Wolcott; George W. Wolcott; Hester A. Wolcott; Thomas I. Wolcott; Martha Francis Wolcott, under 21yrs.; Benjamin T. Wolcott, under 21yrs.; and Edward M. W. Wolcott, under 21yrs.

WALLING –pg. 243; April 1867. Andrew J. Walling petitioned for a division of the real estate owned by Capt. Isaac Walling, dec'd.
Entitled to 1/6 share each: Andrew J. Walling, William Walling, Lydia A. Wolcott, Isaac H. Walling, and Celia L. Strong.
Entitled to 1/6 share total: Emma Force, under 21yrs.; William Force Jr., under 21yrs.; and Elias Force, under 21yrs.

SCHENCK –pg. 245; April 1867. The distribution of the estate of John P. Schenck, dec'd., identified John P. Tunis, Charles Tunis, and Daniel Tunis as children of Rhoda Tunis, dec'd., although the record referred to them as J., C., and D. Tunis. Note: See Book R, pg. 3, April 1864.

NEWCOMB –pg. 251; April 1867. Andrew J. Newcomb, a minor over 14yrs., son of Suther Newcomb, chose Calvin W. Newcomb as his guardian.

BRAILLARD –pg. 251; April 1867. Emile Braillard and Adella Ambruster, minors over 14yrs., children of Francis Braillard of N.Y., dec'd., chose their mother, Francois Braillard of Williamsburg, N.Y. as their guardian.

BRAILLARD –pg. 252; April 1867. Francois Braillard requested guardianship of her son Henry E. Braillard, a minor under 14yrs., son of Francis Braillard, dec'd., late of N.Y.

HEYER –pg. 252; April 1867. DeWitt C. Heyer, a minor over 14yrs., son of Joseph C. Heyer, dec'd., elected Koertenius C. Heyer as his guardian.

MCCORMICK –pg. 253; April 1867. Catherine M. McCormick of N.Y. City, N.Y., a minor over 14yrs., chose Bridget M. McCormick of N.Y. City, N.Y. as her guardian.

HERBERT –pg. 254; April 1867. Martha E. Herbert, a minor over 14yrs., elected John O. Herbert as her guardian.

YOUNGS –pg. 254; April 1867. Margaret A. Youngs requested guardianship of her children John Youngs, Benjamin Youngs, Theodore Youngs, Eveline Youngs, and Joseph Youngs, minors under 14yrs., children of John Youngs, dec'd.

BENNETT –pg. 255; April 1867. Catherine E. Bennett requested guardianship of her children Sarah A. Bennett, Ellen Bennett, Thomas Bennett, Theodore H. Bennett, and Richard B. Bennett, minors under 14yrs., children of Thomas Bennett, dec'd.

BENNETT –pg. 256; April 1867. John H. Bennett, Catherine E. Bennett, and Jeremiah Bennett, minors over 14yrs., chose their mother, Catherine E. Bennett, as their guardian.

CONK –pg. 279; April 1867. Matilda Conk, a minor over 14yrs., dau. of William Conk, dec'd., chose Albert B. Hall as her guardian.

CONK –pg. 279; April 1867. Albert B. Hall requested guardianship of Deborah Ann Conk, Charles Conk, Anthony Conk, and Aaron Conk, minors under 14yrs., children of William Conk, dec'd.

SCHANCK –pg. 286; April 1867. Robert C. Schanck, a minor over 14yrs., son of John Schanck, dec'd., elected John W. Ely as his guardian.

ALLEN –pg. 286; April 1867. Mary E. Allen requested guardianship of her dau. Mary H. Allen, a minor under 14yrs., dau. of Robert H. Allen, dec'd.

RAVATT –pg. 288; April 1867. George W. Ravatt, a minor over 14yrs., son of William S. Ravatt, dec'd., chose David B. Stout as his guardian.

WOLCOTT –pg. 289; April 1867. Benjamin S. Wolcott, a minor over 14yrs., elected his father, Benjamin Wolcott, as his guardian.

WOLCOTT –pg. 290; April 1867. Martha F. Wolcott, a minor over 14yrs., elected her father, Benjamin Wolcott, as her guardian.

SHEPHERD –pg. 290; April 1867. Kate Shepherd, a minor over 14yrs., dau. of Joseph Shepherd, dec'd., chose her mother, Elizabeth Shepherd, as her guardian.

SHEPHERD –pg. 291; April 1867. Annie Shepherd, a minor over 14yrs., dau. of Joseph Shepherd, dec'd., chose her mother, Elizabeth Shepherd, as her guardian.

SCHANCK –pg. 293; April 1867. Morris H. Schanck, a minor over 14yrs., son of John Schanck, dec'd., elected Daniel Conover as his guardian.

SCHANCK –pg. 293; April 1867. Daniel Conover requested guardianship of Charles Schanck, a minor under 14yrs., son of John Schanck, dec'd.

THORNE –pg. 305; April 1867. Ann Eliza Thorne and Ellen S. Thorne, minors over 14yrs., children of Thomas W. Thorne, dec'd., chose Thomas W. Thorne as their guardian. Note: two separate entries on the same page.

HENDRICKSON –pg. 306; April 1867. Charles P. Hendrickson, a minor over 14yrs., son of Enoch C. Hendrickson, dec'd., chose his mother, Achsah E. Hendrickson, as his guardian.

HENDRICKSON –pg. 307; April 1867. Wilson Hendrickson and Sallie E. Hendrickson, minors over 14yrs., children of Enoch C. Hendrickson, dec'd., chose their mother, Achsah E. Hendrickson, as their guardian. Note: two separate entries on the same page.

HENDRICKSON –pg. 308; April 1867. Achsah E. Hendrickson requested guardianship of her dau. Hannah Hendrickson, a minor under 14yrs., dau. of Enoch C. Hendrickson, dec'd.

HENDRICKSON –pg. 316; Sept. 1867. Stout P. Hendrickson petitioned for a division of the real estate owned by Enoch C. Hendrickson, dec'd.
Widow: Achsah E. Hendrickson, entitled to her dower.
Entitled to 1/8 share each: Stout P. Hendrickson; Henry P. Hendrickson; Catherine Wells, wife of John C. Wells; Joseph P. Hendrickson; Wilson Hendrickson, under 21yrs.; Charles P. Hendrickson, under 21yrs.; Sarah E. Hendrickson, under 21yrs.; and Hannah Hendrickson, under 21yrs.

RAVATT –pg. 318; Sept. 1867. John S. Ravatt petitioned for a division of the real estate owned by William S. Ravatt, dec'd.
Widow: Emma Ravatt, entitled to her dower.
Entitled to 1/6 share each: John S. Ravatt; Elizabeth Ravatt; James Ravatt; Daniel Ravatt, under 21yrs.; and George W. Ravatt, under 21yrs.
Entitled to 1/6 share total, all under 21yrs.: Catherine Ravatt, William Ravatt, and Uretta Ravatt.

SHEERER –pg. 321; Sept. 1867. Sarah Cornell requested guardianship of her children Ella F. Sheerer, Aurora E. Sheerer, and Oliver E. E. Sheerer, minors under 14yrs., children of Joseph Sheerer, dec'd.

WALSH –pg. 325; Sept. 1867. Daniel A. Holmes requested guardianship of Edward Walsh, a minor under 14yrs., son of Caroline M. Walsh of Philadelphia, Pa.

REID –pg. 331; Sept. 1867. Charlotte R. Reid requested guardianship of her children Arthur F. Reid and Elwood Reid, minors under 14yrs.

WOOLLEY –pg. 353; Sept. 1867. James H. Marks and his wife, Catherine, petitioned for a division of the real estate owned by Adam Woolley, dec'd., late of Howell Tshp.

Widow: Mary Woolley, entitled to her dower.
Children: Catherine Marks, wife of James H. Marks; Elizabeth Clayton, wife of Reading
Clayton; Joseph Woolley; Jerusha Hall, wife of Sylvester Hall; Alfred Woolley; Rhoda Ann
Rogers, wife of William Rogers; Adam Woolley, under 21yrs.; Hannah Matilda Woolley,
under 21yrs.; Sarah Woolley, under 21yrs.; William Woolley, under 21yrs.; and Lydia
Woolley, under 21yrs.

LOKERSON –pg. 362; Sept. 1867. David Lokerson petitioned for a division of the real estate
owned by John Lokerson, dec'd., late of Freehold Tshp.
Widow: Alice Lokerson, entitled to her dower.
Entitled to 1/8 share each: David Lokerson; Susan Irons, wife of Aaron Irons; Caleb
Lokerson; Hugh B. Lokerson; Peter C. Lokerson; Thomas Lokerson, under 21yrs.; Jane
Lokerson, under 21yrs.; and Sarah Lokerson, under 21yrs.

CARMAN –pg. 365 - 368; Sept. 1867. The commissioners reported on the distribution of the estate
of Eden B. Carman, dec'd. They still held the share owed to Charles Martin because they
were unable to determine if he was living or not. Charles Martin had one sibling, his sole
heir, Caroline D. Gorham, wife of William R. Gorham. Caroline D. Gorham died intestate on
Oct. 29, 1860, leaving seven children, viz., John E. Gorham, Daniel Gorham, Caroline P.
Gorham, Mary Louisa Gorham, Thomas J. Gorham, Ida E. Gorham, and Charles M. Gorham.
All her children were living, with the exception of Charles M. Gorham who died June 15,
1867, unwed and intestate. The court ordered Charles Martin's share distributed amongst the
children of Caroline D. Gorham, dec'd.

GORHAM –pg. 368; Sept. 1867. William R. Gorham of N.Y. requested guardianship of his dau. Ida
E. Gorham, a minor under 14yrs.

JOBES –pg. 372; Sept. 1867. Ester A. Jobes, now Ester A. Manning, administrator of the estate of
Robert Jobes, dec'd., applied to sell the deceased's real estate to pay his debts.

RUE –pg. 374; Sept. 1867. James A. Rue, a minor over 14yrs., son of John M. Rue, chose his
mother, Mary E. Rue, as his guardian.

RUE –pg. 374; Sept. 1867. Mary E. Rue requested guardianship of her dau. Mary M. Rue, a minor
under 14yrs., dau. of John M. Rue.

PULLEN –pg. 381; Sept. 1867. Benjamin J. Pullen, heir of Stockton Pullen, dec'd., petitioned to
have the court assign the dower for Lydia Pullen, widow of the said Stockton Pullen, dec'd.
Heirs who were notified of the petition: Gilbert Pullen, Charles K. Pullen, Sarah Johnson,
Johnson Pullen, Adaline Haye, Rebecca Holloway, Charlotte Bodine, Mary Jane Larrison,
Susan J. Pullen, Mary Stackhouse, Charlotte Ely, and Isabella Pullen.
Heirs who were not notified of the petition: William Pullen, a resident of Ohio; Samuel
Pullen, a resident of Pa.; Charles K. Pullen, a resident of Ind.; Augustus Pullen, a resident of
Calif.; Rebecca A. Pullen, a resident of Philadelphia, Pa.; and Clark D. Pullen, a resident of
Philadelphia, Pa.

SCHANCK –pg. 386 - 387; Dec. 1867. John B. Crawford and his wife, Henrietta, along with John
E. Longstreet and his wife, Christianna H., petitioned for a division of the real estate owned
by both John Schanck, dec'd. and Jane Ann Schanck, dec'd., late of Marlboro Tshp.
Children entitled to 9/56 share each: Henrietta Crawford, wife of John B. Crawford; and
Christianna H. Longstreet, wife of John E. Longstreet.
Child entitled to 2/56 share: Elizabeth Morford, wife of Thomas Morford.
Children entitled to 9/56 share each: John Schanck; Robert C. Schanck, under 21yrs.; Morris
H. Schanck, under 21yrs.; and Charles Schanck, under 21yrs. This grouping of shares was
given as 9/46 in this record and corrected in subsequent records to the 9/56 shown. Note: See
Book S, pg. 470, Dec. 1867 for a more information on these heirs.

FORCE –pg. 388; Dec. 1867. Thomas S. R. Brown requested guardianship of William S. Force and
Elias C. Force, minors under 14yrs., children of Elizabeth Force, dec'd., late wife of William
S. Force.

EMMONS –pg. 401; Dec. 1867. Alexander S. Barkalow requested guardianship of Charles P.
Emmons and Mary Elizabeth Emmons, minors under 14yrs., children of William B. Emmons.
Note: In subsequent records, Alexander Barkalow's middle initial was given as 'L.' A
repetition of this record in Book S, pg. 435, Dec. 1867 reported Alexander L. Barkalow was
the step-father of the children.

QUACKENBUSH –pg. 416; Dec. 1867. James S. Quackenbush, a minor over 14yrs., son of Peter Quackenbush, dec'd., chose Sarah J. Quackenbush as his guardian.

ALLGOR –pg. 419 – 433; Dec. 1867. Caroline Allgor of Wall Tshp. petitioned the court to declare her husband, Devine Allgor, mentally incompetent. He had been deprived of reason for more than six months and was confined to an asylum on June 1, 1867. Caroline Allgor, 44yrs. old, and Devine Allgor, 47yrs. old, were married for 26yrs. They had one living child, Mary Catherine Allgor, 22yrs. old.

CAMP –pg. 439; Dec. 1867. James Camp, a minor over 14yrs., son of David Camp, elected Sarah A. Woodward as his guardian.

PIERCE –pg. 440; Dec. 1867. Mary Ann Pierce, a minor over 14yrs., dau. of Asher Pierce, chose Ann Newman as her guardian.

PIERCE –pg. 441; Dec. 1867. Ann Newman was appointed guardian of Rachel Lavinia Pierce, Josephine Pierce, and Jacob E. Pierce, minors under 14yrs., children of Asher Pierce.

JONES –pg. 441; Dec. 1867. John Jones, a minor over 14yrs., son of Rachel Jones, chose Benjamin V. Dey as his guardian.

PARKER –pg. 442; Dec. 1867. George A. Parker was appointed guardian of Mary Ella Parker and John H. Parker, minors under 14yrs., children of Charles Parker.

PARKER –pg. 442; Dec. 1867. James H. Parker and Charles A. Parker, minors over 14yrs., children of Charles Parker, elected George A. Parker as their guardian.

THE TERM DATES WERE OUT OF SEQUENCE FOR THE REMAINDER OF BOOK S, BUT THE PAGE NUMBERS REMAINED IN SEQUENCE.

SCHANCK –pg. 443; Dec. 1868. Anna Schanck was appointed guardian of Georgiana Schanck and John W. Schanck, minors under 14yrs., children of Garret Schanck.

FROST –pg. 443; Dec. 1868. William V. Wilson was appointed guardian of Matilda Frost, William Henry Frost, and Lydia Frost, minors under 14yrs., children of Elijah L. Frost.

CONOVER –pg. 444; Dec. 1868. James W. Conover was appointed guardian of Henry Conover, Sarah W. Conover, and Ida L. Conover, minors under 14yrs., children of Eliza L. Conover.

VANDORN –pg. 444; Dec. 1868. John Baird was appointed guardian of George H. VanDorn, a minor under 14yrs., son of David M. VanDorn.

VANDORN –pg. 445; Dec. 1868. Ellen C. VanDorn, a minor over 14yrs., dau. of David M. VanDorn, chose John Baird as her guardian.

STOUT –pg. 445; Dec. 1868. Sidney Walling was appointed guardian of Sarah Stout, a minor under 14yrs., dau. of John B. Stout.

WOOLLEY –pg. 446; April 1868. Mary M. Woolley was appointed guardian of Sarah Woolley and Lydia Woolley, minors under 14yrs., children of Adam Woolley.

ESTELL –pg. 446; April 1868. Israel Reynolds was appointed guardian of George B. Estell, a minor under 14yrs., son of John A. Estell.

LOKERSON –pg. 447; Dec. 1867. Thomas S. Lokerson and Jane Lokerson, minors over 14yrs., children of John Lokerson, elected Alice Lokerson as their guardian.

LOKERSON –pg. 447; Dec. 1867. Alice Lokerson was appointed guardian of Sarah Lokerson, a minor under 14yrs., dau. of John Lokerson.

ROGERS –pg. 448; Dec. 1867. Eleanor A. Morris was appointed guardian of John M. Rogers, Vananzo Rogers, and George Patterson Rogers, minors under 14yrs., children of John M. Rogers.

ROGERS –pg. 448; Dec. 1867. James E. Rogers, a minor over 14yrs., son of John M. Rogers, chose Eleanor A. Morris as his guardian.

SCHANCK –pg. 449; Dec. 1867. John Schanck, a minor over 14yrs., son of John Schanck, elected Daniel Conover as his guardian.

ESTELL –pg. 451; April 1868. John H. Estell, Mary C. Estell, and Charles A. Estell, minors over 14yrs., children of John Allen Estell, chose Israel Reynolds as their guardian.

HIELD –pg. 451; April 1868. Ann S. Hield, a minor over 14yrs., dau. of William Hield, chose Mar L. Mount as her guardian.

PALMER –pg. 452; April 1868. Samuel G. Palmer, a minor over 14yrs., son of John Palmer, chose Charles P. Robbins as his guardian.

HIELD –pg. 452; April 1868. Mark L. Mount was appointed guardian of Norma S. Hield, a minor under 14yrs., dau. of William Hield.

WOOLLEY –pg. 453; April 1868. Hannah Woolley and William Woolley, minors over 14yrs., children of Adam Woolley, elected Mary M. Woolley as their guardian. Note: two separate entries on the same page.

WOOLLEY –pg. 454; April 1868. Adam P. Woolley, a minor over 14yrs., son of Adam Woolley, chose Mary M. Woolley as his guardian.

HULME –pg. 456; Sept. 1868. John L. Hulme was appointed guardian of Mary E. Hulme and Sarah M. Hulme, minors under 14yrs., children of Anna M. Hulme.

SMOCK –pg. 456; Sept. 1868. Forman Stillwell was appointed guardian of Ella Smock, a minor under 14yrs., dau. of John P. Smock.

PERRINE –pg. 457; Sept. 1868. Martha S. Perrine was appointed guardian of David M. C. Perrine, Mary E. Perrine, Thomas A. Perrine, Margaret I. Perrine, and Gilbert W. Perrine, minors under 14yrs., children of Gilbert W. Perrine.

VANMATER –pg. 457; Sept. 1868. John VanMater was appointed guardian of Charles VanMater, a minor under 14yrs., son of Benjamin VanMater.

PROVOST –pg. 458; Sept. 1868. Lewis W. Brown was appointed guardian of Lilian Provost, a minor under 14yrs., dau. of William Provost.

MCGEE –pg. 459; Sept. 1868. Charles R. McGee was appointed guardian of Kate L. McGee, a minor under 14yrs., dau. of Jacob McGee.

PATTEE –pg. 460; Dec. 1868. John Hilands was appointed guardian of Daniel Pattee, a minor under 14yrs., son of Mary Pattee.

COVERT –pg. 461; Dec. 1868. Daniel Covert was appointed guardian of George Covert, Cornelius C. Covert, and Mary A. Covert, minors under 14yrs., children of George W. Covert.

BROWN –pg. 461; Dec. 1868. Conrad Winters was appointed guardian of Catherine Brown, Matthew Brown, Eleanor Brown, and Mary Brown, minors under 14yrs., children of Philip Brown.

KEENER –pg. 462; Dec. 1868. William H. Keener was appointed guardian of Lucretia A. Keener, a minor under 14yrs., dau. of Catherine Keener.

WEST –pg. 462; Dec. 1868. Thomas West was appointed guardian of Emma West, a minor under 14yrs., dau. of Mary E. West.

SMOCK –pg. 468; Dec. 1867. Peter S. Smock petitioned for a division of the real estate owned by John R. Smock, dec'd., late of Middletown Tshp. The petitioner, Peter S. Smock, was entitled to 4/5 share and Ella Smock was entitled to 1/5 share.

SCHANCK –pg. 470 - 472: Dec. 1867. The distribution of the estate of John Schanck, dec'd., and Jane Ann Schanck, dec'd., reported the said Jane Ann Schanck, dec'd., was the late wife of said John Schanck, dec'd. In her lifetime, Jane Ann Schanck, dec'd., purchased the shares of Gordon Schanck and Elizabeth Conover, both children and devisees of John Schanck, dec'd. All children receiving shares were both devisees of John Schanck, dec'd. and heirs of Jane

Ann Schanck, except Elizabeth Morford. Elizabeth Morford was the dau. of Jane Ann Schanck, dec'd., by her former (unnamed) husband. As such, she was the heir of Jane Ann Schanck, dec'd., but not a devisee of John Schanck, dec'd. Note: See Book S, pg. 386, Dec. 1867 for original entry.

Children of John Schanck, dec'd.: Gordon Schanck, Elizabeth Conover, Henrietta Schanck, Christianna Schanck, John Schanck, Robert Schanck, Morris Schanck, and Charles Schanck.

MOUNT –pg. 485; April 1868. William S. Mount petitioned for a division of the real estate owned by Jane R. C. Mount, dec'd., late wife of Andrew Mount.

Entitled to 1/4 share each: William S. Mount; Josephine A. Gray, wife of Boyce Gray; and Georgia A. Worrall, wife of Lawrence Worrall.

Entitled to 1/8 share each: Andrew M. Platt, under 21yrs.; and William M. Platt, under 21yrs. Samuel K. Platt was entitled by curtesy to a lifetime estate in the shares due Andrew and William Platt. Andrew Mount was entitled by curtesy to a lifetime estate in the entire estate. Note: The deceased's name also appeared as Jane C. R. Mount.

BORDEN –pg. 489; April 1868. Josiah Borden petitioned for a division of the real estate owned by George Borden, dec'd.

Widow: Susan Borden, entitled to her dower.

Entitled to 1/5 share each: Josiah Borden; Francis Borden; Charlotte Longstreet, wife of George Longstreet; and Garret B. Borden.

Entitled to 1/10 share each: Charles Borden, under 21yrs.; and Randal Borden, under 21yrs.

HOWLAND –pg. 492; April 1868. Thomas Worthley and his wife, Ophelia Worthley, petitioned for a division of the real estate owned by Stewart Howland, dec'd.

Widow: Hannah Bishop, entitled to her dower.

Entitled to 5/20 share each: Ophelia Worthley, wife of Thomas Worthley; Peter Howland, under 21yrs.; and Susan Howland, under 21yrs.

Entitled to 1/20 share: Henry S. Howland (sold the other 4/20 of his share).

Entitled to 4/20 share: Edward Wardell, by purchasing shares from Henry S. Howland.

BOOK 1

1882 – 1885

WALLING –pg. 9; Jan. 1882. Distribution of the estate of Hannah Walling, dec'd., divided her
  estate by shares.
  Entitled to 4/15 share: Thomas M. Walling.
  Entitled to 3/15 share: Martha M. Ryder, formerly Martha Walling.
  Entitled to 8/15 share: Henrietta Scott, a minor and dau. of Hannah Scott, dec'd.
  Henry D. Scott was noted as the late husband of Hannah Scott, dec'd.

FIELDS –pg. 12; Jan. 1882. Distribution of the estate of Britton Fields, dec'd., divided the estate by
  shares.
  Entitled to 1/5 share each: Theodore Fields, John Fields, William Fields, and Ruth A. Sickles.
  Children of Henry E. Fields, dec'd., entitled to 1/5 share total: Reluis, Myron H. Fields and
  Effie Fields.
  Henry E. Fields, dec'd., also left a widow, Mary L. Fields. Note: Reluis' surname was not
  given in this record. See Book 1, pg. 75, Oct. 1882.

MUCHMORE –pg. 19; Jan. 1882. Minnie Muchmore was appointed guardian of Richard
  Muchmore, a minor under 14yrs.

IVINS –pg. 22; Jan. 1882. Mary L. Ivins was appointed guardian of Harry S. Ivins and Frank E.
  Ivins, minors under 14yrs.

APPLEBY –pg. 22; Jan. 1882. Charles E. Appleby was appointed guardian of Theodore F.
  Appleby, a minor over 14yrs.

APPLEBY –pg. 23; Jan. 1882. Charles E. Appleby was appointed guardian of Addie M. Appleby
  and Richard Henry Appleby, minors over 14yrs. Note: two separate entries on the same page.

SCHOCK –pg. 26; Jan. 1882. Rosa F. Schock was appointed guardian of Matthias F. Schock and
  Charles C. Schock, minors under 14yrs.

BRINLEY –pg. 27; May 1882. Francis M. Brinley and Edward Brinley petitioned for a division of
  the real estate owned by their father, Edward Brinley, dec'd., who died intestate. He left a
  widow and children.
  Widow: Andrewetta S. Brinley.
  Children: Francis M. Brinley; Edward Brinley; John R. Brinley, under 21yrs.; and Godfrey M.
  Brinley, under 21yrs.

NEWMAN –pg. 29; May 1882. James Holloway Newman petitioned for a division of the real estate
  owned by his father, Jeremiah Newman, dec'd. Jeremiah Newman, dec'd., left a will,
  probated in 1835, devising his property to his three children, John Lewis Newman, James
  Holloway Newman and Jane Newman. Jane Newman died intestate and unmarried. John
  Lewis Newman died Jan. 15, 1881, leaving a will that left his estate to his wife, Rebecca
  Newman, during her life. After her death his estate was to pass to his grandchildren Lewis
  Layton, Nathan Layton, Sarah L. Layton, and Delia Layton. Rebecca Newman died before
  her husband, and Lewis Layton, Nathan Layton, and Delia Layton also died unmarried and
  intestate. James Holloway Newman, the petitioner, and Sarah L. Layton, the great
  granddaughter, as surviving heirs of Jeremiah Newman, dec'd., were each entitled to a 1/2
  share of his property.

BENNETT –pg. 34; May 1882. John F. Mount of Brooklyn, N.Y., as guardian of Jennie R. Mount
  and Gracie H. Mount, also of Brooklyn, N.Y., petitioned the court for the money due his
  wards from the estate of William H. Bennett, dec'd., late of Monmouth Co., N.J. His wards
  were the only children of Evelina Mount, dec'd., who was a dau. of Sarah Hart, dec'd. The

said Sarah Hart, dec'd., was a legatee in the will of the William H. Bennett, dec'd.

MAINES –pg. 35; May 1882. James Maines petitioned for a division of the real estate he owned as
tenants in common with his siblings and their heirs.
Siblings holding 1/4 share each: James Maines, the petitioner; Catherine E. VanDorn; Lavenia
Crawford; and William Maines, dec'd. The said William Maines, dec'd., left two children
who were also deceased, viz., David W. Maines, dec'd., and Elizabeth V. Hooper, dec'd.
Elizabeth V. Hooper, dec'd., left a dau., Nellie Hooper. David W. Maines, dec'd., left a
widow, Eliza Maines, and a son, David W. Maines Jr. Nellie Hooper and David W. Maines
Jr. were entitled to 1/8 share each.

CONOVER –pg. 37; May 1882. William Craig Conover was appointed guardian of Margaret L.
Conover, a minor under 14yrs.

THOMPSON –pg. 38; May 1882. Samuel Thompson was appointed guardian of Mamie Thompson,
a minor over 14yrs.

BARNEY –pg. 48; May 1882. Janet L. Barney was appointed guardian of George A. Barney, a
minor over 14yrs.

ROBERTS –pg. 49; May 1882. Distribution of the estate of Elbridge G. Roberts, dec'd., who died
intestate leaving a widow and children.
Widow: Margaret Roberts.
Children: Mary E. Anderson, wife of Galusha Anderson; and Edward E. Roberts.

THOMASON –pg. 52; May 1882. Forest H. Parker of N.Y. City, N.Y., as guardian of Eveline T.
Parker, Jennie P. Parker, and Forrest H. Parker Jr. of N.Y. City, N.Y., requested payment of
the money due his wards as heirs of their uncle Dr. Thomas J. Thomason, dec'd., late of
Monmouth Co., N.J. who died intestate.

SCHANCK –pg. 66; May 1882. Micah Schanck was appointed guardian of John C. Schanck and
Mary P. Schanck, minors over 14yrs. Note: two separate entries on the same page.

GERAN –pg. 75; Oct. 1882. Jesiah P. Geran was appointed guardian of Carroll V. Geran, a minor
under 14yrs.

FIELDS –pg. 76; Oct. 1882. Mary L. Fields was appointed guardian of Aurelius Fields, Myron H.
Fields, and Effie L. Fields, minors under 14yrs.

BRAY –pg. 80; Oct. 1882. Margaret V. Bray was appointed guardian of Harriet W. Bray, a minor
under 14yrs.

DAVISON –pg. 81; Oct. 1882. Distribution of the estate of John W. Davison, dec'd., who died
leaving a widow and children.
Widow: Ann Davison.
Children: Edward G. Davison; Mary Jane Lawyer, wife of Alfred Lawyer; John J. Davison;
Annie A. Robbins, wife of Timothy Robbins; Savillian Davison; and Matilda R. Davison.
Another son, Charles E. Davison, was presumed dead after being absent from N.J. without
contact for 25yrs. or more.

GOLDEN –pg. 82; Oct. 1882. Caroline Golden was appointed guardian of Lou Golden, a minor
under 14yrs.

BURTIS –pg. 82; Oct. 1882. Hannah A. Burtis and James T. Burtis were appointed guardians of
Emily S. Burtis, a minor under 14yrs.

BROWN –pg. 90; Oct. 1882. Distribution of the estate of William Brown, dec'd., revealed he left a
widow and children.
Widow: Harriet Brown.
Children, all minors: William R. Brown and Minor Brown.

GOLDEN –pg. 94; Oct. 1882. Caroline Golden was appointed guardian of Harry B. Golden, a
minor over 14yrs.

BORDEN –pg. 101; Jan. 1883. Emma Caminade, wife of Frederick Caminade, petitioned for a
division of the real estate owned by her parents, Joseph W. Borden, dec'd., and Mary Borden,

dec'd. Joseph W. Borden died intestate in 1865 and his wife, Mary Borden, died intestate in
1881.
Children: Emma Caminade, wife of Frederick Caminade; and James H. Borden.
Grandchildren, who were children of their dau. Margaret S. Curtis, dec'd.: Harry Darcy
Curtis, 13yrs. old; and Frederick W. B. Curtis, 10yrs. old.
Margaret S. Curtis, formerly Margaret S. Borden, wife of Henry H. Curtis, died intestate in
1878.

LAMBERTSON –pg. 109; Jan. 1883. Eunice Lambertson was appointed guardian of Hartweld
Lambertson, Flora E. Lambertson, David H. Lambertson, and George W. Lambertson, minors
under 14yrs.

CASLER –pg. 118 – 121; Jan. 1883. Henry Casler petitioned for a division the real estate owned by
his father, Peter Casler, dec'd., who died intestate on May 14, 1882.
Widow: Elizabeth Casler, due her dower.
Children: Joseph Casler; Henry Casler, the petitioner; John P. Casler; Theodocia Lupton;
Margaret A. Throckmorton; Mary E. Cooke; Peter Casler; Adelia Martin; Aaron Casler;
Rufus T. Casler; Sarah E. Borden; and Harriet A. Wikoff.
Grandchild, child of his son William Corlies Casler, dec'd., who died in 1877: Mary E.
Casler.
Grandchildren, children of his dau. Emily Williams, dec'd., who died in 1874: Mary Emma
Williams, 18yrs. old; and William Edward Williams, 16 yrs. old.
Grandchildren, children of his son Edward Casler, dec'd., who died in 1872: Laura Edna
Casler, 14yrs. old; and Joseph Edward Casler, 12yrs. old.
John P. Casler, son of the said Peter Casler, dec'd., died leaving a widow, Elizabeth Casler.
Peter Casler, son of the said Peter Casler, dec'd., died leaving a widow, Julia Casler. Note:
See Book 1, pg. 299, May 1884.

MATTHEWS –pg. 129; Jan. 1883. Ellen Franklin, wife of Thomas E. Franklin, was appointed
guardian of Ella Matthews, a minor over 14yrs., wife of Alfred Matthews.

BEERS –pg. 135; Jan. 1883. Distribution of the estate of William Beers, dec'd.
Children of his brother John N. Beers, dec'd., entitled to 1/6 share each: John J. Beers, Ann
Tilton, and Elizabeth VanBrackle.
Children of his half-sister Elizabeth Crawford, dec'd., entitled to 1/8 share each: William S.
Crawford, John J. Crawford, Ann Holmes, and Elizabeth Crawford.

CARHART –pg. 139; Jan. 1883. Louisa J. Carhart was appointed guardian of Samuel L. Carhart, a
minor under 14yrs.

COOPER –pg. 146; Jan. 1883. The record was a decree on the final settlement of the accounts for
the estate of Jonathan P. Cooper, dec'd., who was the illegitimate son of Rachel Cottrell. His
last will revoked all prior wills, and expressed his desire to have his estate divided according
to the laws of N.J. governing the estates of intestates. He was survived by his mother and his
adopted dau., Emma A. Borden, widow of Randall R. Borden, dec'd. Emma Borden was
adopted by Jonathan P. Cooper and his wife, Lillias Cooper, under the laws of Ohio.

DUNN –pg. 149; Jan. 1883. Mary Dunn was appointed guardian of John Dunn, a minor under
14yrs., and Andrew Dunn and Letitia Dunn, minors over 14yrs. Note: three separate entries
on the same page.

CHATTLE –pg. 164; May 1883. Thomas G. Chattle was appointed guardian of John H. Chattle, a
minor under 14yrs.

MORRIS –pg. 165; May 1883. Timbrook Morris was appointed guardian of Mary Emma Morris, a
minor over 14yrs., wife of Jno. A. Morris.

WILLIAMS –pg. 167; May 1883. Andrew J. Williams was appointed guardian of William Edward
Williams, a minor over 14yrs.

EMMONS –pg. 180; May 1883. Benjamin F. Emmons petitioned for a division of the real estate
owned by his father, Stephen Emmons, dec'd., who died leaving a widow and children.
Widow: Mary A. Clayton, formerly Mary A. Emmons, entitled to her dower.
Children: Benjamin F. Emmons; Samuel Conover Emmons, a minor; and Jennie H. Emmons,
a minor.

SEWING –pg. 187; May 1883. William Sewing was appointed guardian of Anna Sewing, a minor under 14yrs.

THISTLE –pg. 202 – 203; Oct. 1883. Samuel B. Thistle of Matawan Tshp. petitioned for a division of the real estate owned by Samuel E. Thistle, dec'd., and for the appointment of guardians for his heirs who were minors residing outside N.J.
Widow: Margaret Thistle, entitled to her dower.
Entitled to 1/8 share each: Samuel B. Thistle, petitioner; Hannah E. Thistle; William E. Thistle; John H. Thistle; Emma Thistle; Amelia Thistle; Edward Thistle, a minor over 14yrs., a resident of N.Y.; and Charles Thistle, a minor under 14yrs., a resident of Ill.
The fathers of Edward Thistle and Charles Thistle were both deceased, and neither had a mother or guardian residing in N.J.

GREEN –pg. 204; Oct. 1883. George H. Green was appointed guardian of Forrest Green and Isabella Green, minors over 14yrs., and Charles C. Green, a minor under 14yrs. Note: three separate entries on the same page.

TAYLOR –pg. 208; Oct. 1883. Lydia L. Taylor was appointed guardian of Maria L. Taylor and Sarah E. Taylor, minors under 14yrs., and Ray Taylor, a minor over 14yrs. Note: two separate entries on the same page.

REILEY –pg. 210; Oct. 1883. Catherine E. Bernard petitioned for a division of the real estate owned by Thomas Reiley, dec'd., and Eliza Reiley, dec'd.
Entitled to 1/3 share each: the petitioner, Catherine E. Bernard, and her sister Elizabeth A. Rainear, wife of Albert C. Rainear.
Children of the petitioner's sister Mary Sutton, late Mary Reiley, dec'd., late wife of Charles W. Sutton, entitled to 1/3 share total: Charles Sutton, 6yrs. old; and Thomas Sutton, 4yrs. old.

EMMONS –pg. 213; Oct. 1883. Mary A. Clayton and her husband, Edward Clayton, were appointed guardians of Samuel C. Emmons, a minor over 14yrs., and Jennie H. Emmons, a minor under 14yrs. Note: two separate entries on the same page.

DENISE –pg. 214; Oct. 1883. Louisa A. Denise was appointed guardian of Charles M. Denise, a minor under 14yrs.

DENISE –pg. 217; Oct. 1883. Fannie H. Denise was appointed guardian of Mabel W. Denise and William H. Denise, minors under 14yrs.

TALLMAN –pg. 222; Oct. 1883. Catherine Tallman was appointed guardian of Ellis J. Tallman, a minor over 14yrs., and George L. Tallman, a minor under 14yrs. Note: two separate entries on the same page.

STILLWELL –pg. 236; Jan. 1884. Joel Stillwell was appointed guardian of Sarah E. Stillwell, a minor under 14yrs.

GORDON –pg. 241; Jan. 1884. Charles I. Gordon was appointed guardian of Alice F. Gordon, late Alice F. Thompson, a minor over 14yrs.

BOUD –pg. 248; Jan. 1884. The record was an order demanding bond from the administrator of the estate of John M. Boud, dec'd., late of Monmouth Co., N.J. Mary E. Boud took the administrator's position on Oct. 17, 1882 and then married Edward Koman of Bergen Co., N.J. on Feb. 4, 1884, before completion of her duties as administrator.

WILSON –pg. 249; Jan. 1884. Anthony A. Wilson was appointed guardian of Gertrude A. Wilson, a minor over 14yrs.

SUTTON –pg. 262; Jan. 1884. Charles W. Sutton was appointed guardian of Charles Sutton and Thomas Sutton, minors under 14yrs.

TRUMP –pg. 263; Jan. 1884. Margaret K. Trump was appointed guardian of Margaret W. Trump, a minor under 14yrs.

STRYKER –pg. 264; Jan. 1884. David H. Stryker was appointed guardian of Florence V. Stryker, a minor under 14yrs.

WHITE –pg. 274; Jan. 1884. Robert B. White was appointed guardian of Mary B. White, a minor over 14yrs.

DENISE –pg. 278; May 1884. Lillian M. Denise was appointed guardian of Edwin S. Denise, a minor over 14yrs.

SATTERTHWAIT –pg. 287; May 1884. Emma L. Satterthwait was appointed guardian of Elizabeth K. Satterthwait, a minor under 14yrs.

LEONARD –pg. 290; May 1884. Emeline Leonard was appointed guardian of Edward H. Leonard, a minor under 14yrs.

MONTANYE –pg. 295; May 1884. Distribution of the estate of Charles Montanye, dec'd., showed he left a widow, Rebecca Montanye, and one child, May Franklin, wife of G. H. Franklin. Note: In the header, the surname was spelled Monyanye.

CASLER –pg. 299; May 1884. The record was a supplement to distribution of the estate of Peter Casler, dec'd. Theodocia Lupton died in N.Y. leaving two children, viz., Edward F. Lupton and Mary Hankins, wife of Morris Hankins. Note: See Book 1, pg. 118 – 121, Jan. 1883.

SCULTHORPE –pg. 301; May 1884. Distribution of the estate of James Sculthorpe, dec'd., named his widow and children.
Widow: Mary Sculthorpe.
Children: James Sculthorpe; Nicholas V. Sculthorpe; Elizabeth A. Emmons, wife of Tylee L. Emmons; Elias Sculthorpe; and Thompson G. Sculthorpe.

BROWN –pg. 310; May 1884. Thomas T. Brown petitioned the court to assign the dower for Jane Brown, widow of Vincent Brown, dec'd.

CONOVER –pg. 313; May 1884. William M. Conover petitioned for a division of the real estate owned by his father, Edward M. Conover, dec'd., who died leaving a widow and children.
Widow: Margaret A. Conover.
Children: William M. Conover, the petitioner; Peter F. Conover; and Hannah B. Buck, a minor, wife of Henry W. Buck.

SMITH –pg. 314; Oct. 1884. Distribution of the estate of Garret L. Smith, dec'd., revealed his only heirs were his siblings and the children of a deceased sister.
Siblings: Sarah M. Patterson, wife of James B. Patterson; Rebecca Smith; Zilpha Smith; Elmira McBribe, wife of George McBribe; Susan J. Patterson, wife of Henry A. Patterson; and David O. Smith.
Children of his sister Catherine Ann Patterson, dec'd.: Huldah Patterson, Sarah C. Patterson, Henry Patterson, Charles Patterson, and Ann Elizabeth Patterson.

WOOLLEY –pg. 316; Oct. 1884. Distribution of the estate of Jordan Woolley, dec'd., showed he left a widow and children.
Widow: Margaret Woolley.
Children: Thomas R. Woolley; Clay Woolley; Penn Woolley; Ada W. Shanghuessy, wife of Michael W. Shanghuessy; Mary J. Slocum, wife of Edward R. Slocum; Sarah Woolley; Margaret Woolley; and Annie Woolley, a minor under 21yrs.

WOOLLEY –pg. 317; Oct. 1884. Margaret Woolley was appointed guardian of Annie E. Woolley, a minor over 14yrs.

STELLE –pg. 320; Oct. 1884. Distribution of the estate of Elizabeth L. Stelle, dec'd., who died intestate, showed her only heirs were her siblings and one niece.
Siblings: James D. Stelle; Isaac B. Stelle; Martin D. Stelle; Caroline E. Darnell, wife of Joseph Darnell; Susan D. Arnold, wife of Joseph M. Arnold; Sarah D. West, wife of John W. West; Annie Robbins, wife of Ridgeway Robbins; Adalaide Tindel, wife of Perrine Tindel; and Benjamin F. Stelle.
Child of her brother William D. Stelle, dec'd.: Elizabeth Stelle.

THROCKMORTON –pg. 320 – 321; Oct. 1884. Distribution of the estate of Sydney Throckmorton dec'd., revealed the names of his children.
Children: Susan A. Throckmorton; Lydia A. Randall, widow of _____ Randall, dec'd.; Sarah J. Throckmorton; Samuel Throckmorton; and William H. Throckmorton.

CONKLIN –pg. 335; Oct. 1884. Matilda Conklin was appointed guardian of Annie Conklin, a minor under 14yrs.

SILVER –pg. 343; Oct. 1884. Catherine V. Silver was appointed guardian of William V. Silver and Frank L. Silver, minors over 14yrs. Note: two separate entries on the same page.

FROM PAGE 344 TO PAGE 347 THE TERM DATES WERE OUT OF SEQUENCE, BUT THE PAGE NUMBERS REMAINED SEQUENTIAL.

THOMASON –pg. 344; May 1882. Distribution of the estate of Dr. Thomas J. Thomason, dec'd., identified his heirs.
Widow: Anna M. Thomason.
Brother: William W. Thomason.
Children of his sister Mary E. G. Parker, dec'd., all minors: Evelina T. Parker, Jennie P. Parker, and Forrest H. Parker Jr.

BROWER –pg. 347; May 1884. Distribution of the estate of Jane Ann Brower, dec'd., who died intestate leaving a brother, nieces, and nephews as her heirs. Note: The first page of this record was dated for the term of May 1884, and the second page for Oct. 1884. The recording date was Jan. 2, 1885.
Brother: Charles Farrington.
Daughter of a deceased sister (not named): Maria E. Morris.
Son of his brother Alanson Farrington, dec'd. (whereabouts unknown for 30yrs., presumed dead): Abraham Farrington.
Children of a deceased sister (not named): Melissa Cornell and William H. Dimond.
Children of a deceased brother (not named): Elias P. Farrington, William Farrington, Elizabeth Griffen, and Mary A. Norris.

SWEET –pg. 353; Jan. 1885. Louisa S. Ryall Sweet, a minor over 14yrs., dau. of Lt. Col. Henry B. Sweet and his wife, Louisa Sweet of London, England, chose Thomas W. Ryall of Monmouth Co., N.J. as her guardian.

CRAWFORD –pg. 354 – 363; Jan. 1885. William S. Crawford petitioned the court to declare his brother John J. Crawford mentally incompetent. John J. Crawford, 55yrs. old, was a widower whose wife died about 1874. Shortly thereafter, he began to act strange and was placed in an asylum five years later.
Siblings: William S. Crawford; and Ann Holmes, wife of Joseph Holmes.
Children: Caroline Crawford, 25yrs. old; James Crawford, 23yrs. old; John Crawford, 21yrs. old; Mary Crawford, 19yrs. old; Emeline Crawford, 16yrs. old; Theressa Crawford, 15yrs. old; Harriet Crawford, 12yrs. old; and Ester Crawford, 10yrs. old.

STELLE –pg. 376; Jan. 1885. Cornelia Stelle was appointed guardian of Lizzie Stelle, a minor under 14yrs.

HERBERT –pg. 383; Jan. 1885. Distribution of the estate of William H. Herbert, dec'd., identified his widow and children.
Widow: Mary Beecroft, formerly Mary Herbert.
Children: Mabel Herbert, under 14yrs.; and Mary Grace Herbert, under 14yrs.

WYATT –pg. 390; Jan. 1885. Alice Edith Wyatt, a minor over 14yrs., chose Henry Wyatt as her guardian.

ROGERS –pg. 394; Jan. 1885. Distribution of the estate of John Rogers, dec'd., who died intestate, revealed only nieces and nephews remained as his heirs.
Children of his sister Elizabeth Allen, dec'd.: Lydia M. Cafferty, wife of Enoch Cafferty; and Joel Allen.
Children of his brother William Rogers, dec'd.: VanRoom Rogers, Eden Rogers, and Elwood Rogers.
Children of his sister Ester Middleton, dec'd.: Daniel Middleton and Mary Ann Middleton.
Children of his sister Catherine Frazer, dec'd.: Lydia Frazer and Franklin Frazer.
Children of his brother Daniel Rogers, dec'd.: John W. Rogers, James B. Rogers, and Ferdinan Rogers.
Children of his sister Sarah Steward, dec'd.: Nathan R. Steward; Eli Steward; Thomas Steward; John W. Steward; Mary A. E. DuBois, wife of James DuBois; Joseph R. Steward; Sarah Griscom, wife of Job Griscom; William Steward; Charles P. Steward; Samuel Steward; George W. Steward; and Alfred Steward.

STILWELL –pg. 397; Jan. 1885. Distribution of the estate of John S. Stilwell, dec'd., identified his widow and children.
Widow: Francis A. Stilwell.
Children: Emeline L. Crawford, Daniel I. Stilwell, Henry C. Stilwell, Holmes M. Stilwell, Catherine M. VanMater, Mary S. Stilwell, and Anna B. Ackerson.

BRADLEY –pg. 399; Jan. 1885. Distribution of the estate of William J. Bradley, dec'd., named his three children as heirs.
Children: Thomas Bradley, Allan C. Bradley, and Margaret B. Leppelman, wife of E. J. Leppelman.

POLHEMUS –pg. 401; Jan. 1885. Distribution of the estate of Tobias Polhemus, dec'd., identified his heirs.
Widow: Sarah Polhemus, who since died testate.
Children: John Polhemus; George W. Polhemus; Achsah Larrison, wife of Henry Larrison; and Anna Maria Hendrickson, wife of George Hendrickson.
Grandchildren who were children of his dau. Mary Forsyth, dec'd., late wife of Pearson Forsyth: Emma Terhune, wife of ____ Terhune; Annetta Havens, wife of John Havens; and Martha Forsyth who died after her grandfather Tobias Polhemus, dec'd.
Grandchildren who were children of his son Charles H. Polhemus, dec'd., and his wife, Edith, who was still living: Ella A. Nelson, wife of Sheffington Nelson; Tobias Polhemus; and William Polhemus.

CONOVER –pg. 406; Jan. 1885. Anna M. Conover was appointed guardian of Annie T. Conover, a minor under 14yrs.

BUCK –pg. 408; Jan. 1885. Hannah B. Buck, late Hannah B. Conover, a minor over 14yrs., chose Henry W. Buck as her guardian.

ERRICKSON –pg. 412; Jan. 1885. Distribution of the estate of Permelia Errickson, dec'd., who died intestate, reported no husband, parents, siblings, nieces, or nephews survived her. Her only heirs were first cousins.
Children of her uncle Peter Errickson, dec'd.: George P. Errickson, and Margaret Quackenbush, wife of John A. Quackenbush.
Daughter of her uncle Thomas Errickson, dec'd.: Lydia Truax, wife of Bills Truax.
Children of her uncle Samuel Errickson, dec'd.: Margaret Julien, wife of Oliver Julien; Parmelia Cross, wife of William Cross; and Elizabeth Franklin, wife of ____ Franklin.
Children of her aunt Susan Coon, dec'd.: Phebe Ann Brown, wife of Paul S. Brown; and Jane E. West, widow of Daniel West, dec'd.
Children of her uncle Timothy Errickson, dec'd.: Susan Errickson, dec'd., who died without issue; and Eliza Keepers, dec'd., who left a dau., Eliza Keepers, whose whereabouts was unknown.
After the death of Permelia Errickson, Parmelia Cross died in 1889, Elizabeth Franklin died, and Jane E. West died April 1, 1889.

STILWELL –pg. 416; Jan. 1885. Ann Augusta Stilwell, a minor over 14yrs., chose Forman Stilwell as her guardian.

NEWMAN –pg. 418; Jan. 1885. Distribution of the estate of Nelson Newman, dec'd., identified his heirs.
Children: Joseph H. Newman; Catherine J. White; Abby A. Height, wife of James Hiram Height; and Augustus B. Newman.
Since the death of her father, Abby A. Height died leaving a husband and a child, Susan Taylor.

REYNOLDS –pg. 424; May 1885. Mercy Jane Havens petitioned for a division of the real estate owned by her mother, Ann Maria Reynolds, dec'd., who died intestate in 1872 leaving children and grandchildren.
Children: Mercy Jane Havens, the petitioner; and Tylee L. Reynolds.
Grandchildren who were children of her dau. Mary Ellen Cooper, dec'd.: David Edward Cooper, a minor; and Laura Cooper, a minor.

HOFF –pg. 426 – 433; May 1885. Elijah Hoff of Raritan Tshp. petitioned the court to declare his mother, Phiatta Hoff (sometimes called Zenetta Hoff), mentally incompetent. Phiatta Hoff, widow of George Hoff, dec'd., had been in an asylum for several years.
Brother: Aaron Bedle.

Son: Elijah Hoff, 54yrs. old.
Granddaughters: Arletta Dresser, 22yrs. old, and Phiatta Wingate, 20yrs. old.

WHITE –pg. 440; May 1885. Caroline F. White was appointed guardian of Olive E. C. White, a minor under 14yrs.

CLAYTON –pg. 441; May 1885. William Clayton was appointed guardian of Garrie Clayton, a minor under 14yrs.

ELY –pg. 446; May 1885. Distribution of the estate of John Perrine Ely, dec'd., listed his heirs.
Brother: Enoch Ely.
Half-sisters: Mary Ely, wife of James Ely; and Charlotte Reid.
Children of his sister Sarah Ann Johnson, dec'd.: Necorsuli Johnson; Mary Ellen Ely, wife of William Ely; and Elizabeth Rue, wife of Joseph Rue.

TAYLOR –pg. 457; May 1885. William P. Taylor petitioned for a division of the real estate owned by his father, Nelson Taylor, dec'd., who died intestate in 1883.
Widow: Lydia A. Taylor, entitled to her dower.
Children: William P. Taylor, the petitioner; Barzilla Taylor; Jane A. Sherman, wife of John B. Sherman; Ray Taylor; Maria Louisa Taylor, under 21yrs.; and Sarah E. Taylor, under 21yrs.

SMITH –pg. 462; May 1885. James VanCleaf petitioned for a division of the real estate owned by Mary Smith, dec'd.
Entitled to 2/7 share: James VanCleaf.
Entitled to 1/7 share each: William VanCleaf; Maria VanPelt, widow of Alexander VanPelt; and Hannah J. Hyer, wife of Edgar Hyer.
Children of Catherine Walling, dec'd., entitled to 1/42 share each: Daniel Walling; Spafford Walling; James Walling; Stephen Walling; and Catherine Dexter, wife of Charles Dexter.
Children of Martha J. Lambertson, dec'd., a dau. of Catherine Walling, dec'd., entitled to 1/42 share total: Edward Lambertson, Thaddeus Lambertson, John Lambertson, Stephen Lambertson, and Amelia Lambertson.
Children of Elizabeth A. Crawford, dec'd., entitled to 1/14 share each: William H. Crawford and Carrie E. Cornish, wife of Robert Cornish.

DEY –pg. 481; May 1885. Distribution of the estate of Joseph W. Dey, dec'd., identified his children and grandchildren.
Children: Sophia H. Walker, wife of Eebon F. Walker; William L. Dey; Annie Dey; Samuel M. Dey; Mary E. Dey; Ellie F. Dey; and Kate W. Dey.
Grandchild who was the only child of his dau. Susan Clayton, dec'd.: Garrie Clayton.

BOOK 2

1885 – 1888

SICKLES –pg. 5; Oct. 1885. A settlement of accounts on the estate of Charles Sickles, dec'd., revealed he left a widow, Elizabeth Sickles, and one child, Alice E. Sickles.

OSBORN –pg. 8; Oct. 1885. Orders to show cause noted, in his lifetime, Abraham J. Osborn, dec'd., was also known as James A. Osborn.

DANGLER –pg. 22; Oct. 1885. Mary Dangler, administrator of the estate of Daniel Dangler, dec'd., was ordered to pay out the proceeds. Daniel Dangler, dec'd., was survived by a widow, one child, twenty-two grandchildren, and one great grandchild.
Widow: Mary Dangler.
Child: Miriam Bennett, wife of William Bennett.
Grandchildren who were children of his dau. Hannah Woolley, dec'd.: Elvine Howland, wife of Zenas M. Howland; Tenty White, wife of James White; Elizabeth Durham, wife of ___ Durham; Daniel Woolley; Susan Truax, wife of Charles E. Truax; Christina Conk, wife of ____ Conk; and Mary Tilton, wife of William Tilton.
Great grandchild who was a child of Bloomfield Woolley, dec'd., son of Hannah Woolley, dec'd.: Clarence Woolley, a minor left behind by his father, said Bloomfield Woolley, who left the state of N.J. and hadn't been heard from for 12 – 14yrs.
Grandchildren who were children of his son Joseph Dangler, dec'd.: Joseph C. Dangler; Mary Elizabeth Parker, wife of ___ Parker; Debby Young, wife of ___ Young; Annie Mountenbeck, wife of Thomas Mountenbeck; Eleanor Scott, wife of Webster Scott; Abby Metzgar, wife of John Metzgar; and Frank Dangler.
Grandchildren who were children of his son Daniel C. Dangler, dec'd.: Daniel Louis Dangler, Ruth Hannah Wardell, Joseph L. Dangler, and James Hunter Dangler.
Grandchildren who were children of his dau. Elizabeth Ann Howland, dec'd.: Alice Carey, wife of William Carey; Eseck Wolcott Howland; Catharine Elizabeth Kirby, wife of Joseph Kirby; and Mary Ellen Kirby, wife of Louis Kirby.

VANANTWERP –pg. 33; Oct. 1885. Margaret VanAntwerp was appointed guardian of Frederick G. VanAntwerp, under 14yrs., Florence VanAntwerp, over 14yrs., and Dudley S. VanAntwerp, over 14yrs. Note: three separate entries on the same page.

BRUSNAHAM –pg. 36; Oct. 1885. David Brusnaham petitioned for a division of the real estate owned by Martha Brusnaham, dec'd., who died intestate. She was the widow of Edward Brusnaham, dec'd.
Children: David Brusnaham; Anna VanSchoick, wife of William VanSchoick; Ella S. Pearce, wife of Edward Pearce; Dennis S. Brusnaham, a minor between 14yrs. and 21yrs.; and Mary E. Brusnaham, a minor between 14yrs. and 21yrs.

PATTERSON –pg. 38; Oct. 1885. Charles E. Patterson, a minor over 14yrs., chose James H. Patterson as his guardian.

PATTERSON –pg. 39; Oct. 1885. Cora Patterson, a minor over 14yrs., elected James H. Patterson as her guardian.

CRUSER –pg. 41; Oct. 1885. The distribution of the estate of Ellen C. Cruser, dec'd., revealed her heirs.
Children: James Scudder; William V. Scudder; Charles Cruser; Alexander Cruser; John Cruser; and Emeline S. Rue, wife of Peter Rue.
Grandchild who was the only child of her dau. Mary Wyckoff, dec'd.: Anna Wyckoff.

ROBERTS –pg. 47; Oct. 1885. The distribution of the estate of Nathaniel H. Roberts, dec'd., named his children.

Children: Thomas J. Roberts, David Jones Roberts, Frederick Roberts, Nathaniel H. Roberts, William M. Roberts, and Mary Ella Roberts.

KETCHUM –pg. 48; Jan. 1886. Charles H. Vanderveer, guardian of Elizabeth F. DuBois, late Elizabeth F. Ketchum, filed a record of his accounts.

LITTLE –pg. 51; Jan. 1886. Grenville B. Little was appointed guardian of Emily C. Little, a minor under 14yrs.

SMITH –pg. 55; Jan. 1886. The distribution of the estate of Mary Smith was given in shares that did not add up correctly.
Heirs entitled to 1/7 share each: William L. Terlain, William VanCleaf, Hannah J. Heyer, and Maria VanPelt.
Heir entitled to 2/7 share: James VanCleaf.
Heirs entitled to 1/42 share each: Daniel Walling, Spafford W. Walling, James Walling, Stephen Walling, and Catharine Dexter.
Heirs entitled to 1/210 share each: John Lambertson, Edward Lambertson, Stephen Lambertson, Amelia Lambertson, and Thaddeus Lambertson.
Heirs entitled to 1/14 share each: William H. Crawford and Carrie E. Cornish.

LIPPINCOTT –pg. 61; Jan. 1886. Distribution of the estate of Rachel Lippincott, dec'd., identified her children.
Children: Samuel B. Lippincott; Peter Lippincott; James M. Lippincott; George D. Lippincott; Emily Lippincott; Sarah Jane Obre, wife of ___ Obre; and Elizabeth W. Hampton, wife of James H. Hampton.

COOPER –pg. 68 - 69; Jan. 1886. The accounts for the estate of James G. Cooper, dec'd., who died intestate, identified his heirs.
Sister: Maria Thorpe, wife of ___ Thorpe.
Children of his brother William S. Cooper, dec'd.: William E. Cooper and Joseph D. Cooper.
Children of his brother Joseph Cooper, dec'd.: Henry C. Cooper and Thomas Cooper.
Child of his sister Rachel Cooper, dec'd.: Martha Cooper.

HULST –pg. 70; Jan. 1886. The distribution of the estate of Peter Hulst, dec'd., identified his heirs.
Widow: Hannah Hulst.
Grandchildren who were children of his son John D. Hulst, dec'd.: Sarah Mead, wife of Rev. Elias Mead, administrator of the deceased's estate; and Georgiana Hulst, under 21yrs.

REMSEN –pg. 73; Jan. 1886. The distribution of the estate of John Remsen, dec'd., identified his heirs.
Widow: Jane Remsen, now Jane Hubbell, wife of Anson Hubbell.
Children: Carrie A. Frantz; Bessie R. Humphrey; Edward W. Remsen, under 21yrs.; and John Howard Remsen, under 21yrs. Note: See Book 2, pg. 155, May 1886.

BIRKHOLM –pg. 77; Jan. 1886. The appeal on the accounts for the estate of Hans C. Birkholm, dec'd., described family relationships. Hannah A. Wardell, formerly Hannah A. Birkholm, widow of Hans C. Birkholm, was currently the wife of Charles Wardell. Hans C. Birkholm died intestate on Aug. 2, 1855, leaving the previously mentioned widow and one child, William H. Birkholm, who was then about two months old. Hannah A. Birkholm was remarried to Charles Wardell before 1867.

HURLEY –pg. 85; Jan. 1886. The distribution of the estate of Samuel Hurley, dec'd., identified his heirs.
Widow: Mary Hurley.
Children: Catharine Estel, wife of David L. Estel; Hettie Emmons, wife of Tunis Emmons; Rebecca Brahm, wife of Brazilla Brahm; Permelia Brown, wife of Tylee Brown; Benjamin G. Hurley; Joseph Hurley; Andrew J. Hurley; and Robert S. Hurley.
Grandchildren who were children of his son Samuel Hurley Jr., dec'd.: Annie Newman, Elizabeth Havens, and Jane Hurley.

MORRIS –pg. 90; Jan. 1886. The distribution of the estate of William Morris, dec'd., who died intestate, identified his heirs.
Children: Jacob S. Morris; Lucien Morris; Mary C. Roswell, wife of Charles W. Roswell; Rachel E. Laird, wife of William H. Laird; Sarah J. Emmons, wife of John H. Emmons; and Hannah Smith, wife of James T. Smith.
Grandchildren who were children of his son James Morris, dec'd.: Edward B. Morris; Jacob

S. Morris; and Harriet S. Minton, wife of William Minton.

TAYLOR –pg. 91; Jan. 1886. The distribution of the estate of Nelson Taylor, dec'd., identified the recipients by shares.
Widow: Lydia L. Taylor.
Entitled to 1/6 share each: William P. Taylor; Barzilla Taylor; Jane A. Sherman, wife of John B. Sherman; Ray Taylor; Maria L. Taylor; and Sarah E. Taylor. Maria L. Taylor and Sarah E. Taylor were wards of Lydia Taylor.

GROVER –pg. 92; Jan. 1886. Sarah M. Grover was appointed guardian of Ida Grover and Rachel Grover, minors under 14yrs.

EDWARDS –pg. 97; Jan. 1886. Charles L. Edwards, a minor over 14yrs., elected Mary C. Edwards as his guardian.

SCOBEY –pg. 115 – 122; May 1886. James S. Scobey of Matawan Tshp. petitioned the court to declare his wife, Sarah J. Scobey, mentally incompetent. The couple had lived together in Matawan Village for eleven years, and she had been deprived of reason for four months. A relative claimed Sarah was between 68yrs. and 69yrs. old.
Other relatives: half-brother William A. Dunlap of Matawan, 52yrs. old; half-brother Alfred S. Dunlap of Richmond, Ind., 54yrs. old; half-sister Herimon Dunn, 58yrs. old, wife of Ezra A. Dunn.
Only child: Charles Merritt, 35yrs. old, in an asylum in Denvers, Mass.

HULST –pg. 125; May 1886. Theodore F. Jackson of Brooklyn, Kings Co., N.Y., guardian of Georgianna Hulst of Long Island City, Queens Co., N.Y., petitioned for delivery of money owed his ward from the estate of Peter Hulst, dec'd.

BEACH –pg. 126 – 134; May 1886. Annie B. Farrier of N.Y. City, N.Y. petitioned the court to declare her father, 62yr. old Henry D. Beach of Shrewsbury Tshp., mentally incompetent. He had been deprived of reason for four years. In June of 1884, he married Emily V. A. Beach, formerly Emily V. A. Gibson, who was still alive.
Step-daughter: Zoe A. Langley, late Zoe A. Gibson, dau. of Emily V. A. Beach from a prior marriage.
Brothers: Alfred E. Beach of N.Y. City, N.Y., and Moses S. Beach of Brooklyn, N.Y.
Only surviving child: Annie B. Farrier, wife of John M. Farrier.

QUACKENBUSH –pg. 142; May 1886. A settlement of accounts was filed by John W. Herbert as guardian of the deceased Lizzie J. Quackenbush, late Lizzie J. Butler, late wife of Elmer J. Quackenbush.

REMSEN –pg. 146 – 154; May 1886. Edward H. Ward Jr. and his wife, Sarah E. Ward, petitioned the court to declare Sarah's brother Henry S. Remsen mentally incompetent. He had been deprived of reason for 20yrs. Sarah E. Ward, 46yrs. old, and Henry S. Remsen, 49yrs. old, were the only surviving children of their deceased parents.

REMSEN –pg. 155 – 156; May 1886. A report on the division of the real estate owned by John Remsen, dec'd., stated Jane Hubbell, late widow of John Remsen, dec'd., purchased the shares of heirs Carrie R. Frantz, wife of A. E. Frantz, and Bessie R. Humphrey, wife of Wilson S. Humphrey. Note: See Book 2, pg. 73, Jan. 1886.

WOOLLEY –pg. 165; May 1886. Clarence Woolley, a minor over 14yrs., chose Annie E. Woolley as his guardian.

CURTIS –pg. 170 – 178; May 1886. Abraham O. Curtis of Wall Tshp. petitioned the court to declare his father, Osborn Curtis, mentally incompetent. He suffered apoplexy in 1885 that left him deprived of reason. His wife, Susan E. Curtis, 57yrs. old, was married to him for sixteen years.
Children and heirs of Osborn Curtis: Abraham O. Curtis, 44yrs. old; Hannah Borden, 42yrs. old; Asa Curtis, 39yrs. old; Lucinda VanLear, 36yrs. old; and Henry A. Curtis, 28yrs. old.

REYNOLDS –pg. 187; May 1886. Distribution of the estate of Enoch Reynolds, dec'd., identified heirs both living and dead.
Widow: Margaret Reynolds, died about Dec. 25, 1885.
Children: James C. Reynolds, dec'd.; Margaret Holman, wife of John H. Holman; Huldah Ely, wife of William Ely; Maria Tantum, dec'd.; Theresa (aka Charity) Tantum, dec'd.;

Enoch Reynolds, dec'd.; and Paul Reynolds, dec'd.

BARRETT –pg. 190; May 1886. Distribution of the estate of William E. Barrett, dec'd., identified his heirs.
Widow: Laura A. Barrett.
Children: Laura E. Oddie, Pauline E. Mansfield, Virginia A. Chadwick, William L. Barrett, and Lucy W. Barrett.

CONROW –pg. 206; Oct. 1886. Garret DuBois Conrow, a minor over 14yrs., chose John Conrow as his guardian.

CONROW –pg. 206; Oct. 1886. John Conrow was appointed guardian of Albert Conrow, a minor under 14yrs.

THOMASON –pg. 206 – 207; Oct. 1886. Distribution of the estate of Dr. Thomas J. Thomason, dec'd., identified his heirs.
Widow: Annie M. Thomason.
Brother: William W. Thomason.
Children, all minors, of his sister Mary E. G. Parker, dec'd.: Eveline T. Parker, Jennie P. Parker, and Forrest H. Parker Jr.

SAGNES –pg. 207; Oct. 1886. Samuel S. Sagnes was appointed guardian of Fannie M. Sagnes, a minor.

SHACKLETON –pg. 209; Oct. 1886. Adelaide Shackleton, a minor over 14yrs., elected Cordelia M. Shackleton as her guardian.

SHACKLETON –pg. 210; Oct. 1886. Fannie E. Shackleton, a minor over 14yrs., elected Cordelia M. Shackleton as her guardian.

OSBORN –pg. 215; Oct. 1886. Euphemia Osborn was appointed guardian of David L. Osborn and Viola M. Osborn, minors under 14yrs.

IVINS –pg. 223; Oct. 1886. James L. Ivins and John W. Ivins, minors over 14yrs., chose Margaret Ivins as their guardian. Note: two separate entries on the same page.

IVINS –pg. 224; Oct. 1886. Annie M. Ivins, a minor over 14yrs., chose Margaret Ivins as her guardian.

IVINS –pg. 224; Oct. 1886. Margaret Ivins was appointed guardian of George G. Ivins, a minor under 14yrs.

LAWRENCE –pg. 229; Oct. 1886. Mary Corlies and the minor Bessie D. Lawrence petitioned the court to appoint Henry Corlies, husband of said Mary Corlies, guardian of Bessie, born Sept. 18, 1875. Bessie's father left N.J. two or more years earlier without providing for her, and Mary Corlies was her nearest relative.

CURTIS –pg. 231; Oct. 1886. Harry Darcy Curtis and Fred W. B. Curtis, minors over 14yrs., elected Henry H. Curtis as their guardian. Note: two separate entries on the same page.

PROBASCO –pg. 236; Jan. 1887. Edward D. Probasco and Rachel S. Probasco, minors over 14yrs., chose Christopher Probasco as their guardian. Note: two separate entries on the same page.

MUHLENBRINK –pg. 243; Jan. 1887. Mary Muhlenbrink was appointed guardian of Henry A. Muhlenbrink, a minor under 14yrs.

SOFFEL –pg. 243; Jan. 1887. Lewis A. Soffel was appointed guardian of Arthur R. Soffel, a minor under 14yrs.

VANDORN –pg. 246; Jan. 1887. Horace B. VanDorn petitioned for a division of the real estate owned by Garret VanDorn, dec'd. Horace B. VanDorn, the petitioner, was entitled to 1/2 share. Petitioner's nephew Alvin H. Cady and niece Francis H. Cady were entitled to 1/4 share each. Elizabeth VanDorn, widow of Garret VanDorn, dec'd., was entitled to her dower.

TRUSWELL –pg. 248; Jan. 1887. Hannah A. Truswell was appointed guardian of Josephine Truswell and Frederk Truswell, minors under 14yrs.

ROBBINS –pg. 248; Jan. 1887. Distribution of the estate of Elizabeth M. Robbins, dec'd., showed she left sisters, nieces, and nephews.
  Entitled to 1/6 share each: sister Letitia Thompson; and the heirs of sister Rachel Robbins, dec'd.
  Children of Abigail S. Miller, dec'd., entitled to 1/12 share each: Charles H. Miller and George Miller.
  Children of Lucy Kirby, dec'd., entitled to 1/18 share each: Rebecca Kirby; Susan B. Aull, wife of Joseph Aull; and Elizabeth O'Hagan.
  Children of Susan Borden, dec'd., entitled to 1/18 share each: Josiah Borden, Charlotte R. Longstreet, and Garret Borden.
  Children of George Robbins, dec'd., entitled to 1/12 share each: Mary R. Holmes and Rebecca F. Gaddis.

EMMONS –pg. 249; Jan. 1887. The distribution of the estate of William Emmons, dec'd., who died intestate, named his five surviving children, viz., John H. Emmons, Sarah Carson, William H. H. Emmons, Elizabeth A. Burlew, and Benjamin Emmons.

REILLY –pg. 250; Jan. 1887. John F. Reilly and William E. Reilly, minors over 14yrs., chose Johanna C. Reilly as their guardian. Note: two separate entries on the same page.

REILLY –pg. 251; Jan. 1887. Johanna C. Reilly was appointed guardian of Mary A. Reilly, a minor under 14yrs.

TAYLOR –pg. 254; Jan. 1887. Hattie B. Taylor, a minor over 14yrs., elected Lydia M. Taylor as her guardian.

TAYLOR –pg. 255; Jan. 1887. Lydia M. Taylor was appointed guardian of James J. Taylor, a minor under 14yrs.

WHITE –pg. 257; Jan. 1887. A decree for the distribution of the estate of Christopher White, dec'd., revealed his siblings were his only heirs.
  Siblings of Christopher White, dec'd.: Charles White; Jediah White; Remington White; Henry White; Lorenzo White; Elizabeth Brown, wife of Halstead Brown; Emeline VanBrunt, wife of Benjamin VanBrunt; and Hannah Sculthorpe, wife of George Sculthorpe.

VANMATER –pg. 258; Jan. 1887. Anna M. VanMater and Joseph H. VanMater, minors over 14yrs., chose Joseph I. VanMater as their guardian. Note: two separate entries on the same page.

VANMATER –pg. 259; Jan. 1887. Joseph I. VanMater was appointed guardian of Jessie A. VanMater and Frederick A. VanMater, minors under 14yrs. Note: two separate entries on the same page.

BEEKMAN –pg. 264; Jan. 1887. Abram J. Beekman was appointed guardian of Mary V. Beekman, Lidie H. Beekman, Anna S. Beekman, and Jennie B. Beekman.

JOHNSON –pg. 275; Jan. 1887. Distribution of the estate of Catharine Johnson, dec'd., revealed she died intestate leaving two brothers, and eight nieces and nephews.
  Brothers: Joseph Patterson and Stilwell Patterson.
  Children of her sister Maria Allen, dec'd.: Charles Allen and Phebe A. Vanderveer.
  Child of her brother John Patterson, dec'd.: Phebe C. Williams.
  Child of her brother John Patterson, dec'd.: John W. Patterson.
  Children of her brother Robert Patterson, dec'd.: John R. Patterson, George C. Patterson, Rachel P. Finch, and Herman E. Patterson.
  Note: Two brothers were named John in this record, and a full 1/6 share was awarded to their progeny.

JOWITT –pg. 277; May 1887. Rev. Jos. F. Jowitt was appointed guardian of Constance Mary Jowitt.

SWITSER –pg. 287; May 1887. Clara A. Mason and Lewis Switser petitioned for a division of the real estate owned by Anna C. Switser, dec'd., property allotted to her in the division of the estate of Gustav (Gavine) Drummond.
  Heirs of Anna C. Switser, dec'd.: George T. Switser; Clara A. Mason, wife of William P. Mason; Ella M. Southwick, wife of Francis H. Southwick; and Elizabeth S. Mason, wife of William P. Mason.

George T. Switser died around July 26, 1886, intestate, leaving a widow, Corrine C. Switser, and three minor children, viz., Lewis H. Switser, Charles S. Switser, and George Switser. Note: In subsequent records the surname was spelled Switzer.

ROBBINS –pg. 293; May 1887. Charles Robbins was appointed guardian of Chilion Robbins, a minor under 14yrs.

RUE –pg. 301; May 1887. Annie H. Rue, a minor over 14yrs., chose Mary H. Rue as her guardian.

RUE –pg. 301; May 1887. Mary H. Rue was appointed guardian of Joseph H. Rue, a minor under 14yrs.

REED –pg. 311; May 1887. Distribution of the estate of Rebecca C. Reed, dec'd., identified her heirs.
Mother: Cornelia A. Reed.
Siblings: James Bowne Reed; John L. Reed; and Mary E. Parker, a widow.
Nieces: Sallie B. Reed; and Mary A. Wells, wife of David Wells.
John L. Reed had since died intestate, and his share went to his legal representatives. Within the record, the middle name for James Bowne Reed was also given as Brown, and the family surname was spelled both Reed and Reid.

WELLS –pg. 312; May 1887. Lucy H. Wells was appointed guardian of Addie May Wells and Mary H. Wells, minors under 14yrs.

BORDEN –pg. 312; May 1887. Charles E. Borden was appointed guardian of Lillias May Borden, a minor under 14yrs.

CONOVER –pg. 313 - 320; May 1887. Mary Ann Conover petitioned the court to declare her brother Robert R. Conover of Freehold Tshp. mentally incompetent. Robert R. Conover, 52yrs. old, son of John M. Conover, dec'd., was mentally incompetent since birth. Only sibling: Mary Ann Conover, 46yrs. old, wife of John C. Conover.

WOODRUFF –pg. 328; Oct. 1887. Henry M. Woodruff, a minor over 14yrs., chose Samuel V. Woodruff as his guardian.

MEGILL –pg. 332; Oct. 1887. Sarah M. Megill, a minor over 14yrs. and wife of Theo. Megill, elected John T. S. Hall as her guardian.

HALL –pg. 333; Oct. 1887. John T. S. Hall was appointed guardian of John S. Hall, a minor over 14yrs.

HALL –pg. 333; Oct. 1887. John T. S. Hall was appointed guardian of Clarence L. Hall and Bertha M. Hall, minors under 14yrs.

SIMPSON –pg. 338; Oct. 1887. Horace E. Simpson, a minor over 14yrs., chose Charles H. Simpson as his guardian.

SIMPSON –pg. 338; Oct. 1887. Charles H. Simpson was appointed guardian of Leonard E. Simpson, a minor under 14yrs.

DRUMMOND –pg. 343; Oct. 1887. Distribution of the estate of Peter Drummond, dec'd., who died testate on March 17, 188_, revealed the deaths of some of those who received a legacy from him. Legatees Rachel West, Bathsheba Drummond, and Abigail Drummond were still alive. Abigail Drummond married Charles Braeutigain, and Bathsheba Drummond married John G. Kim. Residuary legatee Hannah Drummond was alive and married John Hopper. Legatees Lydia Drummond and Taber Chadwick died before the said Peter Drummond, dec'd. Residuary legatee Elizabeth Drummond married Henry C. J. Schroeder and died before the said Peter Drummond, dec'd., leaving four children, viz., Anthony D. Schroeder, John E. Schroeder, Henry E. Schroeder, and Ernest Schroeder, dec'd., who died before said Peter Drummond, dec'd. Residuary devisee Ann Drummond married Lewis Switzer and died before the said Peter Drummond, dec'd., leaving five children: Clara A. Mason, wife of William Mason; Elizabeth S. Mason, wife of William P. Mason; Ella M. Southwick, wife of Harry Southwick; George T. Switzer; and Lewis J. Switzer Jr., dec'd.

GROVER –pg. 345 – 351; Oct. 1887. Jehu P. Applegate, County Auditor, asked the court to assign a guardian for William V. Grover of Eatontown Tshp., a legatee of James Grover, dec'd., and

an inmate of the state asylum since Feb. 7, 1881 at the county expense.
Wife: Jennie Grover.
Siblings: Cornelia Ann Hubbard, 70yrs. old; Abigail Leonard, 68yrs. old; Sarah Conover, 65yrs. old; John B. Grover, 60yrs. old; Caroline F. Morton, 45yrs. old; Henry C. Grover, 43yrs. old; and Joseph Grover, 40yrs. old.

TAYLOR –pg. 357; Oct. 1887. Anna Leila Taylor, a minor over 14yrs., elected Eliza J. Taylor as her guardian.

WILSON –pg. 370; Oct. 1887. Distribution of the estate of the widow Adaline Wilson, dec'd., identified her surviving heirs.
Children: Daniel Wilson and Lydia Ann Walling.
Granddaughter who was a child of her dau. Elizabeth Curtis, dec'd.: Elizabeth C. Walling.
Grandchildren who were children of her son John W. Wilson, dec'd.: George W. Wilson and Lillie Borst.
Great grandchildren who were children of Bertha Wingate, dec'd., a dau. of said John W. Wilson, dec'd.: Norma Wingate, Roy Wingate, and Stella Wingate.

COYNE –pg. 380 – 387; Jan. 1888. Thomas Coyne of Middletown Tshp. petitioned the court to declare his brother Patrick Coyne mentally incompetent. Patrick Coyne, 50yrs. old, deprived of reason for several months, was an inmate of the asylum. He owned no real property, but he received a pension of $36 per month from the US Government for military service in the last war. He lost a leg at Antietam.
Brothers: Thomas Coyne, 60yrs. old; Michael Coyne, 57yrs. old; and William Coyne, 52yrs. old.

CLAYTON –pg. 401; Jan. 1888. Mary J. Clayton was appointed guardian of John H. Clayton, a minor under 14yrs.

DEANS –pg. 415; Jan. 1888. William P. Yallalee, as guardian of Allen J. Yallalee and Charles H. Yallalee of Brooklyn, N.Y., petitioned the court to have the executor of the estate of David Deans, dec'd., turn over the money owed his wards who were legatees of the estate.

DEANS –pg. 416; Jan. 1888. R. Frank Clark, as guardian of William S. Clark and Herbert D. Clark of Alameda, Calif., petitioned the court to have the executor of the estate of David Deans, dec'd., turn over the money owed his wards who were legatees of the estate.

WILD –pg. 417; Jan. 1888. Distribution of the estate of Mary L. Wild, dec'd., revealed she left two children as her only heirs, viz., George H. Wild and Mary E. Bardon.

BENNETT –pg. 419; Jan. 1888. Final distribution of the estate of Thomas Hulet Bennett, dec'd., revealed the names of his heirs.
Widow: Isabella Bennett.
Children: James C. Bennett and Mary E. Eustace.
Grandchildren who were children of his son John T. Bennett, dec'd.: Mary Matilda Bennett and John T. Bennett. John T. Bennett, dec'd., left a widow, Margaret Bennett.

TRACY –pg. 424; Jan. 1888. Susan ("Susie") L. Tracy, a minor over 14yrs., chose Elizabeth R. Tracy as her guardian.

TRACY –pg. 425; Jan. 1888. Alfred Tracy and Cora Belle Tracy, minors over 14yrs., chose Elizabeth R. Tracy as their guardian. Note: two separate entries on the same page.

TRACY –pg. 426; Jan. 1888. Elizabeth R. Tracy was appointed guardian of Joanna Tracy, a minor under 14yrs.

MANAHAN –pg. 427; Jan. 1888. Aurelia Manahan and Jane A. Manahan, minors over 14yrs., elected William H. Manahan as their guardian. Note: two separate entries on the same page.

MANAHAN –pg. 428; Jan. 1888. Elmira Manahan, a minor over 14yrs., chose William H. Manahan as her guardian.

MANAHAN –pg. 428; Jan. 1888. William H. Manahan was appointed guardian of Frederick T. Manahan, a minor under 14yrs.

CARSON –pg. 438; May 1888. Mary C. Carson was appointed guardian of Matilda C. Carson and

Adelia M. Carson, minors under 14yrs.

CAMPBELL –pg. 449; May 1888. Distribution of the estate of William Campbell, dec'd., identified his surviving children.
Children: Richard B. Campbell, Nathan Campbell, William H. Campbell, and Adaline Haviland, wife of Jacob Haviland.

WELLS –pg. 455; May 1888. Distribution of the estate of William W. Wells, dec'd., disclosed the names of his heirs.
Widow: Eliza Wells.
Children: Susan A. Sanford and Nellie J. Wells.
Grandchildren: Addie M. Wells and Mary H. Wells, both minors and wards of Lucy H. Wells.

BOOK 3

1888 – 1891

TANTUM –pg. 11; May 1888. Distribution of the estate of Theresa ("Charity") Tantum, dec'd., showed she was survived by her husband, Morrison B. Tantum.

STRIKER –pg. 59 – 61; Oct. 1888. Distribution of the estate of Philip Striker, dec'd., revealed his only surviving heirs were nieces and nephews.
Child of Henry Striker, dec'd., entitled to 1/5 share: Sarah Randall.
Children of Elias Striker, dec'd., entitled to 1/50 share each: Ann Woolley, William Striker, Joseph P. Striker, Elias Striker, James Striker, Louisa Sutphin, and John Striker.
Child (only surviving) of Henry Striker, dec'd., a son of Elias Striker, dec'd., entitled to 1/50 share: William H. Striker.
Children of Samuel Striker, dec'd., a son of Elias Striker, dec'd., entitled to 1/100 share each: Melvina Anderson and Samuel Striker.
Child (only surviving) of Caroline Buckelew, dec'd., a dau. of Elias Striker, dec'd., entitled to 1/50 share: Olivia White.
Children of John Striker, dec'd., entitled to 1/35 share each: Cyrenius Striker; Charles Striker Ellen Emmons; and the representatives of Phebe Long, dec'd., who died after Philip Striker, dec'd.
Children of Samuel Striker, dec'd., entitled to 1/245 share each: John Striker, Jacob Striker, Joseph Striker, Forman Striker, Kate McCafferty, Jane A. Polhemus, and Monroe Striker.
Children of Elizabeth Bodine (afterwards Elizabeth Davison) dec'd., entitled to 1/105 share each: William H. Bodine, Cyrenius Bodine, and Joseph Bodine.
Children of Ann Stillwagon, dec'd., dau. of Jno Striker, dec'd., entitled to 1/140 share each: Mary Emmons, John H. Stillwagon, Catharine L. Stillwell, and Elizabeth C. Smith.
Children of Joseph Striker, dec'd., entitled to 1/45 share each: Maria Sutphen, Margaret A. Sutphen, Henrietta Sutphen (within the record, this surname also given as Gordon), David H. Striker, Forman C. Striker, and Caroline Sutphen.
Children of Sarah J. Hunsinger, dec'd., entitled to 1/90 share each: Jane Ann Dayland and Mary T. Hopper.
Children of Charlotte Sanford, dec'd., entitled to 1/225 share each: Delia Sanford, Gussie Sanford, Lidie Sanford, Belle Sanford, and Emma Sanford.
Children of Elizabeth Davison (afterwards Elizabeth Bailey), dec'd., entitled to 1/225 share each: George Davison; Lillie Smith; Jane Davison; William H. Bailey, a minor; and Howard Bailey, a minor.
Children of Margaret Chambers, dec'd., entitled to 1/25 share each: Mary Horton, Charles Chambers, and Margaret A. Perry.
Child of Elizabeth Calder, dec'd., entitled to 1/50 share: Margaret Kerr.
Children (surviving) of Sarah Z. Striker, dec'd., a dau. of Elizabeth Calder, dec'd., entitled to 1/100 share each: Sarah Z. Scobey and Robert C. Striker.
Children of Caroline Blancard, dec'd., entitled to 1/75 share each: Mary Ann Jansen, Charles Blancard, and Jessie Ostrum.

ROSS –pg. 70; Jan. 1889. William B. Ross was appointed guardian of Thomas Ross, a minor under 14yrs.

CONOVER –pg. 70; Jan. 1889. Annie A. Conover was appointed guardian of Josie M. Conover and William V. Conover, minors under 14yrs.

WALDEN –pg. 74; Jan. 1889. James Russell Walden, a minor over 14yrs., elected Jeter Walden as his guardian.

WALDEN –pg. 75; Jan. 1889. Jeter Walden was appointed guardian of Lulu C. Walden and Marilla F. Walden, minors under 14yrs.

COUSE –pg. 76; Jan. 1889. Mary D. Couse and William J. Couse of Farmingdale, Mon. Co., N.J., minors over 14yrs., chose Evi. A. Willson of Deckertown, Sussex Co., N.J. as their guardian. Note: two separate entries on the same page.

COUSE –pg. 77; Jan. 1889. Evi. A. Willson requested guardianship of Lulu W. Couse, a minor under 14yrs. Her mother, Emily Couse, relinquished her right to guardianship.

COUSE –pg. 79; Jan. 1889. Distribution of the estate of Peter Couse, dec'd., who died intestate, named his heirs.
Widow: Emily Couse.
Children: William J. Couse, Mary D. Couse, and Lulu W. Couse.

MEGILL –pg. 81; Jan. 1889. Stephen S. Megill, a minor over 14yrs., elected his mother, Calicia A. T. Megill, as his guardian.

MEGILL –pg. 82; Jan. 1889. Calvin H. Megill and William K. Megill, minors over 14yrs., elected their mother, Calicia A. T. Megill, as their guardian. Note: two separate entries on the same page.

RAVATT –pg. 84; Jan. 1889. Charles E. Ravatt and Fannie D. Ravatt, minors over 14yrs., chose their mother, Sarah E. Dey, and her husband, John Dey, as their guardians. Note: two separate entries on the same page.

MEAD –pg. 86; Jan. 1889. Elias Mead was appointed guardian of Roger L. Mead, Marvin H. Mead, and Telford C. Mead, minors under 14yrs.

DALTON –pg. 91; Jan. 1889. Frank Dalton was appointed guardian of Mattie R. Dalton, a minor under 14yrs.

MANEY –pg. 94; Jan. 1889. Katherine Kelsy and Michael Kelsy petitioned the court for a division of the real estate owned by Thomas Maney, dec'd., who died intestate several years ago.
Widow: Margaret Maney.
Children: Margaret Conrey, wife of Michael Conrey; Catherine Kelsey, wife of Michael Kelsey; Nora Collins, wife of Austin Collins; Johanna Maney; Thomas Maney; John Maney; and Austin M. Maney, under 18yrs.

SICKLES –pg. 110; Jan. 1889. Distribution of the estate of Alfred Sickles, dec'd., who died intestate, identified his only heirs as siblings, nieces, and nephews.
Siblings of Alfred Sickles, dec'd.: John H. Sickles; Eliza Ann Emmons, widow; Bradford Sickles; and Forman Sickles.
Children of his brother William Sickles, dec'd.: Eleanor J. Leighton, wife of Conover S. Leighton; Laura Hester, wife of Earl L. D. Hester; Irene Salt, wife of Joseph Salt; and William I. Sickles.
Child of his sister Sarah J. Chambers, dec'd.: Edgar Chambers.

WALN –pg. 113; Jan. 1889. Distribution of the estate of Sarah Waln, dec'd., who died intestate, identified her heirs.
Surviving children, entitled to 1/5 share each: John R. Waln and Sarah W. Hendrickson. Deceased children whose representatives (unnamed) were entitled to 1/5 share each: Richard Waln, dec'd., who died before his mother; and Nicholas Waln, dec'd., who died after his mother.
Heirs of her son Joseph Waln, dec'd., entitled to 1/45 share each: Sallie R. Satterthwait; William W. Waln; Frank Waln; Richard Waln; Alfred L. Waln; Robert W. Waln; Elizabeth W. Waln; Joseph Rogers Waln; and the representatives of Mary W. Waln, dec'd., who died intestate on May 22, 1888.

WOOLSTON –pg. 127; May 1889. Paul L. Woolston, a minor over 14yrs., elected Rebecca S. Woolston as his guardian.

WOOLSTON –pg. 128; May 1889. Blanche C. Woolston, a minor over 14yrs., elected Rebecca S. Woolston as her guardian.

MORTON –pg. 138; May 1889. Elwood S. Morton of Red Bank, Shrewsbury Tshp., a minor over 14yrs., chose his father, Walter H. Morton, as his guardian.

BOWNE –pg. 140; May 1889. Ellen C. Bowne, a minor over 14yrs., elected Anna W. Bowne as her

---

guardian.

LAWYER –pg. 141; May 1889. Distribution of the estate of Mary J. Lawyer, dec'd., named her siblings as her heirs.
Siblings: John J. Davison; Syvillian Davison; Anna A. Robbins; Matilda R. Horner; and Edward G. Davison who died intestate after his sister. Charles E. Davison, another brother, was presumed dead after being absent from N.J. for over twenty years without any word from him.

RAVATT –pg. 146; May 1889. Distribution of the estate of William S. Ravatt, dec'd., identified his heirs.
Widow: Emma Ravatt, who died after the death of her husband.
Children: Elizabeth Taylor, wife of Reynolds Taylor; James K. Ravatt; Daniel Ravatt; and George W. Ravatt.
Grandchildren who were children of his son William Ravatt, dec'd.: Euretta N. Cheney, Catharine L. Willett, and William Ravatt.
Grandchildren who were children of his son John S. Ravatt, dec'd., who died after his father: William S. Ravatt; John H. Ravatt; Charles E. Ravatt, under 21yrs.; and Fannie D. Ravatt, under 21yrs. John S. Ravatt, dec'd., also left a widow, Sarah E. Ravatt.

HOLMES –pg. 147; May 1889. Henry L. Holmes, a minor over 14yrs., chose Chrineyonce S. Holmes as his guardian.

HOLMES –pg. 148; May 1889. Jonathan I. Holmes, a minor over 14yrs., chose Chrineyonce S. Holmes as his guardian.

PERRINE –pg. 154; May 1889. Distribution of the estate of unwed and mentally incompetent Matthew Perrine, dec'd., identified his siblings and their children.
Sisters: Hannah Mount, still living; and Margaret Hendrickson who died Dec. 22, 1888, testate.
Children of his brother John J. Perrine, dec'd.: Mary E. Imlay, wife of William Imlay; Lydia Smock, wife of Henry D. Smock; and Newell Perrine, who was presumed dead after a prolonged absence.
Child of his brother Stephen Perrine, dec'd.: William D. Perrine.
Children of his sister Caroline Baird, dec'd.: David Baird, Mary Ewing, Joseph P. Baird, Samuel T. H. Baird, and Margaret E. Robbins.
Children of his sister Mary Hankinson, dec'd.: Phebe Snyder, Elizabeth P. Hoff, William W. Hankinson, and John P. Hankinson.
Children of his brother William J. Perrine, dec'd.: Peter F. Perrine; Stephen P. Perrine; Francis Rosten Perrine; Joseph Perrine; and Sarah Ellen Allen, wife of Jasper H. Allen.

BROWN –pg. 156; May 1889. Distribution of the estate of William Brown, dec'd., revealed he was survived by children and grandchildren, but no widow.
Children: John Lefferts Brown, Wainright W. Brown, Parmela VanBrackle, and Zilpha Maria Morford.
Grandchildren, all minors, who were children of his dau. Rebecca W. Roberts, dec'd.: George Roberts and Dora Roberts.

PATTERSON –pg. 158; May 1889. Distribution of the estate of John H. Patterson, dec'd., identified his nieces and nephews. His will left a legacy to Susan Howland that passed to his surviving nieces and nephews after her death. The legacy included the children of his half-brother William Patterson, but excluded Joseph Patterson, a son of his brother Caleb Patterson. Susan Howland died March 5, 1889.
Children of Susan Richmond, dec'd.: Lydia Richmond, Mary Davis, and Annie Hoff.
Son of Eliza Patterson: Charles Stillwagon.
Children of Josephine Patterson: Harriet P. Patterson, Maria Patterson, Catharine Patterson, and Elizabeth Patterson.
Children of Maria Robins, formerly Maria Patterson: Amos Patterson (later given as Amos ___), Marietta Orr, and Ellen Tice.
Children of Caleb Patterson: John H. Patterson, Charles Patterson, and William B. Patterson.
Children of William Patterson: Theodore Patterson, Elisha Patterson, and Annie Hampton.

BEALE –pg. 160 – 162; May 1889. Fred A. Beale petitioned for a distribution of the estate of Maria P. Beale, dec'd., who owned real estate in Eatontown, Tshp. The real estate was held as tenants in common by the petitioner, Fred A. Beale, his brother John E. Beale, and their three nephews Thomas E. Stearns, Joel W. Stearns, and Arthur K. Stearns (sons of the petitioner's sister Elizabeth Stearns, dec'd.). This was a series of four records, in which the third record named Joel W. Stearns the husband of the late Elizabeth Stearns, dec'd.

WHITE –pg. 167; May 1889. Distribution of the estate of Brittan White, dec'd., identified his widow and children.
Widow: Caroline White.
Children: Washington White; Juliett Slocum, wife of Mahlon Slocum; Andrew J. White; Lewis F. White; Eastwood White; and Brittan R. White.

ROBERTS –pg. 168; May 1889. George Roberts, a minor over 14yrs., chose Leonard D. Roberts as his guardian.

COE –pg. 169; May 1889. Alice B. Coe, a minor over 14yrs., elected her mother, Mary Ann Coe, as her guardian.

COE –pg. 170; May 1889. Ada Coe, a minor over 14yrs., elected Mary Ann Coe as her guardian.

LEONARD –pg. 177; May 1889. Joseph Leonard petitioned the court for a division of the real estate owned by his father, Joseph Leonard, dec'd., who died intestate on March 11, 1883 leaving children.
Children: Joseph Leonard, John Leonard, Adeline Hendrickson, and Edward Leonard.
Subsequently, the son John Leonard died testate on March 11, 1889, leaving a widow, Emma Leonard, and no children. The son Edward Leonard, a minor, died intestate and unmarried. The dau. Adeline Hendrickson, and her husband, James W. Hendrickson, died intestate leaving three children, minors under 14yrs., viz., William Hendrickson, Emma Hendrickson, and James Hendrickson.

MEIRS –pg. 190; May 1889. Distribution of the trust fund established by Apollo Meirs, dec'd., for his daus. Sarah Tilton and Martha Tilton, and their heirs.
Surviving children of Martha Tilton, dec'd.: Elizabeth T. Ellis, Sarah A. Bordon, Lawrence Tilton, Martha A. Satterthwaite, Mary A. Wright, Caroline I./T. Worden, and George W. Tilton.
Surviving child of Sarah Tilton, dec'd.: Charles M. Tilton.
Children of Apollo M. Tilton, dec'd., son of Martha Tilton, dec'd.: William H. Tilton, Ella Hart, and Charles M. Tilton.
Children of Unity M. Waln, dec'd., dau. of Martha Tilton, dec'd.: Richard C. Waln, George Waln, and T. R. Waln.
Children of John M. Tilton, dec'd., son of Martha Tilton, dec'd.: Isabell Hendrickson, Mary A./H. Appleton, Sarah E. Coleman, Albert Tilton, and William Tilton.
Children of Abraham Tilton, dec'd., son of Martha Tilton, dec'd.: Joseph Tilton and Julia Weed.
Children of William Tilton, dec'd., son of Martha Tilton, dec'd.: Susan H. Leming, Anna E. Steward, Mary V. Chafey, Emma B. Pullen, Sarah Lee, Florence Bird, and Martha M. Chafey.
Note: The record used two different middle initials for Caroline Worden and Mary Appleton.

CURTIS –pg. 200; Oct. 1889. Harriet E. Curtis, a minor over 14yrs., chose Harriet E. Curtis as her guardian.

STEARNS –pg. 205; Oct. 1889. Joel Stearns, guardian of Arthur K. Stearns of Brooklyn, N.Y., petitioned the court to have the commissioners pay the money owed his ward from the estate of Maria P. Beale, dec'd.

LEONARD –pg. 211; Oct. 1889. Emeline Leonard, widow of Joseph Leonard, dec'd., relinquished her right to dower in exchange for a sum of money.

WHITE –pg. 213; Oct. 1889. An order to show cause on the estate of William White, dec'd., revealed he died intestate in Brooklyn, N.Y. leaving a widow, Jane White, who had died. He was survived by siblings and their heirs.
Surviving siblings: Hugh White; Eliza Hagerman; Abigail White; Hannah Campbell, wife of Anthony Campbell; Bloomfield White; Eleazer White; and Atlantic White.
Children of his sister Margaret VanPelt, dec'd.: William H. VanPelt and Elbert H. VanPelt.
Children of his sister Alice Thompson, dec'd.: Charles Thompson and Minnie Thompson.
Children of his brother George White, dec'd.: Deborah White; Ellsworth White; Francis White; Adele White; and Lillie White, between 14yrs. and 21yrs. old.
The brother Hugh White had since died, testate, leaving a widow, Susan A. White. The brothers Bloomfield White and Eleazer White had also died, both intestate.

CLAYTON –pg. 234; Oct. 1889. Elizabeth Hall, formerly Elizabeth Clayton the administrator of the estate of James Gordon Clayton, dec'd., applied to sell his real estate to pay his debts.

HANCE –pg. 236; Oct. 1889. Tillie Hance was appointed guardian of Daisy Hance and Lester Hance, minors under 14yrs.

ELY –pg. 246; Oct. 1889. Carrie Ely, a minor over 14yrs., elected Huldah Ely, wife of William Ely, as her guardian.

BRUSENHAN –pg. 256; Jan. 1890. Mary E. Cooper, formerly Mary E. Brusenhan, protested the handling of her estate by her guardian, John B. Shumar.

HANCE –pg. 259; Jan. 1890. John W. Hance and David Hance petitioned for a division of the real estate owned by their grandfather Edward Hance, dec'd., whose will, dated June 12, 1867, left property to his son Isaac Hance. Isaac Hance died Aug. 19, 1884, leaving three sons, viz., John W. Hance, David Hance, and James Hance. The said James Hance died intestate on Aug. 30, 1888, leaving a widow, Tillie Hance, and two children, viz., Daisy Hance and Lester Hance.

NEWMAN –pg. 262; Jan. 1890. Marietta Allen and her husband, John M. Allen, petitioned for a division of the real estate owned by Sarah Newman, dec'd. Sarah Newman, dec'd., left a will, probated April 2, 1878. Her daus. Lydia Howland and Marietta Newman were then both unmarried women. Lydia Howland married John M. Allen, and died June 25, 1888, leaving one child, James M. Allen, a minor under 14yrs. Marietta Newman married the said widower John M. Allen on Oct. 13, 1889.
Children of Sarah Newman, dec'd.: Marietta Allen, wife of John M. Allen; Rebecca DuBois, wife of Charles H. DuBois; John S. Newman; and Curtis Newman.
Grandchild of Sarah Newman, dec'd.: James M. Allen.

SHERMAN –pg. 265; Jan. 1890. Emma Sherman was appointed guardian of George T. Sherman and Richard L. Sherman, minors under 14yrs.

HUMANN –pg. 271; Jan. 1890. Charles H. Humann petitioned for a division of the real estate owned by his father, Benjamin Humann, dec'd., who died intestate Aug. 31, 1888.
Widow: Fanny Humann.
Children: Charles H. Humann, the petitioner; and Louis Humann.
Grandchildren, all minors, who were children of his son Frederick W. Humann, dec'd., who died intestate Sept. 20, 1889: Florence Humann, Mamie Humann, and Benjamin Humann. Frederick W. Humann, dec'd., left a widow, Catharine Humann.

ALLEN –pg. 284; Jan. 1890. John Lee Allen, a minor over 14yrs., chose Edmund W. Allen as his guardian.

BROWER –pg. 285; Jan. 1890. Alonzo Brower was appointed guardian of Sadie Brower, a minor under 14yrs.

WHITE –pg. 290; Jan. 1890. Distribution of the estate of Jane White, dec'd., who died in Brooklyn, N.Y., reported her surviving heirs were siblings and offspring of siblings.
Siblings: Samuel Whitlock; George Whitlock; Andrew Whitlock; James Whitlock; and Isabella McDonald, widow of George McDonald.
Only child of her sister Cornelia Hays, dec'd.: Emma Hovell, wife of Thomas Hovell.

HOLZINGER –pg. 296; Jan. 1890. Wilfred Holzinger and Walter Holzinger, minors over 14yrs., chose Augusta Holzinger as their guardian.

ERRICKSON –pg. 304; Jan. 1890. Distribution of the estate of Permelia Errickson, dec'd., revealed her only heirs were first cousins.
Children of her uncle Peter Errickson, dec'd.: George P. Errickson; and Margaret Quackenbush, wife of John A. Quackenbush.
Surviving child of her uncle Thomas Errickson, dec'd.: Lydia Truax, wife of Bills Truax.
Children of her uncle Samuel Errickson, dec'd.: Margaret Julien, wife of Oliver Julien; Parmelia Cross, wife of William Cross; and Elizabeth Franklin, wife of _____ Franklin.
Children of her aunt Susan Coon, dec'd.: Phebe Ann Brown, wife of Paul S. Brown; and Jane E. West, widow of Daniel West, dec'd.
Deceased children of her uncle Timothy Errickson, dec'd.: Susan Errickson, dec'd., who left no issue; and Eliza Keepers, dec'd., who left one child, Eliza Keepers, whose whereabouts

was unknown.

Parmelia Cross died in 1889. Elizabeth Franklin died after the said Permelia Errickson, dec'd. Jane E. West died April 1, 1889.

CLAYTON –pg. 339; May 1890. William B. Clayton, a minor over 14yrs., chose John W. Clayton as his guardian.

HANCE –pg. 355; May 1890. Susan B. Hance petitioned for a division of the real estate in Middletown Tshp. owned by her father, Louveniers S. Hance, dec'd.
Children: Susan B. Hance, the petitioner; Elizabeth A. Hance; and Howard I. Hance.

LONGSTREET –pg. 373; May 1890. Annetta Allen, as next of kin, petitioned the court to appoint a guardian for Selby Longstreet, Louis F. Longstreet, Annetta Longstreet, and Margaret H. Longstreet, minors under 14yrs. whose parents were deceased. Other next of kin lived outside the USA. The wording of the record implied the children lived in Canada. The court appointed James J. Reed as their guardian.

ALLEN –pg. 377; May 1890. John M. Allen was appointed guardian of James M. Allen, a minor under 14yrs.

ALLEN –pg. 380; May 1890. Forman O. Allen and George J. Allen, minors over 14yrs., chose Samuel E. Allen as their guardian.

SLOAN –pg. 382; May 1890. Asenath Sloan was appointed guardian of Charles C. Sloan, a minor under 14yrs.

VANMATER –pg. 386; Oct. 1890. Anna M. Campbell, late Anna M. VanMater, a minor over 14yrs., elected Samuel S. Campbell of N.Y. City, N.Y. as her guardian.

BROWN –pg. 386; Oct. 1890. Benjamin F. S. Brown was appointed guardian of Jennie Mable Brown, Charles S. B. Brown, and Herbert F. Brown, minors under 14yrs.

BATEMAN –pg. 394; Oct. 1890. W. Clayton Bateman, a minor over 14yrs., chose Lucy J. Bateman as his guardian.

BATEMAN –pg. 395; Oct. 1890. Clara Bateman, a minor over 14yrs., chose Lucy J. Bateman as her guardian.

BATEMAN –pg. 395; Oct. 1890. Lucy J. Bateman was appointed guardian of Herbert J. Bateman, Bernice A. Bateman, and Mildred Bateman, minors under 14yrs.

COE –pg. 398; Oct. 1890. William Coe and Henry Coe petitioned for a division of the estate owned by William Coe, dec'd. As heirs of William Coe, dec'd., they and their sisters, Alice Coe and Ada Coe, owned the property together. Note: See Book 3, pg. 400; Oct. 1890, where Mary A. Coe was identified as the widow of William Coe, dec'd.

WARNER –pg. 414; Oct. 1890. Distribution of the estate of Jacob Warner, dec'd., stated he left his entire estate to his children, some of whom had died, leaving the estate to be divided between children and grandchildren.
Children of Jacob Warner, dec'd.: William H. Warner; Catharine West, wife of John West; Clementine West, wife of Abram H. West; and Nelson T. Warner.
Grandchildren who were children of his son George Warner, dec'd.: James E. Warner; Mary E. Warner, now Mary E. Smith; Charles Warner; and Owen W. Warner.
Grandchildren who were children of his dau. Margaret West, dec'd.: Lawner B. West, Frank F. West, Elliott M. West, and Clementine Crouter.
Grandchild who was a child of his dau. Mary A. Tallman, dec'd.: Mary E. Ousterman.
Grandchildren, all minors, who were children of his son Jacob Warner Jr., dec'd.: Lillie Warner, George Warner, Trueman Warner, and Frank Warner.
Owen W. Warner had since died, unwed. Lawner B. West had been absent from N.J. for over seven years, whereabouts unknown.

MEGILL –pg. 417; Oct. 1890. Distribution of the estate of Britton Megill, dec'd., named his widow, Louisa Megill, and children, George B. Megill, Benjamin Megill, William H. Megill, and John Megill.

REYNOLDS –pg. 419; Oct. 1890. Distribution of the estate of Hiram B. Reynolds revealed he left a

widow and nine children.
Widow: Jemmima Reynolds.
Children: Mary Anderson, wife of James Anderson; Hannah DeBow, wife of Charles DeBow; Rachel Thompson, wife of Charles Thompson; Jane Down, wife of George Down; William P. Reynolds; Phebe A. Callahan; Walter Reynolds; Ely Barker, wife of James Barker; and Anna M. Anderson, wife of Garret Anderson.

HENDRICKSON –pg. 421; Oct. 1890. Distribution of the estate of Holmes Hendrickson, dec'd., identified children and grandchildren.
Children: Pierson H. Hendrickson, Sarah J. Woolley, and Addie M. Hendrickson.
Grandchildren, all minors, who were children of his son Henry P. Hendrickson, dec'd.: Lizzie B. Hendrickson and Lottie Hendrickson.
Grandchildren, all minors, who were children of his son James W. Hendrickson, dec'd.: William Hendrickson, Emma Hendrickson, and James Hendrickson.
Grandchildren, all minors, who were children of his son Uriah S. Hendrickson, dec'd.: Benjamin S. Hendrickson, Sarah M. Hendrickson, Robert L. Hendrickson, and Susie Hendrickson.

WARNER –pg. 429; Oct. 1890. George T. Warner, a minor over 14yrs., elected Catharine Warner as his guardian.

WARNER –pg. 430; Oct. 1890. Lillie M. Warner, a minor over 14yrs., chose Catharine Warner as her guardian.

WARNER –pg. 430; Oct. 1890. Catharine Warner was appointed guardian of Trueman N. Warner and Frank W. Warner, minors under 14yrs.

CROUTER –pg. 431; Oct. 1890. Clementine Crouter, a minor over 14yrs., chose James H. Crouter as her guardian.

CONOVER –pg. 436; Jan. 1891. Distribution of the estate of Dr. Robert R. Conover, dec'd., showed he left a widow, Ann M. Conover, and one child, Annie F. Conover, a minor.

COX –pg. 437; Jan. 1891. Charles M. Cox and Louise S. Cox, minors over 14yrs., chose Ella S. Cox as their guardian. Note: two separate entries on the same page, but Ella Cox's middle initial given as P in the second record.

HANCE –pg. 438; Jan. 1891. Howard I. Hance, a minor over 14yrs., elected Susan B. Hance as his guardian.

HENDRICKSON –pg. 440; Jan. 1891. Lydia Hendrickson was appointed guardian of Benjamin S. Hendrickson, Sarah M. Hendrickson, Robert L. Hendrickson, and Susie Hendrickson.

ALLEN –pg. 441; Jan. 1891. Samuel E. Allen and Howard Osborn petitioned the court to assign them as administrators of the estate of Adelaide Allen, dec'd. Notice of their request was sent to relatives.
Children of Adelaide Allen, dec'd., all under 21yrs.: Forman O. Allen, George J. Allen, Chauncey Allen, Elizabeth V. Allen, and Cornelius S. Allen.
Mother of Adelaide Allen, dec'd.: Elizabeth Osborn.
Siblings of Adelaide Allen, dec'd.: Abraham Osborn; Jane Hubbell, wife of Anson Hubbell; Franklin Osborn; Cornelius Osborn; Anna O. Parker; and Frances O. Jaques, wife of George B. Jaques.

DISOSWAY –pg. 447; Jan. 1891. May C. Disosway, a minor over 14yrs., chose Susan E. Disosway as her guardian.

MEGILL –pg. 448; Jan. 1891. Distribution of the estate of John H. Megill, dec'd., named his widow, Calicia A. T. Megill, and children, William K. Megill, Calvin H. Megill, and Stephen S. Megill.

SHARP –pg. 457; Jan. 1891. Estelle Sharp, a minor over 14yrs., dau. of Samuel R. Sharp and the late Catharine Sharp, dec'd., of Philadelphia, Pa., requested Frederick Parker of Monmouth Co., N.J. be appointed guardian of her estate in N.J.

BOOK 4
1891 – 1894

CLAYTON –pg. 19; Jan. 1891. Elizabeth B. Clayton was appointed guardian of James M. Clayton
   and Harry H. Clayton, minors under 14yrs.

HIGGENSON –pg. 26; Jan. 1891. Stephen Higginson was appointed guardian of Frank Stanley
   Higginson, a minor under 14yrs.

SPAULDING –pg. 27; Jan. 1891. Distribution of the estate of Julia A. Spaulding, dec'd., revealed
   she was survived by a husband, a sister, and the children of deceased siblings, but no children
   of her own.
   Husband: Henry F. Spaulding.
   Sister: Grace W. Holmes.
   Surviving children her brother Peter Wikoff, dec'd.: Benjamin C. Wikoff; Charles Wikoff;
   and Elizabeth Hopper, wife of Ruleff F. Hopper. Said Peter Wikoff, dec'd., and his dau.
   Susan Smock, dec'd., late wife of Garret V. Smock, both predeceased Julia Spaulding.
   Children of her sister Hannah Hendrickson, dec'd.: Samuel W. Hendrickson; William H.
   Hendrickson, dec'd.; Hannah Hedden, dec'd., late wife of John Hedden; and Alice Romaine,
   dec'd., late wife of James H. Romaine.
   Child of Alice Romaine, dec'd., dau. of Hannah Hendrickson, dec'd.: William Romaine.
   Children of Julia Finkle, dec'd., dau. of Hannah Hendrickson, dec'd.: Morford Gordon and
   Lettie Gordon, children by her former husband, Morford Gordon, dec'd.
   Child of her brother Garret R. Wikoff, dec'd.: James Wikoff.
   Children of her sister Alice Woolley, dec'd.: Owen Woolley and Ann Kingsland.
   Child of her sister Charity Corlies, dec'd.: Alice Croxson, dec'd., who left a child, Mary
   Giffing, wife of John Giffing.
   Children of her sister Elizabeth Hendrickson, dec'd.: Edward Hendrickson and Elizabeth
   Hoxsie.

VANKIRK –pg. 33; Jan. 1891. John S. VanKirk, a minor over 14yrs., chose John VanKirk as his
   guardian.

ACKERSON –pg. 40; Jan. 1891. Belle C. Ackerson, a minor over 14yrs., elected Cornelius
   Ackerson as her guardian.

HANCE –pg. 42; Jan. 1891. Sarah Hance, a minor over 14yrs., elected Sarah J. Hance, wife of John
   Hance, as her guardian.

HEADDEN –pg. 53; May 1891. Jonathan Headden was appointed guardian of Katie Headden,
   Rebecca C. Headden, Alexr. N. Headden, and John M. Headden, minors under 14yrs.

MURPHY –pg. 62; May 1891. Margaret Murphy was appointed guardian of Mary E. Murphy, a
   minor under 14yrs.

FORSYTH –pg. 65; May 1891. Distribution of the estate of Pierson K. Forsyth, dec'd., revealed he
   left a widow and children.
   Widow: Mary H. Forsyth.
   Children: Nettie I. Havens, wife of John W. Havens; Emma E. Terhune, widow; and Charles
   G. Forsyth.

RAIGUEL –pg. 71; May 1891. Abbie F. Raiguel was appointed guardian of William O. Raiguel, a
   minor over 14yrs., and Marquerite A. Raiguel, a minor under 14yrs. Note: two separate
   entries on the same page.

BAUMAN –pg. 82; May 1891. Annie E. Bennett petitioned for a division of the real estate owned by her grandmother Annie E. Bauman, dec'd. All the heirs were grandchildren, children of her dau., Adeline M. Stiles, dec'd., late wife of Thomas T. Stiles of Philadelphia, Pa. Children of her dau. Adeline M. Stiles, dec'd.: Annie E. Bennett, wife of Theodore M. Bennett; Frederick B. Stiles, over 14yrs.; John Edward Stiles, over 14yrs.; Elizabeth L. Stiles, under 14yrs; and Mary M. Stiles, under 14yrs. The last four named were all residents of Philadelphia, Pa.

HANCOCK –pg. 109; Oct. 1891. Walter Hancock, a minor over 14yrs., chose George C. Hancock as his guardian.

MILLER –pg. 120; Jan. 1892. Distribution of the estate of Simon Miller, dec'd., stated he left a widow and children.
Widow: Christina Miller.
Children: Margaret Bender, wife of Otto C. Bender; _____, formerly Mary Vandergrift; and Albert Miller, a minor.

HOOK –pg. 123; Jan. 1892. Annie M. Hook was appointed guardian of Margaret M. Hook, Edith L. Hook, George T. Hook, and Christina Hook, minors under 14yrs.

SHINN –pg. 126; Jan. 1892. Hannah A. Shinn was appointed guardian of Walter T. Shinn, a minor under 14yrs.

NANZ –pg. 127; Jan. 1892. An Order to Show Cause stated John Jacob Nanz died on Nov. 14, 1891, leaving a widow, Margaritte Nanz, and three minor children, viz., John Jacob Nanz Jr., Kathrina B. F. Nanz, and Louisa M. F. Nanz.

QUACKENBUSH –pg. 128; Jan. 1892. Annie L. Quackenbush, a minor over 14yrs., elected Jacob M. Quackenbush as her guardian.

CONOVER –pg. 151; Jan. 1892. Distribution of the estate of Charlotte Conover, dec'd., who died intestate and unmarried, revealed her next of kin and heirs.
Siblings: Cornelia Thorton and Sidney Conover.
Children of her brother Simpson Conover who was presumed dead after no word in 20yrs.: Jessie Goodwin, wife of H. K. Goodwin; Libbie Booth, wife of G. A. Booth; Flora Conover; and John S. Conover.
Children of her sister Mary C. Schanck, dec'd.: Lydia H. Conover; Maggie P. DuBois, wife of William H. DuBois; Eliza V. VanMater, wife of Henry VanMater; and John C. Schanck.
Child of her sister Emily Butler, dec'd.: Mary C. Hyer, wife of Peter V. Hyer.
Child of her brother John V. Conover, dec'd.: Mary E. Higgins.

SLOCUM –pg. 162; Jan. 1892. Henry Britt Slocum, a minor over 14yrs., chose Rachel L. Slocum as his guardian.

SLOCUM –pg. 163; Jan. 1892. John Howard Slocum and Nettie Jarvis Slocum, minors over 14yrs., chose Rachel L. Slocum as their guardian. Note: two separate entries on the same page.

SLOCUM –pg. 163; Jan. 1892. Rachel L. Slocum was appointed guardian of Bessie T. Slocum and Chester A. Slocum, minors under 14yrs.

WIKOFF –pg. 173; May 1892. Distribution of the estate of Maria Antoinette Moore Wikoff, dec'd., identified her surviving heirs as cousins.
Cousins: L. Charlotte G. Woodhull of Freehold, N.J.; Sarah S. Throckmorton of Freehold, N.J.; Anna M. Woodhull of Freehold, N.J.; Henry W. B. Woodhull of Berkeley Place, Brooklyn, N.Y.; John Woodhull of Freehold, N.J.; Gilbert T. Woodhull of Lincoln, Pa.; Spafford P. Woodhull of Newark, N.J.; S. C. Ross Smith of Philadelphia, Pa.; Maria P. Smith of Baltimore, Md.; Cooper Smith of Philadelphia, Pa.; Anna C. Glenn of Baltimore, Md.; Hannah W. Woodhull, dec'd.; and Letitia C. Backus, dec'd.

SOMMERS –pg. 177; May 1892. Mary E. Sommers, a minor over 14yrs., elected Richard Sommers as her guardian.

SUSSMAN –pg. 188; May 1892. Isidor Sussman was appointed guardian of Leroy Sussman and Clarence Sussman, minors under 14yrs.

PROUT –pg. 195; May 1892. Distribution of the estate of James D. Prout, dec'd., showed he was survived by a widow, Hannah M. Prout, and one child, Charles D. Prout, a minor.

KEEFE –pg. 210; May 1892. Mary Ann Keefe requested guardianship of her children Lizzie D. Keefe, Thomas F. Keefe, Catharine M. Keefe, and James Henry Keefe, minors under 14yrs. They were children of her late husband Patrick Keefe, dec'd.

MORTON –pg. 231; Oct. 1892. Distribution of the estate of Ann Morton, dec'd, who died intestate on June 29, 1881, named her heirs.
Siblings: Prudence Allen, formerly of Lincoln, Nebr., then a resident of Laporte, Tex.; Samuel I. Allen who died May 31, 1882 leaving children; Mary Allen of Allenwood, N.J., a widow; and Joseph I. Allen of Allenwood, N.J.
Children of Richard I. Allen, dec'd., who died Feb. 26, 1843: Joseph F. Allen of Lower Squankum, N.J.; and Sarah A. Rice, wife of William Rice of Manasquan, N.J.
Children of Elizabeth Morton, dec'd., who died March 12, 1846: Walter H. Morton of Allenwood, N.J.; Peter C. Morton of Allenwood, N.J.; John L. Morton, dec'd., who died April 16, 1883; Joseph A. Morton, dec'd., who died March 24, 1863; and Sarah Ann Morton, dec'd., who died March 6, 1846 without issue.
Children of the said Joseph A. Morton, dec'd.: Thomas A. Morton of Manasquan, N.J.; Robert M. Morton of N.Y. City; and Charlotte E. Morton of Manasquan, N.J.
Children of the said John L. Morton, dec'd., late husband of Sarah H. Morton of South Amboy, N.J. (still alive): James A. Morton of Allenwood, N.J.; Maria Elizabeth Newman, wife of Wilson Newman of Belmar, N.J.; Tabor Frank Morton of South Amboy, N.J.; Clara Newman, wife of Andrew Newman of Belmar, N.J.; Harriet H. Morton of Belmar, N.J., over 14yrs.; David A. Morton of Belmar, N.J., over 14yrs.; and Sarah Morton of South Amboy, N.J., under 14yrs.

KING –pg. 245; Oct. 1892. Leslie W. King, a minor over 14yrs., chose Victoria King as guardian.

KING –pg. 245; Oct. 1892. Victoria King was appointed guardian of William F. King and Effie V. King, minors under 14yrs.

TAYLOR –pg. 248; Oct. 1892. James J. Taylor, a minor over 14yrs., elected Morford Taylor as his guardian.

KIRBY –pg. 252; Oct. 1892. James A. Kirby was appointed guardian of Wm. E. Kirby and Harry C. Kirby, minors under 14yrs.

MCGARRY –pg. 253 – 254; Oct. 1892. Distribution of the estate of Mary McGarry, dec'd., revealed the names of her siblings as her heirs. Her parents were deceased, and she left one illegitimate son, William McGarry, who was not considered a legal heir.
Siblings: Ann Bambrick; Bridget McGarry; and John McGarry, dec'd., whose heirs were to receive his share.

CHATTLE –pg. 254; Oct. 1892. John H. Chattle, a minor over 14yrs., chose his mother, Emma A. Chattle, as his guardian.

CHATTLE –pg. 255; Oct. 1892. Louise S. Chattle and Adah Chapter Chattle, minors over 14yrs., chose Emma A. Chattle as their guardian. Note: two separate entries on the same page.

CHATTLE –pg. 255; Oct. 1892. Emma A. Chattle was appointed guardian of William M. K. Chattle and Joseph Chattle, minors under 14yrs.

HOLMES –pg. 273; Jan. 1893. John S. Holmes was appointed guardian of Catharine L. Holmes and Joseph H. Holmes, minors under 14yrs. Note: two separate entries on the same page.

BOWNE –pg. 275; Jan. 1893. Mary A. Bowne was allowed to continue as executor of the estate of John E. Bowne, dec'd., despite her having married Samuel F. Roberts.

FISHER –pg. 277; Jan. 1893. Grace E. Fisher and Delford M. Fisher, minors over 14yrs., chose Elizabeth M. Fisher as their guardian. Note: two separate entries on the same page.

FISHER –pg. 278; Jan. 1893. Malcom P. Fisher, a minor over 14yrs., chose Elizabeth M. Fisher as his guardian.

MURPHY –pg. 284; Jan. 1893. Michael H. Murphy was appointed guardian of Mary E. Murphy, a minor under 14yrs.

KELSEY –pg. 285; Jan. 1893. Michael Kelsey petitioned for a division of the real estate owned by

James Kelsey, dec'd. As heirs of the said deceased, he, his sisters, and the children of his
deceased brother held the land as tenants in common.
Michael Kelsey's sisters: Catharine Desmond, wife of Patrick Desmond; and Mary Ann
Flannigan, wife of John Flannigan.
Children of Michael Kelsey's brother James Kelsey Jr., dec'd.: Annie Kelsey and James
Thomas Kelsey.
Note: In Book 4, pg. 286, Jan. 1893 Michael Kelsey and his sisters were entitled to 1/4 share
each and the children of James Kelsey, Jr., dec'd., were entitled to 1/8 share each.

KELSEY –pg. 286; Jan. 1893. Mary Kelsey, widow of James Kelsey, dec'd., consented to a
division of her late husband's estate.

THOMPSON –pg. 289; Jan. 1893. Albert E. Thompson, a minor over 14yrs., elected Peter V.
Thompson as his guardian.

THOMPSON –pg. 290; Jan. 1893. Louis W. Thompson, a minor over 14yrs., chose Peter V.
Thompson as his guardian.

THOMPSON –pg. 290; Jan. 1893. Peter V. Thompson was appointed guardian of Mabel I.
Thompson, James S. Thompson, and Fredk. P. Thompson, minors under 14yrs.

CHATTLE –pg. 301; Jan. 1893. Thomas H. Chattle petitioned for a division of the real estate
owned by his grandmother Elizabeth W. Chattle, dec'd., who died in 1892 leaving her
property to her grandchildren who were children of her dau. Emma A. Chattle who was still
alive.
Children of Emma A. Chattle: Thomas H. Chattle, the petitioner; George M. Chattle; William
M. K. Chattle; John H. Chattle; Francis E. Chattle, then Francis E. Hopkins; Mary A. Chattle,
then Mary A. Tibbs; Emma K. Chattle; Anna D. Chattle; Louise S. Chattle; Adah S. Chattle;
and Josepha Chattle.

OSBORN –pg. 312; Jan. 1843. Ellison Osborn, a minor over 14yrs., chose his mother, Mary R.
Osborn, as his guardian.

HENDRICKSON –pg. 318; Jan. 1893. Thomas S. Hubbard, uncle of George O. Hendrickson,
James H. Hendrickson, and Charles E. Hendrickson, minors under 14yrs., requested
guardianship of said minors. Their mother, unnamed, relinquished her right to guardianship.

LONGSTREET –pg. 321; Jan. 1893. Henry H. Longstreet was appointed guardian of Henry M.
Longstreet, a minor under 14yrs.

HENDRICKSON –pg. 323; Jan. 1893. Distribution of the estate of Samuel T. Hendrickson, dec'd.,
who died intestate, identified his heirs.
Widow: Emma B. Hendrickson.
Siblings: James H. Hendrickson; Alchey Elizabeth Conover, widow; and Maria C.
Hendrickson.
Children of his brother Tobias C. Hendrickson, dec'd.: Alice E. Hendrickson, Samuel T.
Hendrickson Jr., and George C. Hendrickson.

MARTIN –pg. 326; May 1893. Catharine Bumster petitioned for a division of the real estate owned
by her sister Annie Martin, dec'd., who died unmarried and intestate.
Sisters: Catharine Bumster; Ellen Hogan, wife of Patrick Hogan; Margaret Riehill, wife of
William Riehill; and Mary Meaney, wife of Martin Meaney.
Children of her brother Thomas Martin Jr., dec'd.: Mary Darcy, 20yrs. old, wife of Thomas
Darcy; and Katie Martin.
Child of her sister Eliza Magee, dec'd., late wife of John Magee: Peter Magee, 15yrs. old.
The said Eliza Magee, dec'd., died intestate in 1878, and her husband was still alive.

TOMPKINS –pg. 337; May 1893. Distribution of the estate of Benjamin F. Tompkins, dec'd.,
revealed his heirs as siblings and children of his siblings.
Siblings: George W. Tompkins, Sarah A. Weed, and Josephine Tompkins.
Children of his brother Walter B. Tompkins, dec'd.: Harry Tompkins and Ida Tompkins.
Children of his brother Elijah Tompkins, dec'd.: Elijah E. Tompkins and Georgiana Flynn.

BRUTTING –pg. 351; May 1893. Distribution of the estate of George Joseph Brutting, dec'd.,
identified six heirs: John George Brutting, John Brutting, Joseph Brutting, Charles Joseph
Brutting, Barbara Brutting, and George Brutting.

HESS –pg. 355; May 1893. William Hess was appointed guardian of Drusilla Hess, a minor under 14yrs.

HURLEY –pg. 366; May 1893. Zilpha C. Hurley, administrator of the estate of Elias P. Hurley, dec'd., married Samuel M. Rue.

SUTTON –pg. 366; May 1893. Grace E. Sutton, a minor over 14yrs., elected her father, William J. Sutton, as her guardian.

SUTTON –pg. 367; May 1893. William J. Sutton was appointed guardian of Mattie E. Sutton, Harry H. Sutton, and William J. Sutton, minors under 14yrs.

PITTENGER –pg. 367; May 1893. Edward F. Pittenger, a minor over 14yrs., chose John C. Pittenger as his guardian.

THOMPSON –pg. 376; May 1893. Jamesetta Thompson, a minor over 14yrs., elected Robert R. Thompson as her guardian.

DUNN –pg. 378; Oct. 1893. Distribution of the estate of Edward Dunn, dec'd., identified his heirs.
Widow: Ellen Dunn, who had since died.
Brothers: Michael Dunn and James Dunn.

PARKER –pg. 389; Oct. 1893. Cornelia B. Parker and Clarence H. Parker, minors over 14yrs., chose Mary E. Parker as their guardian. Note: two separate entries on the same page.

PARKER –pg. 390; Oct. 1893. John R. Parker and James A. Parker, minors over 14yrs., elected Mary E. Parker as their guardian. Note: two separate entries on the same page.

PARKER –pg. 391; Oct. 1893. Mary E. Parker was appointed guardian of Nellie W. Parker, a minor under 14yrs.

ROCKHILL –pg. 400 – 401; Oct. 1893. Distribution of the estate of Emma F. Rockhill, dec'd., identified her children and grandchildren.
Children: Anthony R. Rockhill, Elizabeth M. Hart, Hannah E. Rogers, Mary E. Curtis, Malinda Worthley, Lydia E. Sandford, Francis W. Rockhill, and Addie H. Beatty.
Grandchildren who were children of her son William C. Rockhill, dec'd.: Llewellyn Rockhill and Herbert Rockhill.

BENAWAY –pg. 404; Oct. 1893. Distribution of the estate of John Benaway, dec'd., identified his widow, Martha Benaway, and his child, Mary Mulligan of Hampton, Mass.

REYNOLDS –pg. 415; Jan. 1894. Distribution of the estate of Elias H. Reynolds, dec'd., identified his children and grandchildren.
Children: Mercy J. Havens, wife of James H. Havens; and Tylee L. Reynolds.
Grandchildren: Edward Cooper; and Laura Smith, formerly Laura Cooper.

THROCKMORTON –pg. 425; Jan. 1894. William S. Throckmorton was appointed guardian of his son John Ellis Throckmorton, a minor under 14yrs.

TROUTMAN –pg. 433; Jan. 1894. Geo. M. Troutman, a minor over 14yrs., chose Susan A. Troutman as his guardian.

TROUTMAN –pg. 434; Jan. 1894. Mary B. Troutman, a minor over 14yrs., elected Susan A. Troutman as her guardian.

TROUTMAN –pg. 434; Jan. 1894. Susan A. Troutman was appointed guardian of Godfrey L. Troutman and Nathaniel W. Troutman, minors under 14yrs., children of George M. Troutman, dec'd.

TROUTMAN –pg. 435; Jan. 1894. Susan O. Troutman, a minor over 14yrs., chose John J. Troutman as her guardian.

TROUTMAN –pg. 435; Jan. 1894. John J. Troutman was appointed guardian of his dau. Ivy A. Troutman, a minor under 14yrs.

TROUTMAN –pg. 436; Jan. 1894. John J. Troutman was appointed guardian of his son Diamond

M. Troutman, a minor under 14yrs.

SMITH –pg. 437; Jan. 1894. Distribution of the estate of Lewis Smith, dec'd., who wrote his will in 1864, identified heirs not named in the will.
Children of his dau. Jane Hathaway, dec'd.: William Hathaway; Mary Green; Annie Green; Benjamin Hathaway, dec'd.; and John C. Hathaway, dec'd.
Children of said Benjamin Hathaway, dec'd., who died intestate: Emma Johnston, wife of _____ Johnston; and James B. Hathaway.
Children of said John C. Hathaway, dec'd., who died intestate: Lewis G. Hathaway; Charles L. Hathaway; Jennie Worth, wife of _____ Worth; William C. Hathaway; Harry T. Hathaway and Jay C. Hathaway.

FRICK –pg. 441; Jan. 1894. Fannie A. Frick was appointed guardian of Augustus F. Frick, William F. Frick, and Louis G. Frick, minors under 14yrs., children of Augustus F. Frick, dec'd.

WOLCOTT –pg. 463; May 1894. Distribution of the estate of Benjamin Wolcott, dec'd., identified his children.
Children: Emeline Wemple, wife of Joseph Wemple; Elizabeth Taber, wife of William Russell Taber; John Wolcott; Daniel S. Wolcott; Charles H. Wolcott; Hester A. Bennett, wife of John W. Bennett; Martha F. Wolcott; Thomas Wolcott; Edward M. W. Wolcott; Benjamin W. Wolcott; and Annie Wolcott.

BOOK 5
1894 – 1897

COSTELLO –pg. 3; May 1894. Distribution of the estate of Thomas Costello, dec'd., who died intestate identified his children and grandchildren.
Daughter: Mary Stryker, wife of Holmes Stryker.
Children of his son Patrick Costello, dec'd.: Sarah Costello; Thomas Costello; John Costello; Ella Costello; Mary Costello; and Margaret Costello, a minor.
Children of his son John Costello, dec'd.: Mary Costello; Emma Costello; John Costello; Thomas Costello, a minor; Daniel Costello, a minor; William Costello, a minor; James Costello, a minor; Frank Costello, a minor; Sarah Costello, a minor; and Beatrice Costello, a minor.

DORN –pg. 30; May 1894. Distribution of a trust fund established by the will of Catherine Dorn, dec'd., revealed the principle went to Sarah Johnson, Elizabeth Shepherd, and their heirs after Charity Sweeny died. Charity Sweeny died, and Sarah Johnson and Elizabeth Shepherd were also deceased.
Children of Elizabeth Shepherd, dec'd.: Almira Greer, Mary E. Smith, Kate Shepherd, and Anna C. White.
Children of Helen S. Lufburrow, dec'd., a dau. of Elizabeth Shepherd, dec'd.: Elizabeth S. Lufburrow and Grace Lufburrow.
Daughter of Sarah Johnson, dec'd.: Deborah D. Campbell.
Children of William L. Johnson, dec'd., a son of Sarah Johnson, dec'd.: Morrell Johnson, Eva Douglas, and George Johnson.
Children, all minors, of Anna Card, dec'd., a dau. of William L. Johnson, dec'd.: Charles Card, Annie Card, and Nellie Card.
Child of Rebecca B. Benjamin, dec'd., a dau. of William L. Johnson, dec'd.: Rosie Benjamin.

GRIGGS –pg. 54 - 56; Oct. 1894. Distribution of the estate of John W. Griggs, dec'd., identified his heirs.
Widow: Hannah A. Griggs, who later died on June 24, 1894.
Children: Catharine A. Griggs; Benjamin F. Griggs; Lydia C. Griggs, now Lydia C. Reid, wife of Charles Reid; and Orsemus Griggs.
Children of his dau. Mary A. Buckelew, dec'd., wife of John T. Buckelew, dec'd.: Ada Conover, wife of Holmes Conover; Ella Buckelew, under 21yrs.; Angie Buckelew, under 21yrs.; Lillie Buckelew, under 21yrs.; and John Buckelew, under 21yrs.

PATTERSON –pg. 60; Oct. 1894. Distribution of the estate of Amos Patterson, dec'd., who died intestate on April 21, 1893, revealed Amos Patterson married Clara A. Page on Jan. 31, 1881 and resided with her until Jan. 1, 1883. They had one child, Lillian May Patterson, who was born May 14, 1883. Amos Patterson's widow had remarried and was then Clara A. Peer.

GRIMM –pg. 68; Jan. 1895. Distribution of the estate of Christian Grimm, dec'd., identified those who put in claims for his estate. Jacob Kupferschmied and Johann Ulrich Kupferschmied claimed to be his nephews and only heirs. Their claim was upheld. Susie M. Sutton claimed to be his dau. Her claim was denied.

DREYFUS –pg. 91; Jan. 1895. Distribution of the estate of Lewis Dreyfus, dec'd., who died intestate, identified his heirs as his widow and the children of his brothers James Dreyfus and Joseph Dreyfus. The nieces and nephews weren't separated by father.
Widow: Henrietta Dreyfus.
Children of James Dreyfus, dec'd., and Joseph Dreyfus, dec'd.: Fannie Stern, formerly Fannie Dreyfus; Louise Dreyfus; Fannie Block, wife of Leopold Block; Henrietta Hagenbacher, wife of Isadore Hagenbacher; Gussie Kodziesen, wife of Abraham Kodziesen; Max Dreyfus; and Herman Dreyfus.

CORLIES –pg. 99; Jan. 1895. Distribution of the estate of Tylee W. Corlies, dec'd., stated his
    siblings were his heirs.
    Siblings: Henry Corlies; Frank Corlies; Sarah C. Osborn, wife of Ezra A. Osborn; and Eliza
    H. Townsend, wife of Henry Townsend.

HENDRICKSON –pg. 169; Oct. 1895. Distribution of the estate of Charles A. Hendrickson, dec'd.,
    named his widow and his children.
    Widow: Josephine Hendrickson.
    Children: Ella Hendrickson; John J. Hendrickson; George Hendrickson; Mary E.
    Hendrickson; and Meta B. Hendrickson, a minor.

ROBBINS –pg. 178; Oct. 1895. Distribution of the estate of Chilion Robbins, dec'd., a minor born
    on Feb. 14, 1876, who died intestate and without issue on Feb. 22, 1895, revealed his mother
    and siblings predeceased him. His father, Benjamin Robbins, was a resident of Franklin,
    Ohio.

HULSE –pg. 192; Oct. 1895. A settlement of accounts filed on the estate of John Hulse, dec'd.,
    stated he was also known as John Hulsart.

MCKAY –pg. 205; Oct. 1895. Distribution of the estate of John McKay, dec'd., showed his only
    heirs were his nieces and nephews whose parents weren't identified.
    Nieces and nephews: Nathaniel R. Wilkinson; William P. Wilkinson; Margaret Young; Jane
    Purdy; Margaret Ludlam; and Ann Mason, who had since died leaving no husband or
    children.

PEMBERTON –pg. 217; Oct. 1895. Caroline Pemberton, administrator of the estate of Charles G.
    Pemberton, dec'd., requested discharge from the duties of administrator. The record disclosed
    Charles G. Pemberton was also known as Charles Pemberton or Charles Johnson.
    Administration of the estate was granted to James S. White.

GARDENER –pg. 221; Oct. 1895. Ella Blanche Angelo, executor of the estate of Amanda E.
    Gardener, dec'd., married James Q. Fitzsimmons before completing her duties as executor.

BEARMORE –pg. 233; Jan. 1896. Alvin Bearmore petitioned for a division of the real estate owned
    by his father, William L. Bearmore, dec'd., who died intestate in 1894 leaving children and
    grandchildren.
    Children, entitled to 1/5 share each: Alvin Bearmore, Edgar Bearmore, and William Franklin
    Bearmore.
    Grandchildren whose parents weren't identified, entitled to 1/10 share each: Leander
    Bearmore, 20yrs. old; and Lena Bearmore, 15yrs. old.
    Grandchildren who were children of his dau. Mary E. Allgor, dec'd., late wife of John W.
    Allgor, who died intestate in 1895, entitled to 1/10 share each: Luella Allgor, 12yrs. old; and
    Carrie Allgor, 8yrs. old.

BENNETT –pg. 332; May 1896. Distribution of the estate of Charles A. Bennett Jr., dec'd., stated
    his heirs were his widow and his father.
    Widow: Clara J. Bennett.
    Father: Charles A. Bennett.

JOHNSTON –pg. 342; May 1896. Isaac C. Johnston petitioned for a division of the real estate
    owned by his mother, Mary Johnston, dec'd., who died intestate leaving children.
    Children: Adaline Johnston, in an asylum; Isaac C. Johnston; John L. Johnston; Susie C.
    Johnston; Mary E. Stout; and Cornelia Hawkins. Note: Book 5, pg. 400 – 404, Jan. 1897 –
    Adaline Johnston died on Nov. 10, 1896.

PATTERSON –pg. 358 – 360; Oct. 1896. Distribution of the estate of Jeanette C. Patterson, dec'd.,
    started on this page and was poorly organized. Full identification of the family and heirs
    required the use of the succeeding records for the distribution of the estate of Amelia
    Patterson, dec'd. Jeanette C. Patterson and Amelia Patterson were sisters who died leaving
    their siblings and children of a deceased sister as their only heirs.
    Siblings of Jeanette C. Patterson, dec'd., and Amelia Patterson, dec'd.: John F. Patterson,
    declared mentally incompetent; William F. Patterson; Mary E. Patterson; Virgina Swope, wife
    of Isaac Swope; Alexina Patterson; Peter V. Patterson; and Harriet E. Ravatt, wife of John
    Ravatt.
    Children of their deceased sister Emeline A. O'Niel, dec'd.: Paul O'Niel, a minor; Eulalia
    O'Niel, a minor; Evangeline O'Niel who died unwed and intestate; Cosmo O'Niel; and

Francis O'Niel.

CARPENTER –pg. 387; Jan. 1897. Distribution of the estate of Lawrence Carpenter, dec'd., identified heirs not named in his will.
Widow, Mary Ann Carpenter was recently deceased. Legatee Ada Masker was now Ada M. Duryea. Legatee Jessie Masker was now Jessie Berrien. Legatee Elizabeth Ivins died after the said Lawrence Carpenter, dec'd., leaving children: Charles H. Ivins; Elizabeth (Ivins) Sayre; Albert L. Ivins; Elwood Ivins; and William Ivins, dec'd., who left a widow, Mary L. Ivins, and two children, viz., Harry S. Ivins and Frank E. Ivins.

SCHWARTING –pg. 420; Jan. 1897. Kundegunde Holsten, only living aunt and nearest relative of August Schwarting, asked the court to appoint Clarence G. VanNote guardian of said nephew who was mentally incompetent..

HOLT –pg. 453; May 1897. Distribution of the estate of Annie R. Holt, dec'd., identified her heirs.
Mother: Sarah A. Holt who had since died.
Brother: Joseph C. Holt who was judged incompetent by a court in Dakota Co., Minn.

BOOK 6

1897 – 1900

DANGLER –pg. 20; May 1897. Distribution of the estate of James Britton Dangler, dec'd.,
    identified his widow, Derenda Dangler, and his children, viz., Eva Dangler, Hattie Dangler,
    Sarah Dangler, Samuel Dangler, Ethel Dangler, and Mabel Dangler.

BORDEN –pg. 29; May 1897. Samuel Borden petitioned for payment of his share of a legacy left
    by the will of his father, Sidney P. Borden, dec'd. The petition identified heirs receiving
    shares after the deaths of the legatees. Mary Borden, widow of Sidney P. Borden, dec'd.,
    received a trust for her lifetime. She died Jan. 1895, and the trust passed to Andrew Borden,
    son of Sidney P. Borden, dec'd., for his lifetime. After his death it descended to his heirs. If
    he left no heirs it passed to three siblings Eugenia Borden, Mary Borden, and Samuel Borden.
    Andrew Borden had not been heard from in thirty years and was presumed dead without
    issue.
    Eugenia Borden married Garret Conover and died without issue.
    Mary Borden married Richard Taylor and divorced him before her death. She left three
    children, viz., Andrew Taylor, Mary E. Kugler, and Augustus Taylor, a minor. Note: Book 6,
    pg. 63, Oct. 1897, entered a correction, stating Mary (Borden) Taylor did not divorce Richard
    Taylor, and he was alive.
    Due to the deaths of legatees, 1/3 share of the trust went to Samuel Borden, the petitioner, 1/3
    to the heirs of Mary (Borden) Taylor, dec'd., and 1/3 to all the heirs of Sidney P. Borden,
    dec'd., who were identified as follows: Alexander Borden; Parker Borden; the previously
    named children of Mary Taylor, dec'd.; Julia Walker; and the children of Margaret Atkinson,
    dec'd., formerly Margaret Borden.
    Children of Margaret Atkinson, formerly Margaret Borden, dec'd.: John Borden; Walker
    Borden; Carrie Brown; Amanda Brown; Ann Eliza Zilly, late Eliza Borden; Rebecca Dolan,
    late Rebecca Borden; Annie Yard; and Ida Stewart. Note: See Book 7, pg. 20, Jan. 1900.

SMITH –pg. 35; May 1897. Distribution of the estate of Sarah A. Smith, dec'd., identified her heirs.
    Sister: Adeline D. Staake.
    Child of her sister Harriet C. Gorbett, dec'd.: Henrietta T. Gorbett.
    Child of her sister Martha M. Tileston, dec'd.: William Tileston.

NOYES –pg. 37; May 1897. Distribution of the estate of Ann W. Noyes, dec'd., named her only
    surviving heirs.
    Children of her sister Maria P. Beale, dec'd.: John E. Beale and Fred A. Beale.
    Children of Elizabeth Stearns, dec'd., a dau. of Maria P. Beale, dec'd.: Thomas B. Stearns,
    Joel W. Stearns Jr., and Arthur K. Stearns.
    Children of her sister Sarah A. Turner, dec'd.: Cora L. Turner, Samuel Turner, Isabella
    Moran, and Charles W. Turner.
    Children of her brother William Edward Innett, dec'd.: William Innett and Edward Innett.

COOPER –pg. 51; Oct. 1897. Stanley G. Cooper, a minor under 21yrs. who resided in Philadelphia,
    Pa. with his mother, Caroline A. Cooper, had no guardian in N.J., and his father was
    deceased. The court appointed David S. Crater as his guardian.

COOPER –pg. 52 - 54; Oct. 1897. James E. Cooper Jr. petitioned for a division of the real estate
    owned by his father, James E. Cooper, dec'd.
    Children of James E. Cooper, dec'd.: Linda R. Cassard, wife of Harry L. Cassard; Stanley G.
    Cooper, a minor; and James E. Cooper Jr., the petitioner.

DEBOW –pg. 96 – 99; Jan. 1898. Distribution of the estate of Susan Debow, dec'd., who left a will,
    identified heirs of deceased legatees. This abstract does not reflect all the legacies of her will.
    Her sister Elizabeth MacKinder died June 4, 1887, intestate, in Ill. and left one son, Thomas
    N. Perrine, who also died intestate in Ill., on April 8, 1891, leaving a widow, Mary A. Perrine,

and five children, all residents of Anna, Ill., viz., Daniel W. Perrine, Thomas N. Perrine, Sarah Debow Fasig, William M. Perrine, and James S. Perrine.
Her sister Mary Leavenworth died intestate in N.J. on March 23, 1883.
Her sister Mary Buckley was deceased.
Children of her aunt Hetty Newell: Mary Cook Newell of Iowa City, Iowa; Hetty Newell Watson of Iowa City, Iowa; Elizabeth Montgomery Passmore of Hammonton, N.J.; Sarah Newell Gill, dec'd.; and Lucy Montgomery Stagg, dec'd.
The said Sarah Newell Gill, dec'd., left five children, all residents of Trenton, N.J.: Lucy Lawrence Gill, Albert Livingston Gill, Clarence Newell Gill, Hetty Montgomery Gill, and Joseph Havens Gill.
The said Lucy Montgomery Stagg, dec'd., left five children: Montgomery Stagg of Snow Hill, Md.; Sarah M. Stagg of Brooklyn, N.Y.; Susan N. McMaster of Pocomoke City, Md.; Elizabeth M. Corddry of Snow Hill, Md.; and Robert Newell Stagg of Snow Hill, Md.

CONOVER –pg. 136; May 1898. Henry W. Johnson, surviving executor of the will of Peter P. Conover, dec'd., reported on the distribution of the estate and identified heirs of deceased legatees. Peter P. Conover died Nov. 15, 1890, survived by a wife and children. His widow Margaret Conover died Oct. 1, 1893.
Children from a first wife, unnamed: John H. Conover; and Mary Conover who died Jan. 1898, intestate and without issue.
Children from his second wife, the said Margaret Conover, dec'd.: Elias H. Conover, William L. Conover, and Huldah H. Stillman.
Son Henry Conover, dec'd., predeceased his father and died without issue.
Grandchild: J. Peter Frismuth, son of Henrietta Frismuth, dec'd., his dau. by his first wife.

VANDEVENTER –pg. 164; May 1898. Distribution of the estate of David P. VanDeventer, dec'd., showed he left a widow and children.
Widow: Maria L. VanDeventer.
Children: Florence Secor, wife of Clarence E. Secor; David P. VanDeventer Jr.; M. Josephine VanDeventer; and Raphael VanDeventer.

NEDDLEIN –pg. 169; May 1898. An order to the commissioners regarding the estate of John Neddlein, dec'd., revealed he was also known as John Leonhardt Needlein, Leonhardt Neidlein, Leonard Neidlein, or Leonhardt Nettlein.

OVERTON –pg. 171; May 1898. Julia A. Overton, executor of the estate of William W. Overton, dec'd., married Thomas Reddington.

MEGILL –pg. 186; May 1898. Distribution of the estate of James E. Megill, dec'd., identified his children, viz., Charles H. Megill, Robert J. Megill, John Megill, and Mary C. Tilton, wife of Joseph Tilton.

WOOLLEY –pg. 188; Oct. 1898. Distribution of the estate of Matilda Woolley, dec'd., identified her children and grandchildren, but did not name the parents of the grandchildren.
Children, entitled to 1/7 share each: William H. Woolley; Edward Woolley; Nathan W. Woolley; and Matilda Fowler, wife of William Fowler.
Grandchildren, entitled to 1/14 share each: Charles Haden and Rhoda Haden.
Grandchildren, entitled to 1/14 share each: Frank Ferguson and Anna Ferguson.
Grandchildren, entitled to 1/63 share each: Lucy Tallman, Harry Tallman, Virginia Tallman, Matilda Tallman, Grace Tallman, Maria Tallman, Sarah Tallman, William Tallman, and Minnie T. Tallman.

DICKENSON –pg. 195; Oct. 1898. An order to show cause on the estate of Albert E. Dickinson, dec'd., identified his children as Albert S. Dickinson, Dudley R. Dickinson, and Lucile Dickinson. Dudley and Lucile were minors under 14yrs. of age.

WHITE –pg. 256; Jan. 1899. Distribution of the estate of Eseck White, dec'd., who died intestate, identified his children and grandchildren.
Children: Eseck Henry White, Caroline H. Allaire, and Adaline F. Rogers.
Children of his son John B. White, dec'd.: May E. Howland and Susan B. White, a minor.

BUTT –pg. 272; Jan. 1899. Distribution of the estate of Alice Butt, dec'd., formerly Alice Cherry, named her children.
Children: Peter Cherry; and Joseph Cherry, who died leaving a widow, Elizabeth Cherry, and a child, Elizabeth Cherry, who was a minor.

170 Intestates and Others

BORDEN –pg. 273; Jan. 1899. Distribution of the estate of Randal R. Borden, dec'd., identified his widow and child.
Widow: Emma A. Borden who married George Hutchins, and then died intestate.
Child: Lillie May Borden, a minor.

PARR –pg. 283; Jan. 1899. Distribution of the estate of Henry M. Parr Jr., dec'd., who died intestate, named his heirs.
Widow: Annie Y. Parr.
Children, all minors: Elsie Parr, Gladys Parr, and Henry M. Parr.

CORBETT –pg. 285; Jan. 1899. Martin Corbett and his wife Ellen Corbett protested the appointment of Martin Ward as guardian of their grandson James Corbett, a minor under 14yrs. They claimed they were not notified of the guardianship petition, and Martin Ward was mismanaging the estate. Note: In Book 6, pg. 279, Jan. 1899, Martin Ward's petition for guardianship named the deceased James Corbett and Mary Corbett as parents of the minor.

SOFFELL –pg. 287; Jan. 1899. Christian Soffell filed a complaint against John C. Soffell's guardianship of Julia Soffell and Adeline Soffell, children of Emma E. Soffell, dec'd. John C. Soffel was appointed guardian of the children on Dec. 4, 1894. During the summer of 1898 he disappeared and hadn't returned, or been heard from since. Note: Book 6, pg. 286, Jan. 1899 identified Christian Soffell as grandfather of the minors.

TANTUM –pg. 299 - 300; May 1899. Distribution of a trust established by the last will of James Tantum, dec'd., identified heirs of the trust. The income of the trust went to Lucy Beatty, and upon her death, to her heirs. Lucy Beatty, wife of William C. Beatty, died Jan. 22, 1899 leaving William P. Beatty and Mary E. R. Flock as her heirs.

PARR –pg. 308; May 1899. Annie Y. Parr, guardian of Elsie Parr, Gladys Parr, and Henry M. Parr of Madison, Morgan Co., Ga., petitioned the court for money due her wards.

BEYER –pg. 314; May 1899. Matilda W. Beyer, guardian of Josephine L. Beyer and Marion L. Beyer, both of Brooklyn, Kings Co., N.Y., petitioned for the legacies due her wards from the estates of Elizabeth W. Beyer, dec'd., late of Red Bank, Monmouth Co., N.J., and John Beyer, dec'd., of the same location.

GROVER –pg. 329; May 1899. Distribution of the estate of James Grover, dec'd., revealed names of heirs of legatees named in his will. This abstract does not identify all legatees of the will.
Children of Abigail Leonard: Welling Leonard, John Leonard, and Deborah Woodward.
Legatee Sallie Grover was the wife of John B. Grover.
Children of James Clark Grover, dec'd.: Alice Roberts, Deborah Conover, Emily Wyckoff, Effie G. Lum, Cornelia Leonard, and Stillwell Grover.
Charles Grover, dec'd., son of the said James C. Grover, dec'd., died intestate leaving a widow, Sarah Conklin, and children, viz., Ida Grover and Rachel Grover.
Annie Leonard, dau. of James C. Grover, dec'd., died intestate leaving a husband, Charles T. Leonard.

YERO –pg. 378; Oct. 1899. Distribution of the estate of Emma Yero, dec'd., revealed heirs not named in her will. Emma Yero left her entire estate to William Schanck Jr., and after his death, to his heirs. William Schanck Jr. left the state of N.J. seven years earlier and hadn't been heard from since. He was presumed dead. He was the only child of Catharine Schanck, dec'd., a dau. of Jefferson and Sarah Schanck. Jefferson Schanck and his wife, Sarah, had other children: Jane Schanck Jackson, died without issue; Sarah A. Raynor, still living; and William Schanck, who died intestate after Emma Yero, dec'd., and left children (not named).

BENNETT –pg. 390; Oct. 1899. Distribution of the estate of James C. Bennett, dec'd., named his widow and children.
Widow: Mary C. Bennett.
Children, all minors: Isabella Bennett, Thomas H. Bennett, Mary Bennett, and James C. Bennett.

WORTHINGTON –pg. 393; Oct. 1899. Irene Bateman requested guardianship of the widow of Robert M. Worthington, dec'd., Anna M. Worthington, who was an inmate of the state asylum. Anna M. Worthington received a pension because her late husband had been a Corporal in Co. M, G Regt., Illinois Vol. Cavalry.

SHAFTO –pg. 419; Jan. 1900. Distribution of the estate of Samuel G. Shafto, dec'd., who died intestate and unmarried.

Brother: Thomas Shafto.

Children of his brother John Shafto, dec'd.: Robert Shafto, Anthony R. Shafto, Rolin E. Shafto, George W. Shafto, Monroe Shafto, Cyrus Shafto, Rebecca Day, and Isabella Morris.

Children of his brother Robert K. Shafto, dec'd.: Elizabeth Donahay, William H. Shafto, Andrew M. Shafto, Mary Johnson, and Rena Stout.

Children of his brother William C. Shafto, dec'd.: Isabella Matlack, Elizabeth Githens, Jane Romaine, T. Milton Shafto, and Henry Shafto.

Children of his brother George W. Shafto, dec'd.: Adelia Hurley, Alvin Shafto, Emma Pyle, Jane Morris, Frank Shafto, John G. Shafto, and Isabella Sanborn.

Children of his sister Jane White, dec'd.: Elizabeth Davison and Isabella VanNortwick.

CAMP –pg. 420; Jan. 1900. The court appointed David S. Crater guardian of Preston Camp, Nettie Camp, and Celia Camp, minors and heirs of their mother, Hannah Camp, dec'd., late wife of Daniel Camp (still living). Their mother died after her father, James Brand, dec'd.

BRAND –pg. 421; Jan. 1900. Ellwood Brand petitioned for a division of the real estate owned by his father, James Brand, dec'd.

Children of James Brand, dec'd.: Ellwood Brand; John C. Brand; Deborah A. May, wife of Alex'r May; Caroline Stanton, wife of Benjamin H. Stanton; Forman Brand; Sanford Brand; David Brand; Charlotte Bennett, wife of Henry H. Bennett; Sarah or Sadie Brand, wife of Charles Brand; and James Brand.

Ellwood Brand had also purchased the share of his sister Jane Horner, wife of John Horner. Grandchildren who were children of his deceased dau.(not named), late wife of Daniel Camp: Preston Camp, Nettie Camp, and Celia Camp.

ALLEN –pg. 433; Jan. 1900. Leslie J. Allen petitioned for a division of the real estate owned by David F. Allen, dec'd. Leslie J. Allen, the petitioner, and his brothers, Samuel I. Allen, Edgar D. Allen, and Archibald H. Allen, were each entitled to 1/4 share. Edgar and Archibald were minors.

BOOK 7

1900 – 1902

WHITE –pg. 13; Jan. 1900. Benjamin A. Hagerman requested guardianship of his brother-in-law Forman Edward White, a person deemed mentally incompetent.

BORDEN –pg. 20; Jan. 1900. Alice E. Morris petitioned the court for her share of the estate of Sidney P. Borden, dec'd. Alexander Borden died on Oct. 24, 1899 leaving Alice E. Morris as his only legal heir. William Borden (or Parker), Emma Borden (or Parker), and Albert Borden (or Parker) were named the illegitimate children of Alexander Borden, dec'd. Note: See Book 6, pg. 29, May 1897.

HARNETT –pg. 27; May 1900. Distribution of the estate of Pauline L. Harnett, dec'd., identified her heirs.
Sister: Henrietta T. Murphy.
Children of her brother Edward H. Eckel, dec'd.: Henry Eckel, Edward Eckel, and Annetta Ford.
Half-sisters: Christine Hinsdale and Julie Rosswog (also spelled Rosswod in same record).

BOWNE –pg. 40; May 1900. Distribution of the estate of John A. Bowne, dec'd., who died intestate, identified his heirs.
Siblings: Simon Bowne who since died intestate; Mary A. Reid; Sarah Silver; and Caroline Luff who since died intestate.
Child of his sister Levinia French, dec'd.: John H. French.
Child of his sister Alice Rue, dec'd.: Jacob S. Rue.
Children of his brother William Bowne, dec'd.: Aaron Bowne; Rebecca Culver; David Bowne, dec'd.; and John Bowne, dec'd.

THOMPSON –pg. 65; May 1900. Distribution of the estate of Mary E. Thompson, dec'd., identified her children as her heirs.
Children: Lewis S. Thompson of Red Bank, N.J.; William P. Thompson of Red Bank, N.J.; and Elizabeth T. Preston who died Dec. 3, 1899 and was the late wife of Ralph T. Preston.

HAMPTON –pg. 80 - 82; May 1900. Distribution of the estate of Moses Hampton, dec'd., revealed information about some of the legatees of his will. The record referred to specific clauses of the will; therefore, this abstract may not contain the names of all the heirs of Moses Hampton, dec'd.
Children of Moses Hampton, dec'd., who were still alive: William M. Hampton, Caroline C. Cook, and Lewis M. Hampton.
Daughter Mary Ann Hulick died intestate leaving children: Charles L. Hulick; George A. Hulick; Eunice Maps; and Laura Truax who had died intestate. Laura Truax, dec'd., left two children, wards of A. Taylor Truax, viz., Harry Truax and Chester Truax.
Son James L. Hampton died intestate leaving children: James Monroe Hampton and Mary Etta Dalton. Mary Etta Dalton died intestate leaving a dau., Hattie Dalton, a minor, ward of Frank Dalton.
Daughter Catharine VanDyke died intestate leaving children: William E. VanDyke; Jane Dennis; Hart VanDyke; Elisha G. VanDyke; Sidney C. VanDyke; and Melissa Davis who died intestate leaving two minor children, viz., Roberta M. Davis and Warren L. Davis, wards of William T. Davis.
Daughter Elizabeth Hendrickson died intestate leaving Frank Hendrickson as her only child.
Daughter Jane Fuller died after her father and left a will.
Grandchildren of Moses Hampton, dec'd., parents not given: Moses I. Hampton; Hannah Hampton, now Hannah Eaton; Lucy Hampton, now Lucy Blackwell; and Charles Hampton.

MURRAY –pg. 92; May 1900. Charles H. Boud was appointed guardian of Martha Murray, a resident of the state asylum whose parents were deceased. Her sister Maria E. Murray relinquished her right to guardianship.

LAIGHT –pg. 99; May 1900. Anna M. Laight requested guardianship of her step-children Frederick B. Laight and Julia H. Laight, minors, children of John M. Laight, dec'd.

WEST –pg. 124; Oct. 1900. Distribution of the estate of John R. West, dec'd., identified his children.
Children: John P. West, Rebecca A. West, Harrison West, Adaline Lippincott, Margaret West, and Lucy A. Manahan, dec'd.

LANTHIEER –pg. 130; Oct. 1900. Distribution of the estate of Emeline Lanthieer, dec'd., identified her heirs.
Sisters, entitled to 1/3 share each: Sarah P. Lukens and Catharine A. Grant.
Niece and nephew, entitled to 1/6 share each: Lydia Rudd and Edward L. Burk.

VANBRUNT –pg. 130; Oct. 1900. Margaret Fletcher was appointed guardian of her sister Adelaide VanBrunt who had been mentally incompetent since infancy. Their mother was deceased.

BROWN –pg. 133; Oct. 1900. Distribution of the estate of George W. Brown, dec'd., identified his heirs.
Children: Lizzie Brown, May P. Brown, and Annie B. Brown.
Grandchild: Cora Vanderveer Brown, a minor whose guardian was her mother, Anna Vanderveer Brown.

NEWING –pg. 136; Oct. 1900. Carrie Newing relinquished her right to dower from the estate of her husband, Archer C. Newing, dec'd., late of Ocean Tshp.

WHITE –pg. 152 – 154; Jan. 1901. Theodore F. White petitioned for a division of the real estate owned by his father, Lewis White, dec'd., who died intestate in 1900.
Children of Lewis White: Theodore F. White, William A. White, Joseph White, Winfield S. White, Timothy M. White, and Amanda White.
Children of his son Henry C. White, dec'd.: George H. White, 12yrs. old; Walter R. White, 11 yrs. old; and Mabel White, 14yrs. old. Henry C. White, dec'd., also left a widow, Carrie S. White, mother of his children.

HITCHCOCK –pg. 154; Jan. 1901. Distribution of the estate of William G. Hitchcock, dec'd., listed his heirs as his siblings and the children of a deceased sister.
Siblings: George W. Hitchcock, Julia E. Borden, and Georgianna Stout.
Children of his sister Mira Boyd, dec'd.: Charles H. Boyd, Walter E. Boyd, and Minnie Boyd.

COTTRELL –pg. 164; Jan. 1901. Distribution of the estate of Harriet W. Cottrell, dec'd., identified her children and grandchildren.
Children: Frank P. Cottrell, Louis P. Cottrell, and George Cottrell.
Grandchild: Hattie Cottrell, a minor, ward of her mother, Katie T. Smith.

MARTIN –pg. 175; Jan. 1901. Distribution of the estate of Rhoda Martin, dec'd., a single woman whose parents predeceased her, identified her heirs.
Sister: Eliza G. Martin who since died intestate. Note: In Book 7, pg. 176, Jan. 1901, distribution of Eliza's estate contained the same list of heirs.
Children of her sister Charity Lane, dec'd., who died intestate on Sept. 27, 1882: John Lane who died intestate; Ann Covert who died intestate on Oct. 30, 1886; Hannah Corlies who died testate on Sept. 26, 1897; and Henrietta Hubbard who died intestate on Jan. 12, 1896. The said John Lane, dec'd., left one child, Annie A. Styles. The said Ann Covert, dec'd., left five children, viz., Ella Covert, Belle Covert, Daniel Covert Jr., Charles Covert, and John Covert. John Hubbard, son of the said Henrietta Hubbard, dec'd., was administrator of her estate.
Child of her sister Margaret Ward, dec'd., who died intestate on Jan. 16, 1900: Amy Overin.
Children of her sister Allcha Hurley, dec'd., who died intestate on March 24, 1827: Alexander Hurley and Charles Hurley.
Her sister Catharine VanDyke died intestate on Nov. 27, 1861 leaving children and grandchildren.
Children of Catherine VanDyke, dec'd.: John VanDyke, dec'd., died unwed and intestate on Dec. 7, 1881; Vincent W. VanDyke, dec'd., died intestate on July 10, 1881; Isaac VanDyke, dec'd., died intestate on Aug. 18, 1874; and Hannah DeNyse, dec'd., died intestate on July 10, 1899.
Children of Catherine VanDyke's son Henry VanDyke, dec'd., who died on Dec. 2, 1859: Henry VanDyke, Catharine Fisher, Virginia Conk, and Michael M. VanDyke Jr.

Children of Catherine VanDyke's son Samuel T. VanDyke, dec'd., who died intestate on Jan. 28, 1898: Leonard S. VanDyke, Emma VanDyke, Minnie Quinn, Jessie Sperling, and Hattie Venable.

Children of Catharine VanDyke's son Michael M. VanDyke, dec'd., who died intestate on Sept. 11, 1885: Sylvester B. VanDyke, Sidney B. VanDyke, James O. VanDyke, Eloise Jolins, Lillie B. Davis, and Mary T. Trott who since died intestate.

COVERT –pg. 208; Jan. 1901. Caroline Covert requested guardianship of her husband, Matthew R. Covert, then residing at the state asylum. Matthew R. Covert was a private in Co. B, 3rd Reg., NJ Vol. Calvary during the Civil War and held pension certificate number 728621.

WOOD –pg. 211; Jan. 1901. Distribution of the estate of Louisa Wood, dec'd., identified her heirs.
Brother: James Wood of San Francisco, Calif.
Children of her brother Jacob Wood, dec'd.: William H. Wood, resident of 146 Maple Ave., Red Bank, N.J.; Emma Brady, resident of 385 Third St., Brooklyn, N.Y.; Elmira Morrow, resident 163 West 81st St., N.Y. City, N.Y.; Christie Wood of Hackensack, N.J.; and Irving Wood of Lake St. Catharine, Bermont.
Child of her brother Abram Wood, dec'd.: Susan Schroeder of Red Bank, N.J.
Children of her brother William Wood, dec'd.: Ada Chadwick of Red Bank, N.J.; and Fidelia Ackerman of Red Bank, N.J.
Children of her brother Charles Wood, dec'd.: Charles F. Wood of N.Y. City, N.Y.; and James H. Wood, late of N.Y. City, N.Y., who died March 23, 1901 leaving Augusta E. Wood as his widow.
Children of her sister Mary E. Benson, dec'd.: William Benson of Haverstraw, N.Y.; and Caroline DeBaun of Haverstraw, N.Y.
Children of her niece Malvina Fowler, dec'd., a dau. of her sister Ann M. Stevens, dec'd.: Ardilla Fowler Vail of Yorktown Heights, Westchester Co., N.Y.; Anna W. Naugle, resident #19 Bank St., Manhatten Borough, N.Y.; John Henry Bassett of Yorktown Heights, Westchester Co., N.Y.; and Melvin Bassett of Yorktown Heights, Westchester Co., N.Y.

SLOAN –pg. 239; May 1901. James M. Sloan and Mary A. Poole, siblings of Francis W. Sloan, a minor under 14yrs., requested James Dunn be appointed guardian of their brother. Their mother was deceased, and all other siblings were minors.

COMPTON –pg. 246; May 1901. Distribution of the estate of John S. Compton, dec'd., identified heirs of the legatees in his will. The record may not have reflected the entire will; therefore, this abstract may not contain the names of all his heirs.
1/6 share each to Job Compton and Hannah C. Matthews.
1/6 share to the heirs of Seely Compton: Eliza Thorne, Laura Folks, Abigail Willetts, Mary Compton, Emma Dyer, Irene Compton, and Theresa Compton.
1/6 share to the heirs of Abigail Walling: Annie Walling, Abigail Rockafeller, Deborah Whittaker, Emma Walling, Nettie Walling, and Norah Walling.
1/6 share to the heirs of Huldah Clark: Joseph S. Clark and John C. Clark.
1/6 share to the heirs of Cornelius Compton: Sarah Lawrence, Julia F. Johnson, Mary H. Glass, Amelia F. Roberts, and Arthur Compton.

MATTHEWS –pg. 247; May 1901. A decree for payment from the estate of William Matthews, dec'd., identified Frank Matthews and Hattie L. Matthews as siblings and sole heirs of William Oscar Matthews, dec'd., a nephew and residual legatee of the estate of said William Matthews, dec'd. William Oscar Matthews died unwed and intestate.

VANDERVEER –pg. 250; May 1901. Distribution of the estate of Eleanor Vanderveer, dec'd., revealed she left a will in which she requested a portion of her estate be divided according to the laws governing inheritance. The record identified those heirs.
Children of her brother Tobias Polhemus, dec'd.: Emeline Conover, a widow; Henry Polhemus; Matthias V. D. Polhemus; John Polhemus; Daniel Polhemus; Rachel A. Lloyd, a widow; Sarah Ladd, a widow; and Mary H. Taylor, a widow.
Children of her sister Margaret Schanck, dec'd.: Mary S. Holmes, a widow; Lavinia S. Jones; Eleanor Conover; and Sarah H. Taylor.
Children of Daniel Schanck, dec'd., a son of the said Margaret Schanck, dec'd.: Sarah E. Ely and Margaret Ely.

GILLET –pg. 280; Oct. 1901. Francis M. Gillet requested guardianship of his son Cromwell M. Gillet who was mentally incompetent.

CONK –pg. 288; Oct. 1901. Distribution of the estate of John Conk, dec'd. identified his heirs.

Children of his brother Jacob Conk, dec'd.: Amos Conk, Hannah E. Thompson, Theodore F. Conk, Adalaide Lawrence, Clarkson B. Conk, Margaret A. Ward, and Jane L. Kelly.
Children of his sister Sarah Morris, dec'd.: John Morris, Debbie Morris, and Hannah H. Hubert.

BROWN –pg. 292; Oct. 1901. Margaret Brown requested guardianship of her husband, Oscar S. Brown, who was confined to a state asylum.

MURRAY –pg. 339; Jan. 1902. Distribution of the estate of Susan Murray, dec'd., who died in 1890.
Children: Maria E. Murray; Martha Murray, mentally incompetent; and Susan Murray, since deceased.
Children of her son William Murray, dec'd.: Theodore S. Murray, Julia Murray, William Murray, Harvey D. Murray, Ada Burdge, Jennie Parker, James T. Murray, and Myra Vanderwortt.

PRATT –pg. 345; Jan. 1902. Distribution of the estate of John H. Pratt, dec'd., who died while a resident of Philadelphia, Pa., identified his heirs.
Widow: Julia P. Pratt had since died leaving a will that was admitted to probate in Philadelphia.
Children of his brother Eliphas Perkins Pratt, dec'd.: David P. Pratt and Mary Pratt.
Children of his sister Laura Currier, dec'd.: Edward W. Currier and Addison H. Currier.
Children of his brother Robert W. Pratt, dec'd.: Alice E. Edie, Julia S. McMillan, Lucy M. Duncan, Charles C. Pratt, John A. Pratt, Herbert E. Pratt, Edgar B. Pratt, Laura M. Pratt, Harlan B. Pratt, and Harry H. Pratt.
Children of his sister Julia P. Ballard, dec'd.: Harlan H. Ballard and Winifred B. Blake.

BLOODSALL –pg. 351; Jan. 1902. Distribution of the estate of Caroline N. Bloodsall, dec'd., also known as Caroline N. Stovall, dec'd., identified her heirs as cousins and children of cousins.
Cousins: Ella N. Moore, Sarah I. Francisco, William D. Francisco, Estelle Phillips, Halsey H. Francisco, and Frank E. Francisco.
Children of cousin Henrietta O'Dell, dec'd., formerly Henrietta Blackwell, formerly Henrietta Davis: Aleathea Davis; Maxcy Blackwell; Essie Blackwell, under 21yrs.; and William Blackwell, under 21yrs.

DOLL –pg. 356; Jan. 1902. Distribution of the estate of Jacob Doll, dec'd., identified his widow and children.
Widow: Phillipina Doll.
Children: Jacob Doll Jr., Louisa Mehrtens, Elizabeth Pfaffe Burns, Laura Feigle, and John H. Doll.

MURMAN –pg. 361; Jan. 1902. Distribution of the estate of Anna C. Murman, dec'd., revealed her only heir was Daniel Wretling of Sundborn, Province of Falun, Sweden. The surname Murman was also given as Morman.

LELAND –pg. 375; Jan. 1902. Distribution of the estate of Anna B. Leland, dec'd., stated her heirs were her children, viz., Leslie Francis Johnson, Harry W. Leland, Edwin N. Leland, Annie B. White, and Frank Leland.

WHALEY –pg.376; Jan. 1902. Jane Carhart Whaley, widow of William A. Whaley, dec'd., took cash in lieu of her dower.

REID –pg. 383; May 1902. Distribution of the estate of Aaron H. Reid, dec'd., identified his heirs.
Widow: Armenia M. Reid.
Children: Kate A. Hoffman, a widow; Leona M. Reid, a minor; and Minnie B. Reid, a minor.
Child of his son John D. Reid, dec'd.: Mary Gertrude Burrowes.

MCCLEES –pg. 392; May 1902. Herbert C. McClees, only child of John McClees, was appointed guardian of his father, an alcoholic.

PATTERSON –pg. 434; May 1902. Distribution of the estate of Ann Patterson, dec'd., identified her heirs.
Sister: Margaret Applegate.
Half-brothers: John H. Patterson, Henry J. Patterson, C. Ewing Patterson, and Joseph C. Patterson.
Half-sisters: Rebecca Hendrickson and Lydia Frost.

Child of her brother James H. Patterson, dec'd.: Emma Morford.
Children of her half-brother Samuel H. Patterson, dec'd.: George H. Patterson and Sarah I. Cooper.
Children of her sister Hannah Hopping, dec'd.: James P. Hopping and John J. Hopping.

PIERCE –pg. 439; May 1902. Distribution of the estate of Laura T. Pierce, dec'd., identified her children, viz., Ella Stankeewez, Katie VanHise, Benjamin Pearce, Hannah Elmer, Robert Pearce, and Anthony Pearce.

FORD –pg. 442; May 1902. Distribution of the estate of Randal R. Ford, dec'd., identified his heirs:
Widow: Sarah Ford.
Siblings: William H. Ford and Louisa Sitzer.
Children of his brother John Ford, dec'd.: Horace Ford and William Ford.
Child of his brother Craig Ford, dec'd.: Annie Hendrickson.
Children of his sister Margaret Myers, dec'd.: Leason Myers, Mary Myers, and Horace Myers.

BOOK 8
1903 – 1906

ALLGOR –pg. 6; Jan. 1903. Distribution of the estate of Benjamin Allgor, dec'd., named his heirs.
Widow: Susannah Allgor.
Children: Lydia A. Thomas, Michael H. Allgor, Kate Newman, Harriet Allen, Benjamin E. Allgor, and Mary V. Rogers.
Children of his dau. Ellen B. Hall, dec'd., late wife of S. E. Hall: Walter Hall and Adelbert Hall, a minor.

NALE –pg. 31; Jan. 1903. Distribution of the estate of Norma Nale, dec'd., identified her heirs: her mother, Viola Nale; her sister, Marion Nale; and her half-sister, Helen Nale, a minor. Note: A record in Book 8, pg. 37, Jan. 1903 stated Helen Nale lived in Philadelphia, Pa.

SCHWARTZ –pg. 43; Jan. 1903. Distribution of the estate of Jacob Schwartz, dec'd., revealed he left a widow, Mary A. Schwartz, and four siblings, viz., John F. Schwartz, William Schwartz, Sarah Ludlow, and Margaret Baugham.

WOOLLEY –pg. 50; May 1903. Distribution of the estate of Ludlow Woolley, dec'd., identified his children and grandchildren.
Daughter: Harriet H. Woolley.
Children of his son Nelson Woolley, dec'd.: Mary E. Weeden and Ada Dangler.

HENDRICKSON –pg. 59; May 1903. Distribution of the estate of Mary M. Hendrickson, dec'd., identified her heirs.
Siblings entitled to 1/3 share each: John S. Hendrickson and Ella Hendrickson.
Nieces and nephews (parents not identified), entitled to 1/3 share total: William Hartshorne; Benjamin M. Hartshorne Jr., who since died intestate; Louise Hartshorne; and Susannah P. Hartshorne.

COOPER –pg. 70; May 1903. An order to appear was issued to Louisa Cooper, heir of Caroline F. Evans, dec'd., and wife of Gaston Cooper. Her last known residence was the state of Virginia.

HERBERT –pg. 74; May 1903. Distribution of the estate of Joseph J. Herbert, dec'd., a single man, listed his heirs.
Half-brothers: James H. Howland and Samuel Howland.
Half-sister: Viola H. Kelly, wife of William Kelly.

PAGE –pg. 75; May 1903. The settlement of the estate of Harry W. Page, dec'd., identified his heirs.
Widow: Anna C. Page.
Children: Minnie Iola Page Cline; Edna Claire Page; Mabel Alma Page, a minor; Clarence Leslie Page, a minor; and Hazel Zelma Page, a minor.

WALLING –pg. 108; Oct. 1903. Distribution of the estate of Isaac B. Walling, dec'd., identified his heirs.
Siblings: Aaron B. Walling, Thomas B. Walling, and Mary C. White.
Niece: Laura Walling (parents not named).

O'HAGAN –pg. 109; Oct. 1903. Distribution of the estate of Maria O'Hagan, dec'd., named her heirs.
Children: Mary J. Bohnhof, John J. O'Hagan, William J. O'Hagan, Thomas B. O'Hagan, and Robert E. O'Hagan.

PROBASCO –pg. 122; Oct. 1903. Distribution of the estate of the unwed Mary Jane Probasco,

dec'd., named her heirs.
Siblings: James K. Probasco, Robert S. Probasco, Hendrick Probasco, Rynear Probasco, Joanna Probasco, and Huldah Buck, wife of Andrew J. Buck.

SHREVE –pg. 123; Oct. 1903. Distribution of the estate of William T. Shreve, dec'd., who died intestate, identified his heirs.
Brother: John L. Shreve.
Children of his brother Peter Shreve, dec'd.: Mary E. Donahay, George W. Shreve, Aaron R. Shreve, Peter T. Shreve, and Isaac A. Shreve.
Children of his niece Anna Johnson, dec'd., a dau. of Peter Shreve, dec'd.: Lydia Cutter and Sarah D. Johnson.
Children of his brother Isaac Shreve, dec'd.: Emma Butts, Peter D. Shreve, and Elizabeth Johnston.
Child of his brother Thomas Shreve, dec'd.: Margaret Shreve.

MURRAY –pg. 128; Jan. 1904. Distribution of the estate of Mary C. Murray, dec'd., identified her children.
Children: Mary C. M. Hyde, Ella C. M. VanBrunt, and George C. Murray.

STILLWELL –pg. 131; Jan. 1904. Distribution of the estate of James H. Stillwell, dec'd., identified his children and widow.
Widow: Elizabeth Stillwell.
Children: Britton C. Stillwell, Matilda K. Craig, Jeremiah Stillwell, James H. Stillwell, Joseph M. Stillwell, and Annie M. Pearce.

BROCKLEBANK –pg. 133; Jan. 1904. Amos B. Brocklebank petitioned for a division of the real estate owned by his father, Samuel Brocklebank, dec'd.
Widow: Evlyn L. Brocklebank.
Children: Amos B. Brocklebank; John H. Brocklebank; Charles N. Brocklebank; Adolphus M. Brocklebank; Sarah H. Hendrickson, wife of Charles A. Hendrickson; Mary R. Brocklebank; Martha B. Cooper, wife of Henry Cooper; Alfretta G. Bauer, wife of Charles Bauer; Ada V. Hulsehart, wife of Harry Hulsehart; Harriet E. Harris, wife of John Jay Harris; and Florence Brocklebank, a minor.

CARR –pg. 139; Jan. 1904. Distribution of the estate of Adam Carr, dec'd., identified his children.
Children: John Carr; Richard Carr; Lizzie Lehr, wife of Herman Lehr; Adam Carr Jr.; Sarah Walling, a widow; James Carr; William J. Carr; and Charles Carr.

NIBLETT –pg. 163; Jan. 1904. Distribution of the estate of Henry E. Niblett, dec'd., identified his heirs.
Widow: Arintha Niblett.
Children: Arintha McGuiners, Frank K. Niblett, Lyda Vincent, Charles E. Niblett, Eva M. Schmidt, James B. Niblett, and Henry Z. Niblett.

HEATH –pg. 170; Jan. 1904. George B. Heath, as next of kin, was appointed guardian of Gladys Heath, a minor.

REEDER –pg. 171; Jan. 1904. William B. Allen requested guardianship of his aunt Margaret Reeder who was mentally incompetent.

LIPPINCOTT –pg. 186; May 1904. Distribution of the estate of the unmarried Peter Lippincott, dec'd., named his heirs.
Siblings: Samuel B. Lippincott; George D. Lippincott; James M. Lippincott; Emily Lippincott who died unwed and intestate; Sarah J. Obre; and Elizabeth W. Hampton.

SLOAN –pg. 201; May 1904. Distribution of the estate of John Sloan, dec'd., identified his children.
Children: James M. Sloan; Mary A. Poole, wife of George W. Poole; Annie Sloan; Loretta M. Krug, wife of Montillion Krug; John J. Sloan, a minor; and Francis W. Sloan, a minor.

HAINES –pg. 235; Oct. 1904. Distribution of the estate of Peter Haines, dec'd., identified his heirs.
Widow: Mary Haines.
Children: William Edward Haines, Armenia Fergerson, Lillie Viola Sargent, and Eliza Tooth.

HAVILAND –pg. 245; Oct. 1904. Distribution of the estate of Stephen T. Haviland, dec'd., who died intestate, identified his heirs.

Children: William H. Haviland, Wright F. Haviland, Charles P. Haviland, and E. Combs Haviland.
Children of his son George A. Haviland, dec'd.: Oscar Y. Haviland, Mamie Burroughs, and Raymond Haviland.
Child of his dau. Emma L. Smith, dec'd.: Laura V. Burtis.
Children of his son Amos Haviland, dec'd.: Adaline Chamberlain; Frederick Haviland; Isabel Leron (also given as Levon); Richard C. Haviland; Thomas E. Haviland; Howard Haviland, a minor; Hattie Haviland, a minor; and Nola B. Haviland, a minor.

SWIFT –pg. 249; Oct. 1904. Distribution of the estate of Edward B. Swift, dec'd., identified his widow as Elizabeth V. Swift, and his dau. as Elizabeth B. Swift.

DRENNEN –pg. 253; Oct. 1904. An order to appoint an administrator to the estate of John Drennen, dec'd., revealed he died intestate on Jan. 2, 1904 leaving two sons, viz., John Drennen and Michael H. Drennen.

WOOD –pg. 254; Oct. 1904. An order to appoint an administrator to the estate of Phebe Ann Wood, dec'd., stated she died intestate on Dec. 4, 1903 leaving several nieces and nephews (not named), and three siblings, viz., Caroline Burling, Susan Langdon, and Joseph Langdon.

WOODING –pg. 282; Oct. 1904. Application for letters of administration on the estate of Mary Jane Wooding, dec'd., late of Atlantic Highlands, stated she died intestate on Aug. 3, 1901 leaving children, viz., Alvin S. Wooding and Gertrude A. Hart, wife of Harry A. Hart of Pa.

ASHMORE –pg. 301 – 302; Oct. 1904. The record was a dispute over the administration of the estate of Hannah Maria Ashmore, dec'd., who died intestate leaving children, viz., Elizabeth Ashmore, Theodore Ashmore, Herbert Ashmore, and Edith Wickerham.

NUNNALLY –pg. 327; Jan. 1905. Distribution of the estate of William A. Nunnally, dec'd., identified his heirs.
Widow: Mary A. Nunnally.
Children: Florence Nunnally, William Nunnally, Blakley Nunnally, Raymond Nunnally, and Alma Nunnally.

CATHIE –pg. 347; Jan. 1905. Distribution of the estate of Margaret Cathie, dec'd., who died intestate, identified her heirs.
Children: Adaline Sharp, wife of Samuel F. Sharp; Isabel Earl; Theodore F. Young; and Joseph Young.
Child of her son William N. Cole, dec'd., late husband of Minnie Cole: Elsie Finley, wife of Joseph F. Finley.
Children (all minors) of her dau. Eveline Earl, dec'd.: Wallace Earl, John Earl, Burtt Earl, Effie Earl, Harry Earl, and Elmer Earl.

QUACKENBUSH –pg. 384; Jan. 1905. Distribution of the estate of Holmes J. Quackenbush, dec'd., identified his heirs.
Widow: Aretta Quackenbush.
Child: Gladys May Quackenbush, a minor.

WHITE –pg. 388; May 1905. Distribution of the estate of Uriah White, dec'd., identified his heirs.
Widow: Catharine White.
Child: Hattie Conover.

EMMONS –pg. 390; May 1905. Distribution of the estate of Jonathan Emmons, dec'd., who died intestate, identified his heirs.
Widow: Mary E. Emmons.
Children: Louwella Emmons, Harry A. Emmons, and Grace L. Emmons.

PARMLY –pg. 421; May 1905. Distribution of the estate of Charles Frederick Parmly, dec'd., identified his heirs.
Widow: Emily Neilson Parmly.
Children, all minors: Theodore Neilson Parmly, Ehrick Parmly, and Frederick Dubois Parmly.

LLOYD –pg. 437; Oct. 1905. Distribution of the estate of Emma E. Lloyd, dec'd., who died testate, contained information on the status of some legatees after the execution of her will. The record may not reflect the full contents of her will.
Her niece Emma L. Vanmater married Robert K. Young.

Her sister Catharine L. Forman died in March of 1905.

Emma L. Young, Huldah H. Cooke, Lillian L. Hopping, and William A. Vanmater were listed as the surviving children of Gilbert H. Vanmater and wife, Sarah. The couple had three other children who died leaving issue.

Sarah H. Potter, dec'd., dau. of Gilbert H. and Sarah Vanmater, left two children, not residents of N.J.: Catharine Holmes Potter, a minor over 14yrs.; and Laurence Jerome Potter, a minor under 14yrs.

Daniel G. Vanmater, dec'd., son of Gilbert H. and Sarah Vanmater, left two children: Ethel Vanmater; and Robert A. Vanmater, a minor over 14yrs.

John H. Vanmater, dec'd., son of Gilbert H. and Sarah Vanmater, left three children: Gilbert H. Vanmater, Eliza H. Mannal, and William J. Vanmater.

ROBBINS –pg. 461; Oct. 1905. A decree for distribution of a trust established by the will of Aaron Robbins, dec'd., identified residual legatees of the trust. His will set up a lifetime trust for Louisa R. Davis. After her death, the trust went to her surviving siblings and the heirs of deceased siblings.

Siblings of Louisa R. Davis, dec'd.: Catharine I. Tilton, a widow; Elizabeth R. Waln, wife of Richard C. Waln; Mary I. Ford, a widow; and Aaron H. Robbins.

Child of her sister Eliza Meirs, dec'd.: Louisa A. Denise, a widow.

Children, all minors, of her nephew Charles R. Meirs, dec'd., son of the said Eliza Meirs, dec'd.: Anna E. Meirs, Linda K. Meirs, Idalou Meirs, Lillie A. Meirs, and Charles R. Meirs.

BRAND –pg. 475; Oct. 1905. Distribution of the estate of Elwood Brand, dec'd., identified his heirs.

Widow: Elizabeth Brand.

Children: Lulu M. Brand and J. Ross Brand.

INDEX

Brusenhan
  Mary E., 156
Brusnaham
  David, 144
  Dennis S., 144
  Edward, 144
  Martha, 144
  Mary E., 144
Brutting
  Barbara, 162
  Charles Joseph, 162
  George, 162
  George Joseph, 162
  John, 162
  John George, 162
  Joseph, 162
Buck
  Alice, 93
  Andrew J., 178
  David, 94
  Elizabeth, 25
  Hannah, 25
  Hannah B., 140, 142
  Henry, 93
  Henry W., 140, 142
  Huldah, 178
  James Monroe, 94
  Jane Maria, 94
  John H., 97
  Mary, 93
  Mary Elizabeth, 25
  Peter, 25
  Susannah, 25
  Sylvester, 93
Buckelew
  Andrew L., 80
  Angie, 165
  Caroline, 152
  Ella, 165
  Enoch D., 80
  John, 165
  John P., 80
  John T., 165
  Lillie, 165
  Mary A., 165
  Sarah, 80
Buckley
  Mary, 169
Bullock
  Amos, 71
  Ann, 71
  Elizabeth, 71
  John, 71
  Margaret, 71
  Thomas, 71
Bullus
  John, 25
  William, 25
Bumster
  Catharine, 162
Bunnell
  James, 58
  Lydia, 58
  Mary, 58
Bunting
  Samuel, 51

Burden
  Francis, 47
Burdge
  Ada, 175
  Anna Rosa, 61
  Asher, 61
  Catharine, 61
  Elizabeth, 109
  John, 61
  John L., 109
  Mary Matilda, 61
  Merrick, 44
  Merrick M., 121
  William, 61
Burk
  Abraham, 106
  Edward L., 173
  Sarah, 106
Burlew
  Elizabeth A., 148
Burling
  Caroline, 179
Burns
  Elizabeth Pfaffe, 175
Burroughs
  Mamie, 179
Burrowes
  Mary Gertrude, 175
Burrows
  Edward T., 85
  Joseph T., 85
  Lydia, 31, 91
  Mary, 85
  Richard C., 85
  Thomas, 85
Burtis
  Alice H., 58
  Catharine Ann, 58
  Charles R., 74
  Emily S., 137
  Hannah A., 137
  James T., 137
  Josephine C., 58
  Laura V., 179
  Louisa A., 89
  Lucy Ann, 89
  Margaret, 94
  Peter W., 94
  Rebecca, 36
  Richard, 36
  Richard W., 74, 94
  Sarah A., 94
  Sarah L., 89
  William T., 51
  Zilpha Ann, 89
Burton
  Jesse, 12
  Sarah, 12
Bush
  George, 65
  Keziah, 65
Butcher
  Elizabeth, 32, 47
  Harriet, 47
  Jacob, 40
  Joseph, 32

  Margaret, 47
Butler
  Charles, 64
  Charles K., 96, 98,
    110
  Deliverance, 61, 64
  Emily, 98, 160
  Emily Conover, 110
  Emma Jane, 111
  Isabel, 98
  Isabella, 96
  James, 80
  Jane, 115
  John, 109, 115
  Lizzie J., 146
  Mary, 96, 98
  Mary C., 110
  Rachel, 111
  Rebecca, 80
  Thadius, 111
Butt
  Alice, 169
Butts
  Emma, 178
Byrn
  Eliza, 121
  Garret S., 121
  George P., 121
  James T., 121

C

Cady
  Alvin H., 147
  Francis H., 147
Cafferty
  Abel, 61
  Enoch, 141
  Lydia, 128
  Lydia M., 141
  William I., 61
Calder
  Elizabeth, 152
Callahan
  Phebe A., 158
Cambern
  Harriet, 79
  William, 79
Caminade
  Emma, 137, 138
  Frederick, 137, 138
Camp
  Celia, 171
  Daniel, 171
  David, 133
  Hannah, 171
  James, 133
  Nettie, 171
  Preston, 171
Campbell
  Anna M., 157
  Anne C., 117, 118
  Anthony, 155
  Benjamin, 18, 19, 20,
    21, 23, 26, 29, 36

Catherine, 19, 23, 29,
 44
Deborah D., 165
Delilah, 58
Duncan, 19, 23
Eleanor, 19, 21, 23,
 26, 29
Hannah, 19, 23, 29,
 155
Jane, 18, 26
Jane Haviland, 44
John, 19, 20, 23, 29
Joshua, 58
Lewis, 58
Lydia Ann, 58
Martha, 44
Mary, 81
Nathan, 151
Richard B., 44, 117,
 151
Samuel S., 157
Sarah Winans, 44
William, 19, 20, 23,
 29, 81, 151
William H., 151
Card
 Anna, 165
 Annie, 165
 Charles, 165
 Nellie, 165
Carey
 Alice, 144
 William, 144
Carhart
 Daniel A., 125
 Elizabeth, 113
 Emiline, 92
 Joel, 92
 John, 125
 Leroy, 113
 Louisa J., 138
 Samuel, 92
 Samuel L., 138
 Sarah, 92
 Timothy, 92
 Zephina, 125
Carman
 Eden B., 94, 97, 132
 Eleanor, 94
 Fanny, 97
 Joseph, 94
Carmen
 Ann, 66
Carnaham
 James, 96
Carpenter
 Lawrence, 167
 Lucretia, 43
 Mary Ann, 167
Carr
 Adam, 178
 Amos, 84
 Burroughs, 84
 Charles, 178
 James, 84, 178
 John, 178

John A., 84
Louisa, 84
Richard, 178
William, 84
William J., 178
Carson
 Adelia M., 151
 Disbrow, 42
 Mary C., 150
 Matilda C., 150
 Sarah, 148
Carter
 Jacob, 120
 Marinda, 120
 Mary, 120
Case
 Evilina, 129
 Florence, 129
 William H., 129
Casler
 Aaron, 138
 Edward, 138
 Elizabeth, 138
 Henry, 138
 John P., 138
 Joseph, 138
 Joseph Edward, 138
 Julia, 138
 Laura Edna, 138
 Mary E., 138
 Peter, 138, 140
 Rufus T., 138
 William Corlies, 138
Cassard
 Harry L., 168
 Linda R., 168
Cathie
 Margaret, 179
Caulkite
 Amos, 84
 Ann, 84
 Joanna, 84
 Joseph, 84
 Samuel, 84
 Sarah, 84
Chadwic
 Elvira, 130
Chadwick
 Ada, 174
 Ann, 63
 Catherine, 104
 Francis, 24
 Hulda, 24
 Jackson, 104
 Samuel L., 110
 Taber, 24, 39, 44, 51,
  63, 149
 Virginia A., 147
 William L., 110
Chafey
 Martha M., 155
 Mary V., 155
Chamberlain
 Aaron, 81
 Abijah, 95, 96
 Adaline, 179

Ann, 106
Catherine, 4
Cornelia, 81
Daniel I., 122
Daniel J., 121, 122
Elizabeth, 121
Jesse, 45, 56
John M., 121
Mary, 81
Mary Ann, 58
Mary B., 45
Richard, 4
Samuel B., 45
Susan, 95, 96
Thomas B., 45
William, 4
William I., 106
Chamberlin
 Daniel, 124
 Daniel J., 124
 Elizabeth, 124
Chambers
 Abby, 78
 Ann, 78
 Augustus, 78
 Caleb, 78
 Charles, 152
 Edgar, 153
 Eleanor, 20
 Elizabeth, 20
 Emley, 78
 Ezekial, 78
 George, 78
 James, 78, 81
 Jane, 20, 78
 Job, 78, 81
 John, 20, 78
 Joseph, 78
 Louisa, 78
 Margaret, 78, 152
 Maria, 78
 Rachel, 78
 Robert, 78
 Sarah, 78
 Sarah J., 153
 Solomon, 78
Chandler
 Lewis, 24
Chapman
 Joseph H., 101
Chasey
 Hannah, 64
 William, 64
Chatlier
 Hannah, 75
 John, 75
Chattle
 Adah Chapter, 161
 Adah S., 162
 Anna D., 162
 Elizabeth W., 162
 Emma A., 161, 162
 Emma K., 162
 Francis E., 162
 George M., 162
 John H., 138, 161, 162

Joseph, 161
Josepha, 162
Louise S., 161, 162
Mary A., 162
Thomas G., 138
Thomas H., 162
William M. K., 161,
   162
Cheeseman
   Joseph, 18
   Lucy, 18
Cheney
   Euretta N., 154
Cherry
   Alice, 169
   Elizabeth, 169
   Henry, 115
   John P., 115
   Joseph, 169
   Peter, 169
   William H., 115
Chesney
   Charles C. M., 97
   Charles E. M., 97
   Mary M., 97
   Samuel M. M., 97
Chew
   Hannah, 7
   John, 7
   Mary, 6, 7
   Phebe, 7
   Rachel, 6, 7
   Richard, 7
   William, 7
Chumar
   Harriet, 38
   John, 38
   Rebecca, 38
Clark
   Filey, 49
   George, 100, 115, 116
   Herbert D., 150
   Huldah, 174
   John, 11
   John C., 174
   Joseph, 49
   Joseph S., 174
   Mary, 95, 100
   Micah, 38
   R. Frank, 150
   Sarah, 60
   Thomas, 95, 97
   Thomas L., 95
   Thomas S., 97
   William, 25, 59
   William S., 150
Clayton
   Alice, 98
   Ann, 38
   Ann Amelia, 117
   Ann Eliza, 44
   Catherine, 81
   Cornelia, 40
   Cornelia Ann, 40
   Cornelius, 80
   David, 1, 13, 55, 80

Didamah, 80
Edward, 139
Elizabeth, 33, 49, 115,
   132, 156
Elizabeth B., 159
Ellen, 63
Ellenor, 62, 63
Ellison, 49
Ezekiel D., 98
Garrie, 143
George, 80
Gertrude, 63
Granden L., 125
Hannah, 66
Harry H., 159
Henry D., 98
Hetty, 49
James Gordon, 156
James H., 40
James M., 159
Jane, 63
Jane M., 98
Joel, 13, 81, 122
John, 1, 13, 33, 37, 38,
   49, 51, 63, 80
John H., 150
John M., 98
John W., 157
Jonathan, 42
Joseph, 80
Joseph Riggs, 44
Lucy, 46, 49
Lucy Edith, 33
Lydia, 49, 80
Mary, 42, 44
Mary A., 138, 139
Mary Elizabeth, 63
Mary J., 150
Matilda, 33, 49
Moses, 33, 49
Nancy, 49
Polhemus, 63
Reading, 132
Reuhama C., 125
Robert, 1
Sarah, 33, 37
Sarah E., 124
Susan, 143
Taylor, 63
Thomas, 13, 62
William, 63, 115, 143
William B., 157
William H., 117
Zebulon, 13
Clement
   Caroline, 55
   John, 55
Clements
   Isaac, 80
   John, 80
   William, 80
Clevenger/Clevinger
   Elias, 42, 60
   Lydia, 42
   Mihala, 60
Cline

Minnie Iola Page, 177
Cliver
   Ellenor, 84
   Samuel, 84
Coe
   Ada, 155, 157
   Alice, 157
   Alice B., 155
   Henry, 157
   Mary A., 157
   Mary Ann, 155
   William, 157
Cole
   Aaron, 126
   Minnie, 179
   William N., 179
Coleman
   Anna, 121
   Sarah E., 155
Collins
   Ann Eliza, 66, 81
   Arthur, 66
   Asher, 92
   Austin, 153
   Charles, 79
   Cornelia, 66
   Eli, 61, 79
   Eliza, 79
   James, 61
   Job, 66, 81
   John, 51, 61, 64
   Lydia, 79
   Maria, 79
   Mary, 69, 92
   Nora, 153
   Rachel, 79
   Teresea, 66
   Theresa, 81
   Thomas, 64
   Thomas E., 79
   Zebulon, 108
Combs
   Aaron R., 45
   Catherine, 12
   Elijah, 29, 42, 45
   Elizabeth, 6, 7, 45, 59
   Elizabeth R., 45
   Esther, 45
   Gilbert, 45
   Jemima, 105
   John, 5, 6, 7, 16
   Jonathan, 12
   Joseph, 45, 70
   Maryann, 12
   Nancy, 45
   Solomon, 12
   Thomas E., 45, 105
Comfort
   Ann, 31
   Ellis, 31
Compton
   Arthur, 174
   Cornelius, 36, 72, 174
   Cornelius C., 36
   Deborah, 36
   Hannah, 36

Peter P., 37, 41, 86,
     169
Peter S., 82
Rebecca, 51, 71
Richard, 51
Robert, 35, 45
Robert R., 149, 158
Samuel, 37, 40, 78
Sarah, 44, 70, 150
Sarah Ann, 24, 33, 35
Sarah E., 124
Sarah H., 86
Sarah W., 133
Sidney, 24, 33, 98,
     106, 110, 160
Simpson, 98, 110, 160
Stephen D., 61, 73, 74
Sydney, 35, 91
Theodorus, 40
Tylee, 76
William, 24, 26, 32,
     33, 56
William C., 35
William Craig, 137
William D., 124
William F., 63
William H., 112
William I., 39, 45
William J., 37
William L., 122, 169
William M., 140
William P., 40
William R., 113
William S., 40, 61, 72,
     73, 74, 116
William T., 31, 122
William V., 76, 114,
     119, 128, 152
Conrey
     Margaret, 153
     Michael, 153
Conrow
     Albert, 147
     Garret DuBois, 147
     John, 147
Cook
     Aaron, 51
     Abigail, 38
     Albert S., 123
     Allen, 81
     Ann, 45, 53, 106
     Bloomfield, 123
     Caroline C., 123, 172
     Charles, 51
     Charles H., 123
     Deborah, 51, 62, 81
     George, 10
     James, 3, 5, 29
     Jane, 51, 64
     Jasher, 5
     Jasper, 5
     John, 6, 8, 51, 57, 64,
          71, 75
     Joseph, 5, 55
     Lydia, 5, 6, 51, 58
     Lydia (Borden), 8

Marcy/Mapey, 3
Mary, 28, 29, 51, 71,
     97
Mary E., 123
Mary Hannah, 75
Peter, 28
Rebecca, 51
Samuel, 5, 38
Sarah, 38
Sarah Ann, 75
Thomas, 6, 51, 109
William, 5, 38, 75
William Henry, 51, 57
Cooke
     Huldah H., 180
     Mary E., 138
Coon
     Susan, 142, 156
Cooper
     Abigail, 9
     Alfred, 82
     Benjamin, 3, 9
     Benjamin G., 119
     Benjamin M., 116
     Brittain, 9
     Caroline A., 168
     Catharine, 60
     Charles H., 118, 120
     David, 50
     David Edward, 142
     Deborah, 121
     Edward, 163
     Elizabeth, 7, 9, 120
     Gaston, 177
     George W., 38
     Hannah Ettie, 119
     Henrietta, 97
     Henry, 178
     Henry C., 145
     Ida, 38
     Idah, 30
     Jacob, 119
     Jacob W., 60
     James, 111, 125
     James E., 168
     James G., 38, 145
     John, 30, 38, 76, 117,
          120, 121
     Jonathan P., 138
     Jordan, 120
     Joseph, 145
     Joseph D., 145
     Laura, 142, 163
     Lillias, 138
     Louisa, 177
     Lydia, 76
     Martha, 145
     Martha B., 178
     Mary, 50, 97, 119
     Mary E., 156
     Mary Ellen, 142
     Mary Hannah, 116
     Miles, 82
     Prudence, 97
     Prudence M., 119
     Rachel, 145

Ruth, 24
Samuel, 9, 59
Sarah, 3, 9
Sarah I., 176
Stanley G., 168
Thomas, 145
Uriah, 9
William, 9
William C., 38
William E., 145
William S., 145
Copping
     Anne B., 118
     Charles G., 118
     Emily, 118
     Helen B., 118
Corbett
     Ellen, 170
     James, 170
     Martin, 170
     Mary, 170
Corddry
     Elizabeth M., 169
Corlies
     Abigail, 14
     Benjamin W., 73, 88
     Britton, 14
     Caroline, 71
     Chandler, 75
     Charity, 159
     David, 75
     Deborah, 13, 62
     Edna, 14
     Edward Pennington,
          73
     Elizabeth, 41
     Elizabeth A., 75
     Francis, 120
     Frank, 166
     George, 14
     Hannah, 173
     Henry, 147, 166
     Jacob, 14
     John, 46, 73, 75
     John L., 71
     John P., 41
     Joseph, 14
     Leah, 73
     Margaret, 13
     Mary, 147
     Mary P., 75
     Peter, 73
     Phebe, 14, 73
     Rebecca, 14
     Sarah, 73
     Timothy, 13
     Tylee W., 166
     William P., 75
     William T., 117
Cornelius
     Allen, 14, 16, 18
     Daniel, 16, 18
     David, 18
     Hyram P., 16
     Hyram Parent, 14, 18
     John, 18

Charity, 89
Elizabeth, 89
Gray
  Boyce, 135
  Josephine A., 135
Green
  Ann, 87
  Annie, 164
  Charles C., 139
  Charles H., 81
  Conover, 87
  Elevyn S., 81
  Elizabeth, 81
  Forrest, 139
  George H., 139
  Hannah Elizabeth, 81
  Henrietta, 19, 41
  Henry, 7, 19, 41
  Isabella, 139
  James, 81
  James Oscar, 81
  John, 7, 87
  Josephine, 111
  Lidia, 7
  Lois C., 81
  Maria, 91
  Mary, 164
  Monmouth H., 111
  Nancy, 7
  Orlin H., 111
  Rebecca, 7
  Samuel D., 60
  Samuel R., 60
  Walter S., 81
  William, 87
  Zilphey, 7
Greer
  Almira, 165
Greig
  Catherine M., 78
  George, 78
  Harriet M., 78
  William C., 78
Griffen
  Elizabeth, 141
Griffin
  Charles, 69
  Gloriana, 69
  Joseph, 69
  Mary, 69
  William, 69
Griggs
  Benjamin, 45
  Benjamin F., 128, 165
  Catherine A., 128, 165
  Daniel, 3
  Hannah A., 128, 130,
    165
  John W., 112, 128,
    130, 165
  Joseph, 3
  Leah, 62
  Lydia Ann, 50
  Lydia C., 128, 130,
    165
  Mary A., 128

Orsemus, 128, 165
  William, 50
Grimm
  Christian, 165
Griscom
  Job, 141
  Sarah, 141
Grover
  Charles, 170
  Elizabeth, 104
  Henry C., 150
  Ida, 146, 170
  James, 30, 149, 170
  James Clark, 170
  Jennie, 150
  John B., 150, 170
  John D., 104
  Joseph, 150
  Rachel, 146, 170
  Sallie, 170
  Sarah M., 146
  Stillwell, 170
  William V., 149

H

Haden
  Charles, 169
  Rhoda, 169
Hadsell
  Rice, 43
Hagenbacher
  Henrietta, 165
  Isadore, 165
Hagerman
  Benjamin A., 172
  Eliza, 155
  Elizabeth Ann, 72
  Sarah, 72
Haight
  Ann, 86, 96
  Charles, 86, 96
  Eliza Ann, 91, 96
  Elizabeth, 87, 96
  Furonian, 87
  John T., 87, 91
  John Tyler, 96
  Mary W., 96
  Sarah, 87, 91, 96
  Thomas G., 86, 87, 96
  Trevonian, 96
  William, 86, 87, 96
Haines
  Mary, 178
  Peter, 178
  Reuben, 55
  William Edward, 178
Hale
  Henry E., 95, 96
  Mary, 95, 96
  Mary O., 95, 96
Hall
  Adelbert, 177
  Albert, 56, 68
  Albert B., 130
  Alice, 30

Bertha M., 149
Britta, 56
Caroline, 41, 53
Charity, 89
Clarence L., 149
Cornelia, 34
Edward, 89
Elizabeth, 41, 44, 53,
  156
Ellen B., 177
George W., 53
George Washington,
  44
Harriet, 41, 44, 53
Jerusha, 132
Joanna, 68
Joanna B., 56
John, 21, 30, 34, 41,
  56, 68, 71, 81, 120
John G., 77
John M., 37, 44, 53
John S., 149
John T. S., 149
Mary, 34
Mary Ann, 37, 53
Phebe A., 77
Rhuhania, 56
Rubamah, 68
S. E., 177
Samuel, 37, 41, 44, 53,
  68
Silas B., 56, 68
Sylvester, 132
Walter, 177
Washington, 41
Hallenbake
  Sarah, 112
  William, 112
Halloway
  Catherine, 86
  John, 86
Hamilton
  Angeline, 94
  William B., 94
Hammond
  Ann Amanda, 92
  George, 92
  Jane, 92
  Samuel P., 92
Hampton
  Adaline, 126
  Annie, 154
  Charles, 172
  Elizabeth W., 145, 177
  Hannah, 172
  James, 88, 104
  James H., 145
  James L., 172
  James Monroe, 172
  Julia, 87
  Lewis M., 172
  Lucy, 172
  Margaret, 64
  Moses, 64, 172
  Moses I., 172
  Richard, 88

Elizabeth, 105
Ester A., 132
Euphemia, 106
Hager, 105
Jane, 105
Mary, 105, 106
Mary Elizabeth, 106
Robert, 105, 106, 132
Rosanna, 105, 106
Shepherd, 106
Jobs
Robert, 46
Sarah, 46
Johnes
David, 124
Johns
Elizabeth, 74
Samuel, 74
Walter, 74
Johnson
Aaron, 84
Alfred, 82
Alfred M., 79
Alice, 47
Amos, 84
Amy, 92
Ann Amelia, 127
Anna, 178
Benjamin, 47
Catherine, 76, 97, 148
Charles, 166
Deborah, 56
Edith, 47
Ezekiel, 56
George, 165
George Washington, 48
Gilbert, 92
Hendrick, 84
Henry W., 169
Jacob, 74
Jacob S., 93
James, 48, 82, 93
James H., 79
James N., 93
Johanna, 82
Johannah M., 79
John, 82, 84, 97
John A., 99
Joseph, 79, 82, 84
Judidah, 72
Julia F., 174
Lambert, 102
Leonard L., 116
Leslie Francis, 175
Lucinda, 82
Lydia, 60, 61
Margaret Ann, 74
Maria, 84
Martha, 48
Mary, 60, 76, 97, 99, 171
Mary Ann, 82
Mary Cyrenia, 76
Morrell, 165
Necorsuli, 143

Patience, 127
Peter, 97
Rebecca, 48
Richard, 84
Robert, 76, 97
Samuel, 47, 84
Sarah, 48, 102, 132, 165
Sarah Ann, 143
Sarah D., 178
Stephen, 82
Susan Mary, 97
Thomas, 47, 48
Timothy, 47
William, 47, 60, 84
William A., 84
William E., 56
William H., 79, 82
William L., 165
William P., 111
Johnston
Abraham, 50
Adaline, 166
Benjamin, 1
Catherine, 10, 49
Charles, 49
Daniel, 1
David, 6, 10, 35
Elizabeth, 49, 178
Emma, 164
Euphamana, 73
George, 49, 51
Isaac C., 166
Jacob, 50
James, 49
Joanna, 49
John, 1, 7, 10, 50, 75
John L., 166
Jonathan, 53
Lewis H., 45
Luke, 49
Lydia, 73, 75
Mary, 166
Michael, 73
Pauline, 45
Peter, 19, 73
Rebecca, 35
Sarah, 1, 49
Susie C., 166
William, 73, 75
William G., 49
William P., 111
Jolins
Eloise, 174
Jones
Anna Elizabeth, 98
Catherine S., 127
Christopher, 24, 31
Daniel C., 97, 98
Deborah, 24, 28
George S., 110
Harriet, 51
John, 133
Juli Ann, 51
Lavinia, 110
Lavinia S., 174

Letty Ann, 121
Lloyd, 51
Martha, 97
Mary, 24, 31
Rachel, 133
Robert, 2
Samuel W., 121
Sarah, 31
William, 24, 31
William C., 75
William L., 127
Journey
Catherine, 10
James, 10
Jowitt
Constance Mary, 148
Jos. F., 148
Julien
Margaret, 142, 156
Oliver, 142, 156

K

Karr
Susannah, 32
Kearney
Anastatia, 42
Ann, 41, 42
Catherine, 41, 42
Edmund, 42
Edward, 41
Horatio, 42
James P., 42
Joseph, 46
Mary, 46
Mary Eliza, 42
Thomas, 36, 42
Keefe
Catharine M., 161
James Henry, 161
Lizzie D., 161
Mary Ann, 161
Patrick, 161
Thomas F., 161
Keener
Catherine, 134
Lucretia A., 134
William H., 134
Keepers
Eliza, 142, 156
Kelly
George B., 101
Jane L., 175
John, 86
John B., 101
Mary, 44
Peter B., 101
Viola H., 177
William, 86, 101, 177
Kelsey/Kelsy
Annie, 162
Catherine, 153
James, 162
James Thomas, 162
Katherine, 153
Mary, 162

Michael, 153, 161, 162
Kennedy
Hannah, 54
Ker
Ann, 13
Ebenezer, 13
Euphame, 13
Phebe, 13
Kerr
David, 78
Margaret, 78, 152
Sarah, 78
Thomas, 78
Ketchum
Elizabeth F., 145
Keyser
Deborah L., 100
William, 100
Kim
John G., 149
King
Benjamin, 111
Effie V., 161
John, 20
Joseph, 111
Leslie W., 161
Victoria, 161
William F., 161
Kingsland
Ann, 159
Kinnan
Richard, 1
Kirby
Abel, 9
Catharine Elizabeth, 144
Elizabeth, 58
Ellenor, 58
George, 55, 58
Harriet, 58
Harry C., 161
Israel, 9
James A., 161
Job, 9, 14, 21, 28
John, 32
Joseph, 58, 144
Leberny L., 55
Lebrus L., 58
Louis, 144
Lucy, 148
Maria, 55
Mary Ann, 58
Mary Ellen, 144
Nathaniel, 55
Nathaniel B., 32
Rachel, 58
Rebecca, 58, 148
Robert, 9
Sarah Ann, 55, 58
Thomas, 55, 58
William, 55
Wm. E., 161
Kirkman
Ralph, 112
Kirkpatrick

Nancy Huggins, 3
William, 3
Kisner
Ellen J., 116
William H., 116
Kizer
Deborah A., 119
William, 119
Kline
Jane, 20
Jesse, 20
Knott
Ann, 3
Ann Maria, 48, 56, 113
Anna, 2
Catherine, 2, 3
David, 1, 2, 3
Elizabeth, 6, 48, 56
Hannah, 3
Jacob, 48, 56
Jane, 2, 3
John, 3
Joseph, 3
Lydia, 2, 3
Peter, 1, 3
Knowles
Margaret, 79
Kodziesen
Abraham, 165
Gussie, 165
Koman
Edward, 139
Krug
Loretta M., 178
Montillion, 178
Kugler
Mary E., 168
Kupferschmied
Jacob, 165
Johann Ulrich, 165

L

LaCompt
Elizabeth, 114
Joseph, 114
Mary H., 114
William H., 114
Ladd
Sarah, 174
Lafetra
Almy, 28
Caroline, 96
Charles E., 96
Edmund, 15, 28
Hannah, 40
Harriet, 96
John, 40
Joseph, 26, 70
Josephine, 96
Mary D., 96
Priscilla, 96
Ruth Ann, 96
Laight
Anna M., 173

Frederick B., 173
John M., 173
Julia H., 173
Laird
Archibald, 6
Daniel, 44
David, 44
James, 105
James R., 104
Joseph T., 105, 122
Mary Ann, 104
Mary S., 105
Rachel E., 145
Robert, 105
Samuel, 44, 52, 105
Sarah, 6
William, 9
William H., 145
Lake
Ann C., 103
Elizabeth, 26
John I., 103
William, 26
Lamberson
Catharine Ann, 55
Daniel, 49, 55
Eliza, 49
Elizabeth, 55
Ellenor, 49, 55
James, 55
Maria, 55
William, 49, 55
William C., 49, 55
Lambertson
Amelia, 143, 145
David H., 138
Edward, 143, 145
Eunice, 138
Flora E., 138
George W., 138
Hartweld, 138
John, 143, 145
Martha J., 143
Stephen, 143, 145
Thaddeus, 143, 145
Lane
Abraham, 64
Adaline, 65
Adden Colwell, 72
Alice, 45, 52, 55, 57
Anna, 57
Anna A., 102
Bloomfield, 57
Catharine, 57
Charity, 173
Charles E., 102
Cornelius, 45, 55, 57, 104
Eleanor, 72
Gilbert, 64
Isaiah, 57
Isaiah S., 119
Jacob, 57
James, 64
James H., 106
James Henry, 64

Caroline, 60
Edward, 144
Ella S., 144
Herbert C., 39, 41
Lewis E., 36
Margaret, 39
Mary, 36
Prudence, 36
Robert, 176
Pease
Adam, 5
Adam D., 61
Adam M., 117
Charlotte, 65
Cornelius, 61, 65, 115
David, 65
Harriet, 61
John Nelson, 61
Rhoda, 61
Peer
Clara A., 165
Pemberton
Caroline, 166
Charles G., 166
Pennington
Elizabeth C. H., 27
Perine
Abigail, 11
Hannah, 11
Henry, 11
James, 13
Jeremiah W., 11
John, 11
Lewis, 11
Mary, 11
Perrine
Albert, 103, 104, 109
Alfred, 77, 80
Andrew, 80
Ann, 104
Ann Eliza, 40
Benjamin, 81
Caroline, 103, 104
Catharine Henry, 79
Clark, 25
Cornelia, 103
Daniel W., 169
David, 61, 85
David C., 85
David M. C., 134
Edwin A., 85
Elizabeth, 25, 127
Enoch, 104, 109
Esther H., 35
Ezekiel, 68, 69
Francis R., 128
Francis Rosten, 154
Gilbert W., 134
Hannah, 81
Henry D., 38
Isaac, 112
James S., 169
James W., 77
John, 66, 79, 127
John H., 77
John J., 154

Joseph, 104, 127, 154
Joseph W., 128
Lewis, 103, 104, 109
Lydia, 69
Margaret Ann, 103,
    104, 109
Margaret E. C., 85
Margaret I., 134
Martha, 77
Martha S., 134
Mary, 66, 77
Mary A., 168
Mary Anna, 112
Mary E., 134
Mary Matilda, 79
Matilda, 103, 112
Matthew, 35, 103,
    127, 154
Newell, 154
Peter F., 103, 128, 154
Phebe, 61
Robert, 40
Sarah E., 128
Stephen, 127, 128, 154
Stephen P., 154
Thomas, 77
Thomas A., 134
Thomas M., 35
Thomas N., 168, 169
William D., 154
William I., 77, 80, 128
William J., 154
William M., 35, 128,
    169
William R., 77
Perry
Margaret A., 152
Pervis
Charles, 106
Joseph, 106
Rosanna, 106
Sarah Jane, 106
Pette
Andrew, 81
Pew
Beulah Ann, 128
Phar
Amos, 7
Pharo
Allen, 19, 61
Ann, 61
Anne, 19, 61
Charlotte, 19
Matilda, 61
Orrin, 61
Phebe, 61
Phebe Ann, 61
Robert, 19, 61
Timothy, 19
Phillips
Estelle, 175
Maria, 58
Taylor, 58
Pierce
Asher, 133
Elisha, 80

Jacob E., 133
Josephine, 133
Laura T., 176
Mary Ann, 133
Phebe A., 77
Rachel Lavinia, 133
Sarah, 80
William W., 77
Pierson
Hannah, 25
Henry, 25
Pintard
Ann, 28
Deborah, 95
Glencross, 28
Hannah, 28
John, 28
Samuel, 24, 28
William, 28
Pittenger
Ann Eliza, 71
Christina, 123
Edward F., 163
Ellenor Jane, 66
Elmeretta, 123
John, 67
John C., 163
Lydia G., 123
Mary, 66, 67
Richard, 71, 123
Washington, 123
William, 67
Pitts
Elizabeth, 39
John, 39
Place
Nancy, 69
Platt
Andrew M., 135
Jacob, 77
Jane, 77
Levi, 10
Samuel K., 135
William M., 135
Platues
Mary Ann, 44
Randolph, 44
Pochea
John, 75
William, 75
Poinsett
Hiram, 55
Poland
Allen, 86
Barnes B., 86, 127
Cornelius, 86
Eleanor, 115
John, 86
Mary A., 127
Mary Louisa, 86
Peter B., 86
William, 86, 115
Polhemus
Ann, 128
Ann M., 128
Charles, 128

Charlotte Ann, 84
Chilion, 149, 166
Clark, 67, 70
Clayton, 61, 63, 67,
   70, 86
Eliza (Bailey), 69
Elizabeth, 67
Elizabeth E., 70
Elizabeth M., 148
Ezekiel, 43, 67
George, 84, 148
Jacob, 67
Jacob B., 70
John, 43, 67
John B., 81, 97
Margaret E., 154
Maria, 61, 63, 86
Mary, 67
Mary Ann, 84
Mary E., 70
Phebe, 66, 67
Rachel, 148
Randal C., 122
Rebecca, 43
Rebecca Ann, 67
Richard, 67
Richard C., 66, 67, 70
Ridgeway, 140
Samuel, 67
Samuel C., 70
Sarah, 61, 63, 67, 86
Sarah E., 70
Sarah Jane, 81
Thomas, 39
Timothy, 137
Wikoff, 67
William, 67
William Henry, 81
Roberts
   Alice, 111, 170
   Amelia F., 174
   David Jones, 145
   Dora, 154
   Edward E., 137
   Elbridge G., 137
   Eliza, 69
   Frederick, 145
   Garret, 111
   George, 154, 155
   Leonard D., 155
   Margaret, 137
   Mary Ella, 145
   Nathaniel H., 144, 145
   Rebecca W., 154
   Samuel F., 161
   Sarah, 78
   Thomas J., 145
   William M., 145
Robins
   Caroline E., 124
   Charles, 124
   John B., 114
   Maria, 154
Robinson
   Catherine, 105
   Catherine Maria, 77

Cornelia, 94
Edward, 77
George, 105
Henry, 1
James, 1, 77
John, 77
John Henry, 77
Joseph C., 77
Maria, 77
Martha, 77
Peter, 94
Sarah, 32, 42
Rockafeller
   Abigail, 174
Rockhill
   Anthony R., 163
   Emma F., 163
   Francis W., 163
   Herbert, 163
   Llewellyn, 163
   William C., 163
Rodgers
   Eleanor A., 121
   John M., 121
Rogers
   Abigail, 35
   Adaline, 79
   Adaline F., 169
   Althea, 79
   Althea E., 80
   Andrew T., 49
   Ann, 47, 70, 72, 95
   Asenath, 79
   Azenath, 80, 81
   Azenath O., 81
   Brittain, 12, 13, 42
   Brittan, 43
   Britton, 75
   Caroline, 90
   Catharine C., 64
   Catherine, 35
   Charles, 75
   Daniel, 79, 80, 141
   David, 35, 75, 76
   David I. C., 69
   Deborah Ann, 89
   Deliverance, 49
   Eden, 141
   Edwin L., 89
   Eleanor, 49
   Elihu, 12, 13, 42, 43
   Eliza, 75
   Elizabeth, 31, 43
   Elvira, 79
   Elvira C., 81
   Elwood, 141
   Esther, 35
   Ferdinan, 141
   Forman, 79
   Forman D., 80
   Garret, 12, 13
   George, 35, 75
   George Patterson, 133
   Hannah, 47, 69
   Hannah E., 163
   Isaac, 35, 73

James B., 141
James D., 35
James E., 133
Jeremiah, 42
Jeremiah Newman, 43
Jesse, 35, 79
John, 12, 13, 31, 35,
   70, 75, 79, 141
John M., 49, 133
John W., 141
Joseph, 47
Josiah B., 95
Lucretia, 12, 43
Lydia, 79
Margaret, 79
Martha W., 73
Mary Ann, 47
Mary Jane, 79
Mary V., 177
Michael, 70
Rebecca, 35, 42, 43,
   70, 79
Rebecca Ann, 80
Rhoda Ann, 132
Samuel, 12, 13, 35, 42,
   47
Sarah, 42, 43, 49, 69,
   75
Solomon B., 35
Susan, 35
Susannah, 12, 13
Vananzo, 133
VanRoom, 141
William, 43, 75, 132,
   141
William A., 49
William C., 35, 69
Rolph
   Hannah, 92
   John, 9
   Joseph, 92
Romaine
   Alice, 159
   James H., 159
   Jane, 171
   Phebe, 67
   Theophilus, 67
   William, 159
Roop
   Anna, 107
   Christopher, 108
   Elizabeth, 108
   George, 108
   Hannah, 108
   Isaac, 108
   Jacob, 107, 108
   James H., 108
   James M., 108
   John, 108
   Joseph, 108
   Mary, 108
   Solomon, 108
   Susan, 108
   William, 108
Ross
   Thomas, 152

Margaret A., 113
Maria, 169
Mary, 3, 4
Mary A., 157
Mary E., 80, 123
Matilda, 169
Minnie T., 169
Rachel, 3, 4, 7
Samuel, 4, 7
Sarah, 169
Shade M., 113
Stephen, 3, 4, 7
Virginia, 169
William, 80, 123, 169
William B., 113
Zilpha, 5
Tantum
  Ann, 61
  Elizabeth, 46, 66
  Hartshorne, 61
  James, 170
  Maria, 146
  Morrison B., 152
  Samuel, 46, 66
  Sarah E., 128
  Theresa (aka Charity), 146
  Theresa (Charity), 152
Tapscott
  Catherine, 28
  Elizabeth, 28
  James, 11
  William, 28
Taylor
  Abel R., 89
  Andrew, 168
  Ann, 30, 38
  Ann B., 54
  Ann W., 47
  Anna Leila, 150
  Augustus, 168
  Barzilla, 143, 146
  Charles, 30
  Cornelia Ann, 115
  Daniel H., 115
  David, 47, 115
  Edward, 2, 6, 13, 25, 34
  Eliza, 30, 38
  Eliza J., 150
  Elizabeth, 54, 154
  Ezekiel, 6
  Fanny, 30, 38
  George W., 33
  Grover, 30
  Guisbert, 121
  Hannah, 30, 33
  Hattie B., 148
  Henry C., 102
  Hetty, 38
  Ida, 38
  James, 20, 30, 54
  James B., 121
  James G., 38
  James Grover, 30

James J., 102, 148, 161
Jane F., 128
John, 20, 30, 54
John A., 47, 115
John G., 22, 54
John H., 108
John I., 54
John W., 20
Joseph, 6, 20, 30, 36, 41, 42, 45, 46
Joshua, 6
Lavinia, 115
Lawrence, 6
Lydia, 121, 146
Lydia A., 143
Lydia Ann, 86
Lydia L., 139, 146
Lydia M., 148
Maria L., 139, 146
Maria Louisa, 143
Martha, 20, 46
Mary, 168
Mary H., 174
Mary Jane, 103
Meribah W., 47
Morford, 161
Morford D., 121
Nancy, 20
Nelson, 143, 146
Patty, 30
Phebe, 30, 38
Phebe Ann, 115
Priscilla, 6
Ray, 139, 143, 146
Reynolds, 154
Richard, 103, 168
Samuel, 121
Samuel H., 121
Samuel W., 115
Sarah E., 139, 143, 146
Sarah H., 174
Susan, 142
Violetta, 121
William, 30, 38
William M., 86
William P., 143, 146
Teed
  Nathan P., 129
Tenbrook
  Edmund W., 41
  Jane G., 41
  Mary, 41
  Samuel W., 41
Terhune
  Emma, 142
  Emma E., 159
Terlain
  William L., 145
Test
  Ann, 51
  Jesse, 51
Thistle
  Amelia, 139
  Charles, 139

Edward, 139
Emma, 139
Hannah E., 139
John H., 139
Margaret, 139
Samuel B., 139
Samuel E., 139
William E., 139
Thomas
  Achsah, 100
  Benjamin, 79
  Ezekiel, 89
  Harriet, 79
  Jane, 79
  John W., 89
  Kesiah, 79
  Lydia A., 177
  Maria, 89
  Mary, 79
  Mary E., 89
  Naomi, 79
  Peter, 100
  Rachel, 89
  Sarah, 12, 13
  William Henry, 89
Thomason
  Anna M., 141
  Annie M., 147
  Thomas J., 137, 141, 147
  William W., 141, 147
Thompson
  Acsah, 48
  Albert E., 162
  Alice, 155
  Alice F., 139
  Ann, 68
  Augustus, 110
  Caroline, 39
  Carrie, 129
  Catherine, 110
  Charles, 97, 155, 158
  Charles E., 101
  Cornelius, 39, 72
  Cyrenus, 110
  Elizabeth, 48, 59
  Fredk. P., 162
  George, 13
  Gertrude, 127
  Hannah, 48
  Hannah E., 175
  Hester, 72
  Ida A., 110
  Jackson H., 101
  James S., 162
  Jamesetta, 163
  Jane, 48
  John F., 94
  John L., 94
  Joseph, 68, 127, 129
  Joseph C., 59
  Joseph D., 47
  Josephine, 110
  Letitia, 101, 148
  Lewis S., 172
  Louis W., 162

Charlotte, 56, 57
Gilbert S., 44, 56
Gilbert T., 160
Hannah W., 160
Henry W. B., 57, 160
John, 3, 21, 160
John T., 21, 35, 36, 56
L. Charlotte G., 160
Mary Ann, 21
Nelson, 54
Sarah S., 57
Spafford, 54
Spafford P., 160
William Hedge, 21
William W., 54
Wooding
  Alvin S., 179
  Mary Jane, 179
Woodmansee
  Abigail, 23
  Amela, 10
  Deborah, 17
  Gabriel, 6, 9, 10, 16, 18
  Isaac, 20, 72
  John, 17, 20, 23
  Louisa, 17
  Martha, 17
  Mary, 72
  Reuben, 17, 23
  Thomas, 10
Woodruff
  Henry M., 149
  Samuel V., 149
Woodward
  Alice, 94
  Anthony, 62, 94
  Apollo H., 39
  Caroline, 62
  Deborah, 170
  Elizabeth, 62
  Elizabeth A., 94
  Hannah Ann, 62
  Henry, 39
  Henry Wheelock, 46
  Isaac N., 41, 58, 59, 94
  James W., 46
  Keziah, 62
  Lucy, 33
  Lydia, 39, 46
  Maria, 39
  Mary, 94
  Sarah A., 133
  Tilton, 94
  William, 62
  William Allen, 46
Wooley
  Benjamin, 3
Woolley
  Abigail, 24
  Abraham, 14, 39, 109
  Adam, 14, 24, 41, 45, 53, 54, 71, 109, 131, 132, 133, 134
  Adam P., 134

Alfred, 96, 103, 117, 122, 132
Alice, 112, 159
Ann, 24, 45, 53, 152
Annie, 140
Annie E., 140, 146
Asher, 103
Benjamin, 56
Bloomfield, 144
Britton, 23, 24
Caroline, 39
Charles, 71, 94
Charles Edward, 107
Charles M., 126
Clarence, 144, 146
Clark, 39
Clay, 140
Corlies, 112
Daniel, 7, 8, 9, 10, 24, 144
David, 71
Deborah, 24, 112
Eden, 124
Edward, 169
Edwin, 107
Elihu, 25
Elisha, 59
Eliza Jane, 96
Elizabeth, 24, 45, 53, 73, 107, 124
Ellen, 96
Emeline, 107
Ephram, 11
Francis, 107
George, 71
Hannah, 13, 24, 45, 53, 54, 134, 144
Hannah Matilda, 132
Harriet H., 177
Herbert, 109
Hugh, 10
Indiana J., 113
Indiana Josephine, 112
James H., 113
James T., 126
Jane, 107
Jane Ann, 39, 96, 117
Jedidiah, 8, 10
Jeremiah, 11
John B., 126
Jordan, 95, 99, 100, 140
Joseph, 7, 8, 10, 132
Judiah, 9, 10
Julia Ann, 71
Levi, 58, 109
Lloyd, 39
Ludlow, 177
Lydia, 39, 96, 117, 132, 133
Margaret, 39, 140
Maria, 58
Mariah, 24
Mary, 59, 107, 132
Mary Ann, 107
Mary E., 117

Mary L., 113
Mary M., 112, 133, 134
Matilda, 94, 169
Milton, 112
Montilian, 7, 8
Montillion, 23
Montillion W., 126
Montillon, 24
Nathan W., 169
Nelson, 107, 177
Owen, 159
Penn, 140
Rebecca, 71
Reuben, 39
Richard, 109
Richard Wikoff, 56
Samuel, 13, 112
Sarah, 132, 133, 140
Sarah J., 158
Thomas, 109
Thomas P., 109
Thomas R., 140
William, 14, 24, 53, 73, 103, 132, 134
William B., 112
William E., 117
William Edward, 96, 103
William H., 169
William M., 71
William W., 41, 45
Woolston
  Blanche C., 153
  Paul L., 153
  Rebecca S., 153
Worden
  Caroline I./T., 155
Worrall
  Georgia A., 135
  Lawrence, 135
Worrell
  Charles F., 73, 74
Worth
  Hannah H., 95, 96
  Hannah R., 95, 96
  Jennie, 164
  Josiah S., 95, 96
Worthington
  Anna M., 170
  Robert M., 170
Worthley
  Malinda, 163
  Ophelia, 135
  Thomas, 135
Wretling
  Daniel, 175
Wright
  Ann, 73
  Catherine, 1, 2
  Mary A., 155
  Milton, 73
  Thomas, 1, 73
  William, 73
Wyatt
  Alice Edith, 141

www.ingramcontent.com/pod-product-compliance
Lightning Source LLC
Chambersburg PA
CBHW071856270326
41929CB00013B/2246